Transforming Brazil

Transforming Brazil

A Reform Era in Perspective

MAURICIO A. FONT

ROWMAN & LITTLEFIELD PUBLISHERS, INC.
Lanham • Boulder • New York • Oxford

ROWMAN & LITTLEFIELD PUBLISHERS, INC.

Published in the United States of America
by Rowman & Littlefield Publishers, Inc.
A Member of the Rowman & Littlefield Publishing Group
4501 Forbes Boulevard, Suite 200, Lanham, Maryland 20706
www.rowmanlittlefield.com

P.O. Box 317, Oxford OX2 9RU, United Kingdom

British Library Cataloguing in Publication Information Available

Library of Congress Cataloging-in-Publication Data

Font, Mauricio A. (Mauricio Augusto)
    Transforming Brazil / Mauricio A. Font.
    p.   cm.
    Includes bibliographical references and index.
    ISBN 0-8476-8356-7 (alk. paper) — ISBN 0-8476-8355-9 (pbk. : alk. paper)
    1. Structural adjustment (Economic policy)—Brazil. 2. Brazil—Politics and
    government—1985– 3. Brazil—Social policy. I. Title.

HC187 .F6326 2003
320'.6'0981—dc21

                                                                    2002068142

Printed in the United States of America

♾™ The paper used in this publication meets the minimum requirements of American
National Standard for Information Sciences—Permanence of Paper for Printed Library
Materials, ANSI/NISO Z39.48-1992.

Table of Contents

Tables

Figures

Abbreviations and Acronyms

ACSP — Associação Comercial de São Paulo
(Commercial Association of São Paulo)

ARENA — Aliança de Renovação Nacional
(National Renewal Alliance)

BANERJ — Banco do Estado do Rio de Janeiro
(Bank of the State of Rio de Janeiro)

BANESPA — Banco do Estado de São Paulo
(Bank of the State of São Paulo)

BNDES — Banco Nacional de Desenvolvimento Econômico e Social
(National Bank for Economic and Social Development)

CEBRAP — Centro Brasileiro de Análise e Planejamento
(Brazilian Center for Analysis and Planning)

CEDEC — Centro de Estudos de Cultura Contemporânea
(Center of Studies of Contemporary Culture)

CGT — Central Geral dos Trabalhadores
(General Confederation of Workers)

CIESP — Centro das Indústrias do Estado de São Paulo
(Center of Industries of the State of São Paulo)

CNA — Confederação Nacional da Agricultura
(National Agricultural Confederation)

CNBB — Conferência Nacional dos Bispos Brasileiros
(National Conference of Brazilian Bishops)

CNI — Confederação Nacional da Indústria
(National Industrial Confederation)

CONCLAP — Conselho Nacional das Classes Produtoras
(National Council of Producers)

CONTAG — Confederação Nacional dos Trabalhadores da Agricultura
(National Confederation of Agricultural Workers)

CPI — Comissão Parlamentar de Inquérito
(Congressional Inquiry Commission)

CPMF — Contribuição Provisória sobre Movimentação Financeira
(Financial Turnover Tax)

CPT — Comissão Pastoral da Terra (Pastoral Land Commission)

CUT — Central Única dos Trabalhadores
(Unified Workers' Confederation)

DASP — Departamento Administrativo do Serviço Público
(Administrative Department of Public Services)

FGV — Fundação Getúlio Vargas (Getúlio Vargas Foundation)

FIESP — Federação das Indústrias do Estado de São Paulo
(Federation of Industries of the State of São Paulo)

IDESP	Instituto de Estudos Econômicos, Sociais e Políticos de São Paulo (Institute of Economics, Social, and Political Research of São Paulo)
IMF	International Monetary Fund
INCRA	Instituto Nacional de Colonização e Reforma Agrária (National Institute of Colonization and Agrarian Reform)
IPES	Instituto de Pesquisas e Estudos Sociais (Institute for Research and Social Studies)
ISI	import substitution industrialization
MDB	Movimento Democrático Brasileiro (Brazilian Democratic Movement)
PD	Partido Democrático (Democratic Party)
PDT	Partido Democrático Trabalhista (Democratic Labor Party)
Petrobrás	Petróleos Brasileiros, S.A. (Brazilian Oil Corporation)
PFL	Partido da Frente Liberal (Liberal Front Party)
PMDB	Partido do Movimento Democrático Brasileiro (Party of the Brazilian Democratic Movement)
PNBE	Pensamento Nacional de Bases Empresariais (National Grassroots Business Association)
PND II	Plano Nacional de Desenvolvimento II (National Development Plan II)
PP	Partido Popular (Popular Party)
PPB	Partido Progressista Brasileiro (Brazilian Progressive Party)
PPR	Partido Popular Reformista (Popular Reformist Party)
PRP	Partido Republicano Paulista (Paulista Republican Party)
PSB	Partido Socialista Brasileiro (Brazilian Socialist Party)
PSD	Partido Social Democrático (Democratic Social Party)
PSDB	Partido da Social Democracia Brasileira (Brazilian Social Democracy Party)
PT	Partido dos Trabalhadores (Workers' Party)
PTB	Partido Trabalhista Brasileiro (Brazilian Labor Party)
SRB	Sociedade Rural Brasileira (Brazilian Rural Society)
SUDAM	Superintendência para o Desenvolvimento da Amazônia (Superintendency for the Development of the Amazon Region)
SUDENE	Superintendência para o Desenvolvimento do Nordeste (Superintendency for the Development of the Northeast)
UBE	União Brasileira de Empresários (Union of Brazil Businessmen)
UDB	União Democrática Brasileira (Brazilian Democratic Union)
UDN	União Democrática Nacional (National Democratic Union)
UDR	União Democrática Ruralista (Rural Democratic Union)
URV	Unidade Real de Valor (Real Value Unit)

Preface

My previous work on Brazilian social change and development emphasizes a long-term historical perspective that blends political, economic, and social factors. The challenge of exploring that country's current dynamics became irresistible when Fernando Henrique Cardoso became president. His ideas as a prominent intellectual suggested that as leader of the nation he would take the task of setting Brazil on a new course in earnest. What kind of reforms would be adopted? Would they succeed? Would they endure? Why? I just could not miss the chance to follow the action.

The chapters in this volume, completed as Cardoso's presidency approached its end, just days after the 2002 elections, probe social and political change in several domains, blending structural and conjunctural perspectives, and hence they can be only approximations. The emphasis is more on assessing the extent of change than in providing complete explanations. Even then, the passage of time is essential for a mature perspective. But enough is known, I claim, to sketch a portrait of Brazil as a society involved in a complex transformation, one that challenges the view of Brazil's democracy as frozen.

The first chapter reviews the intellectual context surrounding the Brazilian reforms. Chapter 2 discusses how stabilization set the stage for privatization, economic liberalization, and other reforms. Chapter 3 concentrates on state reform and political dynamics, focusing on democratization as it defines the institutional context. Chapter 4 explores social reform and the conditions shaping collective action, civil society, and interest representation, paying special attention to popular collective action. Chapter 5 probes elite mobilization and contention. Chapter 6 returns the discussion to development strategy, probing the extent to which Brazil is experiencing a transition from *dirigisme* to a liberal development regime. Chapter 7 closes the volume by drawing conclusions with respect to political dynamics and prospects for Brazilian democracy and the reform process. It explores the appropriateness of a structural realignment model to help make sense of such major shifts as Brazil is experiencing.

These chapters aim at clarifying the character and likely durability of the reforms, Brazil's transformation since the 1980s, and the changing policymaking context. Particularly after the crisis of 1998–1999, a significant number of Brazilians came to wonder about the wisdom of the liberalizing agenda. In this context, the Workers' Party electoral victory of 2002 seemed like a rejection of the reform process of the eight previous years. However, declaring that "Brazil has changed, the Workers' Party has changed, and I have changed," Luiz Inácio Lula da Silva and his party confirmed their support for a good number of the priorities and programs already in place. How to account for and what to make of the Brazilian debate and the pace of reforms are important issues that need to be considered to assess their durability and the underlying dynamics of change in Brazil.

This book synthesizes personal observations and studies that span two decades. The limelight is on the post-1985 period of political and economic reform. My earlier and current work on Brazil from a long-term or historical perspective—to be synthesized in the forthcoming companion volume, *Brazilian Dirigisme: Rise and Twilight* —informs the analysis.

I have benefited from the advice and hospitality of many Brazilian institutions, policymakers, and colleagues. At the Ministry of Planning, Minister Martus Tavares, José Paulo Silveira, and several members of the staff provided stimulating accounts of current planning. At BNDES, Francisco Ferreira and Fabio Gambiagi provided ideas and information. Staff at the Brazilian Institute of Geography and Statistics (IBGE) and other statistical agencies took time from their busy schedules to discuss substantive matters with me. I acknowledge advice from Albert Bildner, Eduardo Graeff, Juarez R. Brandao Lopes, Danielle Ardaillon, Anthony Pereira, Maria Hermínia Tavares de Almeida, and the late Vilmar Faria, among many. I am very grateful for the assistance of Bildner Center staff. Rosa Maria Conceição and Marco Afonso provided superior research assistance. Sandra Black and Andrés Salas were very helpful in editing and laying out graphic material. Claudia Carvalho helped in compiling the bibliography. I acknowledge support from Queens College, The Graduate Center, the PSC-CUNY program at the City University of New York, and the Hewlett Foundation.

| CHAPTER 1 | *A Reform Era in Perspective* |

B
razil's reputation as a laggard in matters of economic liberalization through the early 1990s is still in need of a full explanation, but so is the subsequent era of reform. The country experienced considerable reform in the 1990s, particularly during Fernando Henrique Cardoso's two terms as president (1995–1998, 1999–2002). This volume examines policy changes and trends to probe the scope and depth of the Brazilian reforms, the support for them among key actors, and their broad implications.[1]

As the 1990s opened, most Latin American countries were already adopting or had recently embraced various measures to liberalize their economies, redefine the role of the state, and explore new ideas about development. Pioneering Chile introduced in the 1970s, and enhanced during the democratizing period that followed military rule, a massive program that included privatization, trade liberalization and the opening of the economy, foreign investment, deregulation, and social security reform, as well as stabilization and fiscal adjustment.[2] Argentina, Bolivia, Mexico, and several other coun-

1. Bresser Pereira (1996) provides an early sketch of the Brazilian reforms through the early years of the *Plano Real*, placing them in a comparative context and highlighting the great crisis of the 1980s. A reference point for the study of reforms in Latin America, Bresser Pereira's work blends economic and political analyses, calling attention to shifting policy perspectives in response to crises of the state and of the economic model. See also Sola (1993a, 1993b, 1994a, 1994c, 1998).

2. Hira's (1999) account emphasizes the role of ideas and epistemic communities in the Chilean reforms. These reforms were originally adopted in the context of military rule (1973–1990) by a team of economists trained at the University of Chicago. For that reason, they were soon baptized as "neoliberal," often with pejorative intent. After 1990 the coalition of Christian democratic and social democratic parties known as "Concertación" gave the Chilean reforms a different tone, though staying the course with respect to the basic economic model. Subsequent liberalizing policies throughout Latin America and Brazil came to be generically branded as "neoliberal," in part because of the historical context provided by the Chilean case and international pressures for fiscal or structural adjustment. There is considerable imprecision in this regard, since social democrats, Christian democrats, and other political movements and organizations throughout the region have sought distinctive approaches to reform.

tries followed suit in the 1980s and early 1990s, even if in the end their policies lacked the scope or success of Chile's. Brazil, however, marched to a different beat.[3] It stuck to *dirigisme* during the entire period of military rule (1964–1985) and through the first phase of the democratizing era. The first attempt at reform in the early 1990s aborted due to opposition in Congress and the impeachment of President Fernando Collor in 1992. This situation changed decisively with the Cardoso presidency, though the successful stabilization plan of 1993–1994 had begun during the Itamar Franco government (1992–1994). The Cardoso government's policy drive aimed at fundamental transformations, and by the end of the decade Brazil seemed to be on its way to major change. But a series of events following the financial crisis of 1998–1999 set back the reform agenda. The last months of Cardoso's second term would bring new financial pressures and new political dynamics from the election of an opposition president.

While the Cardoso administration pursued reforms with singleness of purpose, their character, depth, and durability, as well as the ability of Brazilian democracy to set a new development path, remain at issue. From that perspective, the time frame for the analysis of reform processes in Brazil begins in 1985, when democratization formally began after twenty years of military rule. In this context, the scope and sustainability of the reform effort since 1994 and the prior timidity in policy making are key issues to be examined. This volume probes the historical context of the reforms, their character, and their relationship to the process of democratization. While a main focus is how political and institutional conditions shape reform making, the reciprocal impact of reforms on democratization is also explored.

Brazilian Reform in Comparative Perspective

The agenda of economic and state reform pursued by Brazilian policymakers after 1994 represented neither the fast-paced, "economic reform first" model of Argentina nor a slow, consensual model such as that of Uruguay.[4] In Argentina, Carlos Menem's government introduced fast reforms expecting that positive outcomes would eventually generate massive popular support, while Uruguay's slow and gradual approach concentrated on consensus

3.   Venezuela and Uruguay are also known for hesitant and cautious approaches to economic liberalization (Blake 1998). Venezuela reversed course toward a state-centered regime with the Hugo Chávez election in 1998 and his reelection under a new constitution in 2000.
4.   Economist Jeffrey Sachs was one of the strongest and most persuasive voices urging a "big bang" approach to economic liberalization (Sachs 1994). Supporters of the "reform first" approach generally argue that "if the [market] reforms bring desirable results, they will build a consensus; if they do not, no previous consensus will withstand the negative outcome" (Blake 1998, 2).

building within a democratic framework.[5] The Cardoso administration gave stabilization and economic reform top priority, simultaneously cultivating a broad alliance for political support. The Brazilian model of reform represents a distinctive type in need of assessment.

The singularity of the Brazilian approach to reform emanates in part from its intellectual and doctrinal underpinnings. Chile, Mexico, and Argentina shared a technocratic model that relied heavily on conventional international wisdom about economic policy.[6] The Brazilian reform effort also fed on the global movement toward market-oriented structural adjustment, but the long-simmering internal criticism of the state and the prior economic model shaped it decisively. For years, intellectuals had debated the flaws of the Brazilian state in terms of clientelism, cartorialism, corporatism, and the statist economic model.[7] Critics of dirigisme gradually coalesced around opposition to the centralized regime bequeathed by the Vargas[8] and the military eras, the need for major state reform, and the search for a new approach to development. The evolving strands of policy-oriented analysis converged with the changing international discussion about development. The collapse of socialism in Russia and Eastern Europe and the rise of East Asian "tigers" brought about the ebbing of marxism and other strongly statist doctrines, fueling the search for more market-friendly approaches to development throughout the world. Brazil's reformist stance was in tune with the theme of balancing fiscal responsibility and social policy found in social democratic practice

5.   Argentina's main reform to fight hyperinflation was a monetary policy centered on peso-dollar convertibility (currency board). Harvard-trained Domingo Cavallo was the mastermind of this policy in 1990 and thereafter Argentina defeated inflation for more than ten years, as it also embarked on the massive privatization of publicly owned companies. The apparent success story ended abruptly in December 2001, when a deepening economic and social crisis led to social revolt protesting both the inability of the government to stem the crisis and the cuts in pensions and social spending. A state of siege could not stop the rioting and ransacking, which led to the resignation of President Fernando De la Rúa and Cavallo, who had been brought back as minister of the economy earlier that year to save the Argentine economy. Instead, Argentina entered the most severe economic crisis in its history, one that worsened as the new president declared a moratorium on its large debt and the country faced the end of monetary parity. Clearly, the monetary and fiscal policies implemented by Menem and maintained by De la Rúa had failed miserably, and at extremely high costs. The failure to bring fiscal matters under control was an immediate factor leading to the crisis. Underlying this failure too was the inability of the political class as a whole to agree on effective solutions.

6.   Williamson (1990a) sketches the "Washington consensus." In Brazil, economic liberalism has often been associated with economist, diplomat, and politician Roberto Campos—whose highly readable and candid memoirs, *Lanterna na popa*, provides a revealing assessment of policy debates and personalities through much of the twentieth century (its large size—1,417 pages—did not prevent it from being a best-seller). This association needs careful qualification, since Campos was directly involved in the rise of the Brazilian developmental state and the early history of such institutions as BNDES, while defending the role of the market and crusading against what he saw as excesses in dirigisme in *cepalismo* and marxism.

throughout Europe and North America. The original reform coalition included parties and factions from the center-right and the right,[9] but it would be simplistic to characterize the Brazilian approach as "neoliberal."[10]

Brazilians endorsed the Cardoso program in 1998, when they reelected him to a second four-year term. Privatization, liberalization, economic openness, and other key reforms seemed largely irreversible at that point. However, a few weeks after the election, the international financial crisis caused support for the government to plummet. Political turbulence throughout much of the second term further hindered the reform process. In fact, the original reform coalition would all but collapse by 2001. The formal reform drive would make little progress through the end of the Cardoso era.

This volume relies heavily on the available empirical material to probe the reforms' character and magnitude, the evolving political and ideological debate about them, and the roles of various actors. It compiles available information about changes and trends in diverse policy areas, seeking to identify as accurately as possible the broad contours of the new policies and their impact (see appendixes A-D). The extent to which Brazil is shifting to a new development strategy is a main focus.

Political and Institutional Context

Comparative discussions of economic reform often dwell on the relative merits of democracy and authoritarianism. Brazil hardly proves the alleged

7. Bresser Pereira's (1996, 1997) thesis of a "fiscal crisis of the state" provides an important explanation of the crisis of dirigisme in Brazil and the rise of a distinctive, broadly social democratic, approach. Advocates of this approach often came from the ranks of those associated with dependency theory and marxism—including Mantega (1984), Bielchowsky (1985), Unger (1990), Biderman et al. (1996), Jaguaribe et al. (1989), Baer et al. (1973). Fernando Henrique Cardoso's own trajectory parallels this shift (see selection of Cardoso's writings in Cardoso and Font [2001]). João Paulo dos Reis Velloso and associates organized the National Forum in Rio, an entity that promoted a political project and a broad social pact and political movement tuned to democratization, modernization, the inclusion of the popular sector, and development (Velloso 1990).
8. Getúlio Vargas came to power as leader of the Revolution of 1930. The progressively authoritarian Vargas era (1930–1945) centralized political power and gradually adopted economic statism. The era of populist democracy (1945–1964) inaugurated after 1945, as well as the military regime of 1964–1985) retained political centralization and embraced dirigisme or a statist approach to development.
9. The PFL, the "liberal" party in the coalition, pays lip service to liberalism but is better known for its skills in pork barrel politics and its strong local political machines, often in the Northeast and the North. It has excelled at acting the role of broker between the federal government and local constituencies.
10. Brazil's reform drive would be shaped after 2003 by the turn to the left in Brazilian politics. "Brazil changed, the Workers' Party changed, I changed"—stated Inácio Lula da Silva during the 2002 electoral debate, confirming the ideological turn to the center by him and his party (see, for example, "Eu mudei. O Brasil também," *Veja*, September 25, 2002). This shift, taking political form as this book went to print, is further evidence of the broader intellectual and ideological shifts in Brazilian society.

advantage of authoritarianism in bringing about successful economic reform. In contrast with the Chilean case, the military regime in Brazil (1964–1985) failed to set a new economic course. It maintained the statist and corporatist model and ended in the midst of an economic crisis.[11] Authoritarianism and dirigisme were two sides of the same coin. Brazil faced increasing deficits, high debt, inflation, and eventual crisis through the first phase of the post-1985 democratic era. Corporatism and clientelism share responsibility for gridlock in the adoption of badly needed changes, including social security reform. Many difficulties of the Brazilian economy have their roots in the institutional legacies of authoritarianism traceable to the Vargas era.

The extent to which Brazil's post-1985 democracy has been conducive to sustained reforms is a separate question, one of major significance in assessing the prospects for a long-term shift in the development model. The theoretical case for a negative relationship between democracy and economic reform often emphasizes distributional effects—the short-term cost to "losers" and their ability to oppose, block, and even reverse them (Blake 1998). Distributional effects make reforms inevitably conflictual, while democracy makes it easier for losers to organize and engage in collective action against the reforms. Democratization also creates conditions for popular expectations to grow, regardless of whether appropriate institutional mechanisms are in place to articulate, channel, and process them (Haggard and Kaufman 1989). In that context, the likelihood of timely and effective reforms in a democratic context depends on the formation and maintenance of durable reform coalitions among organized political forces and the institutional capacity to implement the new policies and to absorb and defuse organized opposition. Democracy's advantage in promoting reform and development has often been argued in terms of broad support and reduction in transaction costs to the population.[12]

There is no denying the shortcomings of Brazilian democracy in promoting development during its first phase (1985–1993), as it fell considerably short of success in addressing the mounting economic woes, much less in setting the country on a new development course. The Brazilian transition to democracy was slow, somewhat precarious, and driven by understandings within the elite. The process of gradual and controlled political liberalization begun in 1973–1974 set the stage for the eventual selection of a civilian president in 1985. This was a "transition from above" that maintained considerable continuity with past practices and leaders.[13] Mentalities, practices, and personnel associated with clientelism and corporatism survived, while the constitution of 1988 added a mix of corporatism and decentralized rule that threatened to

11. Font (forthcoming) discusses the rise and demise of dirigisme in Brazil.
12. Montero (1998a, 1998b) identifies gaps in the literature defending democracy in terms of its impact on effective economic reforms.

immobilize the polity. The weak party system and the imbalanced federation were partly responsible for the government's failure to control inflation through the early 1990s and its inability to introduce a new economic model.

Democratization meant intense political competition and huge growth in the electorate. Dozens of political parties were formed after 1985, as Brazil's electorate burgeoned to over 100 million voters. Persisting political and institutional problems included an unsettled form of presidentialism, a system of proportional representation biased against populous states such as São Paulo, weak party discipline, political fragmentation, unbalanced federalism, and enduring forms of clientelism and corporatism. Partly for those reasons, the emergent democracy came to be characterized as restricted or frozen. Whether or not this is an apt characterization, the Brazilian polity of the mid-1990s did face a daunting agenda of political and institutional change to consolidate democratic rule and development.

Democratic policymakers in Brazil faced dynamics and dilemmas of dual transitions—from nondemocratic to mature democratic rule and from autarkic statism to economic liberalization and openness. This context conditioned the processing of the proposals for economic reform. A key sequencing question was whether economic liberalization should precede or follow further political change. Seemingly chronic economic crises placed the fight against inflation and fiscal policy as a top priority. Performance in that regard had been less than impressive before Cardoso's presidency, as eight years of democracy had only worsened inflation and economic woes. The Fernando Collor administration (1991–1992) tried to implement a program of structural adjustment that included economic liberalization, but dramatically failed to set a new course. In an economic sense as well, Brazilian democracy did indeed appear frozen, unable to break new ground in a clear direction.

By the early 1990s it was clear that the country badly needed major political and institutional reforms, but the Cardoso administration opted for economic liberalization over further political reform as its top priority.[14] Declaring Brazil to be a consolidated democracy, his government concentrated on stabilization, fiscal and state reform, the liberalization of the economy, and laying the foundations for a new approach to development. With a host of political and institutional conditions remaining inauspicious to reform, the executive used the decrees known as *medidas provisórias* (MPs) to enact major policy. Meanwhile, the reformers sought to build up state

13. As president of the Chamber of Deputies, historic democrat Ulisses Guimarães should have been named president. Instead, the military pressed for the selection of Vice President José Sarney, a civilian politician considered closer to the regime.
14. However, considering the previous expansion of democracy in Brazil, this approach differs from those of Mexico, China, and East Asia, where economic liberalization was the key initial priority.

capacity. While compelled to rely on pork barrel politics to maintain a reform coalition, the Cardoso government managed to refurbish and insulate from undue pressure the development bank (BNDES), the Finance Ministry, the Central Bank, the Planning Ministry, the Development Ministry, and other key ministries in the social area, particularly those of Education and Health.

In spite of an impressive number of reforms, political conditions prevented the central government from eliminating certain key vulnerabilities in the Brazilian economy. Wary about public perceptions that it ruled by decree, the executive spent a great deal of time articulating political forces. But Congress often hesitated or failed to act on proposed reforms. A steep price was paid in late 1998–1999, when a major international financial crisis hit Brazil. The beginnings of the crisis did not prevent Cardoso's reelection, but his popularity sank with the deterioration of economic indicators after the election. As the crisis deepened, some began to worry about governability itself. Inflation did not return and the economy gradually bounced back, but the crisis inflicted considerable political damage and made the reform process grind to a virtual standstill. As Cardoso's second term began, the president's political capital seemed substantially depleted, and no major initiative appeared within easy reach in the near future. The new cycle of crisis had brought out the central role of politics in the reform process.

The Elite-Driven Polity: Legacy and Dynamics[15]

The role of elites and interelite dynamics in the Brazilian reform process reflects patterns set throughout the country's political history. The modern Brazilian elite emerged as the result of a complex interplay between two powerful sets of forces whose interactions since the nineteenth century have generated patterns of social organization and collective action, marked by heterogeneity and differentiation. One force is the uneven formation of the state, a process made highly multiform by Brazil's enormous size and geographical diversity. The other is the expansion of capitalism, relentless yet even more uneven than state formation. It accounts for the spatially differentiated pattern of economic development and industrialization jelling at the dawn of the twentieth century. This structural heterogeneity had a major effect on elite formation and the form and character of political contention in subsequent decades, altering the balance on which various republican regimes rested. Both sets of forces acquired new meaning with the cluster of processes characterizing globalization. For those reasons, it is prudent and more accurate to speak of regional elites rather than of a well-integrated ruling class.

---

15. This sections summarizes arguments elaborated in Font (1990a, 1990b, 1996, and forthcoming).

State elites—politicians, soldiers, bureaucrats—have surely been more than mere recipients of influence throughout Brazil's history. At various points they organized and led coalitions aspiring to dominance, relying on state power to consolidate their rule around one or another project of national development. Often, the relationship of policies to the logic of capitalism remained far from unambiguous. The shifting roles of politically active elites rarely emanated from well-settled institutions. The armed forces led the transition from empire to republic in 1889. Rebellious regional elites and sectors of the armed forces figured prominently in the political crisis of the 1920s and the Revolution of 1930, as well as the collapse of democracy in 1964. Regionalism and local factors help explain the behavior of state elites and the seemingly pendular movement between centralized and decentralized federalism in Brazilian history.

In Europe, modern state building took centuries and much bloodshed before reaching a plateau of stability in the twentieth century. In Brazil this process was still unfolding as that century ended. The fluidity of institutional and political life helps explain how state elites forge workable coalitions with social and economic actors,[16] as well as mass and elite collective action.

The dynamics of political realignment involving regionally based actors has been at the center of state-making in modern Brazil. In the Old Republic (1889–1930) political stability rested on the *politica dos governadores,* an accord brokered by the political establishments of Minas Gerais and São Paulo specifying that dominant state-level parties and factions would continue to be acknowledged as such by the federal government so long as in return they would grant support to the federal government. Similar understandings governed reciprocal support between governors and between state-level authorities and the political chieftains controlling local government at the municipal level. The nationalist coalition that won in the 1930s was in large measure a modernizing reaction to the economic and political imbalances in the Brazilian federation. As a whole, the state of São Paulo, a major region in itself, offered a distinctive model for what modern Brazil should be. It stood and still stands for a particular path of national development based on private entrepreneurship and the market, as well as openness to immigrants and outside investment. São Paulo's economy furnished the driving force for modern capitalist development in Brazil. Against the backdrop of the effervescence of a society in transition in the 1920s, the political establishment from São Paulo sought to affirm substantial national control. Reaction to the idea of enhanced *paulista* leadership led to an alternative coalition of military strata and emergent regional oligarchies, which eventually settled on a more

16. The conclusion in Haggard and Kaufman (1995) discusses multiple challenges in the Brazilian polity.

centralized and top-down process of modernization after the success of the Revolution of 1930 led by Getúlio Vargas. That coalition provided the agency that presided over the construction of a political behemoth claiming leadership over political and economic policy. Institutional and political innovations during this period shaped Brazil's development and modernization.

Politicians, soldiers, and bureaucrats forged a top-down, often authoritarian, centralizing, nationalist, and corporatist state form that sought to control and simplify political and economic dynamics. Social and economic groups generally went along and struck the best deals they could. The economic elite was no exception. But its various strands continued to pursue their own local interests and identities. In spite of official rhetoric and moves toward centralization and national development, the real Brazil remained an archipelago of diverse regions, peoples, and interests. Elite and social class formation reflected and perpetuated political and structural heterogeneity. Brazil differed from mature liberal industrial democracies not only in the peculiarities and complexity of its political and civil societies, but also in the form and degree of alignment of the polity. Regional elites and agendas were not easily integrated in the context of the federal polity.

However, the alternation between populist democracy, authoritarianism, and related patterns of instability show that the centralizing coalition was not able to provide a stable modern political regime or sustainable long-term economic growth. Crisis brought dirigisme to its knees in the last part of the twentieth century. Rejected by key players, corporatism provided a weak basis on which to reorganize the polity. But no other organizing principle was ready to take its place. The ability of the diverse political actors to come together in the context of transition would prove very difficult. Region and federation continued to be fundamental political categories in the context of lingering issues of national political integration. The odds of democratic consolidation and a modern system for the representation of interests currently rest on new cycles of innovation and coalition formation to balance the federation, both vertically and horizontally. Political integration and stability now need to take into account the large-scale mobilization of the popular sector in the form of powerful labor confederations, a labor party, and other political organizations.[17] With state elites actively seeking new partners and support in civil society, socially embedded, vertical collective action and contention determine what kinds of coalitions are possible and hence what kinds of development strategies might have a higher probability of prevailing.

17. Chapter 4 discusses popular collective action and chapter 5 explores economic elite contention.

The Brazilian polity is still very much in transition. But this process cannot be understood in terms of simple dichotomies. The current trend is toward the consolidation of a sharply decentralized and pluralistic democratic regime. Nationally, the Congress, the presidency, and the courts are vigorously defining and sharpening their new roles, as are their state-level counterparts. Still, democratic deepening is incomplete and subject to powerful crosscurrents. With political and institutional actors at all levels of the federation involved in a process of innovation and adaptation to changes and challenges brought about by other actors and levels, the new federal system has yet to consolidate.

This broad historical and structural canvas puts into context the enduring significance of regionalism and class relations in the dynamics of national integration and the consolidation of the new federal system. As a new century of development dawns on Brazil, São Paulo is still in many ways a main locomotive trying to pull the rest of Brazil into a journey toward a modern capitalist society. As in earlier decades, the degree to which other Brazilians want to join that ride is in question. Diverse political groups have differing visions of what the national development model should be. Socially embedded contention and collective action will help determine what development path Brazil follows in the new century. The immediate challenge is arriving at a working consensus that assimilates various views and interests. Questions remain about how much additional pressure the changing polity can withstand in this regard. Political leaders are called upon to assess risks and make hard choices.

Theoretical and Intellectual Context

Globalization and international pressures have no doubt structured the context shaping Brazil's approach to development, but changing internal intellectual and political conditions have defined the response.[18] The Brazilian shift in doctrine away from autarkic dirigisme and efforts to go beyond the traditional developmental state finds support in the evolution of the international debate about shifts in development strategy and adjustment programs, as well as the growing focus on the impact of internal institutional conditions on economic policy.

18. Haggard's (1990) account of shifts in development strategy highlights the impact of international shocks and pressures on local crises leading to change. Critical historical junctures created by those shocks and pressures shift the local balance of power and create conditions for innovations in institutional life and the development model. Social forces as such have a limited direct role in this model; their effect is mediated by political elites and institutions. This study's emphasis on choices by decision makers is compatible with the structural realignment approach sketched in chapter 7.

Gereffi and Wyman's (1990) comparison of Brazil and Mexico with newly industrializing societies in East Asia highlights how political and institutional factors aided Korea and Tawain's successful adoption of a strategy of export-oriented industrialization in the 1960s after a short phase of protectionism, while the Latin American cases generally clung to import substitution industrialization (ISI) through the early 1980s. Several authors in that volume point to the autonomy and rationality of the East Asian developmental state—explained partly by such factors as Cold War geopolitics and class structure. These macrostructural studies highlight the conditions for success of a more market-friendly approach, though they do not provide a full account of the actual policy-making process.

The analyses in Haggard and Kaufman (1992a) and Nelson (1989, 1990a) on the timing, scope, and consolidation of adjustment programs begin to fill this gap. In that perspective, policy shifts entail the reduction in "rents" or advantages to influential social and economic groups. Strong or autonomous state elites and institutions succeed in neutralizing those interests partly by relying on their strategic relations to global actors. Drawing from the strength of the state institutions they command, state elites mediating between the international and national arenas are more able to define policy agendas and control resources than social interests. The spotlight is on the autonomy, coherence, and effectiveness of the state. In this view, the insularity of politicians from the pressures of interest groups is seen as increasing the likelihood, depth, and success of reforms.[19]

In contrast, Evans (1992) argues that the state's role in adjustment and development policy depends less on autonomy per se than on the embeddedness of state action in networks of dynamic entrepreneurs (see also Callaghy 1989). As exemplified by East Asia, "embedded autonomy" means the effective alliance between politicians and entrepreneurs. This makes possible a cohesive and effective interventionist state that is also able to engender or facilitate the growth of a new entrepreneurial class. According to Evans, the prototypical landlord-based Latin American regimes of the first part of the twentieth century contrast with this configuration. If the state bureaucracy in East Asia was approximate to the Weberian ideal, Latin America's subsequent regimes were prone to clientelism and higher levels of inefficiency and corruption.

The state-centric and embedded autonomy perspectives call attention to the coherence and effectiveness of states and state-society relations, viewing them as the result of long-term processes of institutional change and state-society relations. With regard to Brazil and Latin America, the role of busi-

19. The state's developmental role is emphasized in Evans, Reuschemeyer, and Skocpol (1985). Evans (1992) traces the treatment of this role by Gerschenkron and Hirschman, in contrast with the antistatism of neoliberalism and neoclassical economic theory.

ness elites in these relations needs to be explored in great depth. To posit a single type of state-entrepreneur relation for the entire region can hardly account for the diversity of experiences found there, even within Brazil alone. Emergent entrepreneurs have been implicated in movements, coalitions, and institutional arrangements associated with either traditional export sector prominence, protected industrialization, or new forms of economic liberalization.[20] If shifts in development strategy are linked to variations and changes in elites and elite-based coalitions, other groups and the popular sector need to be taken into account.[21]

A New Role for the State: The Brazilian Debate

Intellectuals and ideas also need to be taken into account, according to the analysis developed in this volume. Within Brazil, the perception that political and institutional conditions were responsible for the country's economic woes grew with the debt crisis of the early 1980s, but had roots in critiques of the central state developed in earlier decades. A number of public intellectuals previously associated with state-centered models began to argue that the economic collapse indicated a more profound fiscal and institutional crisis.[22] The trajectories of three prestigious public intellectuals make this point. Ignácio Rangel, a noted leftist economist associated with the Vargas era, began to argue as early as 1978 that the old model had spent itself and that privatization and state reform were now necessary to restore vitality to Brazil's development.[23] Diplomat José Guilherme Merquior, an influential intellectual from Rio, began a series of critical reflections that took him from a marxist statist position to open advocacy of liberalism. In the process, he identified clientelistic patrimonialism as the source of many of the country's ills, a problem that could be solved only thorough state reform and the liberalization of Brazilian society.[24] Lastly, Fernando Henrique Cardoso himself and several intellectuals who launched the PSDB in the late 1980s experienced intellectual trajectories that led them to focus on state reform and economic liberaliza-

20. Becker (1990), for example, shows that in Venezuela the top business association led a veritable bourgeois social movement in favor of liberalization. According to the author, business's vociferous opposition to statism/dirigisme and demands for privatization and a more independent civil society played a key role in the election of a pro-reform president. But this reform coalition was not sufficiently strong, for the antireform coalition led by Hugo Chávez won subsequent elections and came to implement major institutional changes of its own. Organized business emerged as the main opposition to Chávez's plans for a statist "Bolivarian revolution."
21. Latin American social scientists have tended to treat twentieth-century development dynamics in terms of class, as exemplified in Cardoso and Faletto's (1979) influential analysis. A large literature demonstrates the importance of social classes in the development trajectories and long-term institutional evolution of Western Europe and settler societies (for example, Moore 1967).
22. See also nn. 4 and 5, this chapter.
23. Bresser Pereira and Rego (1993).

tion.[25] A minority at first, these and other voices had a growing impact on the national debate on the role of the state in development.

The Emphasis on Institutions. Within the Brazilian academic world proper of the 1990s, a growing number of social scientists produced critical assessments of the traditional Brazilian state in their search for explanations to the delays and shortcomings of Brazilian stabilization and poor economic performance as a whole. They generated lines of inquiry focused on conditions shaping strategic action by political elites, as well as class or structural realignments. The intellectual and academic debate within and between these currents of thought is interesting in its own terms as an indicator of major change in Brazil. In addition, it illuminates the role of the political and institutional context in the reform process and helps frame more general questions about transitions and transformation.

The first decade of the democratic transition reinforced social scientists' concern with political institutions and political conditions.[26] Of the several institutional conditions that have been taken to explain the poor performance of the 1985–1993 policies, the weak and fragmented political party system and the character of relations between the president and Congress stand out.[27] Brazilian social scientists became increasingly concerned about the ability of the democratizing polity to pick strong and effective presidents. José Sarney and Itamar Franco, the first and third presidents of the democratizing era, were vice presidents who became heads of state only as replacements for the leaders they were supposed to serve. Sarney came to power after the death of Tancredo Neves, the first civilian president, who died before taking office; Franco did so when Fernando Collor was impeached in 1992 on charges of corruption. None had come to power as a leader of a major political party with a national constituency. They could not rein in the national budget or implement tough austerity measures. Neither Collor nor Cardoso, the two presidents who advanced the reform drive the most, came to power as a member of a majority party.

24. For a discussion of Merquior's trajectory and publications, see André Singer, "O enigma Merquior," *Folha de S. Paulo* (Mais), July 15, 2001. This publication also reproduces an influential essay, "O Brasil no limiar do século 21," delivered as a lecture at the Sorbonne shortly before Merquior's premature death in January 1991.
25. For Fernando Henrique Cardoso's intellectual trajectory, see Cardoso and Font (2001). Several essays by Bresser Pereira trace the evolution of his own thinking as well as Brazilian thought in general [www.bresserpereira.ecn.br]. Bolivar Lamounier and other respected intellectuals experienced parallel trajectories.
26. Brazilian authors had been wrestling with institutional analysis for a considerable time before modern institutionalism gained ground in the United States and Europe. A classic in this regard is Faoro (1958).
27. Lopes (1996) and Diniz (1995b) discuss the shifting literature in the early 1990s.

The economic doctrines and assumptions underlying policy-making and embedded in institutional practice help account for the limited success of pre-1994 stabilization policies. Even when they flirted with economic liberalization, the governments of this era remained largely tied to traditional ideas about the statist, protectionist model in place for decades. It was only with Collor's election in 1990 that the need for liberalizing reforms entered the national agenda seriously (Sola 1993b). Almeida (1995a) calls attention to the traditionally strong statist ideology and an institutional context made worse by democratization itself. Import substitution industrialization and state-led development had been hallmarks of Brazilian economic thinking through much of the twentieth century. To Almeida, these ideas shaped the perception of crises and the design of responses, so that state-centered rather than market reforms were perceived as more adequate. The failure of the Cruzado Plan in 1987 began to break the consensus and create space for alternative perspectives.[28] But the statist ideology was still very strong. The more pragmatic Bresser Plan (1987–1988), based on the "fiscal crisis" approach identified with Bresser Pereira's stint as finance minister and one of the most comprehensive plans through the late 1980s, was still insufficient. It would take the ideological shifts accelerating in 1990 and thereafter to eventually permit the implementation of market or liberalizing reforms.

Almeida's own analysis can be seen as part of the change in perspective experienced by Brazilian intellectuals and enhances the case for the significance of ideas and ideology.[29] But there are limitations to how much ideas or ideology alone can explain. Policymakers during the Sarney government (1985–1989) experimented with diverse approaches to inflation and economic crisis.[30] Ideology alone cannot account for these variations in policy,

28. Appendix A identifies the stabilization plans during the period 1985–2002.
29. Like Lourdes Sola, Maria Hemínia Tavares de Almeida is a prominent member of the Department of Political Science at the University of São Paulo and has been part of the main currents of thought in that important state. Brasilio Sallum, Eduardo Kugelmas, and other colleagues at the University of São Paulo have also provided new insights into Brazil's new reform era. At the Instituto Universitário de Rio de Janeiro (IUPERJ), Wanderley Guilherme dos Santos, Eli Diniz, Renato Boschi, and colleagues have probed diverse aspects of transition and reform in Brazil. A long list of specialists at CEBRAP, CEDEC, IDESP, and other research centers, together with the work done in Brazil's large system of universities and its research facilities in the social sciences, have illuminated the country's new approaches to political, social, and economic change.
30. Sallum (1996, 137–52). Sallum describes considerable alternation between "heterodox" and "orthodox" policies. The first approach, identified with economic teams of the PMDB, centered on measures to enhance tax collection and to increase the prices of goods and services of state enterprises, while holding down the prices of private business and service costs of the public debt. The orthodox approach, originating in economists presumably tied to the previous regime (Francisco Dornelles and Maílson da Nóbrega), called for a reduction in the budget to eliminate deficits. Sallum's interpretation of this phenomenon emphasizes the political role of social groups in the context of a shift in the international articulation of the national economy.

since by most accounts it had not changed appreciably at the time. In any case, just to assert the primacy of ideas begs the questions of how a given ideology comes to prevail and how to explain shifts in policy paradigm.[31] Ideology and policy serve important functions in coalition building, and thus need to be considered as factors shaping the politics of reform.

Other authors dwell on the weaknesses and limitations of Brazilian politics, often converging on a broad analytical emphasis on the strength and autonomy of the state. One version of this line of thinking blames excessive populism and rent-seeking behavior for the Brazilian government's inability to enact and implement appropriate policies in the 1970s and 1980s.[32] Several studies agree that post-1985 democratization worsened the policy-making context, as heightened mobilization and pluralization of political representation coincided with or led to decreased overall coherence in the state apparatus.[33] Even Cardoso, a strong critic of traditional Brazilian politics, had difficulties in getting his basic program approved.

Lopes (1996) sketches a broad political economic perspective in which institutional conditions interact with the "web of powerful interests, institutions, and beliefs" inherited from Brazil's relatively successful developmental state of past decades.[34] In effect, he calls for a synthesis of institutional and structural perspectives. In this view, the same conditions explain the failure of the stabilization plans and reforms under Sarney and Collor—particularly weak presidents as a result of a fragmented party system and frail government coalitions. A large number of parties (more than twelve) and weak party identification and discipline make for an ineffectual party system. At the Congress, deputies and senators are more often swayed by the blocs or caucuses known as *bancadas* than by party position. States and regions have strong blocs that often veto major policy initiatives, while state congressional delegations are often able to veto bills that affect their states negatively. These sectional interests often coincide with economic sectors, as in the case

---

31. Hira's (1999) study of competition between structuralism and neoliberalism in recent Chilean history leads the author to a set of stimulating hypotheses linking shifts in ideas or policy paradigms to the fate of epistemic communities in which they are embedded. The latter's degree of organization, cohesion, and relationship to current Zeitgeist affects the likelihood that power holders will adopt their policy paradigms in moments of crisis.

32. Skidmore (1977), Kaufman (1990), Melo (1993b), Lamounier (1994), Bacha (1991), Martins (1994). Gouvêa's (1994) empirical study of the mid-1980s financial reform, in the context of the transition to democracy, portrays the bureaucracy as a distinctive, coherent actor responding to the excesses of politicians and able to lead in matters of policy. The literature on the Brazilian bureaucracy and its role in economic strategies and reforms includes Fernando Cardoso (1975), Bresser Pereira (1978), Evans (1995), Schneider (1991a), and others.

33. Lopes (1996), Almeida (1995a, 1995b), Sola (1993b), Diniz (1995a, 1995b, 1997). The institutional approach finds inspiration in Samuel Huntington's idea that too fast a democratization in transitional societies hampers institutional stability and governability.

34. Lopes (1996, 195).

of the large cattle ranchers. The fragmented party system and the fragile governing coalitions make it likely for presidents to fall back on clientelism to maintain governing coalitions.[35]

The institutional approaches differ substantially, but they generally weave a cluster of political and institutional variables into a pessimistic scenario about the durable prospects for economic liberalization. Brazil's evolving federalism has come to the limelight as a source of problems. The constitution of 1988 strengthened the role of states and localities in fiscal and political matters. With the demise of the traditional developmental coalition and ethos, the federal bureaucracy lost some functions, just as regionally embedded political and socioeconomic interests increased the political pressure. Public enterprises allied with these interests were able to marshal considerable resources at their command to resist liberalization and privatization policies. Efforts to amend the constitution have not proceeded smoothly, leaving an air of uncertainty about the institutional context.[36]

The early process of democratization undermined the policy coherence of the corporatist state and its very capacity to support reforms. The pronounced shift to decentralization meant a considerable loss of control by the central government. The federal government's share of the total budget decreased and those of state and local governments increased (see table 3-4). Fiscal decentralization and the attendant fragmentation of authority added to the difficulties of implementing wide and deep reforms. Moreover, democratization fueled the expansion of powerful interest groups. In the institutional dynamics created by the transition to democracy, subnational politicians often relied heavily on deficit-financed patronage to promote their political careers.

The institutionalists' pessimism about short-term change misses possibilities for change in the existing context. The Brazilian presidency remains a powerful agent for change. In spite of the admittedly difficult institutional

35. Ames (2001) argues that Brazil has too many political actors with veto power, something he attributes to an excessive number of often weak parties.

36. Haggard and Kaufman (1995, 193–98, 209–11) agree with the explanation of the failure of economic liberalization in Brazil in terms of "centrifugal political pressures" linked to the fragmentation of the party system, the heterogeneity or instability of legislative coalitions, and the power of regional political elites. Noting that pressure from labor and business made Sarney change ministers, but could not stop the inflationary spiral, these authors point out that Sarney's Cruzado Plan "was characterized by relatively limited concern for orthodox (macroeconomic) measures, and represented a calculated attempt to outflank or co-opt opponents on the left" (1995, 194). Sergio Abranches, Walder de Góes, Bolivar Lamounier, and other Brazilian social scientists were coalescing in the early 1990s on a politico-institutional analysis of the obstacles to economic reform along these lines (for example, Marks 1993 reports various statements made to that effect at a 1991 conference). To aid the reform process, these social scientists call for measures leading to a more disciplined and manageable party system, an improved relationship between the president and the Congress, addressing the fiscal federalism decreed by the 1988 constitution, and redefining the role of the state.

context, at least two Brazilian presidents in the nineties, Collor and Cardoso, used the resources of the presidency to adopt major reforms and articulated the need for change in economic policy. As the following chapters show, the Cardoso presidency provides a test of how far the federal government can go to advance various reforms.

The Broader Structural Context. Other Brazilian authors shift the focus of attention to the broader structural context and socioeconomic groups. Rejecting the institutionalist call for further state autonomy, Diniz (1995a) maintains that the Brazilian transition to democracy witnessed considerable continuity within the traditionally centralized policy-making system. A very strong executive and a fragile party system survived largely intact into the post-1985 democratizing era, allowing Brazilian presidents to continue to make extensive use of government decrees and provisional measures. Congressional and party fragmentation hence pose no insurmountable resistance to economic reform (see also Fiori 1993). Associating the "strong state" approach with neoliberalism and the neglect of social policies, Diniz dismisses it as too elitist, reductionistic, and prone to technocratic formulas that impede the further development of democracy and the incorporation of popular sectors.

Diniz's alternative explanation for the failure of post-1985 stabilization programs concentrates on the policy implementation stage and underlines the role of politics broadly conceived. The state itself has wide latitude to make policy decisions. The problem is that it is incapable of implementing vital objectives because of the absence of coalitions and alliances supporting the policies. In fact, the Brazilian democratic state often acts unilaterally, even coercively, thus running the danger of being perceived by Brazilians as lacking legitimacy. According to Diniz, major political reform to enhance democracy rather than governability is the most urgent task. A more democratic and decentralized Brazilian state will be more efficient to the extent that it coordinates its actions with interest groups and other actors during implementation.

One challenge to this line of thinking is that the absence of democracy did not prevent past Brazilian policymakers from making and implementing the most diverse policies, including the rise and deepening of developmentalism in the 1950s. Evidence abounds that elite-centered coalitions have traditionally controlled the making and implementation of policy in Brazil, regardless of regime type.

Sallum (1996) incorporates social classes in a structural model that balances the roles of economic elites, organized labor, and political movements. After dissecting the three adjustment attempts during the Sarney administration—the Cruzado Plan (1986–1987), the Bresser Plan (1987–1988), and the Summer Plan (1989–1990)—Sallum concludes that continued inflation and other economic problems in the early 1990s reflected a broad crisis of the developmentalist state. He places the collapse of the developmentalist coalition and the underlying structural crisis at the center of the analysis. In the context of this "crisis of hegemony," members of the old developmentalist alliance retain sufficient power to veto policy initiatives shifting the costs of new policies to them. Pressures to liberalize the economy come from the entrepreneurial class's turn away from national developmentalism and toward liberalism, as well as from the deepening internationalization of the Brazilian economy. In this perspective, the entrepreneurial class seeks autonomy from the traditional corporatist system and presses for the demise of dirigisme. However, labor and other sectors are able to veto any strategy that shifts the costs of adjustment to them. Hence, Brazil is at a structural impasse. This impasse explains the alternation between economic policies and the inability for the polity to implement a breakthrough. The business-centered liberalizing coalition has not been strong enough to defeat the statism defended by public workers, labor in general, and sectors of the middle class.

Sallum illuminates important aspects of the crisis of Brazilian developmentalism and suggests that the country is moving toward a process of political restructuring to sustain a new economic model or development strategy. The analysis succeeds in placing the reform process in a broad structural context. As it recognizes and weaves in the role of global capital, this study confirms the role of national politics and national actors. The idea of a solid developmentalist coalition through the early 1980s is assumed rather than demonstrated. Behaviors indicating the deterioration of the alliance, including the animosity of the business sector toward state efforts to retain authority, were not new. Entrepreneurs had been at odds with the central government in the early 1980s. In the 1970s, they organized a campaign in favor of destatization. Moreover, this interpretation does not easily accommodate attempts at orthodox policy-making before the Cruzado Plan of 1985. The last years of military rule witnessed these policies, though protected business sectors opposed some of them at the time. Brazilian leaders have been able to implement diverse policies at various points.

An Action-Enabling Approach to Reform

Faced with pressing issues and dilemmas, Brazilian reformers would be ill-advised to wait for institutional or structural changes that require a great deal of time. Successful reformers take structural and institutional realities into account to illuminate the hurdles and contours of the road, but focus on achievable goals and values—what Albert Hirschman calls the art of the possible (1963).

From the perspective of reformers acting upon strategic reasoning to achieve objectives, the very complexity, fluidity, and transitional character of the Brazilian polity offers opportunities for action. Vision to recognize opportunities and the ability to act upon them cannot be taken for granted. Presidents that opened a new democratic era in Brazil were often ineffectual in this regard, which helps explain the timidity of the reform drive for nearly a decade after 1985.[37] That changed with Cardoso. His presidency offered a distinctive vision, a coherent package of reforms, and the ability to forge a broad coalition to implement its program in a democratic framework. That government helps make the case for an approach focused on strategic, problem-solving action—just as it provides an opportunity to test its limits.[38]

A premier challenge for Brazilian reformers is the creation and maintenance of stable political coalitions with a relatively large number of diverse actors and levels of government in the evolving and decentralized federation. Political dynamics at the end of the Cardoso administration suggest that the prospects for long-term success in reforming Brazil hinge not only on political vision and leadership, but also on the ability to form a broad political coalition. Coalition formation is shaped by a complex interplay between a set of actors that includes labor as well as entrepreneurs and state elites. Political elites and other leaders, national or subnational, command the stage. Their actions bear directly on policy decisions and the odds of successful negotiation among organized political forces. Together with other historical and political factors, the peculiarities of the Brazilian institutional context help shape the behavior of political leaders and elites and share responsibility for a complex polity that often resists easy alignment.

A complex political and institutional environment shapes public policymaking in Brazil. In this context, new and old forms of interest mobilization,

37. Collor de Mello did present a bold reformist plan for his short-lived presidency. Collor (1989) is an important document reflecting early thinking about reform on the part of policymakers. A team working under the coordination of Minister of Finance Zélia Cardoso de Mello prepared it between April and August of 1989. Candidate Collor presented it to the public in September, a month before the presidential elections of that year. This document of 130 pages provides a sketch of the crisis of the state and specifies policies to bring about administrative reform, fiscal reform, "patrimonial" reform and privatization, and renegotiation of the external debt. It identifies measures to enhance the action of the Banco do Brasil, BNDES, and the Caixa Econômica Federal, and to develop new approaches to the competitive insertion into the world economy, industrialization, science and technology, trade, agriculture and agrarian reform, energy, infrastructure, social development, environment, and culture. This document provides the blueprint for the reform team formed during the Mello presidency, a group that included Zélia Cardoso, Antonio Kandir, Ibrahim Eris, Eduardo Modiano, and other economists and specialists. I thank Zélia Cardoso for a copy of this report.
38. Cardoso and Font (2001) discusses and documents Cardoso's intellectual trajectory.

20

articulation, and intermediation are likely to coexist for some time. The heterogeneity of political forms and an institutional context marked by fragmentation make political articulation difficult and create vulnerabilities for the political system. But they are not necessary impediments to governance and reform. Reformist statecraft can steer the ship of state to benefit from the powerful currents of the changing civil and political society.

CHAPTER 2   *From Stabilization to Economic Liberalization*

W hen prominent intellectual Fernando Henrique Cardoso became finance minister in May 1993, pundits doubted whether his background prepared him for the battle against hyperinflation, the Brazilian economy's most immediate problem. But Cardoso's stabilization plan brought four-digit annual inflation down to 25 percent within twelve months of its start in mid-1993, and gradually lower after that, reaching single-digit levels in 1996. The success of the *Plano Real*—named after the *real*, the new currency it introduced—led to a resounding victory for Cardoso and his Brazilian Social Democratic Party (PSDB) in the 1994 elections. Cardoso's inauguration as president in January 1995 opened a new chapter in Brazilian political and economic history.

The success of the stabilization plan rekindled hope among Brazilians that the country could overcome its economic and political woes. Some viewed it as a key test of the Brazilian process of democratization. Suspense built in the ensuing months around other reforms promised in the Cardoso platform.

TABLE 2-1. Inflation,[a] 1993–2001, in percent

1993	1994: J-J	1994: J-D	1995	1996	1997	1998	1999	2000	2001	2002[b]
2,564	258.7	16.8	18.8	9.4	6.1	1.0	14.3	7.4	9.3	10.7

Source: Ministério da Fazenda
a. Average of four indices: IGP-DI, IGP-M, IPC-FIPE, and INPC.
b. Annual inflation updated until September.

Background

The nine years of ineffectual economic policies in the post-1985 period of democratization provide the immediate background to Cardoso's policies. Three civilian presidents enacted eight stabilization programs that failed to

21

stop inflation, or to steer Brazil in a new direction. Appendix A describes these policy packages. By 1993 the country faced not only economic stagnation but also record inflation. The successive policy failures had deflated high expectations that democracy would quickly usher in a new era of economic recovery.

The Cruzado Plan's failure set the tone for the poor performance of subsequent stabilization plans. Adopted in February 1986, it was the democratic New Republic's first attempt at addressing economic problems that had surfaced since the years of authoritarian rule. Coming on the heels of a period of high hope and expectations, this failure was particularly frustrating and led to a long and difficult period of social learning about the dangers of the traditional state-centered strategy. The Bresser Plan of May 1987 also failed. The 1989 Summer Plan, the last plan to attempt to stabilize the economy in the 1980s, collapsed even faster than its predecessors. Inflation soared. Brazilians began to worry about their ability to contain it.

Meanwhile, the democratizing polity did not break away from the established practices associated with fiscal deficits, including corporatism and clientelism (Kingstone 1999b). The constitution of 1988, enacted under a president distrusted because of his ties to the military regime, enshrined a long list of specific rights and entitlements to a very large list of constituencies, adding rigidity to a policy-making structure that needed flexibility to undertake reforms. This resulted in most reforms necessitating amendments to the constitution, since that charter specifically protects the items in need of reform—civil service, expenditure levels, expensive pension and social security plans. With amendments requiring two-thirds approval in the Congress on two separate votes in each chamber, the political cost of achieving reforms was and remains very high.

Together with the preexisting fragmentation of political opinion and the cleavages within the Brazilian polity, the constitution facilitated the proliferation of parties. Over sixteen were represented in the Congress and a much larger number competed in elections. The poorest regions were overrepresented. Democratic leaders from São Paulo and other large states demanded congressional and political roles fully commensurate with their states' weight in Brazilian society.

The anti-inflation programs adopted by Collor and then Franco until 1993 met the same fate as those of 1985–1989, feeding fear among Brazilians. The Collor team shocked business groups and the country as a whole with a heterodox policy package that temporarily confiscated bank deposits. Wary of inflation, most Brazilians had given it the benefit of the doubt. The Collor government also pushed through major liberalizing reforms.[1] The drive faltered when a corruption scandal immobilized the federal government in 1992, leading to Collor's impeachment on December 30 of that year.[2]

The rising mood of pessimism about the New Republic peaked just before Cardoso's 1993 appointment as finance minister. Five predecessors and many stabilization attempts had failed to bring inflation under control in the two preceding years. Economic problems seemed intractable.

The mounting policy failures through 1993 did have one positive outcome. By late that year a will for change was palpable through the cloud of deepening disillusionment and frustration. The failure to control inflation fed a generalized perception that Brazil faced a major economic and political crisis. There was now a clearer consensus that the traditional protectionist model was exhausted.[3] New ideas began to appear in the policy-oriented intellectual community. Roberto Campos credits Collor and Finance Minister Zélia Cardoso de Mello for "introducing irreversibly in the nation's agenda ... the modernizing themes of privatization, deregulation, and trade liberalization."[4] At about the same time, politics rather than the economy came to be seen as the root of Brazil's economic problems. Progressively, this perception brought about a new awareness of the flaws of the underlying model in place since the 1930s and of the need to change it.

Cardoso's policies succeeded in large part because of the recognition of the need for change and commitment to state reform, the broad political coalition supporting the reform drive, and presidential leadership. The Cardoso presidency represented a watershed in this regard. Cardoso's team conceived the stabilization plan as only the first step in a broader process of adjustment and restructuring. Viewing heavy government spending and large fiscal imbalances as the key factors in the pernicious form of seemingly chronic hyperinflation, the team looked upon structural and fiscal adjustment as a main avenue to state reform. The government's agenda centered on fiscal adjust-

1. Kingstone (1999a), particularly chapter 5, discusses Collor's reforms in depth. Roberto Campos sketches an interesting assessment of the Collor years from a liberal economic perspective, commenting extensively on the modernizing themes introduced—state reform, privatization, deregulation, trade liberalization, and financial reform (Campos 1994, 1,221–62). Campos praises Collor's inaugural speech, which he claims was written by José Guilherme Merquior, then Brazil's ambassador to UNESCO. However, Campos's view is that this fresh approach was undermined by Collor's failure to appoint established liberal economists to key posts.
2. Technically, Collor resigned just before the impeachment vote.
3. See Boschi (1995). According to Campos (1994, 1,236–37), the Collor administration recruited a team of young economists headed by Zélia Cardoso de Mello, Antonio Kandir, and others, many of them relatively inexperienced ex-marxists (some of them had served in the Sarney government). Campos maintains that this team espoused market reforms but was all too willing to use strong government action to accomplish its goals, such as freezing bank accounts. Though accused of being "neoliberal," Collor actually left out true economic liberals and monetarists from his first and main cabinet. In Campos's view, the Collor reforms partly represent a new form of social liberalism associated with Merquior.
4. Campos (1994, 1,238).

ment, privatization, trade liberalization, deregulation, and related reforms. Gone was the emphasis on heterodox policy packages or shocks normally associated with the economic policy of previous governments. The federal government's ambitious agenda of change included a new balance between federalism and centralization, viewing institutional and fiscal reforms as providing support to each other.

The federal government perceived that it faced deeply rooted economic policy challenges. The larger task was to redefine the economic role of the state and to elaborate a new development model. The old economic model had entered a broader crisis by the early 1980s, when gross domestic product (GDP) contracted partly as a result of the oil crises of the 1970s and the debt crisis of 1982. These external shocks widened the cracks in the existing economic model. Sentiment began to favor the shift away from traditional dirigisme and industrial protectionism.

From Stabilization to Liberalization

To answer why and how the *Plano Real* succeeded in fighting inflation while others failed calls for a reconstruction of the plan itself and the conditions under which it was implemented. The new approach learned from previous stabilization efforts.[5] As finance minister and throughout his first administration, Cardoso concentrated on the anti-inflation plan. The initial measures implemented after June 1993 aimed at reducing the large and growing government deficit of almost US$22 billion (on a yearly budget of US$89 billion). Fiscal reforms in 1993 included a budget cut of US$6 billion, measures against tax evasion (a phenomenon thought to cost Brazil US$25–30 billion per year), and calling in overdue debts owed to the central government by the states. Tax collection in 1993 increased considerably and continued to grow in subsequent years. The fight against the budget deficit—the main cause of inflation—had another key victory in late February 1994, when the Congress approved a US$16 billion emergency fund financed through increased tax collection, which ensured fiscal balance for the next two years. Congress

5.   Several economists at Catholic University in Rio (PUC-Rio) stand out in developing theory and practice centered on the idea that Brazil's inflation had an inertial character and required a distinctive treatment. Cardoso drafted several of them into his government—including Pérsio Arida, Edmar Bacha, Pedro Malan, Gustavo Franco, André Lara Resende, and others. Though the *Plano Real* is a hybrid of heterodox and orthodox approaches, it stands as a watershed in policy reasoning. The underlying premise that Brazil could not enjoy growth with inflation (via indexation) was in itself a major shift. The policy team was influenced by heterodox thinking more than by classical liberalism. Liberal Roberto Campos praised the *Plano Real*, though conditioning it on a series of fiscal and state reforms, including privatization and the full development of a new economic vision for the country (Campos 1994, 1,278).

extended the fund for a further eighteen months in November 1995, again in 1996, and subsequently in later years.

The new fiscal approach increased macroeconomic stability. The above measures broke the ground for a stabilization program proper. Approved in late February 1994, the main instrument toward stabilization proper was a new index, the Real Value Unit (URV), which replaced eleven different indices in adjusting salaries and prices. Pegged to the dollar, this index was conceived as a preamble to the adoption of a strong currency, the third step in the plan. With hard currency reserves nearing US$33 billion (up from US$24 billion in 1992, see fig. D-41) and a seemingly solid trade surplus, the government felt it was in a strong position when it introduced a new currency, the *real*, on July 1, 1994. In 1993 the inflation rate had been above 2,500 percent, but by the second half of 1994 it declined to less than 17 percent.

In late 1994, the IMF's president seemed to endorse Brazil's stabilization plan, giving the *Plano Real* additional momentum. This helped enable an agreement to repay US$35 billion of the foreign debt under the terms of the Brady Plan, using U.S. Treasury Department bonds as collateral, and the renegotiation of the entire debt of US$148 billion (fig. D-38). If the fiscal picture improved significantly, the best grounds for optimism came from the economic performance of the Brazilian economy itself. This top Latin American economy, already larger than Russia's and the world's ninth, grew by 4–5 percent in 1993 and 1994 (see fig. 6-2).[6] The private sector had remained remarkably resilient through the sometimes ill-conceived measures of past governments and responded well to the new economic measures.

The export sector was not as large as it should have been, but in 1993 it was responsible for a trade surplus of US$13 billion in the context of increased imports. Exports continued to grow through 1995 (fig. D-35), though growing import levels made possible by the stronger national currency would soon convert this surplus into a deficit. Some warned that Brazil needed to engage in substantial devaluation, but the government disagreed. Instead it argued that the emergent fiscal context created conditions for initiating such reforms as privatization, trade liberalization, and deregulation.

Hopes were high as the Cardoso presidency began in January 1995. Fully aware that he owed the presidency to the stabilization plan, Cardoso continued to give it top priority. The consolidation of the *real* at an annual inflation rate of less than 20 percent in the context of gradual deregulation was a big achievement for that year. By the end of 1996, annual inflation had been brought down to single digits for the first time since the 1950s. It continued to decrease in subsequent years.

6.   The international ranking of Brazil's economy is sensitive to the fluctuations in the value of the national currency. The country's standing would change from ninth in 1994–1995 to eleventh in mid-2002, as the *real* devalued due to mounting external pressure.

The stabilization plan worked well in the short run, but much remained to be done to ensure long-term success. There were compelling arguments for deepening the process of economic liberalization. However, economic obstacles appeared. The original stabilization formula assumed a strong currency and high interest rates. The first restored confidence in the national currency and channeled surges in demand toward imports. High interest rates served to attract capital, encourage savings, and prevent sudden outflows, such as those that accompanied the Mexican peso crisis of 1994–1995 (fig. D-3). But high interest rates put a break on growth, since they made capital expensive for business, while rising imports pressured the balance of trade toward gradually larger deficits. The government began to liberalize the economy in a cautious manner, seeking support for the stabilization effort.

Trade Liberalization

The Collor administration initiated aggressive trade liberalization policies in 1990 with the goal of opening Brazil's closed economy. The Cardoso government maintained the new emphasis on trade liberalization though it did not accelerate it appreciably, opting instead to channel it in the framework of Mercosul.[7] Even if they represented a significant drop from previous levels, Brazil's average tariffs of 14.2 percent in 1994 were higher than the Latin American average of 11 percent.[8] The federal government used tariff reduction partly to fight inflation via cheaper imports and, selectively, as a disciplinary tool against sectors that increased prices too fast. Imports increased after 1993, as the value of the *real* strengthened. But Brazil's average tariffs remained at around 14 percent in 2002.

Major new rounds of trade liberalization proved elusive after 1994, but selective trade liberalization and cheaper imports of consumer goods continued to be part of the stabilization plan and the appreciated currency in the ensuing years.[9] They gradually exposed Brazilian industry to global competition. Brazil's trade liberalization was not as deep or as broad as that of Mexico, Chile, or Argentina. Moderate and sometimes relatively high tariffs in the context of Mercosul continued to protect important industrial sectors.

7. "Mercosul"—an abbreviation of *Mercado Comum do Sul* (the Spanish version is Mercosur, which stands for *Mercado Común del Sur*)—is a customs union linking Brazil, Argentina, Uruguay, and Paraguay, with special status extended to Chile and Bolivia. The common tariff system affords some protection to industrial production within Mercosul. Brazil's trade strategy emphasizes diversification. Besides Mercosul/Mercosur, the country has sought enhanced relations with industrial nations, including the European Community and Pacific Asia.
8. Average tariff rates had been 38 percent in 1989, 25.3 percent in 1991, 21.2 percent in 1992, and 14.5 percent circa 1993 (Campos 1994, 1,235).
9. Policymakers shared a near-consensus that Brazil was not ready for across-the-board economic liberalization. Cardoso himself would argue against overly rapid trade liberalization at the 2001 Summit of the Americas held in Canada.

A surge in imports began to worry trade experts by late 1995, and by mid-1996 Brazil went from a regime of trade surpluses to one of increasing deficits in the current accounts. Critics warned that the economy was becoming increasingly vulnerable to crises such as that of Mexico in 1994–1995, but the government felt it could finance the trade deficit with hard currency reserves and fresh external investment. The Asian and Russian financial crises of 1997–1998 led to a virtual halt of the trade liberalization drive. One of the 1998 responses to the international financial crisis was to raise tariffs to protect the auto industry from the currency devaluations of South Korea and other Asian auto producers. The hope was that Mercosul would provide a sufficiently large market for Brazilian autos and other products. Other tariffs were maintained or raised somewhat.

The economic contraction of the last quarter of 1998 and the currency devaluation that followed it in January 1999 and after led to a slowdown in imports. The trade deficit decreased significantly in 1999, when exports fell by approximately 6 percent and imports decreased by more than 14 percent. The burning question was whether an acceptable trade balance with no inflation could be achieved only by a recessionary policy. The consensus was that fundamental alterations in the mix of expenditures and tax collection were necessary to eliminate or sharply reduce the fiscal deficit and lead to broader policy options compatible with growth. After several years of negative balance, exports larger than imports in 2001 and after led to a positive balance (see fig. D-36). The positive trade balance responded to the devaluation of the exchange rate in 1999 and to export-promotion policies.

Brazilian policymakers will decide the pattern of subsequent trade liberalization in terms of trade accord negotiations with the United States (Free

FIGURE 2-1. Brazil's Share of World Trade

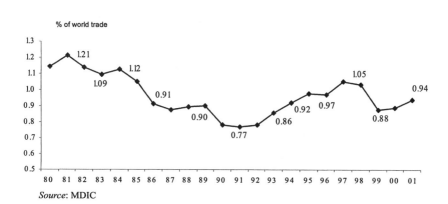

Source: MDIC

Trade Area of the Americas), Mercosul and Mercosul-European Union, and World Trade Organization. In general, export promotion will be emphasized over import liberalization. The substantial devaluation of the *real* through 2002 favors agricultural and other exports. But the new economic model's vulnerabilities with regard to the balance of payment make imperative an explicit export-promotion drive.

Trade is a major challenge for Brazil. Its economy is among the world's ten largest, but Brazilian trade accounts for less than 1 percent of the world's total trade.

Privatization and Foreign Investment

The Brazilian polity had become progressively receptive to the idea of privatization after the 1980s. In the early 1990s, policymakers began to gravitate toward the idea that even a partial sale of the state's 159 public enterprises, thought to be worth over US$190 billion, could bring considerable hard currency to the treasury, while increasing the overall effectiveness of the state and the economy (fig. D-23). The government's resolve to deepen the process of privatization was maintained through the late 1990s.[10]

It had taken the Brazilian political system a long time to decide on such a policy. Some of the early discussions leading to that decision revolved around the issue of increasing administrative inefficiency. In 1979 the Figueiredo government launched the National Program of Debureaucratization and set up the Special Secretariat for the Control of State Enterprises. This initiative did not bring major changes, but it did lead to early steps toward privatization. The 1981 Special Commission for Destatization identified over 100 state enterprises that might be privatized, and a few of the least productive were actually sold between 1981 and 1984. But neither public opinion nor high political circles were fully in favor of privatization. Advocates defended privatization not only to increase economic efficiency, but also as a way of reducing the deficit, political interference in economic decision making, and corruption, while increasing allocation of resources through the market mechanism. Opponents feared lower employment, increasing income concentration, and loss of the national patrimony.

Though the idea of privatization continued to gain favor in the early years of the transition to democracy, it was still seen as only one way of preventing further government expansion. It was not a high priority. Eighteen state enterprises worth US$533 million were privatized between 1985 and 1989. Altogether, the modest privatization of the 1980s amounted to US$780 million.

10. The BNDES website provides much of the essential information on Brazil's privatization program [www.bndes.gov.br]. The crisis of 1998–1999 slowed the privatization process.

The Collor government intensified and formalized the privatization initiative and was the main catalyst for a policy shift in this area. In 1990 it created the National Program of Destatization, charging it with making privatization a central part of a program of economic reform. By 1992 this program had privatized eighteen enterprises worth a total of US$5.38 billion (US$1.36 billion in debt swaps). It also placed a comparable number of companies up for auction, expecting to sell them for more than US$10 billion. Sales concentrated in three sectors—steel, petrochemical, and fertilizers. Collor's impeachment interrupted this process. After first hinting at the suspension of the privatization program, the Itamar Franco administration sold fifteen companies during the period 1993–1994, with receipts totaling US$6.53 billion (US$1.91 billion in debt swaps). The Franco government liberalized sales to foreign investors, allowing for 100 percent ownership. In 1993–1994 the state privatized holdings in the steel industry and readied the Brazilian Aircraft Corporation (Embraer) and three dozen other firms for the auction block. At the end of this period steel had been wholly privatized.

The Cardoso government deepened and broadened the scope of the privatization drive. Within its first two years, it placed the National Program of Destatization under the newly created National Council for Destatization, with both operating within the BNDES. By early 1997, the federal government and some states had sold or were selling off several companies as part of a process expected to yield billions of dollars in the immediate future. Nineteen state enterprises were sold for US$6.37 billion (US$1.294 billion in debt swaps) through 1996.

Privatization peaked in 1997–1998. Total income from privatization by the federal government surpassed US$15–20 billion in both 1997 and 1998. The big test came with the privatization of the Vale do Rio Doce mining complex. Opponents mobilized for a showdown but were not able to stop the sale. This transaction, the largest single privatization transaction in Brazilian history, brought in US$6.858 billion (more than half of which was in debt swaps). In 1997 the Congress approved a new law allowing for the privatization of the huge telecommunications sector. In July 1998 the government sold the twelve

TABLE 2-2. Privatization and Foreign Investment, 1991–2001, in US$ billions

	1991	1992	1993	1994	1995	1996	1997	1998	1999	2000	2001	2002[a]
PND	2.0	3.4	4.2	2.3	1.6	4.8	7.8	2.7	0.1	7.7	1.1	2.0
Telecom	—	—	—	—	—	—	4.7	23.9	0.4	0	1.8	—
Foreign Investment	1.2	3.1	7.3	9.2	6.2	15.5	19.0	28.9	28.6	32.8	22.6	—

Sources: BNDES, Banco Central
a. Updated until October 2002.

companies created in this sector by a division of Telebrás for US$18.998 billion.[11] Concessions for cellular phone service (Band B or digital) brought in US$4 billion in 1997.

By the end of 1998, the sale of 120 state enterprises since 1991 had brought in a total of US$60 billion. Officials proclaimed Brazil's privatization program to be the world's largest, with an additional US$40 billion to flow in within a few years.[12] Meanwhile, state-level governments began their own privatization programs in late 1996, bringing in US$27.5 billion by late October 1998 and a total of US$34.7 billion by April 2001.[13] At that time the total magnitude of the Brazilian privatization effort was US$103.3 billion.

The Brazilian approach to privatization aimed at raising capital and canceling debts, rather than distributing assets as in several East European cases. Privatization alleviated the budget deficit and brought in hard currency to protect the *real*. According to the BNDES, the entity responsible for implementing this complex program, it had also been a success in that the privatized firms began to pay substantial taxes instead of drawing badly needed fiscal resources. Though it still had critics and opponents, privatization had been firmly established as a principle of reform.[14] Still, privatization slowed after 1999—the number of state-owned firms decreased from 252 in 1985 to 103 in early 2000, and remained at 100 in April 2002.[15]

Direct foreign investment followed the ebb and flow of the privatization program. Fresh international capital diminished greatly after the debt crisis of the 1980s. The Collor administration set out to change this situation. Direct private investment grew from US$700 million in 1989 to US$3.1 billion in 1992 and US$7.3 billion in 1993 (see fig. D-40). Growth in foreign invest-

11. This figure includes cellular service, Band A (analog). U.S. dollars are converted from R$22.057 billion at the July 1998 exchange rate.
12. These figures and projections were made by the president of Brazil's Central Bank on November 20, 1998. The second largest privatization was said to be that of the United Kingdom under Margaret Thatcher, which brought in US$40–50 billion.
13. Subnational governments applied these revenues to their own purposes, though with federal pressure to use them for fiscal balance.
14. In November 1998 a scandal broke concerning the illegal wiretapping of high BNDES officials. The recordings suggested that they favored some bids over others. The minister of communications, the president and vice president of the BNDES, and a fourth official resigned. By many accounts, the wiretapping had been released at least in part in the context of rivalries involving the diverse parties and factions vying for power and positions in the second Cardoso administration. This episode slowed but did not stop or cast an aura of suspicion over the privatization program as a whole, which was conducted in a quite transparent way.
15. See table "Evolução do número de estatais" in Ministério de Planejamento website [www.planejamento.gov.br/controle_estatais/conteudo/perfil/evolucao_estatais.htm]. The list of firms awaiting privatization included energy plants, banks, water and sewer utilities, and licensing of Band C cellular telephony (see BNDES website). For a comprehensive list of the state firms in existence in 2002, see website of the Ministry of Planning [www.planejamento.gov.br/contolre_estatais/conteudo/perfil/setor_atividade.htm].

ment resumed in full during the Cardoso presidency—jumping from US$6.2 billion in 1995 to a peak of US$33.3 billion in 2000. By late 1997 and early 1998, the president's agenda included frequent meetings with international business representatives to seek investments in the Brazilian economy.[16]

During its peak years, privatization accounted for approximately a third of foreign private investment. A considerable share of fresh foreign investment has gone into export-oriented industries. In the auto industry, General Motors invested US$1.2 billion in three new plants. Germany's Volkswagen also expanded considerably. Foreign investment has reflected broad confidence in the strengths and promises of the Brazilian economy, as well as emerging opportunities under Mercosul. Fresh foreign capital was also invested in energy, telecommunications, computer technology, construction, and related sectors. United States companies were the single main source, with 16–30 percent of the total. But countries in Europe, Asia, and Latin America were also represented in the wave of investment gathering force in the 1990s.

Toward a New Regulatory Framework

As privatization shifted ownership patterns in several highly concentrated sectors, it revealed the need for a new system. Brazil moved to create modern regulatory agencies in oil, energy, telecommunications, and other sectors that had been highly regulated in the old economic model.[17] The Collor government took some steps toward deregulation, but it was the Cardoso administration that pushed for a more thorough overhaul of the regulatory system.

Prior to 1994, the Brazilian economy coped with high inflation through a complex system of price indexation. By eliminating this system, the stabilization plan itself represented considerable overall deregulation. The deregulating thrust broadened to include rules and practices governing collective bargaining and the government's role in labor relations. When, in response to the crisis of late 1997, labor mobilized to prevent cuts by employers, the federal government refused to get involved. Gaining distance from labor conflicts was a major departure from traditional corporatism in the labor policy

16. Cardoso's schedule in the two-month period that includes December 1997 and January 1998 is typical in this regard. It included the visit to São Paulo of Canadian prime minister Jean Chrétien and a delegation of 375 Canadian business people in January 1998. A few weeks before, President Cardoso spent several days on a state visit to England. At the end of January 1998, Cardoso and some members of his economic team went on a similar trip to Switzerland. At the time, Cardoso was facing international economic pressures and a difficult extraordinary session at the Congress to pass critical economic and state reforms. Because of them, he canceled a visit to Israel that would have followed the trip to Switzerland.

17. There were five regulatory agencies in 2002: National Petroleum Agency, National Telecommunications Agency, National Electrical Energy Agency, National Economic Defense Council, and the Central Bank. These agencies regulate markets and some prices, are led by leaders approved by the Congress, and pursue national policy technically independent of the government.

domain. The government also called for more flexibility in the system of labor relations. In January 1998 the Congress passed a bill creating a new temporary work contract.

The banking crisis in 1995–1996 had moved the government toward a new regulatory structure in the financial sector. The considerable leeway government banks enjoyed in borrowing and spending was only part of the reason for that crisis. Banks owned by states or the federal government controlled over 40 percent of the banking sector.[18] The Bank of Brazil itself had been notoriously free of constraints in issuing bonds or currency to cover deficits. Most state banks became heavily indebted to cover state-level government deficits. Profligacy was a main underlying factor, but the banking crisis of late 1995 was actually triggered by the very reduction of inflation at a point when the number of banks had peaked. The constitution of 1988 so liberalized the process of bank creation that the number of banks in existence grew from 111 in 1988 to 246 in 1995.[19] The elimination of galloping inflation brought down bank returns from 18 percent in 1994 to single-digit levels in 1995. As the "inflation gains" of financial institutions dissipated, banks began to contract or close down. In late 1995, *Medida Provisória* #1179 authorized a set of measures and money incentives designed to encourage mergers. This led to the consolidation of the sector. Though not infrequently criticized at the time, this measure proved to be an asset, making Brazil more resistant to external pressure in 1997–1998.[20] Banks had experienced the erosion of public trust, and hence required special attention. Saving them prevented a financial meltdown. The bank reforms might not have led to fully maximizing the amount of savings turned into productive investments, but it was a success and prepared the Brazilian economy for the financial turbulence it faced after 1998.

18. The comparable figure for Argentina was 50 percent. A promising development in late 1995 was the appointment of respected economist Pérsio Arida as director of the Central Bank, the bank controlling the money supply and regulating credit. On the other hand, also in late 1995, BNDES, the national development bank, lost Edmar Bacha, another highly regarded economist, who had been its president in 1995. Bacha's resignation might have been the result of a turf battle with José Serra, then planning minister and a longtime associate of Cardoso who would become presidential candidate in the 2002 elections.
19. Banks were responsible for 807,000 workers and moved over 26 percent of GDP. *Veja*, November 15, 1995, 32–37.
20. PROER, the Program for the Restructuring and Strengthening of the National Financial System, sought to reduce liquidity and ensure 95 percent of deposits, as it bailed out the banking system via the financing of mergers. PROER financed such mergers as that of the Banco Nacional into Unibanco (R$5.9 billion), the Banco Econômico into Excel (R$4.6 billion), the Banorte into the Bandeirantes (R$.5 billion), and others. PROER's cost between 1995 and 1997 was approximately 2.5 percent of GDP. Comparable programs of financial restructuring in several countries generally had a higher price tag—for example, the program Argentina adopted in 1982 cost 13 percent of GDP.

Crisis and Adjustment: The Limits of Success

In spite of stabilization and related measures of economic liberalization, Brazil remained vulnerable to external shocks. Since its inception, some observers wondered whether the stabilization program might chronically hamper economic growth. The apparent dilemma between stabilization and growth intensified in 1996 when two key deficits—in the budget and in trade—began to grow alarmingly. The worsening trade balance went into the red in June of that year, just as the economy began to pull out of a brief recession. It doubled in a matter of weeks—from a high monthly figure of US$655 million in September to a much larger US$1.3 billion in October. By year's end, the projected current accounts deficit for 1996 was approximately US$23.1 billion, or 3.1 percent of gross domestic product (GDP). In 1997, it was 3.8 percent of GDP.[21] The sharp trade deficit increase of late 1996 seemed to have a direct connection to the faster growth the country had experienced in the preceding months, when the economy had begun to improve. More generally, the deteriorating trade situation tended to confirm fears about the negative short-term impact of the stabilization and adjustment measures on growth.

The budget deficit was the main source of the problem. After growing to 4.88 percent of GDP in 1995, the operational deficit had actually decreased somewhat in 1996, but only to increase again in 1997 and rise sharply in

FIGURE 2-2. Gross Domestic Product per capita, 1980–2001

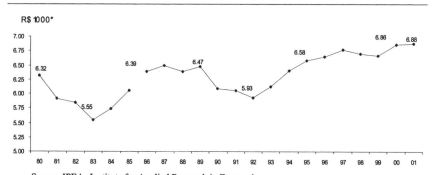

Source: IPEA- Institute for Applied Research in Economics
* 2001 reais. In Dec. 2001: 1 real = 0.45 US dollars.

21. In 1997, Brazil's IBGE introduced long-planned changes in the way GDP (PIB) is estimated. The idea was to make Brazilian measurement closer to international standards. The changes resulted in a GDP of US$805.7 billion for 1997, considerably higher than the US $750 billion based on the previous method. All national statistics using this new base were made smaller. The current accounts deficit of US$33.8 billion, or 4.5 percent of GDP under the old method, became 4.2 percent. See Celso Pinto, "A dança do PIB in 97," *Folha de S. Paulo*, January 18, 1998.

1998, when it reached 7.5 percent of GDP.[22] In combination with the trade deficit, it fueled pressure from currency speculators and deepened the sense of crisis.

Suspense grew in 1998 regarding the prospects of a new attack by currency speculators and the withdrawal of foreign investors. The international financial media openly wondered whether Brazil might be vulnerable to a currency collapse, as had occurred in several Asian countries and Russia.[23] A sharp rise in global interest rates, a drastic devaluation under duress, a contraction in international stock markets, or any combination of these and other factors might lead to a loss of confidence in the fledgling *real* and hence to a rapid outflow of foreign capital. Deepening crises in Japan, other parts of Asia, and Russia gave reason for concern through the elections of 1998.[24]

In this context, deep and broad fiscal adjustment eluded policymakers through the last year of Cardoso's first term. In its absence, key agents in the international financial system deemed the country's financial system vulnerable to collapse. Brazil closed 1998 with barely any economic growth. The high exchange rate stymied policies to promote economic growth. Expensive commercial loans and credits stifled investment. The overvalued exchange rate stimulated imports and decreased exports, sharply worsening the trade deficit.[25] The economy seemed to be trapped in a vicious circle.

22. Unlike the "primary" deficit, the "operational" deficit includes the cost of servicing the debt. The latter is very sensitive to external shocks, such as the international financial crisis of 1997–1999.
23. The Mexican crisis of December 1994 was on everybody's mind at this time. In the Mexican case, the sharp devaluation of an overvalued currency led to the massive outflows of foreign capital, which in turn fed further devaluation and the collapse of stock markets and the financial system. The economy contracted. The "tequila effect" reverberated in the rest of Latin America, including Brazil. Brazilian policymakers had responded to that threat with a policy of a gradual downward adjustment of the exchange rate as well as high interest rates. But to many observers, the exchange rate remained too high, particularly considering that fiscal adjustment had not yet taken place. (See also interview with Rubens Ricúpero, a Brazilian diplomat named secretary-general of UNCTAD, the United Nation's organ on trade and development, in Gilson Schwartz, "Ricúpero aponta riscos de deflação global," *Folha de S. Paulo*, January 18, 1998.)
24. Since at least 1996 and through 1998, Rudy Dornbusch, an MIT professor of economics who had trained some of the economists in the Cardoso team, warned that the *real* was overvalued by as much as 30–40 percent and that the Brazilian government was too complacent and failing to act rapidly to introduce fiscal and other reforms to prevent a crisis. In 1998, economist Albert Fishlow hinted at a financial collapse not unlike those taking place in Asia at the time. Echoing such views, some risk analysts placed Brazil as one of the countries with the highest risk of experiencing a currency collapse in the near future. Many Brazilian economists have challenged this line of reasoning, pointing to factors such as the massive reserves of the Brazilian state, the large export sector, the flow of direct foreign investment, the expansion of trade, and gradual but sustained efforts at stabilization and fiscal adjustment.
25. The core of the current account deficit is the trade deficit, the gap between exports and imports.

The first episode of high anxiety came in the few weeks before the elections of October 1998, when the country lost nearly US$30 billion of its US$60–70 billion in hard currency reserves (fig. D-41). Policymakers had maintained that Brazilian deficits were not exorbitant—that Mexico had experienced its crisis when it had a trade deficit of 7 percent of GDP and a comparable budget deficit, levels Brazil had not reached. But the situation had changed. Brazilian deficits were now in a dangerous zone. The government had claimed to have various policy instruments to manage budget and trade deficits, but it seemed to be running out of options. Had the Brazilian economy enjoyed high levels of international confidence, the obvious alternative would have been the devaluation of the exchange rate. However, policymakers feared that devaluation would contribute not just to inflation but also to the stampede of foreign financial capital.[26]

When the Cardoso administration gave priority to the reelection amendment in early 1997, it gambled that it had sufficient resources to postpone the bulk of the fiscal adjustment until after the election. The severity of the deepening Asian crisis caught the Brazilian government off guard. The crisis of late 1998 made clear that deep fiscal reform could no longer be delayed.[27] The wave of financial and stock market collapses originating in Asia threatened severe damage to Brazil. The country's large deficits in federal budget and current accounts and the notion that its currency was overvalued by perhaps up to 30 percent made currency speculators perceive Brazil to be vulnerable to an attack on the *real*. Driven by capital flight, the stock market fell by more than a third before the government rushed to deploy billions of dollars to defend Brazil's currency.[28] The response to the crisis in 1998 included an accord with the IMF and foreign governments, who supplied up to US$42 billions in loans. This was a potential watershed in relations between Brazil and the IMF, considering that Brazil had previously resisted many IMF pressures. Luckily for Brazil, the crises in Asia and Russia, and an assessment of the importance of the Brazilian case, led to a more flexible position on the part of a now more self-critical IMF. But this was not enough to stave off the

---

26. The underlying factor responsible for the large reserve had been the export sector, in spite of the negative export effects of the overvalued exchange rate.

27. The government had announced adjustment packages before. In 1996, the government had responded to the worsening trade deficit with a package of forty-four carefully targeted policies to stimulate exports by such measures as increasing credits for exporters, reducing finance costs, and giving bank guarantees to foreign companies importing Brazilian goods. Other measures in that package reduced expenditures by US$6.5 billion and led to the hiring of more tax collectors to increase tax collection. The even more urgent package of late 1997 was considerably stronger, but neither had been fully implemented.

28. The government spent nearly US$8 billion in October, but this proved insufficient. The losses were comparable to those resulting from the Mexican peso crisis of 1995 and exchange rate fall in March 1996.

mounting pressures on the *real*, and Brazil continued to lose foreign reserves at a high rate.

The collapse of the fixed exchange rate could not be averted. Capital out-flows, lingering fiscal imbalances, resistance to the record-high interest rates, and growing demands for monetary corrections finally forced the government to float the *real*, leading to its depreciation by more than 45 percent in 1999. The *real* lost ground in 2001 and early 2002, as a consequence of the Argentine crisis and the slowdown in the American economy. The interplay between political uncertainty and external pressure in the context of the 2002 presidential elections would bring down the exchange rate to record lows of nearly four *reais* to the dollar.

As the *real* entered a period of fluctuation and depreciation, the immediate challenge for the government was to maintain both inflation and interest rates on a declining path.[29] Nominal interest rates fell from 45 percent in March to 23 percent in May of 1999. Inflation declined from an annual rate of 16 per-cent in March to 6 percent in April of the same year. The reasons for relative success in this regard include the restoration of investor confidence in the policies of the federal government, a continuing increase in agricultural out-put, and low interest rates in the United States (Cardoso 2001). With the reemergence of the interest rate as a main instrument of monetary policy, the Central Bank had more room for credit expansion. In 2000, Brazil enjoyed a positive export performance and the partial recovery of industrial production.

Several shocks in the last two years of the Cardoso era tested the fiscal edi-fice built since 1993. In 2001, two of these shocks—the financial difficulties in Argentina and a slowdown in the United States' economy, aggravated by the terrorist attacks of September 11—came from the outside. In addition, an energy crisis resulted from the inability of production to keep up with the expansion of electricity consumption at 5.3 percent yearly, compounded by a drought that sharply lowered water levels in Brazil's dams, the source of 90 percent of the country's electricity. Energy investments had averaged US$10 billion yearly in the 1980s and US$6 billion in the 1990s. From 1980 to 1992, installed capacity and demand rose in parallel, but in 2000 the latter had risen by 165 percent while installed capacity had grown by only 119 percent. Crit-ics of the tight fiscal policy argue that the government had neglected the energy sector. The government had been shifting responsibility to the private sector, but opposition to this privatization meant that the government still controlled 80 percent of it. Measures adopted in July 2001 decreased con-sumption and increased supply, but the energy crisis led to a significant reduction in economic growth projections from 3.1 percent to 2.6 percent.[30]

29. See figures D-1 and D-3.

TABLE 2-3. Exchange Rate, *reais* for 1 dollar

	1994	1995	1996	1997	1998	1999	2000	2001	2002
Rate[a]	0.84	0.97	1.04	1.12	1.21	1.79	1.95	2.32	3.75[b]
Variation (%)		15.2	6.9	7.4	8.3	48.0	9.3	18.7	61.6

Source: Central Bank
a. R$/US$ rate for commercial buyers at the end of the period.
b. As of December 12.

Luckily, rainfall in late 2001 and 2002 restored water levels to normalcy and greatly contributed to ending the energy crisis.

Though the lingering crisis in Argentina put considerable pressure on the *real* and the Brazilian financial system, it also highlighted the wisdom of Brazil's new free-floating exchange rate. In Argentina, the fixed peso-to-dollar exchange rate implemented in the 1990s had succeeded in stopping inflation. However, the convertibility plan required large amounts of dollars in the economy that could be financed only via privatization, foreign investment, increased exports, and an increased public debt. Conditions existed for the Argentine plan to perform well for several years, but the fragility of the scheme was revealed when external shocks, insufficient new investments, and the inability to reach fiscal equilibrium generated mounting pressure on the peso. If Brazilian policymakers had reasons to feel good about their policy choices, the differing exchange schemes put a big question mark on Mercosul, the regional integration agreement in which both countries had invested heavily.

Brazil faced new economic woes as the 2002 elections approached. Cardoso and the PSDB chose José Serra, a founding member of the party and close associate to the president, as the official candidate to succeed Cardoso in the 2002 elections. After the definition of the slates in June, polls continued to place Serra far behind the leading candidate, Luiz Inácio Lula da Silva of the Workers' Party (PT). By mid-July, Ciro Gomes, a third candidate presumed to have leftist leanings, moved into second place. The two leading candidates opposed important features of the reforms pursued by the Cardoso government, though Ciro Gomes was considerably less threatening to the middle class and the elite. Uncertainty about the outcome of the elections put growing pressure on the *real*. On July 1, 2002—its eighth anniversary—the *real* price of the dollar reached R$2.90. By the end of the month it reached R$3.39. In mid-October, it reached R$3.90. This was truly a bad omen. Financial analysts wondered openly about the country's ability to pay its pub-

---

30. The energy crisis led to several proposals to address it, including the building of a gigantic dam in the Amazon region (see Larry Rohter, "Brazil searches for more energy: Project again raises exploitation issue in the Amazon Basin," *New York Times*, October 21, 2001, A12.)

lic debt. Brazil's reform drive was heading toward a major test if there were a PT electoral victory.

International financiers worried about the rising Brazilian debt and what that would do to the governments ability to service it. The total public debt increased substantially—topping 50 percent of GDP in 2001—partly as a result of the strategy of relying on very high interest rates to defend the *real* (see table 2-3). The Cardoso administration had also consolidated all public debt in the country, including those of states and municipalities, as well as hidden liabilities. This consolidation was in effect a major contribution to transparency and fiscal control with regard to public accounts. The federal government had also spent considerable effort to convert the public debt from short-term to long-term. Still, in 2002, risk assessments of Brazil's bonds worsened a great deal, as international financiers worried over the size of the budget surpluses related to the debt and the candidates doing well in the polls. Under the circumstances, the *real* would likely continue to lose value. The debt and the exchange rate were both likely to deteriorate further through the elections at the end of the year.

The Elusive Fiscal Model

Brazil's vulnerability to shocks is grounded on the perception that the country has not yet achieved a sustainable fiscal model in spite of increased tax collection. Gross revenue from taxes grew by 13 percent alone between 1996 and 2000—from 28.6 percent to 32.3 percent of GDP. However, pressures on government budgets remained high, as reflected in the chronic operational deficit and the growing public debt (see table 2-4).

Fiscal federalism continues to pose a major fiscal challenge, in spite of substantial improvement during the 1990s. The 1988 constitution guarantees major shares of tax revenues to states and localities. With the federal government controlling a share of receipts, much of the deficit originates at the state and municipal levels (fig. D-28, D-29, and table D-2).[31] Political machines at the local and state levels had been traditionally prone to use public resources to solidify their positions. Through the 1990s, politicians seeking election in the emerging democratic system had relied extensively on state-level banks to favor friends and gain political support, until enhanced federal supervision and privatization helped control the problem. With a bureaucracy of more than 850,000 individuals on payroll at the beginning of the democratization era, the state of São Paulo was a case in point. Two successive administra-

---

31. The federal government collects many taxes but has to transfer a large share to subnational units. Federal tax revenues increased from 18.9 percent of GDP in 1999 to 22.1 percent in 2000, but in 2000 it retained only 16.7 percent of GDP. Amounts transferred to municipalities increased by 20 percent during the same period, while their own tax revenues expanded by 3.52 percent.

TABLE 2-4. Fiscal Balances and Debt, 1991-2001, as percent of GDP

	Primary Deficit[a]	Operational Deficit[b]	Nominal Deficit[c]	Internal Debt	Foreign Debt	Total Debt
1991	2.71	-0.19	-26.75	14.13	24.45	38.58
1992	1.57	-1.74	-45.75	17.44	17.68	35.12
1993	2.19	-0.80	-64.83	17.52	13.64	31.16
1994	5.21	1.14	-26.97	21.58	8.80	30.38
1995	0.27	-5.00	-7.28	25.19	5.64	30.83
1996	-0.09[d]	-3.40	-5.87	29.33	3.90	33.23
1997	-0.87	-4.25	-6.04	30.03	4.29	34.33
1998	0.01	-7.40	-7.93	35.55	6.18	41.73
1999	3.23	-3.41	-9.98	38.99	10.40	49.39
2000	3.51	-1.17	-4.54	39.66	9.77	49.43
2001	3.68	-1.38	-5.23	42.71	10.54	53.25
2002[e]	4.19	-3.28	-8.02	43.69	16.25	59.94

Source: IPEA
a. Primary balance measures government total revenue minus total expenditure.
b. Operational deficit adds payment of real interests to the primary balance.
c. Nominal deficit adds payment of nominal interests to the primary balance.
d. Negative sign denotes the existence of a deficit.
e. Updated October 2002.

tions of the post-1985 democratic era used BANESPA, the state bank originally founded in 1927, to grant easy loans and credits. Because of more than US$10 billion in nonperforming loans in 1995, BANESPA came under the control of the Central Bank and was later privatized. Much of the lending had been authorized by the Orestes Quércia and Antonio Fleury administrations, two of the early democratically elected state governors since the early 1980s. In Bahia, the Banco Econômico also went bankrupt partly because of loans said to favor politicians. For comparable reasons, BANERJ, the state bank of Rio de Janeiro, was readied for the auction block.

The full significance of the fiscal provisions of the 1988 constitution became evident with the adoption of the *Plano Real*. Inflation had been a source of flexibility for the management of state and county budgets. As a sophisticated indexation system, combined with the systematic use of delays in payments, it camouflaged deficits. With the end of inflation, public debts began to soar.

The federal government used the international agreements brokered by the IMF as leverage in its ongoing fiscal negotiations with other actors in the polity, other levels of the Brazilian federation, and the Congress. But fiscal imbalances remained high. Against the backdrop of disappearing primary surpluses over the period 1995–1998, financial markets put Brazilian policymakers under great pressure. Finally, in the context of fiscal war following the election of opposition mayors and governors, Congress passed the Fiscal

Responsibility Law of 2000 (see table B-6). This law increased transparency, accountability, and discipline in public finances. It helped improve budget procedures for fiscal control and implement more effective planning. By putting limits on payroll spending and debt servicing, it represented an essential step forward in stopping the deeply entrenched practice of overspending.

Still, fiscal deficits remained high. Further improvements would need to come from complementary reforms to the social security system and the civil service. Meanwhile, the growth of the public debt added considerable fiscal pressure. In addition, improvements on the states-based value-added tax on goods and services (ICMS) might also be necessary to decrease unnecessary friction among economic liberalization, states.

Conclusion

When the Cardoso administration came to power in 1995, many thought it would emulate that of Juscelino Kubitschek, the development-oriented democratic president of the 1950s.[32] However, conditions were stacked against the refurbishing of the old developmental state. Building on previous experience and social learning, the Cardoso team committed itself to stabilization and economic liberalization. The most prominent early achievements centered on successful stabilization and liberalization. As inflation came under control, Brazil began to make advances in the opening of the economy, privatization, a new approach to regulation, state reform, and changes in the social area. The Cardoso administration represented a turning point with regard to the articulation of a new vision and agenda for the country.

Brazil seemed to have laid foundations for sustainable change and development. However, the expectation for fast growth remained unfulfilled, as a series of crises after 1997 revealed vulnerabilities to external shocks. Brazilians felt that the country should grow at a sustained, faster rate. They cherished stabilization and liberalization, but also demanded growth, jobs, and personal security. The restructuring process had yet to accomplish key goals regarding state reform, fiscal adjustment, tax and administrative reform, and other areas as that year's elections approached. The mood of the country seemed to turn against the reform drive in late 2002.

The government could only have a more active development role with sharply improved fiscal conditions that included a substantial reduction of the fiscal deficit. Given the political complexity of reducing the budget in the context of democratic consolidation, the government had relied heavily on higher tax revenue, privatization, and foreign investment. But the country

32. The Kubitschek government is perhaps best known for building the new Brazilian capital of Brasilia.

had yet to achieve a sustainable new fiscal model as privatization began to wind down and foreign investors worried about the country's vulnerabilities to external shocks.

Change had come slowly and at a high price. Advances regarding stabilization, privatization, trade liberalization were achieved, but much remained to be achieved. The core of the fiscal reform process to be completed centered on the state of the social security and administrative reforms. These policy domains and the broader forces shaping fiscal matters and the policy-making context are discussed next.

CHAPTER 3   *State in Transition*

T he 1990s brought a sea change in Brazilian public opinion concerning the depth and roots of the economic woes since the 1980s. Though Brazilians had generally laid the blame on the debt crisis of that decade, the policy failures of 1985–1993 led many to accept that the country faced a more profound crisis embedded in the political system.[1] Politics itself was the problem. There was a new awareness of how the institutional context shaped economic life. The implied agenda was to overhaul the government apparatus to sharply reduce deficits, waste, corruption, and inefficiency. In 1994, the shift in public sentiment governed the election of Cardoso, who held state reform as a key priority. In effect, the country was immersed in multiple transformations that included the deepening of democratic consolidation, the liberalization of the economy, and the reform of the state. It was not unreasonable to wonder about success in facing such a complex challenge, particularly since Brazil had been a laggard in matters of economic reform and had failed in simpler challenges in the recent past.

The underlying agenda in the post-1985 dynamics of democratization to create a new state form was substantial. The agenda included:

- fiscal restructuring: reforms of the civil service, social security, taxation, and fiscal practices to generate a sustainable new fiscal model;
- a new federalism, a functional balance between the central government, states, and counties;
- stronger and more stable party and electoral systems, as well as the development of a constructive relationship between the president and Congress;
- a functional mode of interest articulation and representation enhancing democratic participation, accountability, modern lobbying, and governance;
- an effective and independent system of courts.

1. See Sola (1994a, 1994b), Diniz (1995a, 1995b), Almeida (1995a), Bresser Pereira (1996). The opposition remained highly critical of neoliberalism, but even the Workers' Party gradually adopted a new tone in economic policy that would be fully expressed in a more moderate and reassuring party platform and strategy for the 2002 elections.

The tall agenda of state reform did not translate easily into change. Key measures presented to the Congress in 1994–1995 lay dormant or defeated in 1997, the third year of Cardoso's first term, while the months that followed were devoted to the passage of a reelection amendment. The second term would not see major reforms and would reveal structural vulnerabilities and difficulties. From the perspective of 1998, the very impetus for structural reform suddenly seemed uncertain. Observers wondered if institutional change was receding from the public agenda. Was the old regime too entrenched to change? Had the success of the *real* lulled Brazilians into complacency? Those questions would demand answers sooner than expected.

The Democratizing Polity: Context and Agenda

Many of the problems of the Brazilian state could be traced to legacies from the Vargas era, including the heavy reliance on clientelism and corporatism to forge a centralized state. Clientelism and corporatism had to be brought under control and their consequences addressed. But the corporatist-clientelistic legacy would continue to shape politics, impeding reform policies and reform-oriented collective action in the post-1985 era of democratization.[2] Moreover, with the gradual changes taking place after 1985, politics was increasingly a mix of the new with the old. New dynamics often interacted with those legacies to affect governability in an unpredictable manner.

The political system as a whole moved toward decentralization and pluralization after democratization opened in 1985, culminating in the constitution of 1988's formalization of decentralized federalism. As democracy became the dominant ideology, new—too many—political parties formed. Social movements, lobbying groups, and other interest associations flourished. These changes enhanced participation and competition, but they also made decision making more difficult. Though major change had taken place by 1994, clientelism and much of the inherited state machinery remained. Would-be reformers had to understand and work within the framework of this transitional system of interest representation and intermediation, as they hoped to change it and bring about major reforms.

The Corporatist Legacy in Comparative Perspective

Contrasting Brazil's traditional corporatist system to the better-known Mexican case helps bring out its peculiarities.[3] Like Mexico, Brazilian corporatism followed a top-down scheme imposed, enhanced, or maintained by self-

2. Hagopian (1996b) makes a strong case for the survival of clientelism. Schmitter (1971) provides a compelling sketch of Brazilian corporatism leading up to the 1970s. In the case of Cardoso, the pace of the reforms was conditioned as well by the priority given to the defense of the *real* and to his own and his party's political consolidation.

described revolutionary and reformist elites during the first part of the twentieth century. In both cases politicians sought to encapsulate interest groups into a framework that enhanced governability by elites bent on consolidating their power within the context of projects of national transformation. Both countries had peak associations seeking to monopolize interest representation for major social classes, including labor and business. And in both societies, nationalistic ideologies and modern repressive apparatuses served to buttress projects of political centralization.[4]

Though twentieth-century Brazilian and Mexican corporatism share a degree of kinship, there are also pronounced differences between these two institutional forms. Brazilian corporatism never had the consistency of Mexico's, where strong one-party rule had led to a highly institutionalized "revolutionary" political class and a stable ruling elite. The Brazilian system was considerably more fluid and unsettled. The original centralizing regime of 1930–1945 adopted authoritarianism to perpetuate itself, but was followed by twenty years of populist democracy and, after the coup of 1964, took the form of the military regime that lasted until 1985. The centralizing rulers from 1930 to 1985, whether authoritarian or democratic, relied on clientelistic corporatism and dirigisme in their attempts to gain legitimacy. Unable to find the legitimacy and institutional strength for stable long-term survival, the authoritarian regime opened a process of political liberalization in the 1970s that eventually led to a full process of democratization after 1985.

Arguably, Brazilian corporatism was never fully consolidated in the twentieth century. The centralizing regimes of the 1930–1985 era lacked the broad legitimacy to effectively integrate Brazil's complex web of interest groups and regions into a durable system of representation and interest intermediation. Unlike in Mexico, intraelite differences prevented the creation of a well-integrated and differentiated national ruling class. Brazil's polity retained a regional and even disaggregated character in spite of the centralization promoted by the armed forces and the bureaucracy. Peak associations and the main interest groups in Brazil retained a problematic relationship with the central government, as well as with processes of mobilization at the grass roots.

In a nutshell, Brazil's corporatism at the beginning of redemocratization in the mid-1980s was much less structured and more fluid than that of Mexico. The state elite—prominent politicians, the armed forces' high command, and top bureaucrats—presided over a bureaucratized but essentially clientelistic

3. Cornelius and Craig (1991) sketch the traditional Mexican corporatism before it began to unravel at the turn of the century.
4. Meant to aid mass mobilization, this form of nationalism in Latin America tended toward populism (appeals to broad cross sections rather than to one class), authoritarianism, and sometimes both.

and protocorporatist system linking regionally based factions and groups into an amorphous and precarious system of coalitions. Brazil lacked a sufficiently stable party system to yield a well-structured hierarchical network of clientelistic relations linking local, state-level, and national political factions into a stable and coherent pattern. In sharp contrast with Mexico's Institutional Revolutionary Party (PRI) and its system of *camarillas,* Brazil's corporatism did not succeed in aggregating class-based interests into a coherent policy-making apparatus.

Political networks retained a more markedly local and regional character under Brazilian federalism throughout the twentieth century, regardless of regime change. The mechanisms of integration into national policy structures were more diverse and subject to change. Clientelistic links to the bureaucracy or the presidency experienced considerable fluctuation from changes in regime type since the 1920s. At least twice, in the thirties and the sixties, pre-existing political parties were destroyed or curtailed by authoritarian and centralizing elites. As a result, Brazilian corporatism retained a more plural, decentralized, informal, and shapeless form than the Mexican.

Its more plural and unsettled character made Brazilian corporatism more protean. The lack of a well-structured single hierarchical principle made Brazilian corporatism a poor vehicle for major policy shifts under a decentralizing process of democratization. Dispersed systems of authority made resistance easier and more diffuse.

On the other hand, the system's malleability could provide opportunities for change if worked by a skillful and resourceful political figure. Though the unsettled and tense form of corporatism created a legacy difficult to ignore, the fault lines of this political system offered some possibilities for shifts in policy. In particular, reformers could engage the diverse political forces to gain momentum for change and reach toward a new political equilibrium.

Democratization and the State

From the perspective of the mid-1990s, the agenda of change seemed ambitious in relation to the system's recent record. Brazil's transition to democracy entailed a slow process of accommodation in which traditional elites and practices survived, adding to the difficulty of change.[5] Democratization's roots are found in 1973–1974, when General-President Ernesto Geisel and a

5. Brazil's democratization has been generally seen as a gradual "transition through transaction" in which the authoritarian regime retained considerable control, particularly in the early stages (Mainwaring 1986b, Martins 1986, Baaklini 1992, ch. 7). Governed by negotiations among sectors of the elite, it exhibited considerable continuity. Democratization moved from initial liberalization to transition and then consolidation. But democracy remained somewhat restricted through the early 1990s in the sense of continuing violence and even repression against the poor and the inability to reverse major trends in inequality and poverty.

core of associates decided to initiate a gradual process of liberalization that eventually became a broader opening or *abertura*. The military never closed the Congress after 1964, and it functioned throughout the military era in a simplified two-party system. At the beginning of the process of liberalization, the opposition Brazilian Democratic Movement (MDB) made headway in Congress, winning important elections in 1974 and 1978. The PMDB, the political party that succeeded the MDB, won other major victories in the first gubernatorial elections of 1982. These victories reinforced the role of state-level political organizations in the struggle for political control—a phenomenon that later reinforced the trend toward decentralized federalism. It took mass mobilization to convince João Figueiredo, the general who followed Ernesto Geisel in the presidency, to agree to civilian rule in the succession of 1985. The PMDB led the struggle for direct presidential elections. To succeed, that party felt compelled to form a coalition with the PFL—a large and disciplined spin-off of the majority government party, the PDS.[6] This broad coalition finally provided the congressional votes in 1985 to elect, even if indirectly, the first civilian president of the redemocratization era, thereby formally opening it. Headway in the Brazilian transition built on pact and compromise.

Odd circumstances interacted with preexisting institutional and political conditions to hamper the pace of political and institutional reform during the critical first years of the new democracy, leading to three vulnerable or weak presidents between 1985 and 1994. Tancredo Neves, the first civilian president, died of natural causes one day before he was to take office. Vice President José Sarney, a politician identified with the old regime and hence of questionable legitimacy to democratic activists, became president and ruled for five years.[7] The democratic leaders who followed Sarney were ill equipped to solve the problems of the Brazilian state. Elected in 1989, Collor de Mello was technically the first democratically elected president in nearly thirty years. This photogenic young leader from one of the smallest states in the country lacked experience and working contacts with other key players in the emerging polity, including the business sector from the Southeast. Collor introduced major reforms, but shocked Brazilian society with a stabilization plan that froze bank accounts for an extended period. Few defended Collor when Congress impeached him in December 1992 on charges of corruption. In turn, Itamar Franco, who went from vice president to president on Collor's downfall, was handicapped by a reputation as a political loose cannon. Prone

6. The PFL included such civilian leaders as Antonio Carlos Magalhães, Aureliano Chaves, José Sarney, Marco Maciel, and the more moderate elements of the old regime. This group demanded the vice presidency in the coalition led by Tancredo Neves. The PFL would make the same demand of Cardoso's PSDB, naming Marco Maciel to that role.
7. The 1988 constitution changed the length of presidential terms to four years.

to mercurial moods and moments of awkwardness, he could not quite shake this image during his stint as president. The public figures that ruled Brazil during six of its nine years of democratic rule after 1985—Sarney, Collor, and Franco—were originally elected as vice presidents as part of compromises in which they did not represent a threat to the president under whom they were meant to serve.[8]

The relationship between the executive and Congress had to be redefined in the changing polity. Since much of the work leading to democratization took place there, Congress could claim to be the political institution leading the transition to democracy. That fueled the movement toward parliamentarism just prior to and during the Constituent Assembly. Though parliamentarism failed, many in Congress continued to see it as the preeminent democratic institution, a perception fueled by the apparent weaknesses of the fledgling presidentialist system.

A civil service rife with clientelism posed major challenges. The problems of the bureaucracy worsened during the first decade of democratic rule, as the civil service and the mechanisms of interest aggregation were weakened by the continued massive reliance on clientelism. *Empreguismo* and other forms of patronage guided the allocation of national offices all too frequently, hampering the effectiveness of the state.[9] The restricted effectiveness of the bureaucracy compelled democratic rulers to rely extensively on political appointments to pass and implement their programs. Turning the bureaucracy into a more effective and less costly operation was of vital importance to design, implement, and maintain effective reforms and new institutional practices.

Of the three democratic administrations prior to 1994, Sarney's was particularly important because of the high expectations surrounding its installation as the first civilian and democratic government since the early 1960s. The Sarney government succeeded in launching the democratic era, but fell short of introducing effective economic reforms and did no better with respect to institutional change. It was also partly responsible for the political climate that led to the patchwork of compromises built into the constitution. Sarney had an uneasy relationship with the Congress, where the historical democrats of the PMDB resented his relationship with the dominant party of the military era. Though the *paulistas* Ulysses Guimarães and Fernando Henrique Cardoso, majority leaders in the Chamber of Deputies and the Senate, respectively, exercised important roles in Sarney's "transitional" government, par-

8.   For a discussion of the problems of the Brazilian polity in the early 1990s see Keith S. Rosenn and Richard Downes (1999).
9.   The pervasiveness of clientelism and pork barrel politics after 1985 is explained in large measure by any ruling coalition's need for support from diverse regions, sectors, and factions.

ticularly in 1986, their relationship to the president deteriorated as politicians sat down to design the new constitution.

Brazilians had great hopes for the Constituent Assembly of 1987.[10] However, against the backdrop of lingering corporatism and clientelism, the intense process of political mobilization surrounding it meant that virtually all interest groups and classes pressed for the inclusion of their interests and demands in the new charter. The new constitution promulgated in 1988 created a complex and unwieldy system of entitlements that in some ways strengthened corporatism and clientelism, blocking the creation of a more functional institutional order. Any change to the long list of clauses in the constitution required a constitutional amendment. The complex process entailed two separate votes in each chamber as well as support from three-fifths of deputies and senators. The constitution itself hindered the kind of flexible policy-making process needed by a reforming polity.

The new charter created a problematic, if not weakened, presidency. The Constituent Assembly debated extensively the adoption of a parliamentary system. Though Cardoso and other congressional leaders supported it, President Sarney, who contemplated reelection, opposed it. Presidentialism remained, but in a diluted form. Congressional leaders distrusting Sarney's background and intentions made sure that reelection was barred and that presidential terms were cut from five to four years. The fledgling New Republic now had a weakened presidency as well as a fractious Congress and a bloated corporatist-clientelistic bureaucracy.

The debate ushered in a period of tense relations between the president and Congress. Sarney relied heavily on presidential decrees known as "provisional decrees" (*medidas provisórias,* or MPs) to advance the executive agenda, a practice that would endure in the years to come. This legislative mechanism had a peculiar history in Brazil. During the military era, the Congress routinely approved the bills presented by the executive. Even in 1983 and 1984, the last years of the dictatorship, 85 percent and 83 percent of such bills shortly became law (most of the others eventually did as well, after more congressional discussion). The proportion decreased to 65 percent during Sarney's first year. Sarney's close, yet fleeting, relationship with congressional leaders in 1986 boosted the approval rate to 93 percent that year. As that relationship soured and the drafting of the constitution intensified tensions between Sarney and the Congress, MPs were used with increasing frequency in 1987–1988.[11] Collor de Mello relied on them extensively—decreeing 114 in 1990—until Congress prohibited him from resubmitting

---

10. This discussion of the politics of institutional change borrows from Martínez-Lara (1996), Baaklini (1992), Sallum (1994).

those already rejected. Subsequent administrations did the same. In September 2001, Congress passed a law limiting the use of provisional measures.

Presidentialism in Transition

The 1989 election took place against the backdrop of an evolving but problematically defined presidency, a fragmented political party system and fractious Congress, and a bureaucracy hamstrung by clientelism. Various groups felt threatened by the candidacy of leftist Luiz Inácio da Silva (universally known as "Lula" in Brazil). Fernando Collor de Mello rode on this sentiment to win the presidency. While driven by great political ambitions and a charismatic public persona, Collor came from a very small party and had weak political bases. Yet, he forged ahead, as if the presidency alone empowered him to bring about major change. Impetuous to the point of recklessness, his government began to draw fire as it adopted highly controversial measures to stabilize the economy and introduce market reforms. Elected on an anticorruption platform, he made himself, his spouse, and his administration vulnerable to major charges of corruption. Working with surprising effectiveness, no doubt due in part to Collor's narrow political base, Congress found him guilty of participating in a vast influence-peddling scheme and impeached him during his third year in office.[12] Impeachment proceedings submerged Brazil in a political crisis that prevented any major initiative from being undertaken or processed during much of 1992 and raised further questions about the presidency and the very process of democratization.

When imminent impeachment drove Collor from office in late 1992, Brazilians were greatly relieved, and worried. The young Brazilian democracy had worked well enough to resolve a major crisis and survive. However, questions lingered about its ability to elect sound leaders, prevent abuses by new incumbents, and foster badly needed structural and institutional change. There would be additional reasons for concern. The impeachment was followed by the weak presidency of Itamar Franco, another vice president originally chosen in part for regional balance and in part because the president he served did not regard him as a threat.[13] Franco was not the best leader for a period of reform. A nationalist with a traditional populist orientation, he was widely perceived as lacking a grasp of major issues and challenges in the national or global economies and the political ability to set Brazil in a new

---

11. Data on executive bills passed and the use of MPs can be found in Baaklini (1992). During the period 1970–1974 (Médici) the rate was close to 100 percent, while for the period 1975–1978, 79 percent of the executive bills were issued as decrees (Baaklini 1992, 117, 119).

12. Strictly speaking, Collor was not impeached; he resigned just before an imminent impeachment vote. Barbara Geddes and Artur Ribeiro Neto (1999) trace corruption in the Brazilian system.

direction. He spent much of his one year in office changing finance ministers and attempting various plans that failed to contain hyperinflation.

The seemingly relentless misfortune with regard to economic and political stabilization led to a feeling of malaise. Brazilians began to harbor doubts about democratization itself. Invidious comparisons with the years of growth and order and the "Brazilian Miracle" under the military were on the rise.[14] In the end, Itamar Franco redeemed himself in the public eye when his choice of Fernando Henrique Cardoso as finance minister led to a successful plan of economic stabilization.

Perhaps because it was young, Brazilian democracy had not brought an abundance of mature democratic leaders, well-organized political forces, or smoothly functioning institutions. The worsening of institutional conditions in the context of democratization was truly worrisome. With deep roots in past practice, clientelism remained entrenched in the political system. Weak political parties and political bases created politically vulnerable democratic presidents prone to dole out favors and concessions to win support. In the context of the fragmentation of the party system, consensus and coherent policy-making were difficult. Narrow political and economic considerations gave political factions and parties incentives to block reform.

If presidential leadership was essential to changing the system, legislative and policy successes were critical to enhancing it. Rival political figures and factions felt tempted to block presidential initiatives. Reforms generally lacked a strong constituency due to their newness or the sacrifices they entailed. In Brazil's institutional and political context, any reformist president hence had little choice but to rely heavily on the temporary executive decrees to introduce economic and political reforms. These MPs could be decreed and renewed indefinitely on a monthly basis, and they thus provided a way of circumventing the difficult process of passing constitutional amendments and other bills. They gave the president leverage over inevitably difficult negotiations with an unruly Congress. But since they clashed with democratic norms, a truly democratic president would have been expected to use them as

13. In a much-discussed, late November 1997 interview published in *Veja*, Collor referred to Itamar Franco, his opponent in 1990, as a "perfect idiot." (At the time, Franco was pondering a run against Cardoso in the 1998 elections and rapidly called a press conference to remind Brazilians of Collor's "past crimes and flawed character.") One of the most visible incidents tending to confirm Franco's reputation as a politician with erratic judgment was a front-page picture of him with a nearly naked young actress, while attending Rio's Carnival. Journalists also poked fun at his bouts of irritability and at his discomfort with extensive foreign travel and meeting with foreign dignitaries. Campos's (1994, 1,253) critical assessment calls attention to Franco's belief in dirigisme, inclination to blame capitalism for the ills of Brazilian society, and less than impressive understanding of international affairs.
14. Open talk of military intervention had surfaced previously in 1987, as the Cruzado Plan implemented by Sarney failed to stabilize prices and restore confidence in the economy (Martínez-Lara 1996, ch. 2, esp. 53–55).

measures of last recourse. Still, how else to lead the nation toward change? The *Plano Real* itself was enacted as an MP and reissued more than five dozen times in seven years before becoming law in 2001. In mid-2001, forty-seven MPs awaited final vote in Congress, with the oldest having been reissued seventy-five times.[15]

The Cardoso Presidency

When Cardoso came into office, his agenda was to consolidate the stabilization plan initiated during his tenure as finance minister, reform the state apparatus, liberalize the economy, and lay the foundations for a new approach to development. The new president's background made him a good candidate to strengthen the presidency and make progress toward those goals. Leading roles in the democracy movement, the Senate, the Constituent Assembly, and the ministries of foreign relations and financial affairs had put him at the center of political networks that included key political factions, entrepreneurs and trade unions, political parties, the military, the university, the media, and civil society. The image was that of a polished and articulate negotiator with a realistic awareness of the workings of the system.

Cardoso and his associates tended to have academic or political backgrounds. They worked to build bridges with business interests and to gain a firmer grasp of economic issues and a broader political base for reforms. Industrialists from São Paulo supported his bid for the presidency. Together with leaders from other business sectors, they generally remained on good terms with the new authorities. The resulting relationship was not quite the "embedded autonomy" described in Evans (1995), either in terms of the contours of a formalized structure or in terms of defining the role of the state in industrial development. Business's generalized perception was that the Cardoso administration represented a new, more pragmatic approach.

Precarious military support had been a major weakness of civilian regimes in Brazil's recent past. As the son of a respected general, Cardoso could count on the goodwill of at least some officers. More important, there were grounds for convergence on development policy. While committed to an expanded role for the market, both retained considerable sympathy for the idea of state action to foster economic development and other national objectives. Unlike those of Chile, the Brazilian armed forces traditionally clung to economic nationalism and had championed the cause of state intervention in pursuit of national goals. This broadened the space for a social democrat such as Cardoso to maneuver. Cardoso's status and potential as a political leader

---

15. Eugênia Lopes, "Falha de acordo ameaça emenda que limita MPs," *O Estado de S. Paulo*, June 2, 2001. See also Chagas (2002).

were also factors. Just before the 1993 selection of Cardoso as finance minister there had been clear rumblings of military anxiety over disarray in the Congress and the prospects of a deepening political crisis. The new government succeeded in arresting the symptoms of decay in the polity and allayed a great many of these fears. In 1999, Cardoso succeeded in reforming the cabinet so that all the branches would be represented by a civilian minister of defense, rather than the military heads of each branch.[16]

Key actors found much to applaud in the president's ability to work with them and other sectors in the Brazilian polity toward developing an approach that balanced market principles and state action in pursuit of national development. They welcomed a president with strong connections to international political and economic actors. Cardoso's stint as foreign minister had consolidated an already impressive international presence and the ability to harness the powers of Brazil's foreign service, one of the most effective branches of the Brazilian bureaucracy, to leverage the increasingly internationalized Brazilian political system and economy. Cardoso came into office as a well-connected statesman able to claim for Brazil a more salient global role in the context of stronger relations with the democratizing regimes in South America, industrial democracies, and international organizations.[17]

Relations with Congress

The Cardoso team's main political strategy was to form a broad strategic alliance with diverse political currents to win the presidency. It recognized the inability of a single party or narrow coalition to muster enough support to implement a serious reform program. The initial successes of the PSDB-PFL-PTB coalition made it easier for the PSDB to expand the governing alliance to include the PMDB and, later, the PPB.[18] In the process, the PSDB sharpened its role as a centrist pragmatic party, willing to form alliances with political forces on both ends of the political spectrum. The main opposition to the

16. The reform extinguished the Estado-Maior das Forças Armadas, the body that had coordinated military policy, as it created a new Ministry of Defense. The Army, Navy, and Air Force thereby lost their previous standing as ministries as well as their membership in the cabinet (Campos 2002).

17. Increased contact with the United States government brought President Bill Clinton to Brazil in April 1997, as part of the "Meeting of the Americas."

18. Bresser Pereira (1996, 224) characterizes the PMDB as "the populist center-left party that commanded the transition to democracy" and the PFL as "a center-right populist party" that splintered from the PDS in 1985. The social democratic PSDB branched out from the PMDB in 1985. In the municipal election of late 1996, the parties in the expanded coalition won 51 percent of the 5,348 races. The PPB was formed in September 1995 from the evolving party structures linked to the military era. The earlier PDS harked back to the Vargas era and in 1964 became ARENA, the ruling party during the military regime through 1984. ARENA/PDS became the PPR during the early stages of democratization. In September 1995, the PPR combined forces with the new PL (Liberal Party) to form the PPB. See Bresser Pereira (1996, 224, n 7a).

center-right coalition came from parties further to the left (especially the PT)[19] as well as rival factions of the PMDB and other groups claiming leadership over the center of the political spectrum.

In principle, the five-party coalition gave the government the ability to have the three-fifths of the congressional votes needed for passage of amendments. In practice, maintaining such majorities is a highly difficult and dynamic affair, since electoral laws make it likely that Brazilian lawmakers will operate with considerable political independence from their parties and presumed doctrines. The lack of party discipline makes it essential to have collaboration across regions, levels of government, and political groups. It entails endless negotiations with leaders of state congressional delegations and dozens of factions in Congress. Sectional and sectoral interests assert themselves in the Brazilian Congress not only through state delegations or *bancadas*, but also through special-interest caucuses. With deputies prone to deviate from a given party's position, coalitions form and reform around specific issues. Achieving coherent policy outcomes requires a skillful executive and sustained political articulation.

The alliance with the PFL entailed major costs, but it was deemed essential. In contrast with its modernizing rhetoric, the PFL retained a reputation as a clientelistic and populist conservative party controlled by traditional elites from the Northeast, one of the most backward regions in Brazil. Through 2001, it was led by Antonio Carlos Magalhães, a skillful, combative, and often resented clientelistic chief from the populous state of Bahia. The PFL was also one of the most effective parties in Congress. PFL leaders are professional politicians with experience in the intricacies of the Brazilian political system and are able to deliver votes in Congress. One of the largest parties in the country, it also represents a strong political base in a politically important region. PFL leaders have provided essential partnership in presidential elections, as well as the passage of all major bills and amendments. In the process, the PFL, known to draw hard bargains, consolidated a central position in the Brazilian political system.

Though Congress has grown in importance in the evolving democratic polity, the president is the one to lead major negotiations and coalition formation around policy initiatives. He must forge ad hoc congressional majorities with diverse factions and leaders to pass specific legislation. These coalitions are

19. Until 1998, the emerging labor parties had not been able to overcome rivalries linked to the political agendas of strong leaders and factions. The PT remained the main base of labor leader Luiz Inácio da Silva, while the PDT was very much associated with Leonel Brizola. These two parties collaborated in the 1998 electoral race, with Brizola running as Lula's vice presidential candidate. Their loss to the Cardoso ticket (with a PFL leader as vice president) frustrated a broader segment of the left than in Cardoso's 1994 victory over Lula. A stable alliance between the PT and PDT would prove elusive through the early 2000s.

often formed selectively, depending on the issue. The ability to make major policy changes is an ongoing balancing act requiring considerable effort and resources as well as skill.

TABLE 3-1. Approved Constitutional Amendments, 1995–2002

Amendment Number	Date	Subject
5	8/15/95	Ends federal gas monopoly
6	8/15/95	Discontinues preferential treatment of Brazilian businesses
7	8/15/95	Permits foreign maritime freight in coastal waters
8	8/15/95	Ends federal telecommunications monopoly
9	11/9/95	Ends federal oil monopoly
10	3/4/96	Extends Social Emergency Fund
11	4/30/96	Permits admission of foreign professors and scientists to Brazilian Universities and Research Institutes
12	8/15/96	Establishes CPMF (Financial Turnover Tax)
13	8/21/96	Instates reinsurance regulation plan
14	9/12/96	Sets minimum tax revenue allotment for education
15	9/12/96	Formalizes procedure for the establishment of new counties
16	6/4/97	Adopts reelection for presidential, gubernatorial, and mayoral posts
17	11/2/97	Extends Social Emergency Fund
18	2/5/98	Redefines military's role in state affairs
19	6/4/98	Modifies laws concerning civil servants' payroll and public agencies' expenditures
20	12/15/98	Reforms Social Security
21	3/18/99	Extends CPMF
22	3/18/99	Creates federal civil and criminal small claims courts
23	9/2/99	Creates the Ministry of Defense
24	12/9/99	Formalizes the method of class associations representation in labor court
25	2/14/00	Imposes limits on municipal legislatures' expenditures
26	2/14/00	Modifies the federal constitution on housing and social rights
27	3/21/00	Modifies tax collection and tax revenue's social contribution
28	5/25/00	Establishes a deadline for contract claims of rural workers
29	9/13/00	Ensures minimum allocation for the Health System
30	9/13/00	Regulates payment of (*precatórios*) judicial debts

TABLE 3-1. Approved Constitutional Amendments, 1995–2002 (Continued)

Amendment Number	Date	Subject
31	12/14/00	Establishes the Fund to Combat Poverty
32	9/11/01	Standardizes the creation, transformation, and termination of public functionaries and public offices
33	12/11/01	Alters fiscal policy toward the energy sector
34	12/13/01	Prohibits the accumulation of remunerated public positions
35	12/20/01	Restricts law suits against deputies and senators (parliamentary immunity)
36	5/28/02	Legalizes corporate firms purchase of shares in media companies
37	6/12/02	Extends CPMF until 2004
38	6/12/02	Incorporates the military police of Rondônia into central government's payroll

Source: Presidência da República, Casa Civil

Congress worked reasonably well with the Cardoso government during his first term. For instance, a great many bills to amend the constitution were introduced by the Brazilian Congress of 1995—278 from deputies, 62 from senators, and 16 from the executive. The record for 1996 and 1997 was comparable. Only a handful of these bills succeeded in being approved. The Cardoso administration convened extraordinary January sessions of the Congress every year since 1997. That of 1998 entailed the debate of twenty-seven bills and fifty-four provisional decrees, as well as the constitutional amendments. Nevertheless, progress was very slow on major reforms until 1998. Partly for that reason, polls in early 1998 showed high levels of dissatisfaction with Congress.[20] The extraordinary session of that year—meeting under the threat of the financial crisis—gave the final approval to a critical civil reform bill and approval for the important social security reform. In general, President Cardoso managed to focus the national debate on the reforms. This situation would change in the second term.

Tactical alliances are needed to maintain the reform drive. The challenge is to find enough leverage and other incentives for a sufficient number of actors to support the government's program. The arrangement can work so long as the executive maintains political capital and credibility. Political losses tend to drain the president and his team of political capital and standing, increasing the difficulty of subsequent initiatives.

20. Leaders of the PFL have proved particularly adept in managing the affairs of the Congress. Antonio Carlos Magalhães, leader of that party, was president of the Senate during the Cardoso government. His son Luis Eduardo, leader of the government coalition in the lower house and rising political figure, died unexpectedly in 1998, the victim of a heart attack.

State governors, who reemerged as major players in the pre-1985 process of political liberalization as well as in the 1988 constitution, have posed special challenges to presidents. Governors and the state-level political establishments they represent exercise significant influence over the congressional delegations or *bancadas* from their states. Many difficult issues regarding the final shape of Brazilian federalism remained unresolved, while the post-1988 decentralized federal system placed great fiscal and political resources at their disposal. Moreover, the opposition won key governorships and mayoralties in the general election of 1999, increasing the tension between Brasilia and other levels of government.

A related crucial new element in Brazilian politics is the emergence of lobbying as a professional endeavor. Lobbying specialists as well as modern social movements have joined professional associations, unions, trade associations, and new nongovernmental organizations (NGOs) in pressing demands on Congress and the executive. The more complex political system is not yet settled. In the fluid political and institutional context, the president has to summon all of his abilities to stay ahead in the complex bargaining process involving diverse actors.

Reforming the State

From the perspective of 1997, the Brazilian presidency was a far cry from that of the early years of the decade. Victory over inflation, the forging of political alliances, and the development of bureaucratic capabilities enhanced its prestige and operability. Observers expected that the government would now make progress in the three policy areas essential to long-term fiscal adjustment—the civil service, social security, and taxation. The first two were needed to reduce expenses and create incentives for better performance, the third to improve the traditionally deficient tax collection system. Together, they would reduce the fiscal deficit, strengthen finances, and reduce disincentives to economic actors. The goal was to create a durable new fiscal model for Brazil.

These reforms aimed at a more efficient and effective state. The business media often referred to the country's fiscal morass as *Custo Brasil*—the cost paid by those doing business in Brazil in terms of substandard infrastructure, a poor educational system, high interest rates, taxes, and other costs that reduced the competitiveness of the Brazilian economy. In other words, the absence of structural reforms and public sector profligacy meant a particularly high cost of doing business in Brazil. The "Brazil Cost" had increased in late 1997 and in late 1998 with the near doubling of interest rates.[21] The overvalued currency, one of the reasons for high interest rates, penalized exports, agriculture, and economic growth. Reforms were ultimately essential to pursue economic growth policies.

The government team packaged much of the three sets of measures as a reform of the state. Full passage of just one or two of the three reforms would have sent a strong signal that the reform drive was on track. But these structural adjustment policies were rather difficult to pass since, like the reelection bill, they required amendments to the constitution. Each reform called for different sets of coalitions and hence a different strategy.[22] Debate was expected to be intense.

The difficulty and political cost of passage in an electoral year made the government demur through 1998. That year, it made the fateful decision of giving top priority to reelection, including the reelection amendment, under the perception that it could delay fiscally vital reforms until after the October-November elections. That turned out to be a dangerous and costly assumption. Faced with the crisis of 1998, accompanied by negotiations with the IMF and international lenders, the Cardoso administration would be forced to launch a major legislative effort at the end of the year, including an extraordinary congressional session in early 1999. Relations with Congress would worsen through the second term, reflecting a significant weakening of the governing coalition.

Reelection Amendment and Political Reform

The reelection amendment required a great deal of political capital to become law. Its debate and eventual passage exemplify the difficulty of constitutional amendments. The issue occupied the front page of major newspapers during several months preceding intense congressional debate in January and February 1997. The ruling coalition did not have the three-fifths of the vote required for congressional approval of the amendment. Support from several factions in the PMDB was essential. But the prospects of a second Cardoso administration threatened the political hopes of other leaders and parties. In exchange for support, the PMDB demanded the key leadership positions in the Chamber of Deputies and the Senate in the new Congress to be constituted in February 1997. For comparable reasons, such positions were also claimed by the PFL and sectors of the president's own PSDB. Former presidents José Sarney and Itamar Franco, both of whom had presidential ambitions, eventually came out against the reelection amendment, as did several leaders in the PMDB and the opposition.[23]

---

21. For the position of business in mid-1996, see "Os vilões do real," *ISTOÉ*, May 29, 1996.
22. See the World Bank's *World Development Report 1997* for an overview of issues and strategies in changing the state.

The Cardoso government had grounds for optimism. It had stabilized the economy as well as the political system. Polls indicated strong approval ratings and presented Brazilians as once again full of hope. The Cardoso team appeared poised to break new ground in the struggle for a new Brazilian state. Having brought a sense of direction to the country, the Cardoso administration emanated confidence about its ability to move the country toward those goals. There were sensible arguments to support the reelection amendment. A four-year presidential term was too short to give a government the chance for a decisive impact in economic restructuring and political realignment. At least one year was required to organize a new government. Any administration would be seen as a lame duck in the fourth year. The rest of the time would not be enough to implement a reasonably ambitious platform. Moreover, the nonrenewable four-year term did not provide incentives for good performance.

Many Brazilians supported this reform, aware that the nonrenewable four-year term had been adopted in unusual circumstances. Still, Cardoso's decision to aim for a second term was a bold gamble. It brought resentment against what appeared to be a power play. Worse, defeat of the amendment would have rendered him a vulnerable lame-duck president right after the vote, thereby threatening the anti-inflation and the reform drives. But victory, on the other hand, would greatly increase the odds of a second Cardoso term, as the amendment would be seen as a referendum on Cardoso's presidency and would enhance the prospects for continuity in policies governing democratization and economic liberalization. Programmatic, political, and personal reasons hence made the constitutional amendment a pivotal affair.[24]

The pro-reform forces unleashed an intense campaign that proved very effective. With more than 60 percent of Brazilians endorsing the amendment, public support added to the impetus of the drive. The first hurdle, committee passage, was overcome with great effort. The second was a first vote in the Chamber, which approved the amendment on January 28, 1997, by a vote of 336 to 17, with most hard-line opponents absent in an attempt to deny quorum. The governing coalition hence got a few more votes than the 308 (out of 513) needed for passage. The proposal still needed to be confirmed by a second Chamber vote, before referral to the Senate. Both votes came in the context of subsequent negotiations about the new presidents of the Chamber and

23. In the state of São Paulo this included Orestes Quércia, a traditional rival of Cardoso and ex-governor of the state of São Paulo. Lula da Silva and the Workers' Party opposed the reform, as did Paulo Maluf and the PPB, though the latter would eventually support Cardoso's reelection. The leaders of the landless movement joined the campaign against reelection.
24. On the other hand, passage of the amendment would provide incentives for delaying major substantive reforms until after the elections.

the Senate. Passage of the reelection amendment reshaped political dynamics.

The Cardoso administration had much less success with regard to the broader political reform agenda. That agenda called for changes in two complementary directions, making the electoral system based on districts and providing incentives for stronger and fewer political parties.

The Brazilian electoral system adopted with the constitution of 1988 relies on state-level majorities to elect chiefs of the executive, counties, states, and Union (president, governors, and mayors), as well as senators. The constitution prescribes a system of proportional representation to elect representatives to the federal Chamber of Deputies and the Senate as well as state and municipal legislatures.[25] Under that system, votes for candidates as well as parties are tallied at the state level. Parties and candidates within each party are ranked using these totals.[26]

Though the number of deputies elected in a given state depends on the size of its electorate, the system of proportional representation is biased against large states. For instance, in the 1999 elections, the small state of Roraima needed 10,406 votes to elect a single deputy, while the state of São Paulo needed 183,719 votes—almost eighteen times more votes to elect a representative. Hence, São Paulo is underrepresented in the Chamber of Deputies. The minimum (eight) and maximum (seventy) number of representatives that are allowed per state aggravates this situation, since the cap applies to populous states. Under this system, some representatives from small states may be elected with 10,000 votes, while some other candidates from large states with 60,000–70,000 votes might lose.

Perhaps an even more important problem with the current Brazilian system is that elected representatives do not feel responsible to any community or constituency, which contributes to party switching. A district-based electoral system would bring elected officials closer to delimited territorial constituencies within each of the states of the federation. It would also make campaigns less expensive, since districts are much smaller than the whole state.

Though some specialists think that a system mixing district and proportional votes has important advantages and would be an important component

25. The electoral system calls for up to two rounds in the election of positions in the executive branch of government. If the first round does not result in a winner with a majority vote, the two candidates with the most votes run in the second round. Winners hence govern with a majority.

26. The electoral quotient to determine the number of seats won by each party is determined by dividing the number of votes by the number of disputed positions—for example, if 1,000,000 electors vote for 100 positions, the electoral quotient for that state is 10,000; therefore, each 10,000 votes earned will represent a chair on the legislative. The number of candidates elected by each party depends on the total votes it receives divided by the electoral quotient.

of the electoral reform, many reformers think that some kind of system based on districts would be better. Many European countries rely on district-based systems, either in pure or mixed ways. This system tends to strengthen big parties and party fidelity. It tends to weaken smaller, urban-based parties in favor of big parties that penetrate cities as well as rural and distant zones. For that reason, reforming the electoral system represents a dilemma for many Brazilians, since many of the smaller parties now active would be unable to compete if reforms are adopted.

Other important changes need to be made in campaign finance and party organization. Campaigns are expensive in Brazil, providing incentives for corruption, particularly political favors in return for financial support. There are no limits to the size of contributions—in the United States, in contrast, the law imposes a limit of US$1,000 per contributor to a candidate according to the federal campaign finance law of 1996. Another proposal extends the requirement of minimum affiliation to a party from two to four years to be eligible for disputing a new election.

These reforms—and others that followed—had not been adopted by mid 2002 and would not be during the remaining months of the Cardoso government. That government's contribution to political change would be more substantive than procedural—including political stability around a broad centrist alliance. Being the first Brazilian president reelected to office and to complete a second term—that is, surviving two terms—was in itself a very significant accomplishment. However, the debate surrounding the 2002 elections made clear that political reform was a priority in the national agenda.[27]

Administrative Reform

Studies of Brazilian development have often highlighted the role of the public bureaucracy.[28] A widespread view of the Brazilian bureaucracy through the 1980s saw developmental administrations such as that of Kubitschek or those of the period of the "Brazilian miracle" as representing an efficacious developmental state able to define and pursue economic growth policies. This perception clashed with evidence of the pernicious legacy of clientelism and populist politics in terms of waste, an ineffectual public bureaucracy, and the crisis of the state.[29] In the late 1980s and the 1990s, in the context of democratization, the balance of the debate would henceforth tip in favor of the latter view.[30]

27. For example, the focused debates among 2002 presidential candidates promoted by the *Jornal do Brasil* identified political reform as a main issue (see "Agenda Brasil" in JB Online [http://jbonline.terra.com.br/destaques/agendabrasil]), though there were important differences among the candidates, with José Serra articulating the most concrete ideas.
28. For example, Gouvêa (1994, III, 165–81).
29. One of the most sophisticated early assessments of clientelism in Brazil came from Hélio Jaguaribe's characterization of the Brazilian state as "cartorial."

The centrality of fiscal profligacy in the economic crises engulfing the country in the 1980s and early 1990s revealed the shortcomings of the civil service.[31] Bloated payrolls and generous pensions to civil service workers often consumed large and growing shares of budgets at all levels of the Brazilian federation. The constitution of 1988 gave public-sector employees with more than five years of service virtual tenure, as well as generous inflation adjustments and pay increases. Well-known abuses came from the *marajás*, the political operators who collected multiple or inflated government checks for jobs and pensions that might not have existed or that they might not have deserved. The federal government's wage bill absorbed 45 percent of the budget, not a particularly high figure, but one with a tendency to grow fast in the mid-1990s.

In fact, states, counties, and cities often had payrolls and pensions accounting for much larger shares of the budget and were responsible for growing deficits. The state of São Paulo, presumably with the most modern bureaucracy, provides an example. It had more than 800,000 employees in the early 1990s. At the municipal level, the chronic deficit of the city of São Paulo alone totaled several billion dollars, much of this due to this problem. In the Northeast, North, and other regions, including the large central state of Minas Gerais, local political machines have been even more prone to rely on massive patronage to solidify their positions. Deficits at the state level were often financed by banks owned by states and protected in the constitution. Incumbents relied extensively on them to raise funds for political support. Again, the state of São Paulo, perhaps that with the best administrative corps, provides telling lessons. Two successive democratic administrations after 1985 used BANESPA, the state bank, to grant easy loans and credits. Because of US$13 billion in nonperforming loans in 1995, BANESPA had to come under the control of the Central Bank and was placed on the auction block in 2000.[32] BANERJ, the state bank of Rio de Janeiro, met a similar fate. Bahia's Banco Econômico went bankrupt partly because of nonperforming loans favoring politicians.

As economic stagnation and inflation wreaked havoc on the prospects for sustained economic development in the early 1990s, public debate concern-

30. For example, Geddes (1994).
31. For example, Bresser Pereira (1996, 224, n 1) acknowledges other studies of the crisis of the state by Rogério Werneck, José Luiz Fiori, and Brasílio Sallum. Sallum (1996) sketches an extended discussion of the crisis of the developmentalist state in the demise of military rule and the transition toward democracy.
32. In the second half of the nineties, the government of Mario Covas successfully implemented a program of fiscal adjustment (cutting the payroll by 120,000 functionaries and controlling salaries) to become the only large state to achieve fiscal balance (see Roberto Macedo, "Covas, a lição e al aula," *O Estado de S. Paulo*, March 8, 2001; Luiz Carlos Bresser-Pereira, "Reforma ou reajuste," *Folha de S. Paulo*, July 25, 1997).

ing the pathologies of the Brazilian state increased, fueling pressure for administrative reform. State reform emerged as a key policy goal. The Cardoso administration appointed a strong minister of administrative affairs, Luiz Carlos Bresser Pereira, an ex-finance minister and a prominent public intellectual from São Paulo, to streamline and modernize the bureaucracy through a newly created Ministry of State Administration and Reform (MARE).[33] The new ministry functioned during Cardoso's first term and produced an overall diagnosis of the problem and ways of addressing it. It supported incremental changes and developed new ideas and proposals for a more competent and dynamic bureaucracy, including partnerships with civil society and the private sector.

To address fiscal deficits and reform the bureaucracy, the government had to amend the 1988 constitution with respect to the inability to lay off civil servants, eliminating a virtual entitlement written into this document. In late 1995, Congress began to discuss a bill to authorize the dismissal of public employees and give public corporations more autonomy from politicians. But this bill lost momentum in 1997, when stabilization and the reelection amendment were the top priorities. Though it seemed that this bill would not be considered until after the election, the international financial and monetary crisis threatening Brazil after October 1997 returned the reform of the civil service and other fiscal adjustment measures to the limelight.[34]

Though massive, the response to external shocks failed to ward off the threat of major crisis. Relentless pressure ensued from the perception that Brazilian authorities were unlikely to take sufficiently tough measures in an election year and that the underlying financial picture could only worsen. The federal government was now compelled to adopt an emergency adjustment package designed to reduce the fiscal deficit by nearly R$20 billion.[35,36] These measures proved insufficient. Pressure on Brazilian finances continued after the November 1997 adjustment package. The Brazilian government felt com-

33. Luiz Carlos Bresser Pereira, who had written extensively on the crisis of the Brazilian state (for example, Bresser Pereira 1996), was charged with reforming it as minister of administration during the Cardoso government.
34. Civil servants at all levels of government could be fired only when found to be stealing or committing "grave" offenses. This virtual tenure was called stability (*estabilidade*). The reform allowed for dismissal when the payroll was too high relative to revenue or on grounds of inefficiency. See *Veja*, February 18, 1998.
35. Some of the measures represented major steps toward structural reform—particularly the increased income taxes (10 percent for top income categories), the nearly 50 percent tax increase on gains from fixed-income securities, and the reduction of the fiscal incentives and handouts to certain regions. The tax increase was less of a political issue than in industrial democracies, since only 8 percent of Brazilians pay income tax and the final measure adopted affected only those in the very top brackets. These measures could be brought about temporarily by executive fiat, but they needed congressional approval. Cardoso cut his presence short at the Ibero-American Summit being held in Venezuela to announce this package on November 10, 1997.

pelled to reassure international capital markets that it was indeed serious about tackling the underlying causes of fiscal and current accounts deficits.

It was in this context that the government announced its third response to the crisis, an all-out effort to pass the dormant civil service reform authorizing cuts in the government payroll. This bill called for layoffs when the payroll consumed more than 60 percent of the revenues of federal, state, or local governments. The odds of congressional adoption seemed no better than 50 percent.

A lot was at stake. Failure would have led to a sharp drop in credibility, as well as the collapse of the anti-inflation plan—not to mention the president's own plans for reelection. Victory, on the other hand, would portray Cardoso as an effective defender of the national economy. The bill affected local and state governments. The president mustered the support of a significant number of governors and mayors, who converged on Brasilia to lobby the Congress. Negotiations with deputies and senators succeeded. On the evening of November 19, the lower house passed the bill on its second and last discussion. The bill moved to the Senate, where it received final approval in the extraordinary session of January-February 1998.

Passage of this bill gave new life to the state reform drive and confirmed Cardoso as the top presidential candidate for the October elections. The night of December 2, when the Brazilian Congress voted on the partial adjustment package, Cardoso and his wife, Ruth, arrived on a five-day state visit to England. As Queen Elizabeth's guests, the couple stayed at Buckingham Palace. Meetings with London financiers and investors in the middle of the crisis reinforced his image as an effective defender of Brazil's economy and a world-class statesman.[37] It was a dazzling performance. Cardoso thereby solidified his image as the modern Brazilian president best able to operate in the international scene. The fate of the civil service reform highlights the role of craftmanship in the making of reforms. The president put lawmakers on the defensive by framing the problem as a crisis induced from abroad and arguing that further delays in enacting reform bills would place Brazil in a

36. The *medida provisória* increasing the personal income tax was officially voted in on December 2, 1997. At that point, the adjustment package looked somewhat different from that announced on November 10, as Antonio Carlos Magalhães led a successful drive to limit the income tax to those earning more than 1,800 *reais* per month and reducing fiscal incentives traditionally granted to the North, Northeast, Manaus, and other areas. The *pacote* cut spending and increased taxes for a total of US$18 billion. Besides the increase in income taxes, the cut in fiscal incentives, and the layoff of 33,000 government workers, the package decreed an increase in gasoline prices, airport use fees, and dozens of specific measures also oriented to discouraging imports and encouraging exports. Programs for agrarian reform, health, education, and welfare were not changed.
37. Cardoso used this visit to convince investors of the soundness of fiscal policy in Brazil. He tried to make the volatility of capital into an international issue in need of debate and declared his party's ideology to be close to that of British Prime Minister Tony Blair.

very vulnerable position and might lead to disastrous results. The crisis served as leverage to advance the reform agenda. Cardoso linked the reform to widening of the reelection amendment to include governors and mayors.[38]

The measures entailed major costs. Brazilians faced further belt-tightening and little economic growth during the electoral year of 1998. Unemployment was expected to rise. There was some softening of support from business and public opinion. Many economists continued to believe that Brazil might also need to devalue its currency even as it projected the image of fiscal austerity to nervous foreign investors.

The impetus for further reform fizzled out in the ensuing months. As the government focused on the reelection campaign, no major legislative initiatives were launched after the electoral season began. Worse, many of the measures approved in December 1997 were not implemented in 1998. The international financial press worried openly about the new slowdown of the reform process, raising questions about a durable commitment to the state reform drive. MARE was extinguished at the end of Cardoso's first term.

International financial investors had yet to render a verdict on the adequacy of the measures adopted thus far. It came sooner than expected. Against the backdrop of intensifying financial crises in Asia and Russia in 1997–1998, the Brazilian currency and stock markets came under formidable pressure from currency speculators. Working under the notions that the Brazilian currency might be overvalued by 30 or 40 percent and that the large fiscal and trade deficits made the current policy unsustainable, they began selling their *real* holdings at an accelerated rate. Just before the October elections, the rate was thought to be US$1 billion per day. Between late August and early November the Central Bank sold nearly US$30 billion of its hard-currency reserves of US$70 billion.[39] The government responded to this dramatic situation by raising interest rates to very high levels. The measure may have attracted hard currency, but it made recession almost certain as consumption and investment spending would be expected to decline. Brazil's worsening crisis threatened to turn into a catastrophe.

This time the Brazilian government had no choice but to resort to the International Monetary Fund, the World Bank, and key G-7 countries. Intense negotiations went on for several weeks. Support was announced in the context of the late-1998 elections, even if negotiations still proceeded for several more weeks.[40] These negotiations led to the drafting of the new adjustment package first announced in late October. The Fiscal Stabilization Program

38. At the same time, Cardoso used the momentum provided by earlier victories to press for passage of other reforms. It went unsaid that it had been the president's choice not to aggressively pursue those bills earlier.
39. See Felipe Patury and Cintia Valentini, "Um cheque de 41 bi," *Veja*, November 18, 1998.

and the new adjustment package of late 1998 emphasized completing the measures only partially implemented in the preceding three years with regard to reforms of the civil service and administration, social security, and taxation. The combination of measures would bring a fiscal adjustment of US$28 billion.[41] The IMF and other international lenders pledged a total of US$41 billion in mid-November, with the official IMF decision not announced until early December. Brazil was called on to maintain and deepen the state reform drive. But the crisis was not over.

The assumption was that political conditions after the late-1998 elections would make the reform process easier. Indeed, though Cardoso was reelected by a wide margin, and voters perceived him as the best leader to deal with the crisis, Brazilians seemed of two minds. They simultaneously reelected a liberalizing president and voted antireform sectors of the opposition into Congress and the governorships of several key states, including Minas Gerais, Rio Grande do Sul, and Rio de Janeiro. These opposition forces coalesced on an antineoliberalism banner just as the Cardoso administration prepared a legislative drive in November and December 1998, and another extraordinary session of Congress during January-February 1999 to debate the enabling legislation for the state reform laws passed earlier in the year. Itamar Franco, the newly elected governor of Minas Gerais and Cardoso's sworn enemy, declared a moratorium on his state's debt. Together with similar demands from other recently elected governors, tremendous pressure built on the *real*. It was in this context of high threat that the government decided to let the currency float freely.

The crisis reverberated for months. But at least a mild version of the civil service bill had passed and a more flexible exchange policy had come into effect. The civil service reform was not as strong as many wanted, and it came at a great political cost, but it helped Brazil move closer to fiscal responsibility.

The Fiscal Responsibility Law of May 2000 is the closest the Cardoso administration came to a capstone of the state reform process (see table B-6). Previous efforts at state reform had succeeded in limiting tenure and creating a more flexible legal framework for public employees. The Fiscal Responsibility Law imposed a limit of 60 percent of the budget for payroll. It autho-

40. For a critique of the IMF's decision to sponsor a large loan to Brazil as well as of Brazilian policy, see Jeffrey Sachs, "O socorro do FMI ao Brasil será mais um fracasso," *Folha de S. Paulo*, November 4, 1998. Sachs and other critics asked for a policy of devaluing the *real*, maintaining free-floating exchange rate, and fiscal adjustment. MIT professor Rudiger Dornbusch, one of the most persistent and vocal critics of the Cardoso administration, also advocated a policy of devaluing the *real*. See, for example, his interview in "Ajuste não reduziu déficit de confiança, diz Dornbusch," *Folha de S. Paulo*, November 3, 1998.
41. The text of the Fiscal Stability Program, a summary, and complementary information appear in special section "Ajuste Fiscal," *O Globo* [accessed on www.oglobo.com.br/].

TABLE 3-2. Social Security Crisis, 1998

	Public Sector	Private Sector	Total
Number of Pensions	3 million	18 million	21 million
Benefits	R$41.1 b	R$53.8 b	R$94.9 b
Contributions	R$6.6 b	R$46.0 b	R$52.5 b
Deficit	R$34.4 b	R$7.8 b	R$42.2 b

Source: Ministério da Fazenda, Programa de Estabilidade Fiscal, 10/28/98

rized agencies of the federal government to withhold funds from non-compliant states and counties and even called for jail terms for offenders. The law increased transparency by forcing all governments to submit reports.

Social Security Reform

The reform of the social security system was a pillar of the fiscal adjustment and state reform initiative. Though it was the single most important item in the state reform drive, no reform proved more costly and difficult. The constitution of 1988 granted public employees unusually generous retirement benefits that included state-funded full pensions after a number of years of service, regardless of age. Workers in the federal government's pension plan could retire at age forty-five with pensions often higher than their last wages. This provided incentives to retire early and seek pensions from other jobs. Moreover, Brazil's demographic dynamics complicated the picture, as the proportion of the population at retirement age was growing quite rapidly, in tandem with the country's demographic transition. There were 16.8 million beneficiaries in mid-1997, twice the number of sixteen years earlier, and the number rose to 17.4 million by the end of the year and 21 million were projected for the end of 1998.[42]

The pension system is divided into three categories: the general plan for private workers (INSS), multiple special regimes for civil service workers, and a complementary program available voluntarily to all workers. About half of the total pension expenditures are paid to civil servants, who account for just 5 percent of the retirees. This expenditure is unlikely to drop during the next ten to fifteen years. Brazil's public pension expenditure of 9 percent of GDP is above the average for the much wealthier Organization for Economic Cooperation and Development countries (OECD 2001).

The rapidly growing cost of the system was unsustainable, according to many specialists. Expenses had more than doubled between 1990 and 1996, from R$18.3 billion to R$42.6 billion. While in 1992 the social security system had generated a 15 percent surplus (used to fund health programs), the

---

42. Of the beneficiaries as of December 1997, 11.5 million were urban and 5.8 million rural. That month, the National Institute of Social Security (INSS) disbursed R$3.9 billion, of which R$3.2 billion (82 percent) went to urban retirees.

system generated growing deficits after 1995, reaching R$42.2 billion in 1998.[43] Public servants accounted for 82 percent of the total deficit in that year, having consumed R$41.1 billion in benefits and contributed only R$6.6 billion in payments. As a result, retirement pensions claimed an increasingly larger share of the national budget. Unless reforms were adopted, the deficit would amount to more than 4 percent of GNP by 2030.[44]

The reforms proposed in 1995 called for a minimum retirement age of fifty-five for men and fifty for women, a new regime of contributions, and other complementary measures. These were sensible measures. But in May 1996 Congress rejected the bill. Mainstream journalists agreed at the time that the main factor for that vote had been the unacceptably opportunistic demands of individual deputies, the prominence of clientelism (*fisiologismo*) in Brazilian politics, and the narrow interests of deputies running for office.[45] Reintroduced, the bill suffered delays through the rest of 1996 and 1997.

A powerful coalition of civil servants, labor, and the left opposed it. This included the Workers' Party and most trade unions. From a political standpoint, social security reform is generally very difficult to achieve. The number and mobilizational capacity of losers (those retired or close to retirement) are typically much larger than those of the initially small and unorganized group of direct winners (young adults entering the labor force).[46] In the Brazilian case, the 17.4 million retirees in early 1998 and the several additional millions expected to retire within a few years added up to a formidable constituency opposing change.

The crisis starting in late 1997 breathed new life into the social security reform bill as well, but there remained reasons to be skeptical about its fate. The amendment reforming the social security system had already been defeated once and powerful constituencies were mobilized against it. The Cardoso administration pressed the extraordinary congressional session of early 1998 to approve it, calling attention to the threat posed by the mounting crashes of currencies and stock exchanges from Asia. A special commission

43. In 2002, the deficit would reach R$70 billion—R$53 billion from the public sector and R$17 from the private sector ("Previdência terá déficit de R$70 bilhões, diz ministro," *O Estado de S. Paulo*, October 31, 2002).
44. See also Marcelo Viana Estevão de Moraes, "A reforma da previdência social," 1997 [www.mpas.gov.br/reforma.html]. At the time, Moraes was secretary of Social Security, Ministry of Social Security and Social Assistance.
45. See, for example, "Os vilões do real," *ISTOÉ*, May 29, 1996. This story had the following phrase as its subtitle: "Guided by personal interests, Deputies break the back of Social Security reform, insist in bargaining over their votes, and threaten the future of the stabilization plan." The story told of one congressman from São Paulo whose price for voting in favor of the reform was that a small university owned by his father be exempt from scrutiny by the income tax office. Another deputy offered a comparable deal for her husband's construction firm.
46. World Bank (1997), ch. 9.

of the Chamber of Deputies forwarded the bill to the full Chamber. An extraordinary session of Congress passed a weakened version of the social security bill in February 1998, in the context of still relatively mild external pressure from the financial crisis. The president mobilized a great deal of his political capital to ensure a positive vote. He framed this reform as a sacrifice needed to defend the nation's economy against a critical global threat. The bill that passed failed to include key changes involving retirement age and benefits.

With reelection on Cardoso's mind, and the Congress concerned with other matters, most analysts had thought that social security reform would not be discussed again until after the elections of October 1998.[47] But the deepening of the external crisis returned social security reform to the spotlight right after the elections. In the last working weeks of 1998, Congress adopted most major pending bills to reform the social security system and even reversed itself with regard to previous votes weakening the initial project. The final legislation voted on and enabled in late 1998 came somewhat closer to the initial bill presented by the president. PSDB Senator Beni Veras, a prominent politician from Ceará, played a key role in steering the bill through Congress.

The main elements of the minireform were (1) a new formula for calculating initial basic benefits, (2) incentives for retiring at an older age, and (3) adjustments of benefits to take into account changes in life expectancy and the aging of the population. Though these changes alleviated the long-term difficulties in the INSS system, they came short of providing an effective solution. As of the early 2000s, much remained to be done with regard to public as well as private social security reforms. In the state of São Paulo, for instance, social security payments accounted for 30 percent of its budget in 2000, with projections for 2006 calling for half of the state budget.

Meanwhile, the reforms had not resolved major inequities in the system. The changes made were still insufficient. In 2002, the accumulated deficit in the private social security program (INSS) in mid-July alone already reached R$6.8 billion. The industrial slowdown accounted for part of the problem, but there was wide agreement that the system needed further reform.

Tax Reform

Prompted in part by external shocks and adjustment programs, a good number of countries in Latin America and other regions implemented substantial changes of their taxation systems during the 1980s. These reforms sought to simplify the tax system, adopt or extend a value-added tax (VAT or IVA),

---

47. Nevertheless, some reformers hoped for a further set of measures to bring public and private employees into the same framework.

TABLE 3-3. Evolution of Federal Taxes

Taxes and Contributions Levied by the Federal Government	Share of Total (Percent)		Variation
	2000	**2001**	**Percent**[a]
Import Tax	4.5	4.9	11.0
Industrial Production Tax (IPI)	10.5	10.1	0.2
Income Tax (IR)	33.4	32.8	1.5
Financial Operations Tax (IOF)	1.8	1.8	5.8
Rural Property Tax	0.1	0.1	-46.1
Financial Turnover Tax (CPMF)	8.7	8.4	0.0
Social Security Contribution (COFINS)	22.1	23.6	10.6
Social Integration Program (PIS/ PASEP)	5.8	5.8	3.8
Net Profit Contribution (CSLL)	5.9	5.0	-10.9
Civil Servant Pension Contribution	2.0	1.9	-4.8
Other Revenues	5.3	5.9	13.3
Federally Collected Revenues (Total)	100	100	3.6

Source: Central Bank
a. Calculated from year to year variation, in R$.

decrease progressiveness, increase collection, and reduce taxes on reinvested profits. If Brazil did not implement comparable reforms through the final years of the military regime, neither did it do so during the three democratic governments in the period 1985–1994. Brazil's fiscal woes resulted in part from a tax collection system characterized by a relatively small number of taxpayers and massive tax evasion.[48]

The Brazilian constitution of 1988 retained essentially the same tax collection system as before, but specified in detail how funds should be distributed between the three levels of the Brazilian federation, guaranteeing states and localities fixed percentages of collections. Moreover, the taxation system itself was now embedded in the constitution and hence required a constitutional amendment to be changed. The charter created strong incentives for constituencies in states and counties to favor the current structure.

From 1993 through 2002 the federal government debated the tax reform, but acted mostly on incremental measures to enhance and rationalize the taxation system. Congress authorized in 1993, and extended in 1995 and after, the special Fund of Fiscal Stabilization (previously named the Social Fund for Emergencies) from funds that would have been distributed to states and localities. In 1996, Congress voted a new tax on idle agricultural land.[49] Defended on the grounds that it provides incentives for land use and protec-

48. For other Latin American countries—including Mexico, Argentina, and Chile—see Ricardo Carciofi, Guillermo Barris, and Oscar Cetrangolo (1994).

TABLE 3-4. Tax Revenue, as percent of GDP

Tax Collected	1996	1997	1998	1999	2000	Variation[a]
All Levels	28.63	28.58	29.33	31.64	32.34	13
Federal Government	18.89	19.21	19.89	21.86	22.09	17
States	8.32	7.90	7.88	8.21	8.78	6
Counties	1.42	1.47	1.56	1.57	1.47	4
Revenue after Transfers	1996	1997	1998	1999	2000	Variation
All Levels	28.63	28.58	29.33	31.64	32.34	13
Federal Government	14.99	15.13	15.16	16.95	16.71	11
States	8.43	8.20	8.32	8.76	9.43	12
Counties	5.21	5.25	5.85	5.93	6.20	19

Source: IBGE
a. Percent increase from 1996 to 2000.

tion of the environment, as well as funds for agrarian reform, this tax imposes 20 percent yearly levies on unproductive land.

The Cardoso administration decided in its early years to focus on strengthening tax collection rather than systematically restructure the taxation system. Since tax evasion had a long history in Brazil, the fiscal picture would improve considerably with better collection procedures. Tax revenues increased by 13 percent between 1996 and 2000—from 28.6 percent of GDP to 32.3 percent in 2000. These figures represented particularly strong growth in relation to the period 1991–1994, when tax collection was 25 percent of GDP. The federal government relied on decrees to increase taxes, often as responses to externally induced financial crisis, as in 1997. The adjustment package announced in late 1998 represented an even larger tax increase, R\$16 billion in 1999, to be accomplished through such items as increasing the financial turnover tax or CPMF (from 0.20 percent to 0.38 percent) and civil servants pension contribution (10 percent on income up to R\$1,200 and 20 percent on income beyond that).[50] When the latter was declared unconstitutional by the Brazilian Supreme Court, the CPMF became even more essential to balance government accounts.

49. The ITR, Imposto sobre a Propriedade Territorial Rural (Rural Property Tax), created conditions for the appropriation of unused land within five years. If no taxes were paid for five years, the total taxes owed would correspond to 100 percent of the value of the property, a condition that would facilitate the appropriation and redistribution of land. In 2000, the federal government passed on to states part of the responsibility for agrarian reform as well as the administration and use of this tax. Expectations were that this tax would generate billions within two years, but revenue for 1996 and 1997 hovered around R\$300 million and decreased in subsequent years. The smaller collection may have been due in part to lower land prices and the stronger *real*.
50. The CPMF, Contribuição Provisória sobre Movimentaçao Financeira (Financial Turnover Tax), was meant as a provisional tax, but by 1999–2000 had become "essential" for the federal government (see, for example, Teodomiro Braga and Paulo Fona, "Reforma tributária na pauta," *Jornal do Brasil*, Economia, May 19, 2000).

   Tax reform emerged as a particularly sensitive issue in the context of the interstate rivalries and fiscal wars exacerbated with the constitution of 1988. The main source of revenue for states is the valued-added tax known as ICMS.[51] For instance, the ICMS accounted for 85 percent of the tax revenues of the state of São Paulo in the late 1990s. Aspects of the ICMS tax led to fiscal wars between the states. A new law of the late 1990s exempted exports and capital goods from ICMS. Producer states such as São Paulo are highly critical of this law, the Kandir Law, because of its impact on tax collection.[52]

   The tax bill debated in 2000 sought to end the fiscal war by homogenizing the ICMS, making exports more competitive, and making tax collection a nonconstitutional matter. This bill had great difficulty making headway in Congress, in the context of intense debate among governors, mayors, and the federal government. Through 2002, the tax system was often criticized because of the expansion of tax as a percentage of GDP, the number of different taxes, the dysfunctionalities of many of them, and the fact that its cumulative impact on productive activities decreased business competitiveness and increased the difficulty of increasing much-needed exports. But the tax bill had not made much progress.

   As the Cardoso era came to a close, there was wide agreement that the tax system needed to be overhauled. Tax collection had become regularized, allowing the government to play a larger role than would have otherwise been the case. And the fiscal crises since 1998 would have been much worse without the increased revenues to the government. Still, the taxation system had flaws that needed to be addressed in the context of the opening of the Brazilian economy and the need to increase competitiveness and exports.[53] Quite obviously, tax reform would remain a difficult matter since there was only partial consensus on concrete measures, the levels of tax collection were adequate, and advocates lacked the political strength and stomach to pass such a difficult constitutional amendment.

---

51. ICMS stands for Imposto sobre Circulação de Mercadorias e Serviços (Goods and Services Circulation Tax).
52. There is considerable controversy over the extent to which the ICMS tax concentrates revenue collection in the southern, industrial states such as São Paulo. The tax is levied at the point of origin instead of destination. But interstate tariffs differ from intrastate tariffs. For instance, sales from São Paulo to Ceará are taxed at only 7 percent by the former. The producer pays the difference (10 percent) between this rate and the intrastate rate in Ceará (17 percent) directly to the state of Ceará. This is in fact a transfer of tax revenues from one state to the other. This scheme generates incentives for redirecting trade and misreporting movements to evade tax and fuels competition among states.
53. Tax reform was an issue in the 2002 presidential elections, with candidates José Serra and Ciro Gomes calling for changing the system to increase the overall competitiveness of Brazilian industry. While Lula had mild agreement with the competitiveness argument, his campaign emphasized increased tax collection.

Conclusion

As the turn of the century approached, the reforms since the 1990s were helping transform Brazil in fundamental ways. The very financial scares had speeded up the approval of a number of reforms, particularly those contributing to fiscal adjustment. In the context of the still maturing democratization process, key actors in the spheres of politics, media, business, and labor focused on the broader national debate about state, economic, political, and social reform. Reformers could point to significant progress in modernizing the state and economy and preparing the country for a more competitive era. But the tall agenda of reform and the vulnerabilities of the economy could easily dissipate the political capital of even a well-consolidated government. The reform process suffered when Cardoso's approval ratings fell precipitously in 1999–2000. The federal government was now forced to reconsider its priorities. An even bigger test would come with the 2002 elections.

The institutionalization of the reforms and a new state form takes many years and hinges on the fate of the democratizing process. In this context, the continuity of the reform process depends in part on institutional dynamics and political actors, including civil society, set in motion as a result of the process of reform itself. The political maturity of civil society and the general public will define the shape of things to come. In this broader canvas, the state reform process tests Brazil's very process of democratization.

Success against inflation and in political stabilization gained Cardoso's PSDB and other pro-reform parties a cardinal position from which to negotiate the adoption of effective answers to pressing problems with other contenders, but it did not translate into a stable political alignment. Sustained state reform and liberalization depend on the political processes and institutional structures being created in the context of democratic consolidation. The relative success of the reforms since 1993 gave the centrist reformers in the PSDB and allied parties an enhanced legitimacy and political role. The sustained period at the helm and the success in bringing inflation down to the lowest rate in more than four decades as well as in stabilizing the policy-making environment have gained them respect, valuable experience, and political presence. The completion of the reforms hinges on the political fate of the reformers and the new policy-making dynamics beyond 2002.

It is sobering that as of 2002 the federal government had been unable to take on an aggressive development-promotion role. Though only effectively adopted in 2001, and in the context of financial threat, the Law of Fiscal Responsibility was a major achievement. But, in spite of the significant effort towards state reform several key reforms had not become law, including the critically important pension or social security reform. Completing the new fiscal model remained essential for a sustainable new development model to emerge. Development activism was on hold, but Brazilian reformers continued to weave ambitious dreams and plans for social and overall development.

CHAPTER 4   *Social Development and Collective Action*

On April 22, 2000, Brazil celebrated the 500th anniversary of the Portuguese landing—or the discovery of Brazil by navigator Pedro Álvarez Cabral, as traditionally observed. The government made elaborate plans to commemorate the event with a yearlong series of public activities, starting with a celebration at the landing site at Porto Seguro in the northeastern state of Bahia on the date of the anniversary. The festivity turned into a fiasco when 2,000 demonstrators organized by the landless movement, Indians, and popular movements opposing the government launched "The March of the Excluded" at the same location and time. The ensuing confrontation, marked by the use of tear gas and some violence, led to 140 arrests and a dozen injures—all of it widely covered by the media. Two high-level federal officials resigned in the aftermath. Whether or not the country faced an identity crisis as a land of ethnic peace, as the *New York Times* reported, this mobilization was a high-profile protest of government policy and social conditions.[1] More important, the vigor of the collective action and the policies at which it was directed both deny credence to views of the post-1985 democratizing polity as a frozen democracy with a timid or ineffectual reform process and little substantive change in terms of oligarchical elite rule, the survival of clientelism and a weak civil society, and the inability to break new ground to address issues of massive poverty and inequality.[2] Bra-

1. For basic coverage see Larry Rohter, "500 Years Later, Brazil Looks Its Past in the Face," *New York Times*, April 25, 2000, A3. A few days later, Indian activists also disrupted a Catholic bishops' mass asking Indians and blacks for forgiveness of the sins committed by the church during the colonial period. They interrupted the ceremony to proclaim that Indians did not grant the forgiveness requested. The minister of tourism and the head of the Brazilian bureau of Indian affairs were forced to resign following the fiasco at the government's celebrations.
2. For example, Weyland (1996a), Sorensen (1993, 47–57), and Skidmore (1999). Weyland emphasizes the inability of democracy to bring major change in social policy, citing institutional dynamics as the main explanatory factor. The essays in Kingstone and Power (1999) offer a positive but tentative assessment of Brazilian democracy.

zilian democracy is now more vibrant, elite influence is decreasing, civil society has gained momentum and is able to challenge the status quo, and poverty and inequality are being addressed in promising new ways.

This chapter puts the spotlight on the interaction between social reform and popular collective action to further probe the depth of changes in Brazilian society. Interest groups, social movements, and civil society as a whole were involved in the construction of policies and institutions in postauthoritarian Brazil, and emerged as important actors with regard to social issues. The erosion of corporatist statism in the 1990s further shaped this process. From the perspective of the 1990s and beyond, the sharpened perception of the need for social development and the considerable agreement on social policy in the context of the reform process stand out, as does the role of the new civil society in articulating demands.

Social Development: Needs

The sheer dimensions and intractability of inequality and poverty in Brazil became increasingly evident as the country deepened its process of democratization. Diverse voices from civil society and government made just this point. At the beginning of the twenty-first century, after more than six years of reform, Brazil remained one of the most unequal societies on earth (Barros et al. 2000a), with over fifty million Brazilians mired in dire poverty.[3] Extreme inequality has been fairly constant for decades, in spite of the gradual increase in per capita income and changes in policy. According to IBGE, the gini coefficient[4] for metropolitan regions of the Northeast of Brazil are considerably worse, while metropolitan regions of the Southeast and South present coefficients similar to that of developed countries.[5] On the other hand, poverty decreased significantly through the 1970s in response to economic growth, as shown in fig. 4-1. After that, poverty rates took downward swings after the stabilization plans of 1985 and 1994. These were one-time effects, with the drop of the mid-1980s nearly wiped out shortly after. Still, in 1999–2000 Brazil had the lowest poverty rate in decades.

---

3.   Henriques (2000) contains a collection of quantitative analyses of poverty and inequality by specialists affiliated with the Instituto de Pesquisa Econômia Aplicada (IPEA). For a qualitative presentation of mainstream Brazilian thinking on social needs and policy, see Barros et al. (2000a, 2000b) and Faria (2000a). Three issues of IPEA's new major bulletin on social policy, *Políticas Sociais: Acompahamento e análise* 1 (2000), 2 (2001), and 3 (2001), elaborate on this point and on the search for more effective approaches to social policy (these reports are also available through the IPEA website).
4.   See definition in fig. 4-2.
5.   Fortaleza, Recife, and Salvador had in 1996 coefficients of 0.6180, 0.6082, and 0.6030, respectively, while São Paulo, Curitiba, and Porto Alegre presented coefficients of 0.5525, 0.5466, and 0.5707 (IBGE, *Pesquisa de orçamentos familiares*, 1996).

FIGURE 4-1. Poverty Incidence, yearly and two-year average trend line

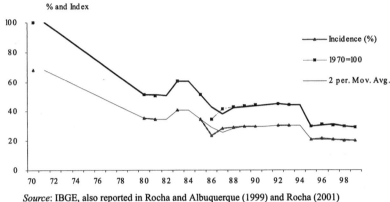

Source: IBGE, also reported in Rocha and Albuquerque (1999) and Rocha (2001)

But poverty remained a major problem. About 31.9 percent of Brazilians were poor in 2000, according to the Institute of Applied Economic Research (IPEA).[6] Approximately 53 million Brazilians live below the government's poverty line—income less than the minimum wage.[7] Economic growth and more effective social policies are essential to reducing poverty in the long run. A growing number of analysts have argued rather persuasively that persistent inequality is also a main cause of poverty and hence more aggressive redistributive measures will be necessary to eliminate dire poverty. In fact, Brazilians seem to have reached a near-consensus that extremely high levels of inequality are incompatible with a modern, humane democracy. Indeed, countries with comparable levels of income per capita show considerably less inequality (see fig. 4-2). Redistribution in the long run can be accomplished through such policies as enhanced access to education and health care, agrarian reform, credits for grassroots entrepreneurship, and the like (Barros et al. 2000b).

Brazil's social needs and social structure reflect long-term fissures and changes. The economy grew quite rapidly during much of the twentieth century. In fact, Brazil was second only to Japan in the growth rate it experienced from 1880 to 1980. The country changed extensively as it moved from a pri-

6. A 2001 study by Marcelo Neri, Centro de Políticas Sociais (Fundação Getúlio Vargas), argues that more than 50 million Brazilians (nearly 30 percent of the population) are very poor or indigent (*Folha de S. Paulo*, July 10, 2001). By indigent, this study means individuals with income of less than R$80 per month. IPEA and other official agencies use a different definition of indigent: those with incomes lower than a third of the minimum salary.
7. Estimates for 2000 indicate 54.1 million Brazilians are "poor"—55.2 percent of rural population, 28.7 percent of the urban, and 22.9 percent of the population in metropolitan areas. See "Índices de pobreza caíram no país após *Plano Real*, diz IPEA," *Folha de S. Paulo*, July 12, 2001.

78   *Chapter 4*

FIGURE 4-2. Inequality and gini coefficient as function of GDP per capita, 1999

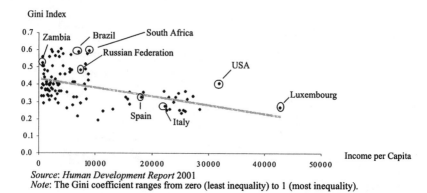

Source: *Human Development Report* 2001

Note: The Gini coefficient ranges from zero (least inequality) to 1 (most inequality).

marily rural society in the 1950s to a highly urbanized one by the mid-1990s, when 80 percent of its people lived in cities. A huge process of internal migration from the poor and rural Northeast to the cities of the Southeast, Brasília, and other growing parts of the Center-West was a key element in the process of urbanization. Though migration not infrequently meant social mobility, the highly skewed social structure inherited from the past endured.

The military regime did not create high levels of poverty and inequality, but certain policies of the 1964–1985 period cemented landlessness and related forms of rural poverty as enduring features of Brazilian society. A majority of Brazilians were still rural in the 1960s. The military's policies of agrarian modernization that gave incentives to large estates—including cheap credit for cattle raising, export commodities, and mechanization—contributed to land concentration. Small producers often lost their land and either migrated or joined the ranks of the landless peasants. Overall, poverty decreased in the period of high growth of the late 1960s and early 1970s, but inequality intensified thereafter as landlessness expanded. Population growth and the debt crisis of the 1980s contributed greatly to blocking social development, and hence to increasing poverty and inequality. Tensions and cleavages rooted in history and region survived the period of authoritarianism. Social exclusion and vulnerability had become deeply ingrained features of Brazilian society.

Brazil had a rather heterogeneous social structure. In fact, income per capita grew in a sustained manner during much of the twentieth century, representing significant economic development. Yet much of this growth was located in the prosperous Southeast, where industry continued to be concentrated. Though the São Paulo metropolitan area eventually lost some ground in this regard, it was there that a huge labor movement and the most important forms of collective action tended to be centered. By 1990, the wealthiest

10 percent of Brazilians held half of the total wealth and had incomes almost thirty times the average for the bottom 40 percent of the population. That year, 30.8 million Brazilians, 21.3 percent of the population, were below the poverty line. More than 63.1 million, or 43.8 percent, could actually be classified as poor. In rural areas, particularly in the Northeast, 43.1 percent were indigent and 70.8 percent were poor.[8]

The country had considerable room for improvement in every measure of social development as the 1990s opened, against the backdrop of considerable differentiation based on region and class. Brazil had low levels of educational achievement, a notoriously deficient public health system, and glaring shortages in housing and sanitation. In 1996, 14.5 percent of Brazilians were illiterate—with the highest rates found in the rural Northeast (45 percent) and the Northeast as a whole (29.2 percent). Still, though Brazil's educational levels were comparable to much less economically developed parts of Latin America, there had been noteworthy improvement. The illiteracy rate decreased from 33.6 percent in 1970, to 25.4 percent in 1980, 20.1 percent in 1991, and 13.6 percent in 2000. The rate decreased by more than 20 percent in a relatively short period of time, an accomplishment that normally takes much longer. Inequalities across income, region, race, and gender also diminished substantially. The improvements were due to urbanization and other demographic and structural factors as well as to changes in the educational system.[9]

From Need to Mobilization

In the democratizing context, collective action has articulated needs into political demands and has become an increasingly important factor in the dynamics of social stratification.[10] Social movements and nongovernmental organizations (NGOs) became significant players making claims about social and political reform in the 1970s and early 1980s, when the modern era of mobilization began. Studying Brazil's evolving social policy and the role of this third sector hence involves a focus on three decades and a shifting focus on the national, state, and local scenes (for example, Doimo 1995).

Labor and land reform issues are prominent on most levels of collective action, though Brazilians from diverse agendas and social backgrounds

8. This paragraph draws heavily from Vilmar Faria and Eduardo Graeff (2000, 17–19).
9. The gini coefficients in the UNDP's *Human Development Report 2002* show a slight increase in income concentration in the period 1997-1998, from .591 to .607.
10. Collective action by workers and "excluded" groups became particularly important in the changing yet uncertain context of the 1990s and is examined in some depth in this chapter. Elite contention is considered in chapter 5. Like all contention, elite behavior is generally shaped by the institutional and political context. In turn, it helps define the contours of the polity affecting collective action by other actors.

TABLE 4-1. Mass Mobilization since 1978, main movements

	Movement	Actions	Claims
1978–1985	Labor Mobilization and Unrest	Strikes, urban rallies	Labor autonomy, democracy, wages adjusted to inflation
1983–1984	Diretas Já!/Campaign for Direct Elections	Urban rallies	Direct presidential elections
1986–1993	Labor Unrest	Strikes	Adjustments to inflation
1986–1988	Various	Rallies, petitions	Shape constitution
1992	Movimento Pela Ética na Política/Pro-Impeachment	Urban rallies	Impeachment of Fernando Collor
1993	Betinho's Campaign	Broad grassroots mobilizing	Press for government and private support for the poor and hungry
1995	Movimento dos Sem Terra (MST)	Land takeovers, sometimes bloody	Land for the landless, political agitation

launched other movements and organizations. Thousands of neighborhood associations and as many as 80,000 "base ecclesiastical communities" (CEBs) (Alvarez 1990) emerged in the context of democratic transition. Millions of Brazilians organized to demand improvements in urban and social conditions (Doimo 1995) and make demands related to democratization—direct elections, influence over the drafting of the constitution of 1988, the impeachment of Fernando Collor, and others. The most visible movements in the 1990s centered on hunger and poverty, the protection of rubber tappers in the Amazon region, the environment, and human rights (Pereira 1999). Land issues occupied center stage in mid-decade.

The emergence and evolution of a democratic state and a modern party system shaped subsequent cycles of collective action. Particularly noteworthy are the consolidation of decentralized federalism, the shift away from corporatism, and the new models of democratic governance that incorporate civil society at all levels of government. Institutional and structural factors shaped popular collective action and its policy impact in a path-dependent manner.[11] The deepening of democratization affected subsequent mobilization and political participation, giving each wave of mobilization a cascading effect but also a somewhat distinctive character.[12] Democratization sharpened the

---

11. This analysis emphasizes the perspective of political institutions, state elites, and social actors. An institutional perspective can help one understand policies as well as patterns of collective action. As shown in chapter 1, such an approach to Brazilian democracy and development has recently flourished.

perception and expression of grievances, leading to the expectation of enhanced social movement activity.[13]

Democratization made collective action easier in several respects. First, it reduced the cost of mobilization. After twenty years of authoritarian politics, the mere political opening encouraged the airing of pent-up demands and grievances. The formal repressive apparatus set up by the military was largely disassembled. It was now considerably safer to organize and articulate demands. Second, changes in civil society helped alter the opportunity structure. Institutional actors in the democratization process and a growing number of national and international nongovernmental organizations interested in poverty and human rights intensified their operations in support of social movements. The Catholic Church's CNBB and Land Pastoral Commission pledged their national reach to aid the mobilization of the landless. Social movements could now count on more resources and support. The media and academia, thriving in democracy, were sympathetic to popular mobilization. Third, uncertain about their own political bases in an evolving institutional and party context, emergent political figures and factions across the board sought the mantle of reformism and receptiveness to social pressure to cement relations with economic interests and voting blocs. Fourth, the shift away from centralization and corporatism to decentralized rule and other forms of interest intermediation affected collective action and contention. The initial stages of mobilization saw many social movements turn against a state traditionally perceived as authoritarian and illegitimate.[14] Until 1988, Brazil operated technically under the centralizing regime in place for decades. The reality was that states and cities were gaining political ground in the process of democratization. The constitution of 1988 put a highly decentralized form of federalism in place. Generally, the political opportunity structure became much more propitious to social movement formation and activity, even if the latter often had a fragmented character.

Following the early burst of collective action during the last years of military rule, particularly the labor strikes of 1979 leading to the creation of CUT in 1983, urban social movement activity subsided at the beginning of the post-1985 democratizing era. This presents a puzzle. The expansion of other

12. Works discussing social movements and related forms of collective action in the context of democratization include Boschi (1987), Mainwaring (1989, 1986a), Ruth Cardoso (1988), Gay (1988), and Avritzer (2000). Gohn (1995) lists major social movements in Brazil in the early 1990s. Garrison (2000) provides a very useful review of surveys and other materials documenting the rise of nongovernmental organizations and a new civil society in Brazil. Weyland (1996a) argues that the process of democratization intensified tendencies toward fragmentation in collective action.

13. Interestingly, social movement activity increased dramatically in the first years of the military dictatorship, when repression was at its highest (Maybury-Lewis 1994).

14. See Frances Hagopian (1998).

channels of interest representation and the pluralization of political life might be partly responsible for the drop in social movement activity after the onset of democratization. Two processes stand out in this regard: the emergence of a vigorous though fragmented political party system and, later, a mode of interest intermediation increasingly marked by an independent third sector with an increasing number of interest groups and nongovernmental organizations. These channeled grievances as well as energies and resources that might have gone toward the creation of social movements. Some social movements actually experienced transformations toward the NGO form as well as the political party.[15]

The dramatic expansion in the number and density of nongovernmental organizations and the creation of a new civil society began in the 1970s and grew steadily in subsequent years, particularly after 1985. By 1995, following rapid expansion, nongovernmental organizations were said to be mobilizing at least US$10 billion, or 1.5 percent of GDP. The Brazilian Association of NGOs (Abong) had 250 members at the turn of the century, but between three and five thousand were thought to exist.[16] A sample of those registered with Abong showed that 60 percent had been founded after 1985.[17] Brazil's Southeast accounts for the majority of the NGOs, particularly the largest.

Democracy made it easier for outside support and international NGOs to become significant forces in Brazil. External support is thought to account for approximately 80 percent of NGO funding. NGO activity has become prominent in particular sectors. For instance, a cluster of twelve or so NGOs focused on the Amazon region adopted the strategy of buying large tracts of land. The Amazonian Association alone acquired control of a portion of the state of Roraima larger than Belgium. Other organizations worked to shape policy toward or to protect local populations. The Amazonian Research Institute relies on a staff of 110 people to assess, often critically, government policy in the Amazon region. By the late 1990s, the Brazilian military, sectors of

15. Even more so than nongovernmental organizations, political parties appear to have attracted even more militants and resources away from social movements. The MST itself began to run candidates in the municipal elections of 2000. One way or another, activists were drawn to electoral activity and other institutionalized channels in the context of the deepening of the democratic polity.

16. Garrison (2000) reviews the evidence and mentions "over 3,000" in his summary (xi) and a credible estimate of 1,041 for 1988 and 4,000–5,000 in 1998 (11). He also cites a 1996 study by the World Wildlife Fund confirming the existence of 725 nongovernmental organizations in the environment field. Garrison agrees with the thesis of a "meteoric rise" of NGOs after the 1980s.

17. This discussion about NGOs draws from a series of articles published by *O Estado de S. Paulo* on July 30-August 2, 2000—including Marta Avancini, "ONGs, sem controle, ganham poder no País," "Controle de ONGs no País é inadequado," "Governo federal adota linhas de atuação de ONGs," "Novo papel do Estado ajuda a explicar crescimento do setor," Tânia Monteiro, "FHC defende debate a respeito do terceiro setor," and Luciana Nunes Leal, "Parceria causa polêmica entre grupos do Rio."

the media, and some political figures became concerned about what they saw as a concerted drive to internationalize the Amazon and the apparent threat this caused to Brazilian sovereignty. Congress ordered a congressional investigation to explore the mode of operation and the foreign links of NGOs.

Because of nongovernmental organizations, the environmental movement had in fact become a major player with regard to policy. The congressional lobby of *ambientalistas* defeated the powerful agricultural caucus on the issue of how much of the Amazon could be preserved. When Congress debated a Code of Forests in May 2000, the *bancada ruralista* wanted to reduce the amount of forests that could be set as preserves from 50 to 20 percent. But the environmental lobby convinced the National Council on the Environment and Congress of the need for a bill setting the figure to 80 percent. Few doubted that NGOs had become consequential players in the environmental policy domain. Brazilian nationalism was tested by the growing role of foreign and international actors, but few envisioned a massive reversal of this process.

After the mid-1990s, the federal government favored the expansion of the third sector as a way of deepening Brazilian democracy, a factor that helps account for the transition of NGOs from "near clandestine status a decade ago to being valued and visible development actors today."[18] It viewed nongovernmental organizations as essential parts of a civil society organizing itself—"an efficient way to aggregate wills around specific proposals to pursue the public interest."[19] Since the 1990s, the federal government has sought to rely extensively on partnerships between itself and the third sector, viewing the rise of NGOs as a worldwide phenomenon rather than as evidence of state weakness. Comunidade Solidária led the way in efforts to create a new legal framework for incorporating the third sector, including legislation to recognize a new type of legal entity, civil society organizations (Public Interest Organizations in Civil Society or Oscip),[20] to stimulate the involvement of third sector organizations in social policy.[21] The Ministry of Education reported partnerships with 230 businesses and NGOs. Comunidade Solidária supported the creation of an NGO to design and implement a literacy program. The partnership with this NGO was to serve as a model for others. Critics of the new relationship between the government, NGOs, and the private sector lamented the loss of militancy among social movement organiza-

18. Garrison (2000, 51). Garrison notes the pattern of collaboration between spheres of government, nongovernmental organizations, and the World Bank.
19. Tânia Monteiro, "FHC defende debate a respeito do terceiro setor," *O Estado de S. Paulo*, July 30, 2000.
20. Marta Avancini, "Controle de ONGs no País é inadequado," *O Estado de S. Paulo*, July 31, 2000.
21. Garrison and Abreu (2000) describe the work of several civil society organizations in the fight against AIDS, emphasizing partnership with various levels of government.

tions.[22] Other levels of government have also actively promoted or embraced the rise of the new civil society.

The extent of civil society support for the entire reform approach seemed in doubt at moments of economic crisis, particularly in the context of political party competition. The 1998–2000 period was critical, as public opinion and some civil society organizations withdrew their support from the government. In 2000, the central government faced an uphill battle to ensure its very survival and the continuity of the reform drive. As that crisis receded through early 2001, Brazil faced new crises: the erosion of the exchange rate linked to the Argentinian crisis, an energy shortage initially thought to be of major proportions, and the economic turmoil of 2001–2002. These moments of vulnerability provide opportunities for assessing the significance of oppositional collective action and the extent of support for the reform program.

The Labor Movement and the New Urban Scene

The revival of strikes in 1978–1980, followed by the tripling of labor unrest in 1983, made the labor movement a key actor in the dynamics of democratic transition.[23] The modern labor movement emerged among the auto workers of São Paulo.[24] Like Luiz Inácio da Silva, many of them were immigrants from the Northeast. Two labor confederations were organized in 1983, the Central Única dos Trabalhadores (CUT) and the Central Geral dos Trabalhadores (CGT). A third, Força Sindical (FS), was born shortly later.[25] CUT has been the most active and political of the labor organizations. As left-leaning Brazilians mobilized around labor issues, the pool of potential recruits for other social movements decreased, partly explaining the drop in nonlabor social movement activity after 1983 (Sandoval 1998).

The new unionism differed above all in terms of relations with the state. It rejected the co-optative leadership (*pelegos*) of the corporatist system. Early decisions by the post-1985 democratic governments, reinforced by the con-

22. See Luciana Nunes Leal, "Parceria causa polêmica entre grupos no Rio," and Marta Avancini, "Governo federal adota linha de atuação de ONGs," *O Estado de S. Paulo*, August 2, 2000. In Rio, the movement "Os Verdes" contrasted with the professionalized "Onda Azul." The latter was involved in government-sponsored programs. Several civil society organizations linked to the ministry or state-level secretary of labor carried out training.
23. Sandoval (1993, 1998) provides a well-researched and theoretically contextualized account of strike activity from the late 1970s through the early 1990s.
24. More precisely, automobile workers in the adjacent region known as ABC—the cities of Santo André, São Bernardo, and São Caetano—were the most mobilized.
25. The two CGT's—Central Geral dos Trabalhadores and the Confederação dos Trabalhadores—were associated with the old, corporatist system. The FS apparently came from independent unions and workers previously affiliated with CGT. FS distanced itself from the CUT in supporting general government policy on the grounds of the national interest and a discourse about partnership (see Martins and Cardoso 1993, Cardoso 1999a and 1999b).

stitution of 1988, democratized the election of labor leaders, curtailed government control of elections in trade unions, and ended the legal restrictions on labor confederations. Brazilian workers now had more freedom to organize in pursuit of their interests and redefine the terms of the relationship between labor and the state. This contributed heavily to the erosion of corporatism across diverse spheres of interest representation. The reshaping of civil society created new possibilities for the formation of political coalitions.[26]

A prominent role in the struggle for democracy gave labor the momentum it needed to claim to be a potentially dominant political force in the country. Born free of government tutelage, CUT emerged as the leading labor confederation in São Paulo and decided to seek direct political representation through a political party. After it formed the Workers' Party (PT), the PT-CUT exercised considerable influence in the Constituent Assembly of 1987–1988 and has been a major contender in each of the elections since 1985.[27]

The 1990s were not as auspicious. The political surge of the Workers' Party began to ebb early in the decade, when the party saw its national political ambitions frustrated. Defeats in the presidential elections of 1990 and 1994 were particularly painful, since labor leader Luíz Inácio "Lula" da Silva commanded early polls in both elections. As the elections of 1998 approached, the PT ran Lula again, but with Leonel Brizola of the PDT as vice president. The PT-PDT alliance lost to the Cardoso ticket by a wide margin. The channeling of working-class demands through a militant party came at a cost in terms of labor unity. Sectors of the labor movement not sharing CUT's socialist ideology either remained in CGT or joined FS, both of which were less politicized and more willing to collaborate with the central government.

But labor's political woes were grounded in underlying structural shifts. In 1986, 22 percent of the labor force was unionized, but the rate had fallen to 17 percent in 1996. Though productivity was rising at a fast annual rate of 7.5 percent (Faria and Graeff 2000), economic restructuring was taking a heavy toll in the labor market. The auto industry alone lost 150,000 jobs in the 1990–1997 period. Union revenues dropped by more than half during the same period, and the number of strikes in 1997 was much lower than in previous years.[28]Demand increased for better educated and trained laborers with new and more flexible skills, but the Brazilian labor force was not yet prepared for the challenge.[29] Certain sectors such as banking experienced sharp

---

26. See Sallum (1996, 118–19). For accounts of the labor movement and the Workers' Party through 1990–1991, see also Keck (1992), and Sandoval (1993). Erickson (1977) provides an important analysis of labor mobilization in the context of the corporatism of the Vargas era.
27. Keck (1992), Danaher and Shellenberger (1995).
28. See, "Loteria Sindical," *Veja*, February 25, 1998.

FIGURE 4-3. Labor Force, employment in 2001

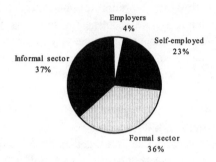

Source: Adapted from OECD 2001
Note: Employment corresponded to 90.4% of the labor force in 2001.

cutbacks. Outsourcing and the informal sector increased, industrial jobs decreased, and the service sector expanded.[30] Labor informality increased, as the informal sector accounted for 40 million workers and workers with formal jobs amounted to 30 million. As Brazilian industry adjusted to global competition by downsizing and relying on subcontracting and flexible employment, the threat or reality of job loss became a great force against militancy. Some workers themselves opened small businesses and abandoned the unions.

Strike activity had peaked in the era of high inflation, when collective action was required to negotiate frequent salary adjustments. The taming of inflation in the mid-1990s partly explains the decline in the union movement. But even at its peak, labor restlessness was a regional phenomenon to a considerable extent. Its core was the industrial workers of the São Paulo metropolitan area, many of them first-generation immigrants from the Northeast. However, as other urban areas attracted industry, even this core sector became less cohesive.

PT-CUT also made mistakes. When the Workers' Party positioned itself against the stabilization program and related measures in 1994, it misjudged the extent of political support for the anti-inflation drive. Public sentiment longed for economic stability and strongly supported the *Plano Real*. Labor now appeared as clinging to traditional positions and unable to respond to the economic realities and challenges of the 1990s.

After the mid-1990s, the central government began to de-emphasize corporatism in favor of a liberalized regime of labor relations based on freely nego-

29. More than half of the Brazilian population had not finished elementary education (see www.itis.com.br/brasil/desemprego.htm; see also *Veja*'s interview with sociologist José Pastore [accessed on www2.uol.com.br/veja/170698/p_011.html]).
30. Without official papers; therefore, without access to basic social benefits.

tiated contracts (including fixed-term contracts), free association, collective bargaining, and the right to strike. Complex labor regulations were simplified. The central government began to abstain from direct involvement in negotiations between owners and workers. The preexisting labor system was now in flux. Alternative unions formed, often with a focus on the defense of economic gains. The result was a labor movement with multiple organizational foci and leadership.

Incorporation into the political system meant that labor could not claim exclusion to justify violent protest. Its role in the political party system obviated the need for noninstitutional protest activity. Labor-related organizations and social movements seeking to restore militancy began to wane in political significance. By 1998 the Workers' Party sought to form broader alliances and coalitions. Though the tactical coalition with Leonel Brizola and the PDT that year ended in failure, the party began to cast a wider net in 2000. It justified that move in terms of forming a broad opposition to the liberalizing reforms. It joined protests by affected business sectors and entered into conversations with other political currents. At the same time, the party and CUT supported protest activity by the militant landless movement, a radical political current that had gained ascendancy in the countryside. The PT and CUT hence were using a two-pronged effort to oppose the market-oriented reforms advocated by the Cardoso administration. The PT and other parties of the left gained ground in the 2000 municipal and gubernatorial elections, particularly in large cities.

Labor remains a formidable political force. As in recent elections, early in the electoral season Lula reemerged as the natural candidate for the 2002 presidential elections. The PT offered a moderate platform. Party leaders argued that they would embrace a different economic or development model, but its precise features remained unclear. With regard to the Workers' Party, the outcome of the elections would no doubt hinge in large part on the clarification of that question relative to the proposals of other candidates.

Other Urban Movements. Of the many urban social movements flourishing after 1985, the campaign against poverty founded by sociologist Betinho is one of the most visible and pivotal.[31] This movement reversed the trend toward erosion of social movement activity. It began in 1993, when activists from preexisting social movement organizations decided to organize a mass movement against poverty. The Committee of Citizen Action against Poverty and for Life (Comitê da Ação da Cidadania Contra a Miséria e Pela Vida) came to be known as "Betinho's campaign" in honor of its leader. A hemophiliac who contracted AIDS in a blood transfusion, Betinho made a public vow to devote the rest of his life to the struggle against poverty. Brazilians responded warmly to this appeal. Together with the labor movement and other forms of collective action, this movement helped redefine the Brazilian polity of the democratic era. The fate of this movement confirms the capacity of the Brazilian polity to facilitate as well as to constrain collective action. The antipoverty campaign added to the pressure for enhanced social policies. When the central government organized the antipoverty program known as Comunidade Solidária, Betinho was drafted into its council and the official campaign against poverty, though he would subsequently withdraw. The movement began to refocus by 1997. Betinho's worsening health and eventual death left the movement without a leader with national and international standing. Its loose organization made it very difficult for the movement to thrive nationally without an inspiring leader. Some of its militants joined political parties, but the movement's broad network of sympathizers and supporters allowed it to survive. It tends to concentrate in Rio, where it originated, and has become an active part of civil society, often acting in partnership with community organizations and businesses.[32]

Brazilian cities have witnessed extensive mobilization on a wide range of issues.[33] Many observers have characterized this phenomenon as a struggle for citizenship. Others have seen the diverse movements as a battle for human rights. Both characterizations underline the role of mobilization in the broadening and deepening of the process of democratization.

31. Betinho's name was José Herbert de Souza. The movement against hunger and poverty emerged from the mass mobilization of Citizen Action, a movement that pressed for the impeachment of Fernando Collor. Betinho was a Catholic activist born in Minas Gerais who joined the Goulart government in 1963. After 1964 he sought exile in Uruguay, Chile, Toronto, and Mexico City, where he deepened his studies in sociology. His reputation was that of a leftist activist who believed in democracy ("democracy without adjectives"). His brother Henfil, a much admired caricaturist of the 1970s and 1980s, used his brand of journalism to press for amnesty and the return of all Brazilian exiles, including his brother. (Also a hemophiliac, Henfil contracted AIDS and died from it several years before Betinho). Upon returning in 1979, Betinho launched the Brazilian Institute of Social and Economic Analysis (IBASE), an organization to support grassroots mobilization. Some of the impetus for Betinho's campaign came from the CNBB, led by Luciano Mendes de Almeida. Betinho's campaign had a loose, decentralized structure. After his death in 1996, the movement lost much momentum, though it continued to exist. See Roberto Bissio, "Betinho: The Conscience of a Society," n/d (accessed on http://www.capside.org.sg/souths/twn/title/betin-cn.htm).

32. See IBASE website (www.ibase.org.br).

33. Farah (1998a) highlights how local governments have stimulated mobilization by experimenting with diverse programs seeking to broaden opportunities for the participation of new community actors in the design and implementation of local public policy. Several of these projects are structured as networks linking civil society, government agencies, and other institutional actors. These are sometimes known as commissions or councils. Farah lists several examples, including the Permanent Commission for Monitoring Working Conditions in Mato Grosso do Sul (391) and others in education, health, housing, and other areas. Conde (1998) sketches a comparable approach in Rio's projects designed to turn favelas into neighborhoods. For a discussion of Viva Rio, a movement to promote personal security in Rio, see Fernandes (1998). Two of the self-declared pillars of that movement are partnerships and local associationism, both of which encompass mobilization. In other words, these projects seek to build local social capital as part of the policy-making process.

Agrarian Mobilization and Reform

Collective action around land issues experienced sustained growth through the 1990s and into the new millennium. Two competing organizations, the National Confederation of Agricultural Workers (CONTAG) and the Landless Workers Movement (MST) dominate the scene. CONTAG, the oldest of the two, emerged as the main agrarian organization representing rural laborers in the framework of the corporatist system. Though its leaders sought to reinvent the organization in the democratizing political system, they soon faced strong competition from the MST, whose struggle for agrarian reform and political change relies on aggressive tactics, such as land invasions, occupation of government facilities, and massive marches and demonstrations.

The Landless Workers Movement's first phase sought to build a national movement. By 1994, when the PT lost the elections and the Cardoso administration deepened the reform drive, the MST enacted a dramatic surge in tense, and not infrequently bloody, land takeovers. By 1997 this wave of collective action and the related social conflict provided a formidable challenge to the federal government.[34] The increasing militancy of the landless and advocates of agrarian reform surely negates the notion of a major slowdown in social movement activity in democratizing Brazil.[35]

The MST perfected the tactic of land takeovers involving hundreds or even thousands of individuals, many in family groups. Gathering on some adjacent public space or remote area during weeks or days preceding the land invasion, they would march on a given property and lay claim to it. The landless movement pursued a strategy of confrontation with local authorities and landlords as well as the federal government. Collective action was accompanied by radical political statements. Besides mass land occupations, the MST experimented with other forms of protest and agitation, including the temporary occupation of government buildings, mass rallies and marches, media campaigns, and other tactics. The MST grew rapidly. By 1996–1997 it represented the main focus of social tension in the country. At that point, the majority of Brazilians supported it.

The government's initial response included some land redistribution, promises for further land distribution, and the establishment of new agencies to track and address the land issue. The MST was not satisfied. In the months preceding the 1998 elections, this movement seemed to have declared war on

---

34. A pivotal event was the April 17, 1996, massacre by state and local police forces of seventeen farmers in the state of Pará. These farmers were part of a massive demonstration supporting land takeovers and agrarian reform. The press reported at least forty wounded and an equal number of people disappeared. This event was widely reported in the international media.
35. For background on agrarian mobilization see Maybury-Lewis (1994), Pereira (1997).

the Cardoso administration itself. As they pondered a mature response, the Brazilian authorities probed for a fuller understanding of agrarian dynamics. Indeed, a historical and institutional perspective is needed to put this somewhat unexpected and rare movement in perspective, and to illuminate the interaction between the changing institutional context and localized socioeconomic cleavages in shaping social movement activity. In Brazil, large estates relying on slavery—or peon labor, though the latter was much less prevalent than in the rest of Latin America—dominated much of the countryside through the nineteenth century, with impoverished peasantries in many other parts of the country. This legacy was responsible for the high indices of inequality in land distribution and rural poverty in the Northeast. The historical phenomenon of poverty rooted in massive landlessness hence applied in particular to the North, Northeast, and most parts of the states of Minas Gerais and Rio de Janeiro. The southern part of the country provided an important contrast. Relatively small and medium-sized farming carried on by European and Japanese colonists or settlers flourished in major parts of São Paulo, Paraná, Rio Grande do Sul, and Santa Catarina since the last third of the nineteenth century. In any case, massive landlessness is perplexing considering the huge and relatively unexploited Amazon frontier—five million square kilometers (nearly 60 percent of the country's landmass). The Amazon frontier worked at best as a symbolic safety valve for conflicts in the adjacent Northeast, the part of the country traditionally exhibiting the most dramatic rural contrasts, problems, and conflict.[36]

Modern agrarian conflict came to the Northeast in the first half of the 1960s, when peasant leagues demanding agrarian reform surged into the sugar zone of Pernambuco. Partly in response, the Goulart government, the last in the 1945–1964 democratizing experiment, made moves toward the adoption of an agrarian reform. Though the military coup of 1964 put a lid on the situation, the agrarian question was now on the national agenda. In fact, the military's agrarian regime shaped agrarian developments henceforth (see also Houtzager 1998; Pereira 1997; Maybury-Lewis 1994). First, as sheer repression led to the break up of the radical leagues, the military incorporated rural unions into the corporatist system of interest representation in place since the Vargas era. Second, the modernizing military government enacted in 1965, and enhanced in subsequent decrees, a series of laws oriented toward an eventual agrarian reform. Known collectively as *Estatuto da Terra* (Land Statute), the agrarian reform legislation was at least as strong as any adopted under the democratizing governments through 1996.[37]

---

36. Rural mobilization tended toward millenarian or religious forms (for example, *Canudos*) as well as quasi banditry.

Third, the military adopted a massive program of regional development in the Amazon in 1966. Three components stand out: promotion of large-scale mining and agrarian projects, the construction of the Transamazonian highway, and a colonization program to settle five million *nordestino* homesteaders in the Amazon region. Starting in 1968, the government began to grant generous subsidies to large mining, cattle, and even industrial schemes.[38] The idea was to promote a large agro-industrial complex oriented to external markets. Ranchers began to claim vast expanses of land. Without access to the markets of the rest of the country, these projects could have only a limited impact. The building of the Transamazonian highway in the 1970s sharply increased the appeal of this region to new projects and settlers. And in 1970 the government founded the National Institute of Colonization and Agrarian Reform (INCRA) with the avowed goal of settling millions of farmers from the Northeast, the poorest region in the country and home to several of the generals ruling Brazil.

Military receptivity to land reform is explained in part by the prominence this issue had gained in the 1960s. A reformist logic argued that Latin American countries needed to redistribute land to avoid revolution, such as that in Cuba. The generals in power hoped to gain legitimacy by linking land distribution to the monumental plan for national and regional development. The new measures were part of a master plan to modernize agriculture and turn Brazil into a world power. The agrarian project became part of the official discourse on transforming Brazil.

But the colonization and development of the Amazon region turned out to be far from a peaceful and orderly process. The waves of land projects and migrants put considerable pressure on Indians, rubbertappers, and others who had adapted earlier to the Amazon environment. Both groups were relatively weak or small. The often bloody conflicts surrounding the penetration of the Amazons echoed distantly to most Brazilians, who tended to live near the Atlantic coast. Social conflict intensified when many of the small-scale homesteaders entered into land conflicts with large cattle ranchers. Between 1980 and 1996, as the military regime gave way to democratization, land conflict resulted in nearly 1,000 deaths—often denounced as killings or murders by the media and most observers. The absence of clear land titles fueled

37. The *Estatuto da Terra* was only partly implemented by the military regime, but it provided the main context governing subsequent approaches. The Constituent Assembly of 1987–1988 discussed putting more teeth into the agrarian reform legislation based on the *Estatuto da Terra*, but the cattle growers of central Brazil, mobilized into the UDR (União Democrática Ruralista), joined forces with other opponents to block progress in that regard.
38. A 1966 law created Sudam, a massive regional development scheme involving highly generous tax and other incentives in the area defined as "Amazônia legal" (legal Amazônia), a landmass encompassing the states of Acre, Amapá, Amazons, Pará, Rondônia, Roraima, Tocantins, and large parts of Maranhão and Mato Grosso.

the conflict. With titles all too frequently gotten through bribery in local and state-level registries, violence was precipitated alternatively by efforts at eviction and land occupation. In many cases, the relatively weak presence of national law enforcement made direct confrontation the likely way to settle issues of land possession or use. In this context, landowners either formed alliances with local and state police forces or built their own private forces.

Democratization created political conditions for land reform to resurface as a policy issue in 1985. Though trends in the countryside might have been expected to defuse the agrarian question, the rural poor were now more ready for political battle than at probably any other time in the country's history. Largely during the military era, they had organized 2,700 rural unions mobilizing nine million laborers. The 785 rural unions in existence in 1964 grew to 1,753 in 1972, 2,068 in 1975, and 2,732 in 1985. The number of unionized rural workers more than doubled between 1970 and 1974, doubling again to 6.9 million in 1980 and reaching 9.4 million in 1985.[39]

It is puzzling that much of this mobilization took place during the years when political repression was toughest. Maybury-Lewis (1994) sketches an institutional answer to this question. Brazilian corporatism specified that only one union per county could hope to gain legal recognition from the government—thereby monopolizing representation. In this context, the military's decision to extend to rural workers some of the services previously given only to urban workers triggered considerable competition to form unions and gain legal status. The argument about the impact of institutional structures on collective action is borne out in Pereira's analysis of the transformation of peasant leagues into trade unions in Pernambuco, partly as a reflection of the welfare programs the government was extending to workers (Pereira 1997). The leadership of CONTAG, the corporatist peak association for rural workers formed after 1968, had come to be perceived as legitimate by its rural constituencies.[40]

Yet other contextual factors—or the broader political opportunity structure, in the language of collective action theory (Tilly 1978)—help explain the explosive growth of rural unionization from the late 1960s through the 1980s and beyond. This was an era in which various new or recent nongovernmental organizations linked to the Catholic Church had a direct role in promoting

39. See Maybury-Lewis (1994, 119, 120). When, led by CONTAG, the Third National Congress of the rural workers met in 1979 to decide on a strategy in the context of the democratic transition, the representatives of the 2,275 rural unions in existence approved the use of strikes and other tactics to press for higher wages, autonomy from the corporatist system, agrarian reform, and other measures (Houtzager 1998). The Movimento Sindical dos Trabalhadores Rurais (MSTR) was the formal organizer of this gathering (Houtzager 1998).
40. For a useful analysis of the formation and trajectory of CONTAG through 1979 as well as the evolution of agrarian policy, see Houtzager (1998). CONTAG's website [www.contag.org.br] provides basic information about this organization.

consciousness-raising "base ecclesiastical communities" (CEBs), agrarian unions, and the legal defense of farmers. The Catholic Church strongly supported the MST via the CNBB and the Christian base communities. Inspired by Catholic liberation theology, the Conference of Brazilian Bishops developed a strong critique of Brazilian capitalism and declared itself to be an advocate of the poor. Turning words into deeds, it authorized the creation of the Pastoral Land Commission (CPT) in 1975, a highly militant and effective agency that gained considerable ground, developing a national network of local commissions and support groups.[41] Catholics in the southeast and south were on occasion also supportive of more conservative movements and helped rural workers organize around different principles.[42]

NGOs and other external actors hence help explain the new mobilizational drive of the landless. Political parties increased their role subsequently, in the context of competition for rural support. Though parties were relative latecomers in addressing land redistribution issues, democratization fueled agrarian activism. The Constituent Assembly of 1987 prompted strong calls for agrarian reform legislation.

This radicalization was somewhat anachronistic in the sense that urban migration and the rapid modernization that the country and Brazilian agriculture had been experiencing made the arguments in favor of radical agrarian reform less compelling, particularly the notion of land expropriations with minimal or no compensation (Sorj 1988). More than thirty million rural individuals migrated to cities between 1960 and the 1980s, thereby turning what had been an agrarian society into a highly urbanized one.[43] Rapid urbanization created incentives for the further commercialization and intensification of agriculture. Considering, in addition, the opening of the huge Amazon frontier, an explanation of the pro-agrarian reform mobilization surrounding the Constituent Assembly of 1987–1988 and the increasingly militant movement is far from obvious.

41. Cousineau (1995) provides an overview of the role of the CEBs in the struggle for land in the Amazon region. The CEBs are groups of lay people who study the Bible using methods derived from Paulo Freire's *Pedagogy of the Oppressed* and go on to apply their lessons and reflections to their own lives. She describes in substantial detail the roles of priests, sisters, and lay members of the CEBs in protecting farmers, mobilizing into unions, and implementing land occupations. In turn, the CPT provides lawyers to defend farmers in land litigations, help with the legal issues of organizing, and the like. In general, the Catholic Church thus has a direct institutional role (CPT) and an indirect role (through CEBs) in promoting social change. In addition, religious beliefs themselves, according to Cousineau, motivate resistance by providing coherent interpretations of the roots of rural social conflict. Substantial external funding from Germany and the Netherlands helped finance the mobilizational drives of the CPT on behalf of the landless.
42. For example, Maybury-Lewis (1994, chs. 4, 6).
43. See also Maybury-Lewis (1994, 29).

Martínez-Lara (1996) explains the agrarian reform's prominence in terms of Tancredo Neves's need to use agrarian reform as an issue to solidify the antiauthoritarian coalition. But rural mobilization beginning in the 1960s had made the agrarian reform movement a force to be reckoned with. Reflecting this context, CONTAG refocused in 1983, making land reform its main goal and land occupation its main tactic. Rural conflict escalated due to a strong landlord response that included the launching of militant antireform organizations such as UDR and the jelling of a *bancada ruralista* in Congress.

The Landless Movement. The MST became very active in the first years of democracy. In Rio Grande do Sul and Paraná, small farmers were made landless by their expulsion from Indian reservations, the construction of the Itaipu dam, and, more important, pressures from agro-business mobilized for land. By the mid-1980s several of these groups came together to launch the MST. The First National Gathering of the MST took place in 1984 in the city of Cascavel, Paraná.[44] The Constituent Assembly of 1987 brought the land reform issue to the forefront. The debate centered on rural property rights. Another issue was whether the law should exclude productive private land from expropriation. Though the constitution of 1988 ended up taking a mild position on agrarian reform, the MST continued to mobilize.

Sentiment for agrarian reform increased in the mid-1990s, fueled in part by the militancy of the MST and continued rural conflict. Many rural unions joined the Landless Workers Movement, as CONTAG lost considerable political prominence.[45] The MST had emerged as a well-organized and thriving national organization claiming to represent nine million workers through chapters in most Brazilian states and regions. National or regional MST

44. The MST maintains a website with considerable background on the movement [www.mst.org.br]. An account found therein identifies the meetings held in 1982 and 1983 in Goiás and Santa Catarina as key moments leading to the emergence of the MST as a differentiated organization with regard to the mobilizational drive of the Pastoral Land Commission (see, in particular, "O desenvolvimento do MST"). The latter document cites João Pedro Stédile, a key MST leader, giving credit to CPT and University of São Paulo sociologist José de Souza Martins for support. About the meetings leading up to the first national meeting in 1984, Stédile writes, "The whole business was very much integrated with the CPT, which supported the struggles making contacts and obtaining infra-structure" (see "O desenvolvimento do MST" [http://www.mst.org.br/historico/historia7.htm]). In this account, the 1984 meeting in Cascavel emerges as the moment in which the MST as such was formed (the original name was Movement of the Landless Rural Workers). A year later, in 1985, the MST organized in Curitiba, Paraná, its First National Congress of the Landless. The second, third, and fourth national congresses would be held in 1990, 1995, and 2000. The Fourth National Congress of the MST (Brasília, July 2000) defined the ideology of the movement as socialist and its main goal to be the radical transformation of Brazilian society.
45. MST stands for "Movimento dos Trabalhadores Rurais Sem Terra" or "Movimento dos Sem-Terra." But some takeovers had loose links to the national movement and members often used other names to identify themselves.

activists plan and organize local land occupations and other acts of protest and resistance, providing legal assistance and general support.

The MST posed a major challenge to Brazilian authorities in the 1990s, though the very status of the land issue and the tactics of the MST have led several observers to question the political potential of the new movement. Writing just before the late 1990s peak of rural conflict, Maybury-Lewis discounts the revolutionary potential of the rural movement, emphasizing that modern state structures such as Brazil's are "tactically flexible and peopled with managers often as well-versed in revolutionary theory as would-be revolutionaries [and are] elaborately arranged to co-opt, encapsulate, or, if necessary, repress them" (1994, 214). This author argues that many unions have a moderate or even conservative orientation, owing to their local allies and institutional contexts.

But the modernization of agriculture posed the biggest challenge to agrarian mobilization. A "new agriculture" resulted from the application of new technology and government policy.[46] Between 1985 and 1996, production grew 30 percent while the agricultural labor force contracted by 23 percent. Yields—productivity of land—increased at an annual average of 1.85 percent since 1987. Grain harvests of 51 million tons in 1980 had grown to 71 million tons in 1989 and over 90 million tons by 2000–2001. Together with political dynamics, the modernization of agriculture has led to higher standards of living for employed rural workers, as well as broader access to social security and health insurance. But overall unemployment increased in the countryside in response to mechanization and pressure from larger producers.

Sugarcane agriculture provides a case in point. This sector had experienced major expansion since the 1970s, when Brazil's auto industry responded to state incentives to manufacture cars running on alcohol extracted from sugar. But conditions accelerating in the 1990s led to a new era of transformation. The mechanization of sugar harvesting in more than 50 percent of the country's cane fields translated into a contraction of the labor force from 1.2 million to 700,000. In the case of the sugarcane producers of Pernambuco, the modernization of productive systems resulted in the shift from quasi peasantry to proletarian (Pereira 1997). Meanwhile, the central government sharply cut the system of incentives to sugar. Joblessness heightened social tensions and migration to towns and cities.[47]

The Brazilian countryside remains rather diverse and heterogeneous. If anything, uneven modernization appears to have actually reinforced the traditionally strong pattern of regional agrarian differentiation.[48] Brazil had differ-

46. Maílson da Nóbrega, "A nova agricultura," *Folha de S. Paulo,* April 21, 2000. Nóbrega notes that the new, more efficient agricultural sector was also favored by trade liberalization, which cheapened imported machines and equipment. The sharp contraction of state subsidies to inefficient producers also helped, according to this observer.

entiated land tenure systems based on different crops and relationship to markets, land, and wage regimes. These often overlap with racial and ethnic differences. All of these factors combined make coherent national collective action very difficult. The landless movement, which stands in some tension with CONTAG, has shown tendencies to splinter.[49]

Some landless groups have adopted strategies that are at odds with official MST discourse. Some have been inclined to negotiate with landowners themselves, as well as with INCRA and subnational governments.[50] In any case, the MST and other organizations were now key players in a major process of agrarian reform, a position they would be unlikely to cede to other groups.[51] The proliferation of landless organizations in most regions of the vast country created a dangerous situation in which diverse groups and individuals were drawn to the use of violence to gain or preserve ownership of land. The UDR has occasionally accused the federal and state governments of encouraging land takeovers.

By late 1999 the MST had taken on a political role that transcended agrarian reform. It had changed tactics in the context of the 1998 elections and the financial crisis of 1998–1999 to include urban demonstrations, takeovers of government buildings, and the shadowing of official events (as in the case of

47. Simon Romero, "Spoonfuls of Hope, Tons of Pain: In Brazil's Sugar Empire, Workers Struggle with Mechanization," *New York Times,* May 21, 2000, section 3, 1. Brazil abandoned the program of incentives to sugar producers as it increased its self-sufficiency in petroleum—from approximately half to nearly three-fourths of national consumption. Brazil's shift to export its huge sugar harvest of 20 million tons has been a major factor in depressed sugar prices in world markets. The crisis in the sugarcane sector has been a major factor fueling agrarian conflict.

48. This diversity is reflected in the different terms found in characterizations of Brazilian rural laborers. Unlike the peasantries of Europe, Asia, or Africa, Brazil's rural laborers originated as slaves and peons of landed estates, or as European and Japanese immigrants arriving after 1870. They can be small holders, *sitiantes (minifundistas)*, *posseiros* (homesteaders or squatters, with substantial differentiation), wage workers or peons, seasonal migratory workers ("bóias frias"), renters, or sharecroppers.

49. For instance, there were nine different camps of landless workers seeking land in the Pontal do Paranapanema region of the state of São Paulo in early 1998. Five of them gathered dissidents of the MST and at least two of these, in turn, had generated their own dissident groups. These camps or movement organizations attract unemployed urban workers and migratory seasonal workers. Rivalries and competition for the same available lands marked the relations between these groups. The names of these camps were Esperança Viva, Movimento Terra Brasil, Movimento da Paz Sem Terra, Brasileiros Unidos Querendo Terra, Terra Brasil, Terra e Esperança, and Movimento Sem Terra do Pontal (see Daniel Hessel Teich, "Crescem no Pontal grupos alternativos ao MST," *O Globo,* May 1, 1998. See also "Orientação é não dar espaço aos rivais" in the same source). This helps explain why MST leader José Rainha declared an end to the phase of confrontation in that region.

50. Owners of underutilized lands have actually had incentives for some of their lands to be occupied, since the government would then pay a hefty price for the redistributed land. The actual process leading to expropriation required INCRA to declare the lands in question to be idle or nonproductive. Land occupations could hence take place with the prior knowledge if not acquiescence of land owners.

Porto Seguro). A backlash began to be felt shortly thereafter. Many Brazilians resented the violence often associated with MST actions. Public opinion polls showed 80 percent support in 1996, but by October 1999 the comparable figure was 28 percent.[52]

A number of academic critics argued that collectivizing agrarian reform was an anachronism (Martins 2000), since Brazilian agriculture had experienced considerable modernization. To these critics, rural masses often defined their problems more in terms of labor than land issues. Moreover, by the end of 2000, Brazil had record grain harvests, and the government had responded to the agrarian crisis, as discussed below.

New Approaches to Social Reform

Faced with traditionally high rates of inequality and poverty, Brazilian policymakers sought more effective social policies in the post-1985 period of democratization. But deep and lasting effects on social development eluded them. Because of the persistence of often dismal social conditions, a new activism with regard to social reform nevertheless did begin to emerge. This activism marked the constitution of 1988, which universalized a series of rights.[53] The perception that the statist model had spent itself as an engine of development made clear that the preexisting approach to social policy and its reliance on centralization and statism was no longer viable (Draibe 1998). The debate sharpened. In the 1990s, reformers accelerated the search for a new approach to social development. The thinking in the mid-1990s was that the state apparatus needed to be overhauled for it to serve a direct role in innovation in the social area (Faria 2000a). Together with fiscal equilibrium and stabilization, state reform would create conditions for a new approach to social development.

51. In effect, unexpected alliances were sometimes formed to transfer land with payments from the state. (See Bruno Paes Manso and Cynthia Campos, "Aliança do barulho: Fazendeiros e trabalhadores sem-terra transformam latifúndios improdutivos em negócios milionários," *Veja*, January 14, 1998).
52. Maurício Lima, "Marchando para trás," *Veja*, October 20, 1999. The loss in popularity between 1996 and 1999 was due, according to *Veja*, to too much aggressiveness in demonstrations, invasion of productive lands, organizing food riots, and making such far-fetched demands as moratorium on the debt, reversing the privatization process, and the impeachment of Cardoso.
53. Draibe (1998) overviews the evolution of Brazilian social policy since the 1970s. She maintains that only in the 1980s and 1990s did Brazil come to have a national policy with clear objectives, resources, and institutional consistency. To her, the constitution of 1988 and the Organic Law of Social Assistance (LOAS) in 1993 were both decisive in bringing about an integrated approach to social policy based on notions of citizen rights. The new approach came to have institutional existence with the 1993 Program against Misery and Hunger (PCFM) and the Programa de Comunidade Solidária of 1995.

A new approach to social policy began to emerge in the context of the post-1990s liberalizing reforms, as macroeconomic conditions began to improve. The central government was spending a considerable amount of money on social policy—nearly 21 percent of GDP, an amount significantly higher than the 15–18 percent spent before the 1990s (Draibe 1998). The emerging Brazilian approach to social development emphasized human development (education and health), decentralization and the devolution of functions to subnational governments, and partnership with stakeholders and civil society.[54] Agrarian reform and rural development gained salience in this context. The reduction of poverty through stabilization of income, somewhat higher minimum wages, and targeting acute forms of poverty became a major focus. Hamstrung by its inability to give immediate direct priority to growth and job creation, the early Cardoso administration relied on the stabilization program itself and on the strong currency to improve the standard of living of the poor. Real wages increased by 5 percent in 1994 and by 13 percent in 1995, as more than 10 million Brazilians experienced an improvement that took them out of poverty, as it is traditionally defined in governmental statistics.[55] The 30 percent increase in consumption during this period reflected the increase in the minimum wage and the above measures.

Dire poverty or misery decreased through the late 1990s. A study by Marcelo Neri indicates it fell by 1.5 percent from 1998 to 1999, while IBGE data indicate a 5.1 percent drop in 2000 in six metropolitan areas.[56] Meanwhile, the 2001 Human Development Index of the United Nations Development Program reports an improvement in 1999, as Brazil went from seventy-fourth to sixty-ninth position in terms of international ranking (of 162 countries).[57]

Cardoso's first term also emphasized basic improvements in education and health, two areas with a substantial lag in terms of social impact. Observers expected a major thrust in his second term (1999–2002), but a series of crises and threats prevented major new spending and made expectations of rapid turnaround unrealistic. Poverty may have decreased to its lowest levels ever

54. See, for example, *Avança Brasil*, the development-oriented program of Cardoso's second term (see also *Sete anos do real: Estabilidade, crescimento e desenvolvimento social* [Brasil, Presidente, 2001]).
55. Faria and Graeff (2000, 21).
56. Antônio Gois and Fernanda da Escóssia, "País tem 50 millhões de indigentes, diz FGV," *Folha de S. Paulo*, July 10, 2001.
57. Brazil also improved in the UNDP's IPH-1 Index of Human Poverty—from 15.8 percent in 1997 to 15.6 percent in 1998 and to 12.9 percent in 1999. The first UNDP's *Human Development Report*, that of 1990, characterized Brazil as a country with low levels of human development. Health, education, and income per capita are the three dimensions that make up the Human Development Index developed by the United National Development Program (UNDP) and reported yearly in its *Human Development Report*. The index was created in 1990 by the economists Mahbub ul Haq and Amartya Sen, who won the Nobel Prize in 1998 for his contributions to welfare economics.

after the adoption of the *Plano Real*, but it will take several years for current policies to have a full impact.[58] The current approach sets the basis for a new Brazilian approach to social reform. Brazil remained one of the most unequal societies on earth, and the federal government, subnational governments, and civil society felt compelled to focus on new approaches to poverty reduction and social development.

From Agrarian Reform to Local Development. The federal government responded to pressures for land redistribution with a distinctive approach to agrarian reform that emphasizes legalized land titles and turning the qualified landless into independent family farmers. It earmarks funds for legal land redistribution. Nearly 584,655 families received plots of land between 1995 and 2001, according to INCRA, and R$13.3 billion was invested. This was the greatest such effort in Brazilian history. Local development plans accompanied the expropriation and redistribution of land. Several programs—the National Project for Family Agriculture (PRONAF), the Land Bank, the Cocoon Project—provide credits, loans, and other incentives for the development of entrepreneurship among small farmers and cooperatives.[59] The focus is on enhancing the latter's capacity to enter the marketplace and remain competitive. The policies also aim at job creation, decreasing migration flows to cities, and rural development.[60] While promoting commercially viable forms of family agriculture, the policies also work to incorporate agriculturalists and rural workers into the social security program. The Cardoso admin-

TABLE 4-2. Agrarian Reform, 1995–2001

Year	Families Settled	Contracts	Hectares	Investment (R$ bi)	Land Invasions	Deaths in Conflict
1995	42,912	314	1,313,509	1.5	n.a.	41
1996	62,044	433	4,451,896	1.6	397	54
1997	81,944	637	4,394,524	2.6	502	30
1998	101,094	850	2,540,645	2.2	446	47
1999	85,226	782	1,478,536	1.5	455	27
2000	108,986	720	3,861,268	1.8	226	10
2001	102,449	539	1,697,043	2.0	157	14
Total	584,655	4,275	19,737,421	13.2	2,183	223

Source: INCRA

58. The annual poverty rate decreased from 41.7 percent in 1993 to 34.1 percent in 1999. Barros et al. (2000a).
59. The World Bank has helped finance Brazilian agrarian reform.
60. The federal government formed the Center for Agrarian and Development Studies in 1997 to study internal migration flows and rural development.

istration claims a leading role in the agrarian reform effort, while also acknowledging the role of popular mobilization. The measures adopted succeeded in reducing agrarian conflict. Land confrontations resulted in 2,183 deaths in the 1995–2001 period, but a decreasing trend set in after 1996—30 deaths in 1997, 47 in 1998, 27 in 1999, 10 in 2000, and 14 in 2001.[61] The Northeast and the North account for many of the worst incidents of agrarian violence. In Pará alone, 447 deaths were reported for the thirteen years before 2000. The number of land invasions remained relatively high through 1999 and began to decline in 2000.

The agrarian reform process needs to be assessed in the broader context of the transformations experienced by Brazilian agriculture since the 1980s. The relatively closed and statist development model continued to shape Brazil's agriculture through that decade. The industrial model had a built-in bias against agriculture. The emphasis on industrial protection and the overvalued exchange rate constrained agricultural prices and agrarian development. Imported inputs were expensive. Subsidies stimulated agricultural production in targeted sectors favoring domestic consumption rather than exports. The elaborate system of government intervention began to experience alteration in the early 1980s, but it really began to be dismantled only toward the end of the decade.

The liberalization of the Brazilian economy since the 1990s has exposed its agricultural sector to competition, cheaper inputs from abroad, and restructuring. The deregulation and the reform of agricultural prices and credit policies were significant changes in themselves. All the elements of a new agricultural policy regime were not in place yet, but many of the features of the old model had been altered or eliminated by the end of the 1990s.[62] The changes, both structural and policy related, led to a contraction in the agricultural labor force and, less so, the area under cultivation, with significant variation across agricultural sectors. Harvests and profits increased as a result of gains in productivity—due to the more intensive cultivation of areas close to cities, the increased use of technology, migration of skilled farmers from the South to western and northern regions, and the reduced cost of imported inputs.[63] The restructuring of agriculture generated losers as well as winners,

61. From Ministério de Desenvolvimento Agrário, relying on the Land Pastoral Commission (CPT) for 1964–1999 and Ouvidoria Agrária Nacional for 2000–2001 [www.incra.gov.br/reforma/recordes8.htm]. These numbers are higher than those reported earlier in "Dados apontam menos mortes em conflitos," *Folha de S. Paulo*, November 20, 2000, from data by the Land Pastoral Commission.
62. Helfand and Rezende (2001). The debt crisis of the early 1980s led to a reduction of rural credit and the expansion of price supports, aimed at reducing the fiscal deficit and increasing the collection of foreign exchange as well as fighting inflation (3). Helfand and Rezende emphasize that trade liberalization, deregulation of agricultural markets, and changes in rural credit and price policies owed to the fight against inflation rather than to a deliberate plan for agrarian or general development.

contributing to rising tensions in parts of the countryside. The opening of agriculture incurred losses in some sectors exposed to cheaper imports, including seasonal grains from Argentina and Uruguay. Many small farmers in the South went bankrupt.

As with other social programs, the federal government has cast its agrarian reform and rural development efforts in terms of processes of local development emphasizing decentralization, partnerships, and local participation (Abramovay 1998). Noting that insufficient social capital is a recurring feature of disadvantaged areas, policymakers seek to rely on social movements and local NGOs as sources of leadership. A major theme is to promote the development of networks to coincide with regional economies, to stimulate economic cooperation and exchange. County commissions for rural development have been formed in a large number of counties, often with involvement by CONTAG. New strategies of rural development often emphasize the link between local sustainable development and urban or regional systems and dynamics.[64]

Human Development. Education and health, the two basic dimensions of human development, have been the most favored dimensions of social policy since the mid-1990s.[65] Lack of education is a well-known factor in poverty, and Brazil's educational system has been traditionally deficient. Its shortcomings became more glaring in the context of global technological advances and the information revolution. The average schooling of the economically active population just before 2000 was barely 3.9 years—considerably lower than neighboring Argentina (9.5 years), Uruguay (10.5 years) or even Paraguay (5.8 years). As with many other indicators of social development, major regional variations characterize the Brazilian case, with the Northeast, North, and the northernmost parts of the Southeast showing low scores, but other regions, particularly in the South and the Federal District, showing substantially higher scores.

The educational reforms have centered on basic education for students aged seven to fourteen. Rates of enrollment for this group grew from 89 per-

63. See, for example, Baumann (1999a, 25–26); Dias and Amaral (1999). The increase of 59 percent in profit levels between 1989 and 1998 reflected a 22 percent growth in productivity as well as a 31 percent improvement in the relative prices or terms of trade (Baumann 1999a, 26).

64. José Graziano da Silva's Project Rurbano at UNICAMP (University of Campinas) sketches "the new rural Brazil" (o novo rural brasileiro) in these terms and shows the depth of new thinking in this regard. Professor Silva is closely identified with Lula and the Workers' Party. At the University of São Paulo, José Eli da Veiga has also advanced a conceptualization of rural development that emphasizes decentralization, rural education, local social capital, an expansion of measures favoring family agriculture, and more intense efforts at reducing rural poverty and inequality (for example, Veiga [1998] "Diretrizes para uma nova política agrária" [www.dataterra.org.br/semce/zeeli.htm]).

65. See note 54.

cent in 1994 to 96 percent in 1998. By 1999, 3.4 million additional young-
sters had been enrolled in the school system, bringing the rate of enrollment
for that group to 97 percent—up from 82 percent at the beginning of the
decade. Of these new enrollees, 2.3 million were in the Northeast and
530,000 in the North. The goal is to universalize education and to prepare
young people and adults for the new, more demanding labor market.

Measures adopted after 1994 and the creation of the Fund for Teacher
Development (FUNDEF) help explain the primary educational system's
improvements through the late 1990s and into the first years of the new century.[66] FUNDEF designates 15 percent of all fiscal revenue and constitutional
transfers to states and municipalities, with funds transferred directly to school
systems at the state and local levels. Funds are also allocated to poor parents
as an incentive for their children's attendance. The resources are collected at
the federal level and distributed to local units in proportion to the number of
elementary schools and students enrolled. The constitution of 1988 had man-
dated the transfer of tax revenues to local facilities, but many of the resources
thus spent had continued to be applied to political interests and clientelistic
practices, often with an emphasis on political visibility (Caixeta 2002). FUN-
DEF has substantially reduced such practices. It also emphasizes quality
rather than quantity. For example, the number of state schools was reduced
by 21 percent between 1996 and 2000. Counties are becoming more involved
with elementary education. In 1997, they were responsible for 40.7 percent of
the students and states for 59.3 percent, while in 1999 the figures were 49.4
percent and 50.6 percent, respectively.

Critics of FUNDEF argue that this system leaves states and municipalities
with a very narrow margin to finance junior and secondary education.[67] However, secondary and professional education are also receiving attention.
Access to intermediate and university education has traditionally benefited
the upper and middle classes disproportionately. Prior to the 1990s, only 10
percent of students with elementary education reached the secondary level.
Higher levels of enrollment in primary education are generating pressures for
expansion at the intermediate level, where the number of enrolled students
increased from 3 million at the beginning of the decade to 6.7 million in
1998. The programs on the development of secondary education aim at creating 10 million new spaces in high schools. Another on the development of

66. Created in 1996 and nationally implemented in 1998, FUNDEF—Fund for Maintaining and Developing Basic Education and for Teacher's Improvement—increases resources
specifically designated for basic education for children seven to fourteen years old. The
leadership of respected economist and educational leader Paulo Renato de Souza as minister of education throughout the entire two terms of the Cardoso administration was an
important factor in Brazil's educational reform.
67. See "Anos FHC dão prioridade para o ensino fundamental," *Folha de S. Paulo*, October 21, 2002.

TABLE 4-3. Elementary Education, 1995–2000

Grade Advancement Rate		Grade Repetition Rate		School Evasion Rate	
1995	1999	1995	1999	1995	1999
64.5	73.6	30.2	21.6	5.3	4.8

Source: MEC

professional education seeks to create 200 new professional schools to train 500,000 students.

Besides stemming dropout and repetition rates by paying poor parents to keep students in school, the federal government has also increased budgets for food, transportation, health assistance, books, and didactic material to students and teachers, as well as for school televisions and computers. Teacher salaries increased by 13 percent in state and county systems. Gains reached 49 percent on average across the counties of the Northeast.[68]

By 2001, it was clear that the educational reforms were making a difference in the lives of millions of Brazilians, even if the full impact on poverty and inequality would take years (see table 4-3).[69] The literacy rate rose to 85.2 percent in 2002. Illiteracy for individuals ten or more years old dropped to 12.5 percent in 2000 from 19.7 percent in the early 1990s. Comparing the indicators of 1991 with 2000, rural areas improved the most, with literacy increasing by 12.5 percent.

However, policymakers still face great dilemmas in deciding how to accomplish their goals. One of them continues to be the relative emphasis between advanced and basic education. Brazilian public universities are often institutions of excellence. However, the public university system continues to account for more than half of the education budget, while elementary and secondary education, essential for a developing country such as Brazil, and critical for the poor, lack the resources for a breakthrough in performance and contribution to development.[70] Meanwhile, public universities favor the rich and the middle classes, who could afford to pay for private education, with poor and minority students being grossly underrepresented.[71]

68. The Ministry of Education publishes a considerable amount of data on its website, www.mec.gov.
69. For evidence of the reforms' effectiveness, see data in *Human Development Report* (2002) and IBGE.
70. East Asian countries, in contrast, have done much better in providing universal basic education and linking it to fast economic growth and development.
71. The very comprehensive exam that applicants take to apply for acceptance to universities screens out less qualified students, who often come from the underprivileged, since private elementary and secondary education is normally much better than the underfunded public system. The number of applications to public universities is much higher than the number accepted.

Health. Brazil has also made important reforms in its health sector and faces comparable dilemmas. Population increase and the persistence of high rates of contagious diseases have traditionally interacted with comparatively low rates of life expectancy to make the need for better public health blatant. Poor administration and graft in the health sector have been widespread. Coupled with high poverty levels, deficiencies in public access to health care help explain the high mortality rate and incidence of contagious diseases. Poor public health mostly affects the poor, since the middle class and the elite rely on private health care when necessary.

The challenges of public health policy differ from those in education partly because the majority of hospitals are not government owned. The Brazilian health system in the early years of the twenty-first century had approximately 6,500 hospitals and clinics. Of these, 30 percent belonged to the government (federal, state, and municipal), sometimes linked to federal or state universities, while 40 percent were philanthropic hospitals and 30 percent were private.

When the constitution of 1988 proclaimed health to be a universal right, the idea was that Brazilians would be provided with free health care, regardless of age and type of disease. Presumably, public or private hospitals linked to the SUS (Universal Health System) would provide treatment. Created in 1990, the SUS sought to rearrange health services by linking university hospitals belonging to the Ministry of Education with the public and private health networks in states and counties to form a system capable of providing universal health care.[72] The constitution emphasized decentralization, simplified control,[73] and social participation in the operations of the system of universal health care.[74]

The traditionally deficient health system faced budget cuts during 1990–1992 (Singer 2002). The Itamar Franco administration did not improve matters. Delays in paying the private hospitals linked with the SUS system contributed to the sense of crisis and, later, the perception that the system had fallen victim to fiscal austerity. In 1993, the Social Security Ministry stopped the practice of transferring funds from salary contributions to the Ministry of Health. To replace those funds, alternative mechanisms were mobilized with

72. The entire network of public providers (federal, states, and counties) would cover the population in a universal manner, without restrictions (Médici 2002). Like most branches of the Brazilian government, the Ministry of Health provides a great deal of information in its website [http://portalweb02.saude.gov.br/saude/].
73. Although decentralized, the system now has a single control in each sphere of the government, avoiding the previous multiple efforts in place among the structures of INAMPS (National Institute for Health Care of Social Security), the Ministry of Health, and state and county bureaus.
74. More than 80 percent of high-risk procedures (health surgeries, transplants, etc.) are performed in public hospitals and affiliates of the SUS.

resources from the FAT (Fund to Assist Workers) and COFINS (Social Security Contribution) taxes. However, the delay in paying private hospitals persisted. The Cardoso administration increased average health expenditures by nearly 30 percent with respect to the last year of the Itamar administration. In 1997, a peak year, the expenditure per capita reached R$121.[75]

That year, a special or provisional tax expected to yield US$4.5 billion to improve public health went into effect. The CPMF, the financial turnover tax, had a major impact in the financing of health care. Of the R$19.5 billion spent by the Health Ministry in 1998, it financed R$6.7 billion (or 42 percent of the total expenditures). The role of the CPMF in financing health care grew in subsequent years. Initially viewed as a step toward a new health policy that ameliorates some of the worse consequences of poverty, this tax does not provide a permanent cure to the ills of the public health system.[76] The health budget remained inadequate in relation to need and the government's goals after the adoption of the CPMF. Congress passed a constitutional amendment in September 2000 to better fund the SUS.[77]

The Cardoso administration accelerated the process of decentralization of the health system. It increased the role of community participation through the program *Agentes Comunitários da Saúde* (PACS) and instituted a popular family doctor program known as *Saúde da Família* (PSF). The public health system moved to emphasize preventive action and the production of generic medicines at a lower price. More attention was given to the poorest and most remote regions. As states and municipalities increased their share of the total health expenditure from 6 percent in 1982 to 37 percent in 1999 (Médici 2002), the federal level decreased its contribution toward the financing of health care expenditures. New partnerships with civil society have sought to decrease the dependence on funds collected from the federal government. Health Councils are increasing civil society participation in the management of the system in all spheres of government. States and counties are promoting partnerships with civil society in accordance with a new management paradigm that changes the focus from addressing medical problems once they surface, to a combination of actions and services to promote wellness and the prevention of disease.

By 2001, the prevention-oriented PSF had more than 154,000 community agents to assist 91 million individuals in 4,719 counties (out of the approximately 5,500). Since the number of community agents in 1994 had been less

75. In 1995 the government had planned to apply R$80 per capita annually and exceeded this goal. From 1994 to 1998 the expenditures in health ensured an average of R$115.59 per person.
76. One drawback of the CPMF is that it is yet one more cumulative tax on production and distribution.
77. Economist José Serra provided considerable leadership in reforming the health system as minister of health during the period 1998–2002.

than 30,000, there was a fivefold increase in seven years. In 2002, the Health Ministry had nearly forty programs focused on specific diseases, prevention, and professional training for nurses. The family health program provides access to medical and dental consultation with the aim of diminishing the incidence of endemic diseases. A program for women concentrates on cancer prevention and gynecological assistance. Another for the elderly provides medical assistance that integrates leisure and educational activities. The new health system has sought to expand and modernize hospitals and medical centers, including laboratories for sanitary, epidemiological, and environmental vigilance. As the universal health system turned into a national goal, SUS became one of the largest public health chains in the world.

There have been improvements in infant mortality, life expectancy, and control of contagious diseases. Infant mortality has decreased substantially—from 74.2 per thousand in 1980 to 37.5 per thousand in 1996, and 35.3 in 2000 (see also fig. D-12). The North and the Northeast still have very high rates, but the new approach is also making a difference there—between 1994 and 1997, infant mortality in parts of the Northeast experiencing the new policies fell by half. Life expectancy rose from 66.03 to 68.6 years between 1991 and 2000, according to IBGE data (see also fig. D-9), while the *Human Development Report 2002* notes an increase in life expectancy from 67.5 years in 1999, to 67.7 years in 2000.

In the area of contagious diseases, Brazil's AIDS program has received international acclaim.[78] Brazil is one of the few countries to offer free AIDS treatment, while avoiding millions of hospitalizations. The program of prevention, control, and assistance to those stricken with the virus sponsors training and educational campaigns. In 1995, the number of cases of AIDS in Brazil was 11.9 per 100,000 inhabitants. In the following year this number rose to 14 per 100,000, fluctuating by only 0.5 until 1998. After 1999, the trend drastically reverted. In 1999, the Ministry of Health enabled 150 maternity hospitals with the medicine (AZT) to treat AIDS, reducing the transmission of the virus to newborns by 70 percent. In 2000, 90,000 people were treated with appropriate medicine distributed by the Ministry of Health. The national production of comparable and generic medicines had started to guarantee reduction of expenditures and kept the universal policy of access to care. By 2001, there had been a marked increase in the number of women assisted to prevent the disease.

Though still relatively modest when compared to need, the gains in health as well as education have contributed to a higher score on the Human Devel-

78. For example, Stephen Buckley, "Brazil Becomes Model in Fight against AIDS," *Washington Post*, September 17, 2000, A22. See also John Garrison and Anabela Abreu, "Government and Civil Society in the Fight against HIV and AIDS in Brazil," World Bank and IESE, May 2000.

opment Index (HDI).[79] Brazil advanced eight positions since 1990, when it scored 0.713, improving to 0.757 in 2000 and earning the 73rd position in a ranking of 173 countries.[80] This achievement in poverty alleviation earned Cardoso the United Nations Development Program (UNDP) Award for Outstanding Leadership in Human Development in 2002.[81] Critics of the new approach to health point out that the system is still far from meeting demand. Others argue that it often does not allocate resources efficiently—for example, financing high-technology procedures for higher income users who would be able to cover them privately, instead of focusing on basic health for all. In the past, local health facilities were often accused of mismanagement, but the main problem was often the inadequacy of revenue. The CPMF was meant to alleviate the problem, but it is not enough and remains controversial.

A New Approach to Welfare and Social Development. After improving in the 1970s, a decade of economic growth, overall social conditions worsened in the aftermath of the crisis of the 1980s, contributing to the formation of social movements and NGOs demanding citizenship rights and the redress of grievances with regard to basic social policy. In the 1990s, changing civil society and political organizations pressured various levels of government and contributed to new thinking with respect to social policy. That inequality and poverty failed to decrease significantly, while economic slowdown returned in the late 1990s, added to the sense of urgency about social development.[82]

---

79. The HDI ranks nations using averages of three indices measuring health (life expectancy at birth), education (adult literacy rate and enrollment ratio [primary, secondary, and university]), and GDP per capita (purchasing power parity in US$, or PPP). The HDI ranges from 0 to 1, with the most developed countries close to 1 and the least developed closer to zero. Brazil's score of .757 in 2000 placed it among nations in the middle range of human development. It ranked somewhat higher than Latin America as a whole (.747), but lower than Argentina (.844), Chile (.831), Uruguay (.831), Costa Rica (.820), Mexico (.796), Panama (.787), Colombia (.772), and Venezuela (.770)—as well as lower than most English-speaking countries in the Caribbean.
80. IPEA and other branches of the Brazilian government dispute the data used by UNDP and argue that Brazil should have a higher ranking (for example, "Para o governo, números estão defasados," *Folha de S. Paulo*, July 7, 2001). See also F. Barbosa and L. Paraguassú, "Uma década de avanço modesto," *O Globo Online*, July 24, 2002; "Dados estão desatualizados, sustenta IPEA," *Folha de S. Paulo*, July 24, 2002.
81. Cardoso was the first recipient of the UNDP's Mahbub ul Haq Award. The awards committee was chaired by Nobel Prize-winning economist Joseph Stiglitz, a critic of the IMF. See UNDP website, "President Cardoso of Brazil is winner of the UNDP Award for Outstanding Leadership in Human Development" [www.undp.org/dpa/pressrelease/releases/2002/october/15oct02.html]. See also "Com o selo da ONU," *Veja* [http://www2.uol.com.br/veja/231002/p_050.html].
82. Elisa Reis (2000) shows that Brazilian elites as a whole recognized poverty and inequality as top policy problems, though those in the private sector place responsibility on the government.

108   *Chapter 4*

Early in the decade of the nineties, prominent intellectuals and policymakers organizing the Fórum Nacional/Instituto Nacional de Altos Estudos (INAE) started a national debate on new approaches to development and modernization. Several of the resulting publications have contributed to framing the debate on social policy.[83] Reflecting the new context, Brazil's evolving approach to social policy began to center on the concepts of partnerships with civil society, municipalization and decentralization, and a new result-oriented management of social programs.[84]

In 1996, the Council of Comunidade Solidária, a program led by Ruth Cardoso, Brazil's noted social scientist and first lady,[85] began to actively promote a dialogue between government and society to build a new strategy for social development and consensus about specific national priorities in social action. This program was part of the Cardoso administration's effort to support the third sector and promote social development. This entity promoted the search for ways to speed up policy design and implementation. It sought to identify areas of conflict or disagreement and to develop dialogue and research around them. From 1995 to 1998, it focused on 1,369 counties, where it invested R$7.8 billion. The broad discussion involving government officials with civil society, intellectuals and academics, and other specialists is a component of the new national thinking about social policy (see appendix C).[86]

It can be surmised that Brazil was making strides in adopting a new, still emerging paradigm of social development, even if the stabilization and fiscal adjustment priorities imposed limits on spending in the social area.[87] *Avança Brasil*, the general plan of the second Cardoso term, articulated part of the new approach to social policy based on partnerships with civil society and the private sector, decentralization, and a new management style (see appendix C). Social programs have deliberately moved away from *assistencialismo*— the traditional welfare policy emphasizing handouts to the needy—toward

83. The books published by Fórum Nacional include Velloso (1991a) *A questão social no Brasil*; Velloso (1991b) *Crescimento com redistribuição e reformas: reverter a opção pelos não-pobres*; Velloso and Albuquerque (1993) *Pobreza e mobilidade social*; Velloso, Albuquerque, and Knoop (1995) *Políticas sociais no Brasil: descentralização, eficiência e equidade*; and Velloso and Albuquerque (2001) *Soluções para a questão do emprego*. The Fórum Nacional's website [www.forumnacional.org.br/] provides abstracts of these and other publications.
84. See also publications from Ministry of Planning, Management, and Budget, particularly those on *Avança Brasil*.
85. An anthropologist, Ruth Corrêa Leite Cardoso before becoming first lady dealt with social movements, youth, and other aspects of Brazilian society. She used her position in this program to promote partnerships between government at various levels, private business, and NGOs. Comunidade Solidária has supported a literacy campaign and the recruitment of college students in programs to address social problems by working directly in the affected communities.
86. Peliano et al. (1998) discusses Comunidade Solidária.
87. See, for example, Velloso and Albuquerque (2000).

addressing underlying factors. The ministries of Education and Health have developed policies with an eye toward addressing the root causes of poverty and misery.[88] Other ministries and such entities as BNDES and Banco do Nordeste have developed programs to promote microentrepreneurship and microcredit to stimulate employment. The list of over fifty priority projects and programs in *Avança Brasil* includes Entrepreneurial Brazil (*Brasil Empreendedor*), PRONAF and agrarian reform, and various others geared toward the generation of self-employment and microenterprises.

Social spending has been channeled directly to institutions at the local level. This has reduced the traditional mediating role of politicians and functionaries, something too often associated with clientelism, corruption, and waste. While targeting Brazil's poorest counties, Active Community (*Comunidade Ativa*) and the Alvorada Project (*Projeto Alvorada*) have sought decentralized forms of intervention that rely on the participation of local groups and NGOs, often creating programs to help mobilize constituencies. At the same time, the government has passed laws to make the creation and operation of NGOs easier.

In the context of Brazil's decentralized federal polity, county and state-level civil society are involved in a great deal of activism and experimentation at subnational levels. Local governments, often adhering to egalitarian and participative ideologies, are encouraging partnerships with nongovernment groups and organizations. Subnational governments are engaged in efforts to reform state action in the social area, self-consciously embracing a break with the centralized approach of the past.[89]

Conclusion

The social programs pursued since the mid-1990s have met promising, though limited, short-term success. However, policies promoting human and social capital and the removal of structural impediments will take time to bear full fruit. With a large number of Brazilians living under dismal conditions, the results are not yet commensurate with these phenomenal needs. Social development remained a major issue in 2002, when Brazilians elected a new president.

That Brazilians seem to share a near consensus about the need for more effective social policies, including the reduction of poverty and dire misery

88. A noteworthy addition came with the Fund to Combat Poverty (Fundo de Combate a Pobreza), a program with a budget of R$3.1 billion signed into law in July 2001.
89. Farah (1998b) lists new subnational projects conforming to this approach. Farah lists ten main criticisms of the old model and lists projects in education, health, general policy-making, job generation, poverty alleviation, rural development, and others. These projects seek to increase effectiveness and enhance access to public services and participation by new social actors.

and redress of the great disparities in well-being resulting from centuries of social exclusion, provides grounds for guarded optimism. Several new and interesting approaches are being implemented or tried. Sustained and enhanced over time, the best of these will make a major difference.

The dilemma of precisely where to draw the line between competing priorities, a prominent question through the crises of 1998–2002, will shape Brazilian policy-making and politics for years to come. Fiscal priorities will no doubt continue to constrain the design of social policies. To implement redistributive measures while at the same time pursuing stabilization, liberalization, and growth is a great challenge. Each of these goals requires vast amounts of resources. Simultaneous emphasis on all of them is a sure formula for failure, including the return of inflation and fiscal imbalances.

The deepening of democracy and the growing role of civil society organizations, together with economic recovery, are the best hope for sustained progress. Because of these forces, politicians and the elite will have a harder time ignoring the needs of the poor. Truly interesting is the possibility that popular sentiment may be converging with the perceptions of a critical mass of policymakers and stakeholders to sustain the new activism in social policy.

Democratization has further complicated policy-making and the game of politics by bringing new actors into the polity and by sharply decentralizing public authority. A growing number of third sector organizations articulate demands and participate in processes of reform. Parties, social movements, nongovernmental organizations, and related groups add to the formidable array of forces shaping political dynamics. The complex political system will continue to make it a major challenge to act cohesively in terms of a view of the national interest arrived at democratically. Governance problems could prove costly. But decentralized federalism offers opportunities to exercise authority in the pursuit of diverse aims. Decentralization (particularly municipalization), partnerships, changing civil society, and community involvement are contributing to an increasingly pluralistic decision-making system. This tendency is a key dimension of the overall transformation of Brazilian society and polity. It is unlikely that future democratic governments would be able or willing to reverse it. Still, the new institutional framework is under development and needs to be consolidated. Questions about institutional design and the forces shaping it are quite important.

In conclusion, in several social policy domains, the Brazilian polity is experiencing a hitherto unknown level of pluralization of political forms and processes encouraging experimentation and collaboration. The fledgling approach to social policy reinforces the role of NGOs and social movements as active agents at lower levels of government, which in turns reinforces decentralized federalism and democratic governance. Brazilian social development will depend on the new institutional frameworks being built at the local level as much as on the articulation across the three levels of government and between the state and civil society at the national level.

CHAPTER 5

Elites and Reform

I n December 1998, in the thick of yet another financial crisis, the Federation of Industries of the State of São Paulo (FIESP) organized a large gathering at its headquarters on Avenida Paulista to protest policies it claimed to be responsible for Brazil's economic woes.[1] The industrial leaders at FIESP billed the event as an attempt to build a lobby in Congress. The "Pact for Production and Jobs" it proclaimed amounted to a political threat to the federal government. The approximately 500 participants represented not only business, but trade union leaders as well as deputies from the Workers' Party and other opposition parties, including the Communist Party of Brazil.[2] Delfim Netto, a minister of finance during the military regime and now a Brazilian Progressive Party (PPB) deputy, was present. These were indeed strange bedfellows. Organizers saw the diversity of views in this coalition as evidence of widespread opposition to government policy.[3] The agitation of the *paulista* business sector was puzzling. FIESP had previously supported the Cardoso administration. Was business now rejecting the reformist economic model it had endorsed earlier? Was the coalition that brought Cardoso to power coming to an end (Diniz 2000)? Were industrialists turning against the reform drive?

1. The collapse of financial systems in several Asian countries led to crises in several emergent economies, an episode journalists dubbed as the Asian financial crisis (see chapter 2; fig. D-3).
2. The governing coalition did not attend, though five deputies from the PSDB did. Practically all major Brazilian newspapers reported and commented on this story on December 22 or 23, 1998. See, for example, Geraldo Magella, "Pacto une FIESP, PT, Delfim and CUT," *O Globo*, December 23, 1998.
3. E.g, Clóvis Rossi, "Algo de muito errado," *Folha de S. Paulo*, December 23, 1998. In contrast, the traditionally conservative *O Estado de S. Paulo* focused on differences among the participants, including several trade associations (for example, Liliana Pinheiro, "Pacto divide CUT e Força Sindical," *O Estado de S. Paulo*, December 23, 1998). For an academic discussion of this event, see Diniz (2000, 96–100).

FIESP leaders justified their protest in terms of what they saw as the Cardoso administration's insensitivity to their demands. A day after the event, Cardoso made public the appointment of Celso Lafer as head of the new Ministry of Development, Industry, and Trade. The official response to this event left business leaders wondering. A member of a prominent family of *paulista* industrialists, Lafer was cousin to FIESP's president as well as nephew to the late Horácio Lafer, a well-known business leader who had been minister of finance in the second Vargas government.[4] Would this satisfy critics?

Business and Politics

The political role of Brazilian business has been interpreted in rather diverse ways. If some authors have implicated the business sector directly in the periods of authoritarianism and statism in the twentieth century, others have portrayed entrepreneurs as lacking a "hegemonic vocation" or as being too fragmented to be a dominant actor.[5]

Brazilian elites have a long and complex history of mobilization. Their trade associations and other organizations have vigorously contended for power and the ability to shape public policy. Business—particularly industrialists from São Paulo—have been involved in several key political events in Brazilian history. Still at issue is the responsibility of business in the corporatist system instituted during the Vargas era, particularly the Estado Novo (1937–1945), and maintained or enhanced by subsequent regimes through the 1985 democratizing era. Business agitation was a factor both in the collapse of democracy in 1964 and of the authoritarian regime that followed it. The *paulista* business sector was not a key protagonist in the authoritarianism and corporatism inaugurated in 1937. Big business from São Paulo did play a role in the processes of mobilization leading to the military regime of 1964, but it seems to have done so in a reactive rather than active fashion, driven by fears of radicalization and populism during the Goulart regime. In fact, it is

4. At the time of this appointment, Celso Lafer was serving as Brazilian ambassador to the World Trade Organization. A political science Ph.D. from Cornell University and professor at the University of São Paulo, Lafer had been minister of foreign relations in the early 1990s. Within two days, Cardoso also announced the creation of a business council of seven to eleven members selected by the government to work with the new Ministry of Development in elaborating options for business policy. The first appointee was the head of Rio de Janeiro's industrial federation (FIERJ) and sharp critic of FIESP, having called it and industry leaders from São Paulo "parrots" insisting on a backward form of protectionism. Through 2001 there was little evidence that the business council had done much.
5. Works positing a weak, fragmented, or otherwise nonhegemonic bourgeoisie include Weyland (1996a), F. H. Cardoso (1972), and Evans (1979). Diniz and Boschi (1978) emphasize the role of industrialists and other business sectors in public policy after 1937. Kingstone (1999a) reviews the role of business in the early to mid-1990s.

difficult to escape the conclusion that at critical moments throughout the twentieth century, big business from São Paulo has often been marked by periods of estrangement from direct influence over policy-making, in parallel to the historical animosities and tensions between São Paulo and the centralizing regimes since Vargas.[6]

Profound cleavages within the Brazilian elite have historically conditioned the role of business. Brazilian corporatism was top-down rather than the expression of class hegemony; it was imposed by the Vargas regime and the centralizing governments that followed it in an attempt to consolidate a new ruling coalition. It did not come about in response to a demand by the most advanced business groups. Throughout the twentieth century, São Paulo industrialists maintained their allegiance to the fiercely reformist Confederation and Center of Industries of São Paulo (FIESP-CIESP), an organization founded in 1928. Corporatism served the interests of centralizing politicians with weak political bases who wanted to encapsulate socioeconomic actors, particularly those in the state of São Paulo. Organized business interests did learn to work within it, as well as around it if necessary, as was often the case. Corporatist aims of channeling business interest intermediation might have given the impression that big business had firm ascendancy over Brazilian politics, but that was not the case.

The extent to which Brazilian corporatism ever generated fully functional institutional mechanisms for incorporating business into government is debatable. The Brazilian political system failed to provide a durable party system, a key element of successful corporatist regimes.[7] No major political party survived any of the major changes in political regime in twentieth-century Brazil; no dominant party or party system could thus emerge to represent organized business or other interests consistently. The inadequacy of legitimate channels of interest intermediation has been a main factor in the clientelism and even corruption not infrequently associated with contact between business and government.

At the same time, regional and sectoral cleavages interacted with this distinctive institutional framework to generate a fragmented pattern of elite collective action. The corporatism created in the Vargas era generated a segmented scheme of national business confederations for each of the main sectors of the economy—National Confederation of Industry (CNI), National Council for Commerce (CNC), and National Council for Agriculture (CNA). But no overarching structures succeeded in presenting a unified front, and major internal divisions remained within each major sector. The idea of monopolies in national interest representation and mediation implied state-

6. See also Font (1996 and 1992a).
7. Chapter 3 also discusses political dynamics.

level confederations for each sector. Brazilian business never had peak associations comparable to those of fully established corporatist regimes. The
Vargas regime sought to organize such entities. It wanted to transform the
Center of Industries of the State of São Paulo (CIESP) into a state-controlled
Federation of Industries of the State of São Paulo (FIESP). But *paulista*
industrialists were adamant. FIESP and CIESP came to have parallel legal
status. Though FIESP eventually emerged as the politically dominant entity,
it retained autonomy from the federal government. Labels aside, key players
since the 1920s knew that CIESP-FIESP was the largest and most powerful
industrial association in São Paulo and all of Brazil.[8]

Business worked around the official corporatist system in diverse ways. In
contrast with the intentions of the centralizing regime during after the
years of military rule, business continued to seek multiple channels of interest aggregation and intermediation. Acting outside the corporatist system, the
business sector formed various regional and sectoral associations in the
1970s and after (Boschi et al. 2000, Diniz and Boschi 1979). A system of parallel independent business associations emerged. The new organizations
often operated at the state level. Individual entrepreneurs influenced policy
via "bureaucratic" and clientelistic rings (Cardoso 1971). Regardless of official design, state and business came together in diverse ways.

Historically, the centralizing system itself generated tendencies toward
fragmentation (Weyland 1996a). The difficult relationship between the central government and industrialists from São Paulo helps account for the
apparent absence of a hegemonic vocation by the Brazilian industrialists during much of the twentieth century.[9] Like many other members of the *paulista*
economic elite, industrialists tried to preserve their autonomy in the frame-

8. FIESP-CIESP claims to represent São Paulo's industry, an economic sector said to
encompass 116,000 firms, 2.8 million workers, and annual production of US$80 billion in
the year 2000. In fact, 126 state-level associations were registered for the 1998 FIESP
elections and 7,158 firms at CIESP (compare to 1990 data in Kingstone 1999a, 126–27).
FIESP-CIESP maintains an informative website at http://www.fiesp.org.br. This dual structure, with a pre-1930 association and a corporatist-era federation functioning side by side
was also present in the commercial sector, with the Commercial Association of São Paulo
(founded decades before 1930) and the Federation of Commerce of the State of São Paulo
imposed by Vargas's corporatism.

Weyland (1996a) argues that by developing its own channels to the state, FIESP undermined the authority of the CNI as a spokesman for industry as a whole. However, a longer
historical perspective would conclude that the intention of the Vargas regime was to have
the Rio-based CNI take the place of CIESP-FIESP as the main organization of industrialists and the corporatist FIESP take over CIESP's role in São Paulo. In other words, the creation of industrial associations was sharply contested terrain with regard to the political
role of business. From the beginning, CIESP-FIESP fought to retain primacy in the process
of business representation.

9. Cardoso (1971) was one of the earliest works to comment on the inability of Brazilian
business to assert itself politically as a dominant class. See also Weyland (1996a, 53–54,
63–66).

work of the corporatist system imposed by the central government. They relied on clientelism and other forms of interest articulation, dispersing the collective influence of business. The *paulista* economic elite had its own reasons to cherish its regional character in matters of political organization. Brazil was a complex society and business in other states had distinctive interests and formed separate organizations within the corporatist system. *Paulistas* saw as natural that the interests of each region be represented separately, in the framework of a complex, plural polity.

Because of these historical dynamics, Brazil's developmental state through the second part of the twentieth century differed substantially from the pattern of embedded autonomy observed for East Asia (Evans 1995).[10] Embedded autonomy presupposes a state with high capacity and a mutually supportive relationship with the leading business sectors. That characterization could be applied to Brazil only with the utmost care, given the peculiar role of business, the complexities in the system of interest representation, and the vulnerabilities of the state. Corporatism lost its grip over society in the 1980s, once the authoritarian regime collapsed. Weak efforts at refurbishing the system in the democratizing era met with failure.[11]

The era of democratization after 1985 accelerated the pluralization of the part of civil society linked to business. Business mobilization increased markedly. It did so as a response to the transition toward a new political model, the perception within business that the old protectionist model was coming to an end, and business's own view that it had lost influence (see also Kingstone 1998). New associations and lobbies were created. Historical reasons and vested interests converged with organizational inertia to ensure the survival of preexisting associations. The Constituent Assembly of 1987 accelerated the creation of new business organizations.[12] Interestingly, the main business cleavages during the constitutional convention parallel those of earlier times. The Brazilian Union of Entrepreneurs (União Brasileira de Empresarios, or UBE), inspired by the lingering corporatist ethos, sought to organize old and new organizations into a national lobby, but was rent by a high degree of factionalism. FIESP created Forum Informal, a lobby that sought to present a unified *paulista* stance. Relatively smaller businesses formed the PNBE—National Thinking of the Entrepreneurial Grassroots.[13]

10. Evans's earlier formulation (Evans 1979) had seen the Brazilian state as shaped by the pattern of "dependent development." Authors such as Gereffi and Schneider have advanced views of the modern Brazilian state as a "developmental state."
11. Martin (1996a, 1996b) describes the failed attempts at developing neocorporatist "sectoral chambers" in the Collor and Franco administrations. These were finally eliminated in the Cardoso government. For a defense of sectoral chambers and a critique of the Cardoso approach see Alexandre Comin (1998), essays in Francisco Oliveira and Alvaro Comin (1999), and Diniz (2000, 83–88).
12. Weyland (1996a, 63–65); Diniz (2000).

The latter demanded the democratization of business representation and interest intermediation, attacking FIESP's dominant role and corporatism in general. As the Sarney government came to a close, business feared that its position was being eroded by forces it could not control. Industrialists at FIESP reponded by forming the Institute for Industrial Development Studies (IEDI), an organization set up to promote public education and lobby for an industrial policy.[14]

The Collor administration's embrace of liberalizing reforms posed a series of challenges to business. Collor used strong language to challenge the so-called anachronistic and pernicious sectors of the elite.[15] Itamar Franco's two-year tenure was also marked by disdain for business interests and the latter's disinterest in joining an effective ruling coalition.[16]

Business and the Post-1994 Reforms

Business endorsed Cardoso's two presidential campaigns against the Workers' Party's candidate and had a good relationship with Cardoso's government and its reformist agenda. The situation threatened to change in late 1998, as a response to the adjustment package and the externally induced crisis. Industrialists from São Paulo had complained about the overvalued currency, taxes, and trade liberalization. They now cried out against high interest rates, arguing that they posed a major threat to the industrial sector. The Institute for Industrial Development Studies demanded a change in policy and the resignation of the president of the Central Bank, the central figure in monetary policy.[17]

In the recent past, industrialists at FIESP and IEDI have continued to demand a developmental strategy explicitly centered on national industry, sometimes giving the impression that they oppose the adjustment policies

13. Pensamento Nacional das Bases Empresariais. Gomes and Guimarães's (1999) sketch of the PNDB describes it as critical of corporatism and FIESP and as part of a search for a new way of representing business interests as well as a new agenda encompassing political and social, as well as economic, issues. It supported the stabilization program. During the Collor and Franco administrations, PNDB worked toward the idea of a new national pact. The PNDB supported the Cardoso reforms, viewing them as representing its goals with regard to social development and the idea of broad partnerships (see also Gomes and Guimarães 2001).
14. Launched in 1989 by thirty of the top industrial firms, IEDI instantly became an important actor. Like PNBE, IEDI was formed by groups affiliated with FIESP. It included such prominent business or business-related leaders as José Ermírio de Moraes, Celso Lafer, and Paulo Aguiar Cunha. Unlike PNDB, its main demand was an industrial policy. It had considerable influence through 1993, but played no major role after that year, when Cardoso became president, though Celso Lafer would play prominent roles.
15. See President Collor's speech of 1990 [www.collor.com/colpoli.htm].
16. IEDI leader Paulo Cunha, for example, refused Itamar Franco's invitation to become finance minister. Franco, a populist, lacked sympathy for the business sector.

and the liberalizing drive.[18] A new level of political activism coincided with the election of a young businessman as FIESP president in August 1998, when leaders felt that new blood was needed to shake the association out of an autarchic pattern, presumably in place since the 1960s.[19] Many members thought that FIESP had not evolved with the times into a more modern lobbying and service-providing stance—in spite of its 17,000 functionaries, 450 employees, 140 directors, and a yearly budget of more than R$698 million.[20]

The Pact for Production and Jobs was hence part of the struggle of the business sector in favor of an industrial policy, as well as an attempt to turn the page with regard to the perceived situation of degraded business influence. Support by the opposition and the antigovernment tone indicated a feeling of estrangement from policy. FIESP's leadership complained bitterly about the Cardoso administration's failure to meet its demands.

Industrialists were responding to broad crosscurrents and frustrations. The pluralization of the state and the fragmentation of the party system greatly increased the difficulty of articulating and representing interests in the political system. The desire to construct a modern congressional lobby can be explained by the new role of Congress and the need for mechanisms of representation adequate to the changing political-institutional context.[21] But the Brazilian economy was experiencing a profound transformation that threatened the primacy of the old industrial sector. Main elements of that transformation were the expansion of the services sector, the restructuring of

17. In October 1998 IEDI sponsored and made public through the Internet a 130-page comparative study of industrial policy whose main conclusion was that Brazil was doing very little to promote industrial growth, while many governments throughout the world continued to promote industrialization (with a focus on ways to increase productivity, protect strategic sectors, engage in job promotion, and revitalize decaying areas). IEDI managed to engage respected academics in its economic analysis, including UNICAMP's Wilson Cano. IEDI also presented a shorter report to the government demanding an industrial policy. The above comparative study and reports of other activities can be found at http://www.iedi.org.br. In late 1998, that website posted a published note dated November 23 containing a strong attack on Gustavo Franco, the president of the Central Bank. For further discussion of IEDI, see Kingstone (1998; 1999a).

18. Critics blamed government policy for opening the economy to external shocks and pressure. In São Paulo critics included Delfim Netto, past minister of finance, and several editorialists at the *Folha de S. Paulo*.

19. The winning candidate represented traditional big industrial families in the state. The unsuccessful opponent was the president of Sindicato da Micro e Pequena Indústria do Estado de S. Paulo (SIMPI), the association of small and medium industrialists. His main argument was that CIESP-FIESP represented the interests of a few businessmen. Both candidates were concerned about the weakening of the association, which they attributed to increasing competition (due to the opening of the economy) and the ending of salary negotiations with the demise of inflation. Both argued for a reinvigorated FIESP-CIESP and demanded an industrial policy. The in-house candidate advocated a stronger political presence for *paulista* industry. SIMPI represented many more firms than CIESP, but most of these were not registered members. Its president lost the CIESP-FIESP elections by a wide margin—120 to 11 at FIESP and 2,842 to 853 at CIESP. This was the twelfth executive committee elected since 1942.

manufacturing, the rise of a new economy, trade liberalization, and globalization.[22]

It is striking that Brazilian industry as a whole was increasingly unable to speak with one voice on a series of major issues related to the reforms. Both the Federation of Industries of Rio de Janeiro (FIRJAN) and the Rio-based National Confederation of Industry (CNI) supported government policy in 1998 and 1999.[23] Presided by a PMDB senator from the Northeast, the CNI lobbied for an industrial policy, but it agreed with the government about the importance of stabilization and fiscal adjustment policies.[24] The challenge to Brazil was to abandon protectionism and embrace progressive trade liberalization and economic openness, according to CNI. Hence, business needed to evolve toward a global strategic orientation based on enhanced competitiveness. FIRJAN, the main industrial association from Rio, tended to work more closely with the government.[25] Also supporting stabilization and adjustment, FIRJAN leaders favored an industrial policy that differed from that demanded by FIESP.[26] The debate in early 1999 pitted those in favor of maintaining stabilization and fiscal adjustment as top priorities against others wanting a development policy as a main goal of economic policy.[27]

The intense debate among industrialists in the 1990s might be taken to confirm that big business lacked internal class unity (Payne 1994). If business had been unable to directly organize the state in previous authoritarian or

20. See Frederico Vasconcelos, "Antigas lideranças perdem espaço com a reestruturação na maior federação das indústrias do país," *Folha de S. Paulo,* November 1, 1998 (Dinheiro: pages 2–7). For another report on how FIESP needed to modernize to catch up with other industrial associations in Brazil see Luís Nassif, "A aposta na FIESP," *Folha de S. Paulo,* August 28, 1998.
21. Brazilians were aware of the existence of lobbies, but were uncertain about the proper regulatory framework. A 1989 bill to that effect, proposed by PFL's Marco Maciel, still lay dormant in 2001 (Doca de Oliveira and Christiane Samarco, "Regulamentação do lobby tem apoio do líderes do Congresso," *O Estado de S. Paulo,* August 23, 2000; "Legalizando o lobby," *Revista Cidades do Brasil* [www.cidadesdobrasil.com.br/bastidores/bastidores11 .htm]). Meanwhile, the Chamber of Deputies still recognized the existence of sixty-two confederations ("Lobby no Brasil," by Essere Consultoria Política [www.essere.com.br/ lobby_no_brasil.htm]). Gustavo Krieger and André Barreto, "Lobby esconde sua cara em Brasília," *Jornal do Brasil,* August 6, 2001, discusses the changing culture of lobbying in Brasília, including the rise of professional lobbies and the survival of old forms of exercising influence. Though several high-profile cases of corruption in 2000–2001 made it difficult for Brazilians to separate criminal influence peddling from the forms of legitimate political lobbying found in mature liberal democracies, the political system was evolving in that direction.
22. See table 5-1 for data on manufacturing growth rate.
23. The traditional corporatist system specified by law the sectoral affiliation of business at the municipal level, the aggregation of such associations to state-level federations, and the latter's amalgamation into national confederations. In reality, CNI was strong outside São Paulo. The CNI system is traditionally part of the state system. More than those of independent federations in São Paulo and elsewhere, its leaders tend to align themselves with the government.

democratic contexts, it seemed even less capable of doing so in the framework of the political dynamics of democratization and reform. Associational and interest differentiation should not come as a surprise. Brazil's historical pattern of development helps explain the pluralization of organized business interests, including the differences between regionally based associations such as the CNI and FIESP.[28] The institutional framework, often less than coherent, still mattered considerably. Though the Cardoso administration aimed at a transition away from corporatism and toward pluralism and state autonomy, it still faced corporatist practices as it sought to encapsulate or channel the business lobby and change the imperial presidency toward consultation and negotiation (Torre 1996).[29] For example, in late December 1998, the federal government somewhat antagonized the confederations in the corporatist system—CNI, CNA, CNC, Confederation of the Commercial Associations of Brazil (CACB)—when it bypassed them in picking a new leadership for Sebrae (Brazilian Service to Support Small and Medium Business/Serviço Brasileiro de Apoio as Micro e Pequenas Empresas). Sebrae was conceived in the same corporatist framework to promote microentrepreneurship. The government appointed the majority of its governing board. The Cardoso government named a member of the governing PSDB who previously had presided over Superintendency for the Develop-

24. The CNI had released a report, "Competitividade e crescimento: A agenda da indústria," which argued that the four pillars of economic policy were and should be stabilization, competitiveness, industrial policy, and export promotion. Since Brazil had been strongly affected by the international financial crisis of 1997–1998, industry was highly threatened, argued the CNI. But it shared the government view that the main problem for industry was integration into a highly competitive global economy. On December 16, 1998, CNI had launched in Brasília the Business Council Brazil—500 Years (CEB500), with Brazil's president attending the event.
25. The president of FIRJAN had been the one to suggest the creation of a business council during the recent crisis between the Cardoso administration and business, and was the first to be named to it.
26. Chico Otavio, "A idéia é somar forças e não pedir protecionismo: Eduardo Eugênio Gouvêa Vieira," *Globo On*, December 25, 1998. In this interview, FIRJAN's president indicates that the new council should not be concerned with subsidies, protectionism, or macroeconomic policy. The challenge was to improve production, something that could be accomplished with simple measures and complements in infrastructure: transportation, communications, financing, and the like. Members of the business council should be picked according to the "potential in each Brazilian region, that is, in accordance with the vocations in each geographic sector." He also stated that the growth of jobs, production, and exports was more closely linked to firms of medium or small size than with very large ones. This discourse contrasted sharply with that from the leading industry associations in São Paulo, which emphasized large national businesses (many in São Paulo), protection and subsidies, business power, and a major shift in economic policy. See also Patrícia Duarte, "Um conselho para a produção," *Globo On*, December 25, 1998.
27. The episode represented a small crisis in that process. Celso Lafer would not last as head of the new Ministry of Development, Industry, and Trade. A few months later Cardoso appointed a *paulista* businessman, Alcides Tápias, to this cabinet post. In July 2001, Sérgio Amaral, then Brazil's ambassador in London, was appointed to head the ministry.

TABLE 5-1. Mining and Manufacturing Growth Rate, 1992–2000

Year	Physical Production	Productivity	Real Average Wages
1992	-3.7	4.6	11.5
1993	7.5	9.5	6.9
1994	7.6	10.8	5.7
1995	1.8	4.3	8.7
1996	1.7	14.9	3.7
1997	3.9	10.7	1.5
1998	-2.0	8.4	2.0
1999	-0.7	7.6	-2.9
2000	6.5	5.7	-1.1
1992–2000	24.3	107.8	41.0

Source: IBGE, Brazil in Figures (2001)

ment of the Northeast (Sudene) as head, with the other two top positions given to figures from the governing coalition.[30]

Through the end of Cardoso's reformist presidency, industrialists complained bitterly about the absence of a well-articulated industrial policy, the single focus on stabilization and liberalization (rather than on growth), the costs imposed by the constitution of 1988 and its emphasis on workers' rights and curtailments of management prerogatives, the high interest rates, and the taxation system.[31]

The debate about Brazil's international trade alignment had as a main question the priority to be given to Mercosul relative to the Free Trade Area of the Americas (FTAA), an issue that intensified the tensions within the Brazilian

28. The commercial elite had an even more diverse set of interest organizations. As early as the nineteenth century, several states (provinces at that point) had their own commercial associations. The Commercial Associations of Rio and the Commercial Association of São Paulo (as well as the Commercial Association of Santos, the chief coffee port) emerged as the most influential. With the onset of corporatism, the union forced states to have commercial "federations." There were several attempts at forming confederations. By the 1990s, São Paulo had the original commercial association plus a federation and four or five other associations—Commercial Association of the State of São Paulo (ACESP), Association of the Unified System of Commerce and Industry of the State of São Paulo (ASUCIESP), Commercial Association and Autonomous of the State of São Paulo (ACAESP), the Commercial, Industrial, and Autonomous Association of the State of São Paulo (ACIAESP), and others. Merchants spoke with many voices.
29. Boschi, Diniz, and Santos (2000), Martin (1996b). Diniz (2000) chastises the Cardoso government for seeking too much bureaucratic insulation.
30. Led by CNI's Bezerra, business leaders protested the meeting formalizing the above appointments by walking out of it. Ribamar Oliveira, "Composição da direção do Sebrae causa conflito," O Estado de S. Paulo, December 30, 1998; James Allen, "Sérgio Moreira vai ser o presidente do Sebrae e irmã de Eduardo Jorge, a vice," Globo On, December 30, 1998; "Indicação de nova diretoria provoca protesto no Sebrae," Folha de S. Paulo, December 30, 1998.
31. See chapter 3.

business sector and the elite as a whole. Throughout the 1990s, Brazil focused on launching Mercosul. Industrialists supported this process, viewing it partly as a defensive response to globalization and other integration agreements in Europe and North America. The decision to form the FTAA by 2006 implied the accelerated liberalization of trade with all the countries in the Western Hemisphere, including the United States.[32] Agriculture, the financial system, most services, and other sectors have been enthusiastic about the FTAA.[33] However, the traditional industrial sector was in favor of a more cautious approach.

Brazil's ambivalence toward the Free Trade Area of the Americas and the extent of trade liberalization is also rooted in real concerns about access to U.S. markets in such critical sectors as steel and agriculture. In 2001, the U.S. Congress was contemplating a law to protect the steel industry in the United States, a measure that would affect Brazil's competitiveness in that area. Brazilian business and policymakers also wondered about the elaborate nontariff and tariff protection of U.S. agricultural producers. Business sectors were uncertain about their competitiveness—the ability to export. Brazil's share of world trade had decreased, from 1.3 percent in the early 1990s to .89 percent in 2000, according to Garnero (see footnote 33).[34]

Business blamed the government for many of its woes.[35] Industrial producers continued to argue that the tax structure—the "imposto em cascata"— imposed burdens on business activity.[36] In São Paulo, taxes could be 32 percent of production, while the international average was said to be 12–17 percent. In October 2001, a prominent leader of the ruling coalition announced that tax reform would not take place until 2003—that is, after the 2002 elections—leading to indignation from business leaders.[37]

---

32. Table 6-2 provides data on trade patters in the largest FTAA countries.
33. Business leaders led by Mário Garnero led a veritable crusade in favor of the FTAA via the Forum of the Americas/Fórum das Américas, a nongovernmental organization that began sponsoring bilateral negotiations and meetings in 1996. Members and supporters included exporters, investors, executives in multinational corporations, providers of business services, and the newspaper *O Estado de S. Paulo*. Garnero was president of BrasilInvest. The forum had a major international meeting, "Riscos e Oportunidades: Os Novos Desafios da Economia Global e a Alca," in São Paulo in October 2001. This gathering produced the pro-FTAA "Letter from São Paulo" and the creation of an international council. It is remarkable that this event took place when it did, in the context of uncertainty about FTAA generated by the September 11 attack on the World Trade Center in New York City. For basic background about the forum, see Carlos José Marques "A cruzada da integração," *ISTOÉ*, December 4, 1996; Paula Pauliti, "Indústria precisa ser mais eficiente para enfrentar a Alca," *O Estado de S. Paulo*, October 23, 2001, News.
34. In Pauliti, "Indústria precisa ser mais eficiente." See also appendix D, External Sector.
35. As argued by Reis (2000), business also blamed the government for Brazil's high inequality and poverty and shifted to it the responsibility for their reduction—rather than accepting its own role.
36. See also chapter 3.

Business as a whole, particularly industrialists, remained particularly sensitive to economic crises. The agitation of early 2000 was directly linked to the 1998–1999 crisis. Business resented the policy of relying on very high interests rates to combat financial threats.

But business radicalism seemed to fizzle out by mid-year, when interest rates were brought down to 16 percent and the industrial sector recovered.[38] In early August 2000, in the middle of a corruption scandal involving a past secretary to the president, CNI prepared a "Manifest to the Nation" supporting Cardoso. The presidents of the five national confederations (industry, commerce, financial institutions, agriculture, and transportation) supported the document, as did well-known *paulista* business leaders.[39] This followed an expression of support from governors. Business would also be at Cardoso's side in 2001, when political boss and ex-ally Antonio Carlos Magalhães threatened to create a political crisis by charging prominent political figures with corruption. Though ambivalent and perplexed, business supported the reform process.

The behavior of the elite as a whole is particularly critical. Sustained action and political stewardship will be necessary to overcome the doubts and perplexity of a large and growing number of consequential actors. The business sector is pivotal, though its ambivalence about such key policies as trade liberalization and high interest rates has introduced an element of uncertainty about its role. As further discussed in chapter 7, stable political alignment still depends to a large extent on the ability of political elites to prevent rivalries from getting out of hand and come to basic understandings about the country's future. The Brazilian political class as a whole has historically faced regional, ideological, and other cleavages that prevented it from acting cohesively at certain critical periods in the country's history, such as the 1930s and the 1960s. The debate around the 2002 elections confirmed regionalism as an important cleavage.

Business and Social Reform

Empirical studies of the Brazilian elite show business leaders as being highly alarmed about the high rates of poverty and inequality in Brazil, but prone to identify the government as responsible for the problem as well as for finding

37. Empresários se frustam com adiamento de reformas para 2003, *Agência do Estado*, October 23, 2001: Últimas Notícias.
38. For example, Evaldo Nogueira, "A escalada na indústria," *Globo On*, July 9, 2000. Production had reached 80-percent capacity in eleven key economic sectors—the highest level since 1989. Massive new investments of US$10 billion were projected in steel, textile, chemicals, paper, and cellulose (see also "Recuperação ajuda a crise de empregos," *Globo On*, July 9, 2000).
39. Including Olavo Setubal, Antonio Ermírio de Moraes, Emílio Odebrecht, Jorge Gerdau, Claudio Bordella, and Abram Szajman (*Folha de S. Paulo*, August 1, 2000).

solutions.[40] According to those observations, Brazilian elites highlight the centrality of education and growth-oriented policies, but neglect to face the need for redistributive measures.[41] Almeida (2000) speaks of "a deficit in social responsibility" on the part of the Brazilian elite.

The above conclusions were drawn from data gathered in the early and mid-1990s. The evidence that business is becoming more involved with social policy has grown since then. By 2000, several reports and surveys spoke of a new activism to promote the private sector's involvement in social policy. The Academy for Social Development was a pioneer in monitoring business "social responsibility."[42] In 1995, the Group of Institutes, Foundations, and Enterprises (GIFE), a consortium of foundations focused on the strengthening of the third sector, or civil society, was formalized (GIFE 2001). GIFE provided an assessment of the limits of the state's promotion of social development as due in part to the crisis of the state and focused on such ideas as "business citizenship" and "business social responsibility." A 2001 GIFE report (Falcone and Vilela 2001) listed over sixty grant-giving entities, with nearly 70 percent of them being either private foundations or programs of particular businesses. Grants often go to nongovernmental organizations in the social area, particularly for education. Another entity, Network to Promote the Third Sector (Rits) used various means to support the expansion of that part of civil society concerned with social policy.[43]

TABLE 5-2. Business Involvement in Social Programs

REGION	Number of firms	Percent involved	Number involved	Expenditures in *reais*	Year of survey
Southeast	445,000	67	300,000	3.5 billion	1998
South	165,000	46	75,000	320 million	1999
Center-West	60,000	50	30,000		2001
North	24,000	49	11,675		2000
Northeast	88,000	55	48,000	260 million	1999

Source: IPEA, "Pesquisa Ação Social das Empresas" [www.ipea.gov.br/asocial]

40. Elisa Reis's comparative study of elite attitudes with respect to inequality and poverty can be found in Reis (2000). At the time, Professor Reis was coordinator of the Interdisciplinary Program for the Study of Inequality (Nied). Her random sample of 320 members of the elite included business leaders. Almeida's (2000) smaller study of municipal elites tends to confirm these findings. See also footnote 30 and chapter 4.
41. Brazil's periods of growth have not translated into major reductions in inequality, hence supporting the argument for other causal factors.
42. See www.academiasocial.org.br/.
43. Rits's mission is to promote the growth of civil society as a whole [www.rits.org.br]. Its president in 2001 was Rubem Cesar Fernandes, main leader of the Viva Rio movement and nongovernmental organization.

A major IPEA study on business social responsibility further illuminates the new behavior, showing how a high percentage of firms involved themselves in social projects, particularly those focused on communities and children.[44] According to this study, the degree of involvement grows with size and is not greatly sensitive to fiscal incentives. This suggests that social activism on the part of business is determined by factors outside of politics.

Business's growing social involvement is related in no small part to its perceived need to earn societal goodwill. Still, it is part of the evidence of a new sensibility about social issues in Brazilian society. It may also be hoped that it presents the emergence of modern and expanded philanthropy in a country that needs it badly.

Conclusion

Several conclusions can be reached from the above review of business-government relations in the context of the reforms of the 1990s and early years of the twenty-first century. First, though it generally supported the reform process, the Brazilian bourgeoisie's uncertain influence in key policy areas (including taxation and industrial policy) suggests a limited role in organizing political life. But that should come as no surprise. Business seldom exercises direct hegemony in sufficiently complex capitalist societies operating within a democratic framework. The very growth and diversification of the economy, civil society, and the polity meant an increased level of pluralism in Brazil and a fluid relationship between business and state elites. In any case, the political elite and political dynamics are leading factors in the reform process. Second, the erosion of the system of elite representation and mediation centered on the corporatist mode accelerated during the 1990s and after. The change was taking place in part as a response to actions by the presidency and in part as the result of new demands from both labor and business.[45] The central government asserted operational autonomy and made decisions that not infrequently hurt sectors of the business community. With elements of corporatism still in place, interest representation was a mix of the old and the new, remaining a complex and even confusing process. Third, business agitation resulted in part from its own perplexity about institutional change and its own role in the changing political system. If Congress was increasingly important, the executive branch was experiencing growing complexity, including the rise of regulatory agencies. If these processes challenged the articulation of collective interests at the federal level, the Brazilian polity was experiencing substantial decentralization and experimentation at the state and

44. IPEA's research on business social action can be found at www.ipea.gov.br/asocial.
45. Gomes and Guimarães (2001).

local levels, which were now important loci of authority. Fourth, while business actively searched for new ways to exercise influence, few in the business community aimed at restoring traditional corporatism. Business was acting as a pressure group in a complex polity. Some business sectors reaffirmed traditional claims to various forms of protection. But as a whole, organized business had not yet settled on a definitive role in the postcorporatist framework. Fifth, the business community as a whole was increasingly divided on a range of issues, including how to respond to the reform process, globalizing capitalism, and the Free Trade Area of the Americas. In brief, business, like Brazil itself, was experiencing a difficult transition.

In particular, industrialists were seeking to refurbish their role in the changing political and economic context. Industrialists were reacting not only to the reform of the state and the relative operational insulation of government, but also to the deepening reorganization of the Brazilian economy. The restructuring of the old industrial economy, the dramatic expansion of the services sector, and the emergence of a new economy based on the information revolution provided new challenges. If that were not enough, the countryside was also changing, driven by agrarian reform and the new soy frontier in the west and north.[46] The financial crisis of 1998–2000 and the 2002 succession provided tests of the strength of an internal consensus about the new economic model within the organized entrepreneurial class and the economic elite as a whole. Within São Paulo itself, some business groups remain perplexed by the changes and the challenges of an open economy. Important business sectors appeared to support opposition candidates. But the bulk of the evidence confirms their support for the pro-reform candidate.

In 2002 industrialists were probably the most effective business sector demanding privileged access to politics, even if their ability to exercise hegemony over government and civil society was limited. They will remain a decisive force in the reform process. Even then, business as a whole can be expected to speak with many voices on the key issues posed by reform and the opening of the Brazilian economy.

46. Chapter 6 discusses the soy-driven frontier in central and northwestern Brazil.

CHAPTER 6   *Toward a New Development Strategy*

The Brazilian reforms of the 1990s will be judged by how close they came to setting a new development course. Development was, and remains, Brazil's premier challenge.[1] Poor economic performance in the 1980s led the country to question dirigisme and begin a search for alternatives. The liberalizing reforms discussed in previous chapters sounded the death knell for the old development strategy, but they only laid the groundwork for a new approach. The emphasis on stabilization and fiscal restructuring delayed more ambitious statements about a new development model through 1997. The financial shocks of 1997–1999 and 2001–2002 further constrained state action and frustrated expectations for a more assertive development strategy during Cardoso's second term. The victory of the Workers' Party in the October 2002 elections raised uncertainty about support for the reform process and Brazil's new development strategy.

The crisis of 1998–1999 renewed the debate about development, as it delayed the formalization of a new development strategy. Dismissing the reforms as neoliberal, much of the opposition renewed calls for state intervention.[2] Threatened industrial sectors demanded government protection. Editorialists at *Folha de S. Paulo* and other journals echoed arguments about the need to defend the national economy against globalization and neoliberalism. But the crisis further constrained the space for state-led initiatives, as it fueled demands for government intervention. This conundrum would represent a major challenge through the end of the Cardoso government.

New measures and initiatives in social development, economic planning, the modernization of the state apparatus, decentralization, local development, export promotion, and related areas did lay foundations for a new approach to development. Brazil was experiencing a shift toward a new policy paradigm.

1. Essential to fighting poverty and inequality, creating conditions for economic development was also Fernando Henrique Cardoso's main concern as both reformist president and intellectual.

129

But how to reconcile the election results with the idea that Brazilians had rejected the dirigisme surviving through the 1980s?[3] Was Brazil about to reverse course once again?

Background: The Crisis of Statism

A long-term view is useful to put the development strategies adopted after 1990 in perspective and to probe their impact relative to other long-term factors transforming Brazil. The country's economic expansion between 1850 and 1980 had been second only to that of Japan—with GDP and GDP per capita growing at average annual rates of 7.41 and 4.51 percent, respectively. By the end of this period the Brazilian economy had consolidated its position as one of the world's top ten. The income per capita growth was quite impressive, considering the rapid pace of population growth (see figs. 6-1, D-8).[4]

Brazil's great transformation was first driven by the expansion of a coffee-led agricultural frontier, augmented next by industrialization and urbanization after World War I. Rooted in the dramatic pre-1930 expansion, industry grew in a sustained manner over the subsequent decades. The statist development strategy since World War II emphasized state intervention and import substitution industrialization. The government built and ran huge complexes in mining and steel production, energy, airplane manufacturing, and the like, while spending heavily on dams and infrastructure.

Few transformations were more striking than urbanization. While 70 percent of the population still lived in the countryside in 1950, 80 percent lived

2.   The modern Brazilian debate about development began in the 1940s. The memorable 1944 exchange, widely covered by the media, was between industrialist and CIESP-FIESP leader Roberto Simonsen, who defended state intervention to promote industrialization, and economics professor Eugênio Gudin, who adhered to mainstream economic ideas skeptical of state intervention. Developmentalists, the advocates of statism, got the upper hand shortly thereafter and remained preeminent through the 1970s, as most currents of economic thought, including that of liberal economist Roberto Campos, embraced some form of interventionism. Mantega's (1984) overview of Brazilian political economy through the 1970s discusses Celso Furtado, Ignácio Rangel, the "Itatiaia group" (later linked to the Instituto Brasileiro de Estudos Superiores), radical strands of dependency theory, and several marxist authors (see also Bielschowsky 1988). Roberto Campos's memoir overviews the same territory and beyond from a mainstream economic perspective (Campos 1994). Particularly after the 1960s, Campos emerged as a strong critic of statism.
3.   One of the indicators of an overall paradigm shift in Brazilian society as a whole was the ideological and political conversion of the Workers' Party (PT) toward a moderate, centrist position that accepted past privatization, fiscal austerity, the IMF accords, major reforms in the social security and taxation system, export promotion, and the need to give up the party's traditional animus toward business and the embrace of statism (see "Cristãos-novos do capitalismo," *Veja*, September 25, 2002). This new look made the Workers' Party a formidable contender in the 2002 elections. But the federal government, the reformist coalition, and Fernando Henrique Cardoso himself had articulated much of the intellectual and policy ideas leading to the shift in the country's stance.
4.   See also Faria and Graeff (2000).

in cities by the mid-1990s (see fig. D-6). From the 1950s through the 1980s millions of migrants from the Northeast and the adjacent hinterlands changed the landscapes of São Paulo, Rio de Janeiro, Belo Horizonte, Brasília, and other large cities in the southeast and central regions. Rural dynamics remained important, but Brazil was on the way to becoming a nation of urban dwellers. By the late 1980s, middle-sized and small cities took the lead in attracting immigrants. Many of the internal migrants dreamed about industrial jobs, but the fastest growth in urban jobs came from the services sector—food, transportation, communications, and the like. Urban growth meant thousands of new dwellings in need of household services and care. The services sector came to account for more than 50 percent of the economy and much of the growth (Bonelli and Gonçalves 1998).[5] Urbanization and economic transformation shaped the form and density of civil society.

The Brazilian statist model began to face major problems in the 1970s, a trend that accelerated in the 1980s. First, the oil crises of that decade created difficulties leading to the great debt crisis of the 1980s. The development model in place since the 1940s relied heavily on foreign lending to finance investment and technological expansion, with the government channeling loans and direct investment to prime and sustain growth in strategic sectors. The oil price shocks of the 1970s made the debt larger, leading to mounting fiscal deficits and the retraction of foreign capital in the 1980s. Second,

FIGURE 6-1. Economic and Population Annual Growth, 1950–1999

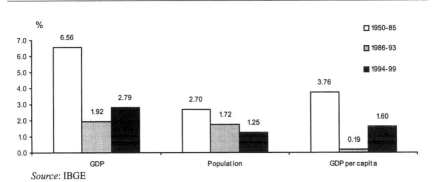

Source: IBGE

though the economic problems were important in themselves, the crisis of the 1980s was evidence of a more insidious crisis of the state.[6]

5. Still, by the early years of the twenty-first century, agriculture would grow faster than manufacturing or services, in part due to grain harvests of 100 million tons that contrasted with those of 57 million tons a decade earlier (see Adriana Carvalho and Roseli Loturco, "O motor que faz o Brasil andar: O capital intensivo e a alta tecnologia fizeram do campo brasileiro uma ilha de Primeiro Mundo que cresceu 8% no primeiro semestre," *Veja*, September 18, 2002).

Third, to many Brazilians the old statist model of development was now spent as an engine of growth.[7] In this perspective, the old semiautarkic model experienced a fatal crisis between 1980 and 1992. The industrial sector itself ceased to have the dynamism of earlier decades. Though this might have reflected in part a near-universal trend toward the service sector, Brazilians were discovering that a significant part of the industry consolidated under protectionism was not competitive. The quality of manufactured goods was often low and prices high. Major restructuring would be needed for the competitive reinsertion in the international economy. As evidence of globalization accumulated, policymakers and business realized that such restructuring was of a magnitude not many had contemplated only a few years earlier. In influential government circles such as BNDES, internal debate had led to support for the thesis of competitive integration into the global economy.

Fourth, in spite of its emphasis on growth, traditional Brazilian statism neglected questions about social development, and the Brazilian public began to regard the high levels of poverty, unemployment, and insecurity as intolerable. Poverty and inequality had firmed up as features of Brazilian society. In 1990, over 40 percent of Brazilians were poor—of which half, or over 20 percent of the population, were considered indigents with nutritional deficiencies. The indices of inequality were among the highest in the world. As recently as 1997, the top 20 percent of Brazilians received 64.2 percent of all income, while the bottom 20 percent received only 2.5 percent. Regional differences in this regard had diminished somewhat, but Brazil at the beginning of the twenty-first century remained internally diverse and structurally heterogeneous (fig. D-14). The Northeast presented the largest problems. Meanwhile, Brazilian cities were experiencing increases in congestion, pollution, crime, and violence.[8] The centralizing regimes since the 1930s relied on growth policies to achieve legitimacy, but economic expansion came about with massive deployment of resources by an often authoritarian government that tended to ignore or neglect popular demands even when it aimed at addressing them. For instance, the early ideas about agrarian reform gave

6.   Bresser Pereira (1992, 1996) provides a comprehensive and focused treatment of how the debt crisis signaled a broader "crisis of the state" and hence the need for major state reform. In Bresser Pereira's account, the crisis of the state immobilized the government and threw into question the idea of the state as a producer of goods and commodities and that of a bureaucracy unaccountable to any actor but itself. The goal of state reform was not a "minimal state," as prescribed by neoliberal doctrine, but a strengthened state able to define and pursue a new development strategy. Bresser Pereira contrasted the social democratic state with that resulting from the policy prescription of the Washington Consensus (see Williamson 1990a)
7.   Bresser Pereira (1996). See also E. Cardoso (2001). Mantega's (1984) overview of the main currents of Brazilian economic thought provides an inventory of some of the early negative assessments in the 1960s and after.
8.   See, for example, Caldeira (2001).

way during the years of military rule to a program to promote cattle ranching in the fringes of the Amazon region, something that did generate growth, but not a great many rural jobs.

Fifth, the political system was wasteful, inefficient, and prone to corruption. Brazilian social scientists extensively documented the evils of clientelism, corporatism, and the patrimonial appropriation of the public sphere.[9] Policymakers spoke of the need to modernize the state apparatus. Business resented red tape and bureaucratic inefficiency, as well as the degree of state intervention in the economy. Through the 1970s, business associations started a campaign for privatization and debureaucratization.[10] Ignacio Rangel and associates at BNDES spoke about the state having reached its limit in terms of its capacity to invest. This led in the 1980s to the first attempts at privatization, including the development of a privatizing methodology that would also be used in the following decade.[11]

Sixth, most Brazilians associated the statist regime with the authoritarian form of centralization inherited from the military. As the hope and reality of political liberalization and democracy grew, so did rejection of a model perceived as politically asphyxiating. Many democrats—intellectuals, students, labor, business, public opinion in general—were united in their distrust of heavily centralized authority.

Of all these factors, the notion that the statist model was exhausted subsumed many of the other criticisms and carried considerable weight with the intelligentsia.[12] Internationally, Brazil lost considerable ground after the 1970s, just as the new wave of globalization accelerated worldwide. The dramatic rise of export-oriented powerhouses in East Asia drove the point home, as Korean and Taiwanese performance surpassed that of Brazil.

Still, the statist mentality ruled through the late 1980s, as shown by the demands made throughout the Constituent Assembly and as reflected in the

9. Luciano Martins (1985) portrays an expanding state with little coherence and lacking as an organized system. Roberto Campos, the founding president of BNDES, often mentioned that the obstacles to change in Brazil came from three Cs: cartorialism, clientelism, and corporatism. Hélio Jaguaribe et al. (1989) held that Brazil's deterioration of the state apparatus and the social crisis were two of the main impediments to development, and he called for a national consensus on how to overcome both. To them, the reform of the state should restore fiscal health, increase the effectiveness of public administration, and bring a regime of moral and public responsibility to state action.
10. Charles Pessanha (1981).
11. BNDES had come to own twenty to thirty relatively small firms for diverse reasons.
12. Latin America as a whole was searching for new approaches to development. For a neostructuralist approach blending a measure of state activism, market policies, and social development see Osvaldo Sunkel (1991). See also Joseph Love (1986). Other currents of thought, to include dependency theory, had produced major criticisms of the Brazilian state. Mainstream economic thought, emphasizing the role of the market in the efficient allocation of resources, had also expanded in Brazilian universities, including Rio's Catholic University, the University of São Paulo, and other institutions.

constitution of 1988. The continuing internal crisis, against the backdrop of
the collapse of socialism in Eastern Europe and the old USSR in 1988–1990,
helped make the case for a new approach. But it was the seemingly uncon-
trollable hyperinflation in the early 1990s, dramatized by the failure of the
Collor government, that finally convinced a critical mass of Brazilians that
change was unavoidable.[13] Though its approach to stabilization failed, the
Collor government began measures to stabilize and open the economy.[14] By
1993–1994, doubts and perplexities had been supplanted by the rejection of
the state as a superinstitution guiding and structuring other institutions and by
the acceptance of the need for a new approach to development (Albuquerque
1995). The change came about through private and public decisions and
actions, rather than via a master strategy. The rationale was clarified within
the intelligentsia and shared within broader circles of an enlightened public
that included academics, policymakers, business leaders, and others.[15]

The new thinking on development aimed at, first, the liberalization of the
economy and the transformation of the productive system. Second, it called
for heavier and more effective spending on basic education and poverty
reduction to give the poor incentives to become contributors and producers.
Third, state reform was needed to generate a smaller, more effective government. State reform and liberalization were seen as the way to arrive at a better
allocation of resources, reduce rent-seeking behavior, attract investment and
technology, and enhance the country's ability to adjust to external shocks.[16]
Such reforms were necessary if Brazil hoped for faster growth and an
enhanced international standing.

The pattern of stagnation followed by inflation in the 1980s might have
been expected to lead to a faster process of social learning about the need for
a new approach to development. However, in spite of the mounting criticism
and pressures to reform, the fledgling democracy had been unable to move
speedily to a new economic model. The first three post-1985 presidencies—
those of José Sarney, Fernando Collor, and Itamar Franco—failed to articulate a new approach to development. The country did experience an aborted
reform drive under Collor, but sheer inertia, the institutional limitations of the
transitional state, and an overloaded political agenda conspired to prevent

13. Roberto Campos and other mainstream authors consider the Collor government as pioneering in taking bold steps toward privatization and trade liberalization (see chapters 1
and 2).
14. Collor (1989).
15. See also chapter 1. As discussed above, liberalizing reforms began in the Collor presidency.
16. Roberto Cavalcanti de Albuquerque (1995). See also J. P. dos Reis Velloso (1994a), J.
P. dos Reis Velloso and R. C. Albuquerque (1994). See also Cardoso (2001) and previously
cited works by Bresser Pereira.

reform.[17] Still, diverse voices now clamored for change. A new mind-set was crystallizing and would be a critical factor in the reform drive.

The Cardoso Era: A Turning Point?

Fernando Henrique Cardoso became president affirming the need for balancing market and state in the pursuit of economic expansion and social inclusion.[18] Aided by the emerging movement toward reform, his presidency represented the first systematic effort at massive reform. Probing how it might represent a durable turning point in Brazil's search for a new approach to development calls for a detailed examination of its main development-related programs.

The programmatic statements of the two Cardoso presidential terms spell out its objectives and plans with respect to development. The official pluriannual plans emphasize health and education to improve human capital, as well as investments in infrastructure and other areas to make Brazil more competitive. Though "Brazil in Action," the name of the first pluriannual plan (1996–1999), focused on economic stabilization and fiscal adjustment, it advanced new ideas about development and social policy.[19]

Avança Brasil, the policy blueprint for the period 2000–2003, identifies concrete policies and programs with regard to state reform, stabilization, sustainable growth and jobs, investment, knowledge and education, poverty and inequality, and democracy and human rights.[20] Government investments in

17. Brazilian intellectuals and policymakers were deeply alarmed about governability and governance issues in the 1992–1994 period. See, for example, João Paulo dos Reis Velloso (1994b), particularly the essays by Bolívar Lamounier, Luciano Martins, and Wanderley Guilherme dos Santos.
18. For Cardoso's ideas about reform as he became president, see Cardoso and Font (2001).
19. Each new Brazilian government submits a plan and budget identifying goals and priorities in public investments. These pluriannual plans are presented to Congress during the second semester of the first year in office to include the following year through the first year of the next administration. The Congress needs to approve the budget. The core plan for Cardoso's first term is "Brasil em ação" (see *Programa Brasil em Ação: Dois Anos* [Brasil, Presidente 1998] and *Brasil em ação: Investimentos e desenvolvimento* [Brasil, Presidente, 1996]). José Serra, Cardoso's first planning minister, designed the pluriannual plans. Antonio Kandir, the second planning minister, transformed general ideas into the forty-two core projects of Brazil in Action.
20. *Avança Brasil*, the plan for 2000–2003, came to include 384 projects and programs, of which 360 were advanced in *Avança Brasil: Mais 4 anos de desenvolvimento para todos* (Brasilia, N/E, 1998). The others were added by Congress. *Avança Brasil* aimed at expenditures of R$1.1 trillion through 2003, resulting in the creation of 8.5 million jobs. A core of fifty projects and programs considered of strategic significance and receiving R$67.2 billion in 2001 are listed in *Avança Brasil: Programas Estratégicos* (Brasil: Ministério de Planejamento, 2001). The last official reports on *Avança Brasil* are found in Cardoso's 2000 and 2001 presidential messages to the Congress (Brasil, Presidente 2000, 2001). Campaign platforms such as *Mãos à obra* help trace government priorities.

national and regional development follow a form of strategic planning focused on nine geographical axes of development. Programs for each of these strategic areas cluster around transportation, energy, and general infrastructure. In most cases, the objective is to enhance connectedness internally and externally. For instance, the completion of the highway connecting Brazil's Amazon city of Manaus to Caracas, Venezuela's capital, and of the gas pipeline to Bolivia are both part of long-term regional plans, while projects aiming at an integrated national grid of electrical power take neighboring countries into account.[21]

Recognizing the importance of stable macroeconomic conditions and a favorable balance of trade, the Cardoso government focused the institutional and financial resources of the federal government on industrial and general economic restructuring. It also gave a great deal of attention to a new role for Brazil in the international economy. Together with the new approaches to social development (see discussion in chapter 4), policies listed in table 6-1 identify in broad strokes the approach of the Cardoso administration.

The emergent approach to development encompasses diverse programs and institutional actors. The tendency has been to rely on existing agencies rather than to create new ones, with a number of key policies also building on prior programs, as indicated in table 6-1. The National Bank for Economic and Social Development (BNDES), the country's main lending institution with regard to development since its launching in the early 1950s, finances projects in accordance with national policy. In late 1994, this bank began to offer lower long-term interest rates to firms in industrial sectors threatened by high interest rates and by imports resulting from trade liberalization and the overvalued exchange rate. The bank has also benefited other sectors and initiatives considered to be of strategic importance.[22] By and large these policies were maintained throughout the Cardoso presidency.

Camex (Foreign Trade Council) traditionally plays a central role in formulating Brazilian trade policy. Housed in the Ministry of Development, it coordinates its credit-granting actions with BNDES. In 1998 the Cardoso administration launched the main export-promotion program with the aim of doubling exports within five years—from US$53 billion to US$100 billion. Brazil's export sector had performed unevenly and unimpressively through 1999. The government declared higher exports a matter of life or death for the country. Manufacturing exports increased somewhat in 2000. One of the truly bright spots is Embraer, the country's airplane manufacturing giant.

21. The energy crisis of 2001 revealed gaps in this plan.
22. BNDES spent R$26 billion in 2001 and R$32 billion in 2002—and a total of R$159 billion for the period 1995-2002 (Guilherme Barros, "BNDES prioriza Sudeste e grandes empresas," *Folha de S. Paulo*, December 25, 2002. See extended discussion of BDNES below.

TABLE 6-1. Development and Industrial Policy

Policy focus	Key measures
Industrial promotion, general	More active BNDES: lower interest rates, increased financing, privatization, direct foreign investment
Sector-specific policies	Automobile (fiscal and financial incentives, Brazil-Argentina agreement), aircraft (Embraer), telecommunications (private-investment promotion), computers (new law, emphasis on research and development); electronics (Manaus Export Processing Zone); support for restructuring of textile, shoe, auto parts, and other threatened sectors
Export promotion	Broadening of credit and lowering of interest rates to industrial producers, particularly exporters, via BNDES, from policy restricted to capital goods sectors; develop export-oriented parks (PNPEs) in interior parts of fourteen states; Special Export Program (PEE)
Competitiveness and productivity	Brazilian Program for Quality and Productivity (PBQP); Competitiveness Forum; Custo Brasil Project and less red tape; design-improvement program; science and technology; tariff reductions for imported capital goods
Small and medium firms	Entrepreneurial Brazil program; expansion of credit and support to small and medium entrepreneurs via Sebrae, Banco do Nordeste, BNDES, FINAME (financing of machines and equipment for industrial production); program to aid export-oriented smaller firms
Rural development	Agrarian reform; integrated local development
International reintegration	Trade liberalization and investment patterns in context of talks with Mercosul, European Union, World Trade Organization negotiations, Latin American integration, Free Trade Area of the Americas
Institutional development	BNDES; Ministry of Planning (*Avança Brasil*); Ministry of Development, strategic planning and professional training for public entrepreneurs, Camex; Ministry of Foreign Relations; Ministry of National Integration; Ministry of Agrarian Reform and INCRA, Ministry of Science and Technology
Subnational	Ministry of National Integration (Sudene and Sudam converted into agencies with new mission, structure, and new approach to regional development and national integration); at state and county levels: tax exemption (ICMS), credit and financial (including fiscal wars), subsidized industrial facilities and infrastructure

BNDES's export-import program favored that firm, thereby enabling it to compete successfully with Canada's Bombardier, its main competitor in aircraft for regional use.[23] As the largest exporter in Brazil, Embraer had foreign sales of US$1.69 billion in 1999. The auto industry, another success story, grew substantially between 1990 and 1999, benefiting from agreements with Argentina as well as other national and subnational policies. These policy initiatives slowly made exports grow.

The Brazilian government supports competitiveness via the innovative Brazilian Program for Quality and Productivity (PBQP), which favors the adoption of international standards, norms, and concepts (such as those from the International Organization for Standards). At the same time, the federal government is more active in financing research and development, as well as in pressing for reduced tariffs for imported capital goods. Applying Mercosul's average of 14 percent to such goods represented a decrease from the 25 percent in place before.

Relatively small firms—micro, small, and medium—account for 30 percent of GDP and 60 percent of new jobs in Brazil, but have traditionally received only 10 percent of credits. This is due in large part to the absence of mechanisms to guarantee loans to small entrepreneurs, who are often without commercial credit. In the 1990s Sebrae gradually emerged as an important actor in promoting small-scale entrepreneurship, including a fund to provide such guarantees. Priority is given to new investments and technology. After 1996, Brazilian states offered exemptions from the value-added tax (ICMS), special credits from state-operated banks, infrastructure, and the occasional sale or concession of lots and warehouses at subsidized prices. On the other hand, small and medium companies were subject to negative side effects of monetary and fiscal policy. The combination of high interest rates and an overvalued exchange rate raised their costs to import and to obtain credit, and they also complained of extra burdens from the tax system.

Brazilian policymakers have also given emphasis to family farming.[24] Applying strategic planning to agriculture, decision makers at the Ministry of Agrarian Development as well as in the Ministry of Agriculture have opted for a conceptualization of rural development that emphasizes the expansion of that sector in conjunction with new approaches to social development, the development of decentralized strategic partnerships, and local participation.[25] The agricultural census of 1995–1996 showed that family farms accounted

23. In 2001, Embraer won over Bombardier in a lucrative contract with American Eagle and other U.S. carriers. Late that year, BNDES lent Embraer US$1.1 billion to finance the sale of up to seventy-five executive jets (twenty-five as a firm order, with options for fifty more) to the U.S. charter airline Indigo (a division of NewWorldAir Holdings). Embraer is the world's fourth largest manufacturer of airplanes and one of the two top makers of regional commuter aircraft.
24. Chapter 4 provides a detailed discussion of agrarian policy.

for 30.5 percent of the country's cultivated area and 37.9 percent of the gross value of production. Family farmers receive only 25.3 percent of all agricultural financing, showing that this sector is relatively effective in applying scarce resources. The list of new programs to promote family farming and sustainable rural development includes the Land Bank (Banco da Terra), the National Program to Strengthen Family Agriculture (Pronaf), the National Program for Education in Agrarian Reform (Pronera), and a reinvigorated National Institute for Agrarian Reform (INCRA). Launched in 2000, the Land Bank reinforces the previously existing INCRA to implement agrarian reform goals by providing direct financing to aspiring farmers who want to acquire plots of land.[26] As with many of the other development-related programmatic areas, the innovation resides in the decentralized and direct character of the intervention and the use of the program as poverty-reducing tool.[27] Pronaf uses BNDES resources and a network of banks to support previously existing agrarian activities, to include those relevant to tourism, the production of crafts, small agro-businesses, and rural services. In the area of technical support, the Brazilian Agricultural Research Corporation (Embrapa) emerged as an effective aid to agricultural and rural development, including the new focus on family farms.[28]

The new approach seeks to redefine Brazil's role in the world economy. The emphasis is on openness and competitiveness—the liberalization of the economy, multilateral and bilateral trade negotiations, and a more assertive engagement in international affairs. Brazil gave a high priority to Mercosul through the 1990s. Mercosul, the customs union with South American neighbors, combined elements of trade liberalization and protection in the context

25. A key entity formulating policy in this area is the National Council for Sustainable Rural Development (CNDRS) at the Ministry of Agrarian Development. The main focus is family farming. This council seeks to articulate policy and programs across ministries and agencies, including comparable councils (*conselhos*) at the state and county levels.
26. INCRA had legal existence since 1970 and was rededicated in 1989, though with limited effective funding. It provides the financing for the settlements related to the bulk of the agrarian reform process. In 1996, the federal government created the Ministry of Agrarian Development, providing INCRA with large funds and placing it under its supervision. Veiga et al. (2001) deepens the discussion of rural development as it probes and criticizes preexisting concepts governing rural life in Brazil and the dual functions of the Ministries of Agriculture and Agrarian Development.
27. Beneficiaries need to have five years of experience in agriculture to be eligible for loans.
28. Embrapa is part of the Ministry of Agriculture and runs the National Agricultural Research System, comprised of thirty-seven research units and a national network of extension services. Its more than 8,500 employees include over 2,000 researchers (many with doctoral degrees). One of its major achievements has been the development of disease-resisting soy bean seeds and agriculture, making it a key player in the dramatic expansion of soy bean production in Brazil. In existence since 1973, Embrapa has been fully supported by the federal government in the 1990s and through 2002. Basic information about Embrapa can be found in www.embrapa.br.

of regional integration. Negotiations with Argentina, Uruguay, and Paraguay in the late 1980s and 1990 led to its formal launching in 1991. Chile, a key prospect, became an associate member, together with Bolivia. Brazil made a major commitment to Mercosul and to enhanced economic relations with its neighbors. Hundreds of Brazilian firms launched subsidiaries in other Mercosul countries, while hundreds of Argentine firms invested in Brazil. Intraregional trade expanded. Renault and other multinationals opened plants in Brazil with an eye toward the Mercosul market. In fact, auto exports accounted for 35 percent of Brazilian exports to Argentina in 2000.[29] Brazil's new international stance builds on enhanced relations with other countries in South America and the European Union. A restructured export sector is emerging in the context of trade and investment policy linked to the country's new international role.[30] Brazil also viewed Mercosul and regional integration as vehicles for interbloc negotiations with the European Union and the Free Trade Area of the Americas. In June 1999 Brazil led the Rio Group to its first summit with the European Union. In 2000, the beginning of negotiations leading to the Free Trade Area of the Americas posed new challenges. In 2003, Brazil and the United States would jointly coordinate the negotiation process.

Cardoso framed his own general ideas about development as a "realistic utopia," aiming at the expansion of democracy and a middle road between the state and market. Brazilian policymakers linked the broad approach to the discussion of progressive governance by social democratic governments in Europe, including the Third Way articulated by sociologist Anthony Giddens and embraced by the Tony Blair administration in the United Kingdom. The emphasis is on balancing the independent roles of state, market, and civil society. In this social democratic perspective, policies focus on fiscal equilibrium and economic stability as well as on state reform and rebuilding of state capacity on basic social development issues, particularly around education, health, and social security (see chapter 4).[31] In this view, technology and the information revolution drive the process of globalization; science and tech-

29. See report in *Veja*, December 13, 2000.
30. The Brazilian government aimed at export levels of US$100 billion annually. Though export increased somewhat in the late 1990s, it was still only US$55 billion in 2000–2001. As a share of total world trade, Brazilian exports had decreased from approximately 1 percent to .8 percent in the twenty years before 2001. In late 2001, the Ministry of Development (MDIC) focused heavily on export promotion, a task for which a new chamber, Gacex, was legally formed. See Antônio Ermírio de Moraes, "Menos burocracia, mais empregos e mais divisas," *Folha de S. Paulo*, September 30, 2001.
31. For a discussion of Cardoso's program in terms of European social democracy see Vilmar Faria and Eduardo Graeff (2000). Cardoso attended the Third Way or progressive governance meetings in Florence (November 1999) and Berlin (June 2000) (see Fernando Henrique Cardoso, "O significado da reunião de Berlin," *Folha de S. Paulo*, June 1, 2000). See also *II Forum Global: Democratic State and Governance in the XXst Century* (Brasil, Ministério de Planejamento, Orçamento e Gestão, 2001).

nology, coupled with basic education to train or retrain the labor force, are hence of vital importance. For a country such as Brazil, the state has to concern itself with economic development, even if defining precise roles remains at issue and the adoption of a traditional industrial policy may be out of the question. The federal government's focus on promoting export-oriented production, small and medium firms, competitiveness, macroeconomic conditions, and the like is likely to endure.

The central government of the 1990s reinvigorated several institutions to achieve its development goals. BNDES, the Planning Ministry, Banco do Nordeste, and Sebrae play particularly important roles in development policy. BNDES, the country's development bank, began a new phase during the Cardoso administration. Founded in 1952 to finance and support the development objectives of Brazil's central government, the bank concentrated on financing projects linked to infrastructure and industrialization during its first phase through the 1970s. A second phase of decreasing budgets and an uncertain mission from the 1980s through 1993 came about in the context of crises associated with the national debt, fiscal imbalances, and inflation. The 1993 stabilization program and the presumption that it would create conditions for a new development strategy ushered in a new phase in the bank's history. Its budget increased 300 percent from 1994 through 1997, largely to accelerate the investment rate, privatization, and exports. BNDES's budget of R$18 billion in 1997 was the largest ever in real terms. A special secretariat was created to promote exports. Meanwhile, the bank streamlined its operations, drastically reducing red tape and embracing norms of transparency and flexibility.[32] The ministries concerned with development and infrastructure include those focused on planning, development, and national integration—with those in the areas of communications, mines and energy, and transportation also being relevant. The Ministry of Education and the Ministry of Health have received particular attention in the framework of social development.

Banco do Brasil and Petrobrás experienced processes of managerial modernization that increased their overall effectiveness. The deregulatory scheme introduced by Petrobrás, subject of a great deal of criticism in the past, is now considered as a factor in its becoming Brazil's first large multinational firm.

Responding in part to calls for a more assertive development policy, the central government inaugurated a new Ministry of Development (MDIC) in 1998.[33] Its mission was to promote industrial production and exports. MDIC

---

32. The BNDES website contains extensive documentation of its activities [www.bndes.br.gov]. Martins (1985) and Campos (1994) provide historical background on this institution. The BNDES operated with considerable operational autonomy and professional effectiveness during the Cardoso administration (see Suely Caldas, "O olho grande no BNDES," *Estado de S. Paulo*, September 15, 2002).

was seen at first as a tool for developmentalists, though its goal to promote competitiveness in the context of industrial restructuring and liberalized trade was short of what they had demanded. In the end, export promotion emerged as its key function. Of several subagencies within this entity, Camex, the trade council or Foreign Trade Council, was perhaps the most important one historically. Other agencies and programs included the export zone of Manaus and a few national institutes concerned with industrial property and industrial quality. Of the new programs launched in 1999 or after, Entrepreneurial Brazil and related programs to promote entrepreneurship at the grassroots level spent billions of *reais* to provide training, advisory services, and financing to smaller firms.[34] Increasing exports and encouraging grassroots entrepreneurship to promote development were important facets of the Cardoso administration's development policy.

During the 1990s, Brazil remained one of the few Latin American countries with a planning ministry concerned with designing and implementing a national development plan. The Planning Ministry was reorganized in the context of the goals of the 2000–2003 pluriannual plan (*Avança Brasil*). That plan was based on a large-scale project aimed at identifying the most important geographic corridors or axes of national integration and development.[35] The nine axes cross the borders of traditional administrative units. Each was to attract investments appropriate to the region to eliminate or reduce obstacles to development in infrastructure, social development (health, education, housing, and sanitation), science and technology, and the environment. Proposed investments of US$165 billion for the 2000–2007 period were to come from the federal government at the approximate rate of US$10 billion per year, with the rest to come from the private sphere.

Sebrae was created in 1990 to support small-scale entrepreneurship.[36] Small and medium-size firms were largely targeted because of their role in

33. The new Ministry of Development, Industry, and Trade (MDIC) was formed out of the old Ministry of Industry and Commerce. Many observers felt that a more assertive development policy would ensue in Cardoso's second term, as stabilization became consolidated in 1993–1997.
34. Other programs were Custo Brazil (late 1990s), the Competitiveness Forum (2000), PBQP (1990s), an export-promotion program (1998), and another to reduce tariffs on imported capital goods.
35. President Fernando Henrique Cardoso's 2002 "Message to the Congress," his eighth and last, provides a simplified presentation of the focus on the axes of integration and development (Brasil, Presidente 2002, 449–57). The nine axes—Northern Arch, Madeiras-Amazon, Araguaia-Tocantins, West, TransNortheastern, São Francisco, Southeast, and South—are defined as territorial spaces delimited in terms of transportation and urban networks as well as dynamic centers and ecosystems. This scheme and its 952 projects place some emphasis on Brazil's western and northern interior as well as the densely populated Southeast, Northeast, and South. These plans also seek to aid Brazil's contact with South American countries, to include the integration of the region (see Brasil, Presidente 2002, 459–62).

job creation, but also because of their potential significance in export promotion and technological innovation. Sebrae is a semipublic entity financed with a .3 percent levy on the payroll of large and medium firms, more than half of them in the industrial sector. With a budget of R$1.4 billion in 1998, this organization is an important mechanism to implement export-promotion and other government policies. By law, the government appoints nine of the thirteen members of its governing board, with the large confederations having the remaining four votes, a legacy of the corporatist system under which it came to life. This agency channels funds and programs through state-level branches in each state, according to population size and social security collected in that state. Sebrae has developed an urban and county focus. It supports businesses in the industrial, commercial, and service sectors.[37] Though the Cardoso government did not create Sebrae, it helped shape its goals and role.

Brazilian development remains deeply affected by regional and local dynamics. Sudene and Sudam, two key development agencies in the old model, became mired in shady practices and bureaucracy and came to be viewed with great suspicion by most Brazilians. With their substantial downgrading in 2001 (see chapter 7), other actors and the new agencies created to take their place gained importance. The Banco do Nordeste, the regional development bank focused on the Northeast, experienced in the 1990s a restructuring comparable to that of BNDES, to focus on microentrepreneurship and local development. Meanwhile, states and even some units of local government have enacted development policies of their own.[38] Brazilian

36. Bonelli (2001). Of the 4.9 million firms created in 1990–1999, 2.7 million were microenterprises, according to Sebrae. As could be expected, the Southeast accounted for 46.4 percent of the 475,000 firms created in 1999. The breakdown for other regions was 20.8 percent for the south, 17 percent for Northeast, 10.2 percent for Center-West, and 5.5 percent for the North (see Sebrae website: www.sebrae.com.br).
37. The Sebrae system employed 4,600 individuals directly and another 2,200 via subcontracting in 2001 (Bonelli 2001). Its budget that year—R$1.2 billion—was spent on providing information, training, and orientation. Sebrae maintains a fund to provide complementary guarantees to commercial credit applications by small-scale entrepreneurs. In 2001, Sebrae serviced 3 million clients, up from 2.3 million the previous year. That year, the state of São Paulo accounted for 22 percent of the cases serviced, with second-placed Minas Gerais receiving 8.2 percent, and third-placed Rio de Janeiro receiving 7.8 percent.
38. Since the early part of the twentieth century, for example, the state of São Paulo promoted extensive road building and infrastructure expansion with an eye toward its own development. São Paulo managed to maintain its own development projects even during the centralizing military regime and continued to do so during the post-1985 democracy. Other units in the southern and southeastern parts of the country have mobilized internal resources to that effect, particularly after the decentralized federalism was deepened by the 1988 constitution (see Montero 1998a, 1998b, 2001). While those in the Northeast have been more likely to rely on resources from the federal government, they too have taken major initiatives on their own (for example, Tendler 1997). For subnational development policies, see also Montero (2001)

development in effect responds to diverse impulses at different levels. Subnational efforts call for separate treatment from national or supranational ones.[39]

Toward a Preliminary Assessment

The perspective of the early years of the new century only allows for a preliminary assessment of the Brazilian reform drive.[40] Reforms in education, health, and other critical systems, as well as those bearing on social capital and institutional change, will require several years to render mature results. Moreover, aspects of the old regime linger and continue to affect performance; it may take considerable time to overcome the legacies of statism, corporatism, and clientelism. Another important caveat is that external shocks and crises continue to affect the Brazilian economy and the reform process. A considerably longer perspective and more methodologically sophisticated analyses in each of the major policy areas will eventually yield a fuller assessment than the approximation now possible.

Still, there is substantial evidence of change and accomplishment. Stopping inflation and creating a more stable economic policy environment, major accomplishments in their own rights, are essential to economic recovery under a new economic model. Macroeconomic conditions and fiscal practices existed by 2001–2002 that, if maintained by subsequent governments, would provide the basis for sustained long-term growth. The approach and measures advanced since the mid-1990s provide the bases for a new development strategy, even if the emphasis on stabilization might have prevented giving social policy the priority it deserves (see chapter 4). Main elements of the fledgling approach include the modernization and refocusing of the state apparatus; a larger role for private capital, both national and foreign; the promotion of microentrepreneurship; decentralization and local development; partnership with civil society; investments in infrastructure; openness, export promotion, and a new role in the international economy.

39. In that regard, there are also signs of important problems with certain policies to promote local economic development. Critics of fiscal wars point out that they lower tax receipts for states, benefit the largest regional economies, benefit multinational corporations and automobile assembly plants, and that benefits probably do not exceed the costs of such programs. The government has attempted to limit such practices, but pressure from the less developed Brazilian states has blocked federal action.
40. Useful preliminary assessments of the reforms of the 1990s can be found in Baumann (1999b) and Lamounier and Figueiredo (2002).

FIGURE 6-2. Economic Performance, 1980–2001

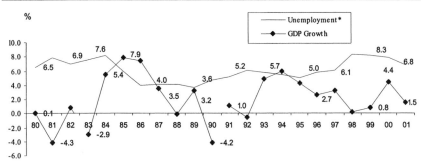

Source: Central Bank
* Unemployment: annual average of the monthly open unemployment rate (30 days).

Expertise has expanded within the civil service—the Finance Ministry, the Central Bank, the Planning Ministry, BNDES, Banco do Nordeste, and related agencies in the economic area. The emerging approach in these and other development institutions reflects a new definition of the role of government, the focus on realistic goals, and the need to curtail the clientelistic gigantism and dirigisme traditionally associated with the Brazilian state. Statism was discredited by its proclivity to economic and political instability. Repeated failures to address the challenges of inflation and the promise of durable economic growth and social equity reverberate in policy circles.

State reform has been a major dimension of the restructuring process. Privatization and liberalization have meant a broader sphere of action for private actors. New patterns of ownership and entrepreneurship are firming up in such key sectors as steel, paper and cellulose, fertilizers, chemicals, petrochemicals, mining, and railroads, telecommunications, and energy.[41] In part to attract modern technology, the economy has been opened up to foreign capital.[42] Such statistics bespeak Brazil's appeal to international investors, as the country redefines its integration into the international economy.

Advances have come at a substantial cost, while Brazil remains vulnerable to external shocks. Measured as income per capita, economic development has been sinuous (see fig. 6-2). The growth rate of 2.7 percent in 1996 was

41. This process helped accelerate the shift toward new forms of corporate ownership and governance, away from the family-owned firm. One study of the 100 largest firms showed that foreign capital grew from 26.9 percent in 1990 to 37.2 percent in 1997, while firms owned by local families decreased from 22.6 percent to 16.5 percent and government ownership changed from 38 percent to 21 percent. The other expanding form of governance was shared ownership with minority control, which jumped from 5 percent to 19 percent. Nelson Siffert Filho (1998). See also "The Buying and Selling of Brazil," *The Economist*, November 9, 1996.

TABLE 6-2. Brazil's Trade Patterns, 1990–2001

Year	1990	1991	1992	1993	1994	1995	1996	1997	1998	1999	2000	2001[a]
Openness[b]	5.5	6.5	7.3	7.4	7.1	6.8	6.5	7.0	6.9	9.2	9.3	11.3
Exports[c]	6.7	7.8	9.2	9.0	8.0	6.6	6.2	6.6	6.5	9.0	9.3	11.6
Imports[d]	4.4	5.2	5.3	5.9	6.1	7.1	6.9	7.4	7.3	9.3	9.4	11.0
Trade[e]	10.8	10.6	15.2	13.3	10.5	-3.3	-5.6	-6.8	-6.6	-1.3	-0.7	2.6

Source: MDIC
a. Estimated.
b. Economic openness is measured by the sum of exports and imports, divided by GDP.
c. Exports Free on Board (FOB) measured as a percentage of GDP.
d. Imports Free on Board (FOB) measured as a percentage of GDP.
e. Trade Balance in US$ billion.

considerably lower than the 4.2 percent of 1995 or the 5.7 percent of 1994. Though it increased in 1997, by 1998 it was close to zero, and it was just 0.5 in 1999. After recovery in 2000, it relapsed into mediocre growth in 2001 and 2002. With external financial pressures mounting in the context of the 2002 elections, the outlook for the immediate future was less than rosy. National and international investors worried about what a Workers' Party victory would mean.

Brazilian industrialists are anxious about their ability to compete. Brazil's role in world trade stagnated in the 1990s, notwithstanding the modest opening of the economy (table 6-2). Brazil's outward strategy involving Mercosul experienced a series of setbacks that added to rising anxiety about the country's process of reinsertion into the global economy. First, Chile began to negotiate a bilateral free trade agreement as the Clinton administration was coming to a close, creating difficulties and disappointments for Brazil. Chile's much lower tariff levels were incompatible with those of Mercosul, but Brazil had thought it would be possible to surmount those difficulties. Chile's decision to in effect speed up negotiations leading to the Free Trade Area of the Americas clashed with Brazil's intention to slow that process. Argentina would pose more formidable challenges. Argentina had fought inflation by pegging the peso to the dollar during the Menem administration. Once Brazil embraced a free-floating exchange rate in 2000, Brazil's currency would tend to depreciate in response to shocks (see table 2-3), while

42. The opening of the economy has led to a marked increase in the presence of foreign corporations. In the six years prior to mid-2000, 1,100 Brazilian firms were sold to multinational corporations. The presence of foreign involvement in the economy tripled in ten years, from 8 percent of GDP to 20 percent. The degree of Brazil's openness to international capital was moderate, as compared to 23 percent for Canada, 24 percent for England and Sweden, 29 percent for Australia, or 27 percent for China. Still, Brazilians were shocked by the speed of the process. See Daniela Pinheiro and Eduardo Oinegue, "Está quase tudo a juros no banco," *Veja*, May 24, 2000.

that of Argentina would maintain its value—a situation benefiting Brazil's exports, since its goods would be cheaper than those of Argentina. Argentina felt it had to adjust its tariff structure. As a serious fiscal crisis mounted in Argentina after early 2001, that tension produced a series of criticisms of the Brazilian monetary and trade regime by Argentina's finance minister, Domingo Cavallo.[43] These setbacks paled in comparison with the financial crisis in Argentina and the collapse of the currency board several months later.[44]

Doubts and fear about Brazil's readiness for further trade liberalization intensified with the approaching negotiations on the Free Trade Area of the Americas and the new multilateral negotiations in the World Trade Organization. Brazil's economic size and position compared to that of North America gave reasons for concern. Though Brazil saw itself as the colossus of the south in a challenging relationship with that of the north, the North American Free Trade Agreement had seemingly strengthened the latter. More important, since Brazil's economy was much more closed than those of the United States, Canada, or Mexico (see table 6-3), it would be making relatively larger concessions, while the degree of industrial competitiveness was more uncertain. As signatory of the 1994 agreement to create a Free Trade Area of the Americas (FTAA), Brazil was committed to support negotiations to further open the economy. But internal support was problematic. Important leaders wondered if trade liberalization was a good thing for Brazil. Only 49 percent of business executives supported FTAA, according to a *Folha de S. Paulo* poll of 2001. In IEDI's view, free trade had been turned into a pernicious ideology.[45] Brazilian exporters were anxious about the extra burdens

TABLE 6-3. Trade in Largest FTAA Countries, 2000

Countries	GDP (US$ bi)	Exports (US$ bi)	Exports (% GDP)	Imports (US$ bi)	Imports (% GDP)
USA	9,882.9	782.4	7.9	1,258.0	12.7
Canada	689.5	277.2	40.2	249.1	36.1
Brazil	587.6	53.6	9.0	55.8	9.4
Mexico	574.5	166.5	29.0	174.5	30.4

Source: World Bank, *World Development Report 2002*

43. In addition, Argentine policy seemed to be leaning toward a bilateral accord with the United States such as that sought by Chile and to support the speed up of negotiations leading to the Free Trade Area of the Americas.
44. From a longer term perspective, the adoption of a fluctuating exchange rate, coupled with the sharp devaluation of the Argentine peso, brought Argentina and Brazil into a more compatible policy framework.
45. See interview with IEDI director Sergio Gomes de Almeida at www.uoo.com.br/fsp/dinheiro/fi1006200107.htm, 2001.

imposed on them by an inadequate taxation system, red tape, relative technological and infrastructural backwardness, limited financial support, and a
poorly trained labor force. They worried about the United States' active protection of sectors in which Brazil was clearly competitive, such as orange
juice and steel. According to José Serra, notwithstanding the United States'
average tariffs of 4 percent, Brazil's top fifteen export products to the United
States faced 46 percent tariffs, while the top fifteen U.S. exports to Brazil
paid 14 percent. Brazil had few reasons to participate in the FTAA unless the
United States negotiated nontariff barriers, antidumping laws, and agrarian
policy. Brazilian officials also worried about hidden protectionism in the
social, environmental, and labor conditionalities that might be included in
trade agreements.

The strain within Mercosul and the FTAA timetable fueled Brazilian concern about the speed at which it would continue to open its economy. Mercosul weakened just when the agenda for negotiating the FTAA called for a
strong common front. The economic and financial crisis in Argentina, the
source of the main pressures on Mercosul, made Brazil's trade policy more
vulnerable. The new government taking office in 2003 faced a truly formidable agenda regarding Brazil's international role.

The external sector posed even greater challenges to designing a new
approach to development. Though the stabilization and fiscal adjustment policies laid foundations for renewed growth and a new development model,
certain features and consequences of that approach through 1999—the overvalued currency, high interest rates, the increasing public debt, and a current
accounts deficit—blocked aggressive growth and social development policies. Success in fiscal adjustment and the adoption of a free-floating currency
later that year created conditions for lower interest rates and export expansion, but the Brazilian economy continued to show signs of vulnerability. The
energy crisis and the Argentine collapse of 2001, internal political turbulence, and the lingering effects of financial crisis after 1998, forced Cardoso's
second presidential term to markedly tone down its more ambitious development goals. Plans through 2003 aimed at an increasingly modest annual
growth rate.[46] But the Cardoso years would come to an end with a frustrated
development agenda.

The debate surrounding the 2002 elections provided a major test of support
for the reform process, as Brazilians sought to draw a balance between
accomplishment and frustration with regard to the policies pursued since the
early 1990s. Social development joined economic growth as a top political
issue (see chapter 4). The *Plano Real* had led to a substantial decrease in pov-

46. The external shocks from the September 11 attacks and the worsening international
economy led to lower growth estimates and performance for 2001 and 2002.

erty right after its implementation, but Brazilian authorities were unable to make a major dent in poverty after that, and inequality remained very high. Such policies as the stabilization program, adjustments in minimum income, and others did lead to noteworthy reductions in poverty right after the inception of the Cardoso presidency and the launching of the *real*. In addition, accomplishments in health, education, and the basic dimensions of human development put Brazil on track in terms of a modern approach to social development. But Brazilians were more alarmed than ever by the country's social and economic problems. Social and economic development emerged as major issues in the 2002 elections and were guaranteed to remain top priorities in the years to come.

In summary, the reforms took bold steps toward the demise of the old autarkic model and laid foundations for the construction of a new development strategy. The achievements included stabilization, but also encompassed major movement toward privatization, the opening of the economy, state and social security reform, deregulation, and trade liberalization. The privatized companies were sold at good prices, and tax revenues generated by these companies are equivalent to their revenues in the preprivatization period.[47] The Brazilian state then moved toward a modern regulatory role in privatized and other sectors.[48] The country as a whole also opened a fresh approach to human and social development, with noteworthy improvements in education and health, decentralization, and the devolution of functions to subnational governments and various stakeholders in civil society. Capping a serious and innovative agrarian reform, the government had laid bases for an approach to rural development that also relied heavily on decentralization, local participation, and partnership with the third sector.

Perhaps more important, the Cardoso administration represents a turning point with regard to the articulation of a new vision and agenda for the country. With multiple changes in progress, Brazil is in the middle of a major transformation. Should the reforms and related change continue to advance and lead to economic growth, they will represent an epochal change in the country's approach to development.[49] However, it is equally clear that the government succeeding that of Cardoso will have a major responsibility in making adjustments to the reform process, addressing unresolved and difficult obstacles, and defining the new Brazilian approach to development of the twenty-first century.

47. Luís Nassif, "Os acertos de FHC," *Folha de S. Paulo*, October 10, 2002.
48. Landau (2002) provides a critical overview of the fledgling regulatory framework.
49. Still, important figures, such as economist Celso Furtado, continued to attack the liberalization drive and defend statism. At the political and ideological level, the Workers' Party and other leftist parties, as well as sectors of the PMDB, advocated or leaned toward state-centered economic models, though they had not really articulated a coherent alternative through the end of 2002.

The Development State, Again?

New ideas, shared by many policy-oriented intellectuals and politicians, might have been key to the adoption of liberalizing reforms in Brazil. But they guaranteed neither operational definitions of the new development approach nor broad and sustained support for it. The evolution of the development debate during the crisis of 1997–1999 through the dynamics of succession in 2002 helps address both questions as well as the context shaping the reform process. If external shocks or crises had contributed to statist reforms in past decades, would they pull in the same direction now? Would a critical mass of organized actors continue to defend the liberalizing reforms?

The international financial crises at the turn of the century, from the spreading Asian crisis of 1997–1998 through the Argentine collapse in 2001–2002, placed the debate about development models in a new light. In particular, the spreading financial collapse posed new issues about broad, market-oriented strategies in emerging economies such as Brazil's.[50] Many blamed structural adjustment packages and the underlying economic policies associated with the International Monetary Fund and the World Bank for increasing vulnerability to external shocks. Crises often resulted from the interaction between international financial conditions and domestic fiscal dynamics. Yet, the crises fueled resistance to globalization and liberalization.[51] In 1997–1998, as the crisis spread from Asia to Russia, the international financial media focused on Brazil, casting it as the next most endangered emergent economy. Indeed, the crisis had a potentially catastrophic impact. Brazil's exchange rate might not withstand the pressure, but letting it fluctuate under those circumstances could lead to a sharp financial crisis and the return of inflation. Debate intensified. As the government pondered a response, the situation worsened. The adjustment measures announced in previous months and years appeared insufficient in the changing context. Electoral competition and the early stages of the crisis had helped reawaken opposition to the liberalizing reforms. *Folha de S. Paulo,* other publications, and several journalists joined their voices to those demanding more aggressive growth and development policies. The government defended the thesis that the crisis was temporary

50. The term "emergent economies" was derived from "emergent markets." The latter referred to countries with sufficient magnitude and dynamic potential to attract substantial foreign capital to their equities markets. Within the international financial community itself, some wondered if the orthodox adjustment policies and the underlying models it had prescribed fueled further deterioration and turmoil.
51. Political reactions to crises seemingly induced by globalization included the overthrow of the Indonesian government by opponents of the economic model. Venezuela elected a new government with an antiliberalization platform. The sharp contractions were taken to challenge even the long-term soundness of the economic models of East Asia, cases that had been considered paradigms for development states since the late 1960s.

and that macroeconomic stabilization and adjustment were creating the conditions for growth to resume in the near future.

Within the government itself, the debate pitted developmentalists against monetarists—those favoring massive incentives and programs to stimulate growth versus others skeptical of such measures because of the threat they posed to stabilization and fiscal equilibrium. For a while, even the governing coalition seemed to be in disarray. With their political eyes on municipal elections in 2000 and general elections in 2002, some allies distanced themselves from official policy, perceiving Cardoso to have suffered a fatal wound. The opposition intensified its attacks, sensing a moment of high vulnerability for the governing coalition. Important sectors of the media joined in the assault. Pressure built for an economic policy oriented to growth and job creation. With demands coming from trade unions and trade associations, the opposition, and the president's own party, the depth and durability of the reform process seemed suddenly in question.

But by early 1999, the threat of immediate crisis dissipated. The *real* bottomed out in February and began to firm up. More important, inflation remained low in spite of the higher exchange rate (fig. D-1 and table 2-3). Still, the internal debate persisted. It came into the open in May of that year. Against the backdrop of political effervescence and the perception that the Cardoso administration might be weakened politically, both the PFL and the PSDB held national conventions in April-May 1999. Potential candidates in the 2002 presidential elections began to maneuver, often with public statements at odds with official policy. A four-day forum organized by BNDES further focused national attention on the development debate. A vigorous internal exchange ensued from a public statement by ex-Minister of Communications Luiz Carlos Mendonça de Barros calling openly for a change in policy from stabilization to development.[52] Finance Minister Pedro Malan and Central Bank president Armínio Fraga, the key officers responsible for monetary stability, responded firmly and fast. Dismissing the new developmentalism as an anachronistic throwback to the 1950s, they argued that development without a stable macroeconomic environment would be a return to past

52. As head of BNDES, Mendonça de Barros had been seen as leading a developmentalist faction within the government and as the future head of a new Ministry of Development in the second Cardoso administration. Though subsequent investigations failed to demonstrate wrongdoing on his part, illegal wiretappings seeming to implicate his office in granting favors to friends forced his resignation in late 1998. His election as a vice president of the PSDB in May 1999 returned him to the political scene, now as a strong ally of developmentalist Mário Covas, the governor of the state of São Paulo. As soon as he won the new party role, Mendonça de Barros gave major newspaper interviews pressing for a shift in policy away from monetarism. The first was to *Folha de S. Paulo*. Another appears in "Mendonça de Barros rebate crítica do ministro," *O Estado de S. Paulo*, May 22, 1999. Mendonça de Barros's comeback was cut short when in the following week a new scandal broke with allegations about improprieties in the privatization program.

mistakes, that much had still to be accomplished to complete structural adjustment, and that economic development should largely be the result of private initiative.[53]

The media framed the debate as one between developmentalists and monetarists. Ministers or ex-ministers José Serra, Paulo Renato Souza, Celso Lafer, and Luiz Carlos Bresser Pereira were in the first group.[54] The broader developmentalist coalition included business leaders Antonio Ermírio de Moraes and FIESP president Horácio Lafer Piva.[55] Malan and Fraga were portrayed as the leaders of monetarism.[56]

The Cardoso administration sought a balanced response. Pimenta da Veiga, one of the president's key political coordinators, staked out a middle course, supporting the idea of a more explicit development strategy, lower interest rates, and "decisive political action" compatible with stabilization.[57] Meanwhile, the federal government chartered the Ministry of Development, Industry, and Trade to give more thrust to its development program.[58] Celso Lafer, its first minister, moved to set the agenda and allay business anxieties. His interview with a leading newspaper emphasized that government policy could play a supportive role in enhancing the export sector.[59] In Lafer's view, the devaluation of the *real,* lower imports, and a resurgence of industrial pro-

53. Rita Tavares e Rodney Vergili, "Malan volta a responder a 'desenvolvimentistas,'" *O Estado de S. Paulo,* May 22, 1999.
54. José Serra and Paulo Renato Souza had full cabinet tenure in both of Cardoso's terms. Luiz Carlos Bresser Pereira ran the Ministry of State Reform in the first term, while Celso Lafer served briefly in the first term and returned in 2001 as minister of foreign relations.
55. "Reforma democratizada," *Jornal do Brasil,* May 22, 1999.
56. Other political actors joined the debate. Industrialists called for Malan to give them more attention, complaining of presumed advantages to banking. Alleging that *paulistas* and the PSDB wanted to monopolize economic policy, PFL president Antonio Carlos Magalhães rose to defend Malan and his policies (Nelson de Sá, "ACM e os paulistas," *Folha de S. Paulo,* May 22,1999; Wilson Tosta, "ACM acusa Mendonça de tentar derrubar Malan," *O Estado de S. Paulo,* May 22, 1999).
57. Eliane Cantanhêde, "Pimenta quer crescimento e estabilidade," *Folha de S. Paulo,* May 21, 1999. Brazilian newspapers widely reported and commented on speeches made at BNDES's Eleventh National Forum of Advanced Studies. Titled "The Global Crisis and the Brazilian Crisis," this meeting took place in Rio de Janeiro, May 17–20, 1999. Rubens Ricupero, ex-minister of finance and head of UNCTAD, took the same side as Bresser Pereira in defending a new national policy oriented to national development and attacked the notion of dependence on foreign capital and finances.
58. "Desenvolvimento: Celso Lafer defende eixos regionais," *Folha de S. Paulo,* April 14, 1999. Besides tax reform, the program emphasized regional axes, an approach reminiscent of the plans of the Juscelino Kubitscheck administration.
59. "Meu DNA vem da produção," *Jornal do Brasil,* May 22, 1999. Lafer, whose Cornell Ph.D. dissertation focused on the history of planning and state action in Brazil, compared Cardoso's two terms to those of two Old Republic (1889–1930) presidents from São Paulo. To Lafer, Cardoso's second term was comparable to that of development-oriented Rodrigues Alves (1902–1906), while the first term was like that of Campos Salles (1898–1902) in emphasizing financial and political equilibrium. These two past presidents had been the architects of the relatively liberal Old Republic.

duction based on de facto import substitution created opportunities for a new model, at least with respect to such sectors as auto parts, toys, clothes, shoes, and machines. The higher exchange rate favored exports. It also created opportunities for industrial promotion via import substitution, following the great expansion of imports that had accompanied the stronger currency. Development policy could hence go beyond stabilization, privatization, trade liberalization, infrastructure, basic social policy to build human capital (health and education), and bureaucratic efficiency.

Soon, the debate about development undermined key leaders. Lafer only lasted a few weeks as minister, as did his successor, Clóvis Carvalho. *Paulista* businessman Alcides Lopes Tápias, the third appointee, took charge of the Ministry of Development in mid 1999 and moved to develop a pragmatic focus on concrete economic issues rather than on grand questions about development strategy. The ministry would focus on export promotion, expanding trade credits, and acting as facilitator to complete the restructuring and modernization of key industrial sectors such as steel, paper and cellulose, and petrochemicals, and supporting relatively small firms. Sergio Amaral, Brazi¹'s ambassador to England and past government spokesperson during Cardoso's first term, would become the fourth appointee, confirming export promotion as a key priority during his tenure in office.[60] A big political question was whether Brazil would adhere to the kind of traditional industrial policy demanded by FIESP.[61]

In effect, the Cardoso administration's approach to development retained a dual character, seeking to balance the views of the two currents of thought in his government. As explained by ex-minister Bresser Pereira, the two wings could be called "internationalists" and "nationalists." The first centered in the Finance Ministry. The nationalists were in such bureaucracies as Itamaraty and the ministries in health, education, and other social areas.[62] Many Brazil-

60. Amaral was named minister of development in 2001.
61. E. Nogueira, F. Oliveira, L. Morais, and S. Emerick, "Fiesp ataca proposta de FH," *Globo On,* June 6, 2000. In mid-2000, when President Cardoso seemed to defend the thesis of a thirty-five-hour workweek, FIESP's president declared the latter "inopportune," claiming that an industrial policy should be Brazil's first priority. Cardoso made the statement about a shorter workweek during a trip to France, a country that had reduced its unemployment rate with such an approach. Cardoso asked trade unions and business to debate the idea, but Força Sindical, CUT, and other trade unions urged the president to take political initiative in advancing the proposal for a shorter workweek. Though the Brazilian constitution limited the workweek to forty-four hours, longer hours were widespread. A reduction from forty-four hours to forty would generate approximately 1.7 million jobs, but just working within the forty-four hour legal limit could generate 3 million jobs, according to CUT (see Liliana Pinheiro, "Hora extra sustenta recuperação da economia," *O Estado de S. Paulo,* June 6, 2000). Shortly after Cardoso's statement, trade unions organized demonstrations and work stoppages in favor of a shorter workweek ("CUT acampa na Fiesp por redução de jornada," *Globo On,* June 7, 2000). FIESP firmly opposed the notion of a shorter workweek.

ians had expected that Cardoso's second term would focus on the adoption of an active development role after the first term's success with stabilization and fiscal adjustment. But such a policy remained elusive. Pressures on the *real* from a series of unexpected problems—Argentina's lingering fiscal crisis, disarray in Brazil's ruling coalition, and a profound energy crisis—virtually ruled out any major change in policy through 2001.

As the Cardoso administration faced its last weeks in office, it was clear that the next government would play a critical role in confirming the course so arduously set since 1994. The debate about the role of the state in promoting development had begun to flare up again in late 2001. Economic development emerged as a key national issue in the October 2002 elections.[63]

Various opposition parties claimed to be the party of growth and development, often arguing that the fiscal priorities associated with the Cardoso team were at fault for the country's woes. The country needed an active government able to speed economic growth and social development. That was the general tone of the positions of most aspiring presidential candidates, including frontrunner Luiz Inácio "Lula" da Silva, Rio's governor Anthony Garotinho, and Ciro Gomes, a former governor of Ceará.[64] Early in the process of succession, even presidential hopefuls from the reform coalition itself sought distance from the policies identified with Minister of Finance Pedro Malan,[65] often calling for policies aimed at growth and job creation. Candidates of Cardoso's own PSDB saw the party's identity as a progressive political force hinging on the social and developmental character of the 2002 political platform. Minister of Health and leading aspirant José Serra defended the thesis of direct state action to advance a policy of national development and joined in dismissing the idea that the market would by itself bring about development.[66] Ceará governor Tasso Jereissati maintained that the minister of finance, presumed to be neoliberal, had too much power and that the Ministry of Planning should expand its sphere of action to promote national development. Pedro Malan, often mentioned as a prospective presidential candidate,

62. "Bresser critica a equipe econômica," *Folha de S. Paulo,* June 1, 2000. Bresser-Pereira was minister of administration and state reform (1995–1998) and, briefly, science and technology (1999) during Cardoso's presidency. He was a member of the Brazilian delegation to the June 2000 meeting on progressive governance held in Germany, together with Celso Lafer, Roberto da Matta, Lídia Goldstein, Sérgio Abranches, Eduardo Graeff, Vilmar Faria, and Cardoso himself.

63. In a poll just days before the October 6 election, voters were deciding how to vote in the presidential elections in terms of the following criteria: economic development (36.5 percent of voters), social and construction programs (19.8 percent), maintenance of the *Plano Real* (15.8 percent), and agrarian reform (15.2 percent) (see "Sensus: desenvolvimento econômico é principal critério de eleitor," *O Globo* 9/30/2002 [http://oglobo.globo.com/oglobo/especiais/eleicoes2002/plantao/45236943.htm]).

64. See, for example, Tina Vieira and Sonia Carneiro, "Mais presença do Estado na economia," *Jornal do Brasil,* October 21, 2001. One of the PT proposals to reduce poverty was a guaranteed minimum income program (No Hunger, or "Fome Zero").

found himself on the defensive, but remained loyal to stabilization and fiscal discipline through the end of Cardoso's government, and did not run for the presidency.

Cardoso sought to diminish the attacks on his policies and to delay the appearance of being a lame duck incumbent through early 2002. He argued forcefully that the selection of a candidate should take place in the second quarter of 2002, while insisting that several figures in the governing coalition might emerge as the official candidate (José Serra, Paulo Renato Souza, Pedro Malan, Tasso Jereissati, Roseana Sarney, or even others). He also embarked on a personal campaign to promote his own political standing. In October 2001, he had a highly successful trip to Europe. The visit included a well-received presentation at a major international conference on democracy in Madrid and an informal weekend meeting with the British prime minister in London. The culmination was a well-crafted speech at France's National Assembly, frequently interrupted by applause and ending with a standing ovation. The acclaim at the French Parliament put an international stamp of approval on Cardoso as a progressive, social democratic statesman. No other figure in Brazil could have hoped for a better performance.[67] Cardoso's speech at the United Nations shortly after his trip to Europe further elaborated and strengthened Brazil's demands for a world order more sensitive to emergent and developing countries, including the relaxation of protectionism against agricultural and other products from such countries. Brazil was a leader in the negotiations for three major trade agreements—Mercosul-Europe, the Free Trade Area of the Americas, and the World Trade Organization. Presidential diplomacy expanded Brazil's choices and leverage, as it cast an even broader argument in favor of solidarious globalization.

65. A new interview with Luiz Carlos Mendonça de Barros in late October 2001 emphasized a new offensive by the "developmentalism and industrial policy" group, an entity said to have been repeatedly defeated in the past by the "liberal orthodoxy group" led by Pedro Malan. Critical of current policy, Cardoso's former communications minister stated that the economic crisis prompted by the plight of the Argentine economy and of the energy sector (he might also have mentioned the worsening global slowdown after the terrorist attacks of September 11, 2001) had reconfirmed the need for active development policy. Barros suggested a convergence on this view on the part of sectors of the PSDB, PMDB, PT, and PFL. The interview appears in Fernando de Barros e Silva, "Sucessão no escuro: 2002 tira o desenvolvimentismo da toca," *Folha de S. Paulo*, October 28, 2001. A few days later, Luiz Carlos Mendonça de Barros's "Meu otimismo está voltando," *Folha de S. Paulo*, November 2, 2001, traces the internal struggles through Cardoso's two terms and closes affirming that Brazil's challenge ahead was not polarization, as advocated by sectors of the left, but sustained growth in the framework of a stable currency. Mendonça de Barros is editor and partner of the website "Primeira Leitura" and *República*, its related publication. He had close historical and ideological links to José Serra and the late Sérgio Mota, two of Cardoso's very close associates and leaders of the developmentalist faction.
66. For example, see speech at the May 2001 convention of the PSDB [www.camara. gov.br/jutahyjunior/discurso.html]. The PSDB website [www.psdb.org.br/] publishes many speeches by party leaders.

If international acclaim enhanced Cardoso's moral and intellectual legitimacy and his role as a statesman, it had the potential also to enlarge his role in the internal succession process and the durability of its economic policy. However, the president's international standing had a limited impact on domestic politics and internal factors continued to shape political dynamics and development policy.[68] The collapse of the reform coalition in 2001–2002 cast a shadow of doubt on the outcome of the upcoming elections.

Brazilians argued heatedly the merits of specific reforms and the country's economic model in the context of the October 2002 elections.[69] The centrality and intensity of the debate raised questions about whether Brazil had completed the intellectual adjustment or transition often associated with successful economic restructuring.[70] Political infighting surrounding the succession debate confirms strains in the original reformist alliance, as well as frustration with economic conditions. Lula and other opposition candidates spoke of changing the economic model.

The line of analysis elaborated in this volume would lead to the expectation of a balance between continuity and change in public policy, notwithstanding the political and ideological rhetoric about changing the economic model. Discernible in the electoral debate and among a critical mass of policymakers and intellectuals was a near consensus about the need to go beyond ideas that had governed Brazil from the 1930s to the 1990s, maintain main reforms already adopted, and support a core of reforms and ideas in the process of implementation.[71] Policy momentum had built up in several issue areas, based on the success of many of the new programs at various levels of the Brazilian federation and the constituencies that had formed around them. In addition, a political movement for reform had jelled as a major national political force in favor of a new approach.

67. Cardoso was the first Latin American head of state and only the tenth foreign leader to address the French National Assembly. Speaking in French, he argued eloquently for a world order with more solidarity, adequate mechanisms to address financial crises, debt relief for poor countries, the opening of markets in rich countries to agricultural goods from poorer ones, the democratization of the United Nations and international cooperation, sustainable development, a Palestine state and the fight against terrorism. The speech and commentary are found in *O Estado de S. Paulo*, October 31, 2001, and *Folha de S. Paulo*, October 31, 2001. (A complete Portuguese version of the speech is found at www.radiobras.gov.br/abrn/integras/01/integra_3010_1.htm). In Europe, *Le Monde* and *El País* published interviews with Cardoso, while *Le Figaro* and other French newspapers reported his visit. In the preceding days, *El País* had published several articles on Cardoso's intellectual role at the Madrid head-of-states conference on democratization.
68. Cardoso's performance at the French Parliament earned him praise from virtually all major Brazilian newspapers, including *Folha de S. Paulo*, which had virtually become an opposition newspaper (for example, see editorial "FHC em Paris," *Folha de S. Paulo*, November 1, 2001).
69. See chapter 7.
70. About intellectual adjustments to transition dynamics see Sola (1993a and 1993b), Bresser Pereira (1996, ch. 18), and chapter 7.

But it was up to the newly elected president and a new Congress to decide the fate of the liberalizing reforms of the 1990s and to decisively shape Brazil's development strategy. The PT and the PSDB, the two leading parties in terms of the race for presidency, had in effect experienced a recent evolution toward considerable convergence in actual policy. The PSDB and its main leaders, including Fernando Henrique Cardoso himself, retained a great deal of sympathy for the idea of assertive state action to advance economic and social goals, with candidate José Serra known as a leader of the "developmentalist" faction. More important, the Workers' Party, by far the most important opposition party during the Cardoso presidency, had shifted toward a considerably more moderate and centrist platform in the months before the 2002 elections.[72]

In terms of political ideas, conditions existed for the Brazilian political class as a whole to reconfigure itself around a new economic and state model regardless of which party gained the presidency. In addition, a number of business leaders endorsed the Lula candidacy, responding well to the PT's new moderate stance and shift from socialism to social democracy.[73] Notwithstanding their often critical tone or vagueness, the PT's platform and Lula's pronouncements called for specific reforms in taxation, fiscal surplus, export promotion, social security, labor relations, microentrepreneurship, the political system, and agrarian reform that seemed to differ only in detail from those initiated in the 1990s. The PT candidate did seem to highlight more decisively, at least in tone, a nationalist ideology based on animosity toward the Free Trade Area of the Americas, but even there the PT did not propose that Brazil should abandon the negotiations.[74]

71. The teams of specialists associated with virtually all frontrunners in the last weeks before the October 6 elections came to agree on such key points as maintaining specific inflation targets (*metas de inflação*) and stabilization as a priority, a fluctuating exchange rate, fiscal austerity, and a substantial primary budget surplus. See, for example, the document by seventeen opposition economists and social scientists convened by Princeton professor José Alexandre Scheinkman, a Brazilian economist affiliated with the Ciro Gomes campaign (in Fernando Dantas, "'Agenda perdida' tenta influir no debate eleitoral," *O Estado de S. Paulo*, September 15, 2002). Also in mid-September, economists at a major BNDES conference expressed similar points. The Workers' Party itself, the main leftist party, embraced a moderate platform that in effect differed only in detail with that of the official candidate José Serra or the Cardoso government.
72. Lula's "Carta ao povo brasileiro" of June 2002 marks the shift toward moderation, a message that Lula began to convey in public appearances earlier that year at the World Social Forum (Forum Social Mundial) held in Porto Alegre, when he and the PT argued that the struggle with regard to globalization was in favor of reforms favoring human and social development, rather than violent revolution to bring about socialism. See also note 3; "Cristãos-novos do capitalismo," *Veja*, September 25, 2002; João Gabriel de Lima e Thais Oyama, "A Rota de Lula para o poder," *Veja*, October 9, 2002; André Petri, "A volta que o mundo deu," *Veja*, October 9, 2002; "Do 'assambleismo' à defesa do pacto, a guinada de Lula," *O Estado de S. Paulo*, October 6, 2002.

If Brazil entered a period of political stability with, as many hoped, an eventual alliance between the PT and the PSDB, it would have auspicious political and ideological conditions to build a new development strategy on achievements and lessons of the recent past.

Conclusion: A Country in Transition

Upon Fernando Henrique Cardoso's election in 1994, prominent members of his party argued that at least two decades of sustained reform were necessary to put Brazil solidly on a new development course. If anything, they might have underestimated the task. Since 1990, the federal government had taken steps to define a new development regime. Considering the breadth and depth of the ideas and changes it implemented or proposed, the Cardoso government in particular represents a watershed in the emergence of a new approach to development in Brazil. Deregulation, trade liberalization, the opening of the economy, privatization, state and social security reform, and related reforms steered Brazil toward a new development strategy. However, too much remained to be accomplished in late 2002 to claim that a new development model was fully in place. By most accounts key reforms remained incomplete, as did the process of transition.

The Brazilian reforms of the 1990s aimed at liberalizing, modernizing, and opening the economy, while deepening the degree of pluralism in the political system. The reforms built on—and hence should be seen as part of—a broader transition born of the process of democratization started in 1985. Brazilian policymakers put forth important reforms in the late 1980s and early 1990s. But it was the Cardoso government in particular that articulated a coherent new vision of Brazilian society and cultivated a broad coalition to advance a package of reforms to reach it. It thereby deepened the multifaceted Brazilian transition to encompass shifts from inward-oriented dirigisme to a more open and liberalized economic regime and from corporatism to a plural and competitive civil society.

73. See, for example, "Eles 'lularam' na reta final: A poucos dias da eleição, empresarios descobrem uma súbita afinidade com o PT," *Veja*, October 2, 2002. This article referred to over 500 business figures, including a FIESP vicepresident and other business leaders, who supported the candidate of the Workers' Party. Lula had cultivated the support of industrialists, who felt that the Cardoso administration had opted for the financial sector over industry. According the story, industrialists also considered Lula to be a conciliator and the candidate most able to focus various sectors on a national project. See also A. Souza e Silva, "A onda vermelha: Cresce o número de empresários pesos pesados que aderem à campanha de Lula, *Istoé*, October 2, 2002. The latter identifies leaders of the Comitê de Empresarios Lula Presidente (the Lula for President Business Committee), which claimed the endorsement of 600 prominent business owners.
74. Lula labeled the FTAA as "annexationist" in the 2002 election debate.

The emphasis on the reform of the state toward decentralization and a larger role for civil society gives this transition a distinctive character. It also points to the difficulty of shifting economic models while bringing about massive political and institutional restructuring. Political and institutional pluralization increase the difficulty of creating durable reforms and having them bind Brazilians in a new compact. That perspective makes clear that national politics remains key to the emergence of a new development regime. Much would depend in both regards on the political dynamics setting in with the election of a new government in October 2002. The shape and deepening of the Brazilian reform process after 2002 depends on the leadership and political dynamics provided by the new government.

That the state remained quite large, taxation rates high, and tariffs relatively steep, while the country remained prone to fiscal imbalances and vulnerable to external shocks, does not invalidate the impact and achievements of the Cardoso government. As the twenty-first century began, the reforms were transforming Brazil in fundamental ways. That government contributed decisively to the Brazilian search for a coherent new approach to development by defining strategic goals and plans, organizing a series of specific projects, modernizing and decentralizing the state apparatus, creating more space and support for civil society, and articulating a framework to reposition Brazil's role in the international economy.

Achievements had at least as much to do with the practice of politics as with implementing a coherent package of liberalizing reforms. The Cardoso government's main concrete realizations—stabilization, privatization, openness to foreign investment, a new regulatory system, economic restructuring, and agrarian reform—owe to decisions and actions by the executive government as well as by such actors as members of Congress, the civil service, civil society, and subnational governments. In addition to returning a sense of normalcy to politics and policy-making from the turbulence that proceeded it, this government helped redefine the debate about development, set the tone for addressing it, engaged major political currents in the process of debate and implementation, and provided the country with a well-articulated social democratic option that differed sharply from the old dirigisme of the Vargas era and from statist proposals associated with Brazilian socialism.

Brazilian reformers are faced with the difficulties of governing and refocusing a large and complex country that has been susceptible to unpredictable elite behavior. They are caught in the furor of demands from the formidable array of forces and actors in civil society empowered by decentralized federalism, democratization, and related political changes. These reformers could take solace from the experience of other countries engaged in multiple transitions, where the emergence and consolidation of a new order has taken many years. The broader comparative framework suggests that the fate of reform and the consolidation of a new economic model depend not only on institutional and political factors, but also on palpable progress in advancing economic and social development. Reforms and politicians associated with recession and crisis will surely lose public support.

The comparative framework also indicates that, in an age of globalization, economic growth depends in part on external forces. The catastrophic or near-catastrophic impact of external shocks that Argentina, Brazil, and other countries experienced since 1997 suggests that considerable work is still necessary to fully understand and harness the forces of globalization in a positive manner. Enhanced international contact and exchange shapes national development patterns. Whether the impact is positive will depend in part on forms of international cooperation able to neutralize or mitigate the destructive aspects of globalization and make robust development strategies possible.

Internally, the fate of the fledgling development strategy will continue to be intertwined with conditions shaping state capabilities and political coherence—that is, with the ability of the polity to redefine itself. In this context, political skill and maturity will be essential to bring together political actors claiming to have widely divergent sets of interests and visions. The extent to which Brazilian democracy as a whole may be up to the task is explored in the next and final chapter.

CHAPTER 7   *Democracy,*
Realignment, and Reform

Brazil experienced changes of considerable magnitude from the 1980s through the early years of the new century. In particular, the reform process of the 1990s brought focus and depth to economic and social policy. The reform process also altered the role of the state and the dynamics of political society as it embraced political and institutional pluralism, the new civil society, and changing state-society relations. Together, these changes confirm the transformation of the Brazilian polity and civil society. Such a characterization contrasts with conventional views of the country's democracy and political system as limited and restricted, in which the legacy of elite authoritarianism conspires with structural factors to constrain participation, democratic deepening, and social inclusion.[1]

By 2002 Brazil was at a turning point in a transformation aimed toward a modern liberalizing polity. But the transition remained incomplete. And though the October victory of the Workers' Party was a reflection of the vigor of Brazilian democracy, it also increased the sense of uncertainty about the direction and stability of the reform process—and politics itself. This concluding chapter further probes the evolving political context and its impact on the reform process. First, it assesses the prospects for democratic governance, looking at factors known to shape processes of democratization. Second, it sketches a structural realignment model to explore in broad historical and analytical perspective the relationship between Brazil's distinctive political dynamics and the reform process.

---

1. For example, Weyland (1996a), Sorensen (1993, 47–57). Freedom House's 1999–2000 survey, *Freedom in the World,* categorized Brazilian society as only "partly free" (rather than "free" or "not free") and experiencing a trend that year toward less freedom (Karatnycky 2000).

Democracy—What Form? How Durable?

Instead of frozen and static, Brazil's democratizing polity is a dynamic and vibrant one, even if still experimental, incomplete, vulnerable, and uncertain—and even if political and economic inequalities, prominent features of Brazilian society since the early days of independence, endure through the post-1985 democratizing era. Enfranchisement and organized political competitiveness, two key dimensions of the process of democratization, grew after 1985 and peaked in the recent past. The 2002 election is very significant in this regard. Nearly 95 million Brazilians voted to elect a new president, governors, two senators per state, and federal and state representatives. In a true feast of democracy, 18,151 candidates from 30 political parties[2] competed for 1,654 political offices across all 27 units of the Brazilian federation.[3] The size of the electorate had grown by 21.6 percent with respect to 1994.[4] In an election marked by freedom and transparency, Brazilians elected a left-leaning president from the opposition and significantly increased the Workers' Party presence in Congress. This was a still relatively rare democratic alternation in power in Brazilian history; it was even more impressive that the major shift toward a leftist president took place in an orderly fashion.[5]

From the perspective of state-society relations, the gradual change from centralizing corporatism to a more pluralistic form of interest intermediation, still fledgling and even precarious, was a main dimension of systemic change through 2002. The constitution of 1988 formalized a highly decentralized

2. Registered voters, the Brazilian electorate, in the 2002 elections numbered 115.2 million individuals—of which 17.8 percent abstained in the first round and 20.5 percent in the runoffs. The rate of abstention was lower than in previous elections. Of the thirty registered political parties, nine were large enough to have congressional delegations just before the elections. Of these, the PFL, PMDB, PSDB, and PT were the largest.
3. Brazil's electoral laws specify two electoral systems. A majority system, used to elect executive positions and senators, selects winners in terms of majority vote; elections for executive positions in which the top runner fails to obtain at least 50 percent of the votes are to be decided in runoff elections between the two candidates with the most votes, as in the 2002 presidential race. Elections for the Chamber of Deputies and subnational legislative bodies rely on a complicated system of proportional representation based on the first election. Voting is mandatory for those between the ages of eighteen and seventy and optional for any other Brazilian older than sixteen. Failure to vote can result in substantial penalties. In 2002, the two election rounds took place on October 6 and October 27. See Madi Rodrigues, "Gigante eleitoral," *Istoé*, October 9, 2002. The 2002 elections, the first to be fully computerized, used over 400,000 electronic voting machines to record the votes of the expanding Brazilian electorate.
4. The Brazilian electorate in 1994 was 94.8 million and grew to 101.3 in 1996, 106.1 in 1998, 109.8 in 2000, and 115.2 in 2002.
5. In a rare display of respect for continuity, the federal government approved funds to finance the work of a large transition team of more than fifty political figures appointed by the Workers' Party. This transition team began to work with the Cardoso administration a few days after the elections.

form of federalism in which states and counties enjoy considerable autonomy. Subsequent political dynamics reinforced this trend. Civil society has expanded a great deal. The ongoing growth of interest organizations, citizen participation, and collective action provides in itself evidence of the expansion of democracy.[6] As multiple organizations compete to represent diverse socioeconomic groups and interests, many policy domains—agriculture, education, health, labor, human rights, the environment, and others—are being restructured in the direction of decentralization and participation. Organized interests press on the three levels of government in diverse, still evolving manners. As interest groups proliferate, so do new forms of lobbying. Television, newspapers and other periodicals, and the new electronic media occupy an increasingly prominent independent space with respect to the political process. Public functionaries and other key players still cherish the benefits and entitlements enjoyed for years, but the evidence points to a significant erosion of traditional corporatism.

The current political system differs considerably from the centralized system in existence during much of the twentieth century. As civil society and decentralized federalism evolve, the overarching institutional framework is beginning to look like a distinctive form of liberal democracy, different from the pluralism of the United States as well as from traditional, top-down corporatism. Various types of partnerships involving government structures at all three levels and interest groups and nongovernmental organizations are part of the evolving system.

Still, this is a political system in transition.[7] The precise contours of the emergent party system and polity remain unclear. In the context of institutional and political change, a difficult reform agenda, and rising demands, it is not unjustified to wonder about institutional coherence, political direction, and even the fate of democracy. Political dynamics took a twist toward further complexity, experimentation, and unpredictability with the election of an opposition president from the Workers' Party in late 2002. Opponents of the liberalizing reforms also gained ground in the Congress and the Senate, though not enough to have effective majorities in the two houses.[8] The PSDB and other pro-reform parties did much better in the races for governor, with PSDB victorious in seven states, including São Paulo and Minas Gerais, the two most populous. The PMDB won in five, the PFL in four, and the PT only in three states with very small populations.[9] The political system was now called upon to generate a different coalition able to guarantee governance and a credible economic strategy more heavily oriented to social development

6. The MST and other movements seeking multiple goals that include radical change share these aims, though their inclination to use force to advance them puts them in a distinctive category. Studies confirming the surge in associative life include Avritzer (2000).
7. See also Hagopian (1998).

goals. One of the first ideas the Workers' Party advanced right after the election was that of a "social pact" between the main sectors of Brazilian society, a concept that resonated with that of corporatism.[10] A reflection of the vitality of Brazil's process of democratization, the Workers' Party government is a major test of the process of democratic development.

The grounds for optimism concerning the emerging democratic system can be readily summarized. First, the new democracy of the 1990s and beyond builds on widespread rejection of the old regime in place before 1985, when authoritarianism was strongly associated with political centralization and dirigisme. Brazilians gained a new realism about state action as the policy failures of the late 1980s and the debate about reform of the 1990s contributed to the demise of the alliance sustaining the old statist regime. Important political and economic actors still embrace the idea of state activism to promote development, but the Brazilian political establishment as a whole warmed up to the idea of opening and liberalizing the economy.[11] In spite of the economic problems after 1998, major players such as the armed forces, business interests, the middle class, and the higher ranks of the bureaucracy do not demand the return of traditional interventionism. Meanwhile, states and large cities are honing new skills in promoting local development on

8.   The first round decided races for the Senate and the Chamber of Deputies. The Workers' Party became the largest party in the Chamber of Deputies, increasing its presence by 50 percent to 91 seats (compared to 84 for the PFL, 73 for the PMDB, 72 for the PSDB, 49 for the PPB, and the rest divided among 14 smaller parties). Opposition parties (PT, PL, PC do B, PSB, PPS, and PDT) increased their congressional delegations by 40 percent—from 134 to 187 deputies. In the Senate, the PSDB lost third place to the PT. The PMDB and the PFL elected 19 senators each, while the PT grew to 14 and the PSDB lost three seats and now had 11. Other parties with five or fewer senators included the PDT (5), PSB (4), PTB (3), PL (3), PPB (1), PPS (1) and PSD (1).
9.   The PSDB elected governors in Goiás, Pará, Rondônia, Ceará, and Paraíba, besides Minas Gerais and São Paulo. The moderate PMDB won in Rio Grande do Sul, Santa Catarina, Paraná, Pernambuco, and the Federal District—hence emerging from the elections with solid control of the South, but only there. The four PFL victories were largely in the Northeast (Bahia, Maranhão, Sergipe) and the adjacent Northern state of Tocantins. Meanwhile, the Workers' Party won only in three states with small populations representing less than 3.5 percent of the electorate—Acre, Mato Grosso do Sul, and Piauí. The PT suffered a bitter defeat in Rio Grande do Sul, a governorship it controlled and expected to win, but lost to the PMDB.
10.   PT intellectuals declared to be inspired by the interclass agreements governing the consolidation of social democracy in Scandinavian societies and later adapted to democratization processes in such countries as Spain. Another corporatist idea floated days after the victory was to bring back the sectorial councils (câmaras setoriais) with which Brazil had experimented in the late 1980s.
11.   Industrialists and labor leaders continue to demand a stronger industrial policy as well as the enhanced ability of government to promote overall development. The policies seem to imply some form of state-centered development. All opposition candidates in the 2002 elections advocated ideas that implied a stronger development role for the state. Official candidate José Serra was himself known as a "developmentalist."

their own. In this context, it appears unlikely that heavy-handed state intervention will return in the near future.

Second, the density of politically active civil society and the increased levels of citizen participation provide reasons for optimism.[12] The enhanced third sector is in itself an important dimension of societal democratization, while the more complex civil society makes relentless demands for political incorporation into a democratic polity.[13] Third, industrialists, much of labor, and other critical social actors learned hard lessons about the costs of authoritarianism, having suffered repression and cooptation, clientelism, top-down policy-making, populism, and misguided policies in the past. The struggle against military rule brought a perceptible change in the political culture in which democracy came to be more valued in itself.[14]

Fourth, political institutions are gradually maturing. Notwithstanding considerable political turbulence, the Congress, the president, and the courts have been redefining their roles along the lines of a liberal polity and gradually solidifying a system of checks and balances.[15] Congress and the courts are more independent than ever, even if Congress is often riven by particularistic interests and the relationship between the president and Congress is in a state of flux—while states and local governments function with great autonomy in the framework of a highly decentralized federalism.[16] In addition, an assertive and independent media acts as watchdog over political life.[17] Last, the end of the Cold War has eliminated an external context that often legiti-

12. IBGE's Pesquisa Sindical 2001 shows that the number of syndicates (trade associations, labor unions, rural associations, and the like) grew by 43 percent in the previous ten years—from 11,193 in 1991 to 15,963 in 2001. The number of labor unions increased from 7,612 to 11,354. Independent or self-employed workers and urban associations grew the fastest. See IBGE, "Sindicatos: Indicadores sociais 2001-primeiros resultados" [www.igbe. gov.br/home/presidencia/noticias/02102002sindicatos.shtm]. The rate of labor unionization (in terms of economically active population) decreased from 24.9 percent in 1990 to 23.58 percent in 2001. In terms of the number employed, the rates increased somewhat from 25.8 percent to 26 percent.
13. Avritzer (2000).
14. Lamounier (1989, 1992a, 1992b). The movement of the Workers' Party toward a moderate and centrist program was accompanied by adherence to democracy in the party's main documents and pronouncements. Candidate Luiz Inácio Lula da Silva was a leader in the early struggle for democracy and was briefly imprisoned by the military in 1980.
15. Brazil's technologically advanced voting system is discussed above. To many Brazilians, another sign of positive political evolution is that traditional political bosses (*caciques*) such as Paulo Maluf, Fernando Collor, Orestes Quércia, Leonel Brizola, Newton Cardoso, and others failed in their bids to return to power; and while Antonio Carlos Magalhães, and Jader Barbalho won seats, they were unlikely to regain the political standing they had enjoyed for years ("O revés dos caciques," *Folha de S. Paulo* editorial, October 9, 2002).
16. The Congress elected in 2002 was very fragmented, perhaps more than any previous one, in spite of the shift toward the left. Such fragmentation of the party system had been an impetus to broad governing alliances in the past. That challenge now fell on the shoulders of the new president.

mized authoritarianism and corporatist ideologies in the name of anticommu-
nism.[18]

These considerations about decentralization, participation and a denser
civil society, change in political culture and institutions, the shift toward a
liberalizing paradigm, and the international context lend weight to the idea
that Brazilian democracy is deepening and is likely to continue to do so in the
foreseeable future. But a few caveats are in order. The ability of the political
system to advance a formidable agenda that includes facing the challenges of
deepening democratization and participation, state reform, change in economic model, and realignment of the polity away from traditional corporatism, all of this in the changing context of globalization, cannot be taken for
granted. To many Brazilians, democracy was hovering on the brink of a governability crisis that might hinder the much-needed reform process.[19] The
2002 elections posed additional challenges since they would intensify ideological debate and might seek to imbue Brazil's reform agenda with an alternative ethos.

In this context, the diverse mobilized interests make demands that tax the
institutional and political capacity of the state to channel and process them
constructively, as shown by the difficulties of the policy-making process during Cardoso's second term in office. Though the reform of the state away
from corporatism and the proliferation of mobilized interests bode well for
democracy in the long term, the issue is whether the country may be reaching
a point in which mobilization exceeds the capacity of the political system to
process demands in an orderly manner.[20] The Cardoso government sought to
frame the widening forms of interest representation and pressures for further
democratization and state reform as part of a process of radicalizing democracy. It cultivated a broad governing coalition to generate political consensus.
The president himself spent a great deal of time and energy articulating these
political coalitions, an effort that even his critics recognize as quite effective.
If specific reforms were often delayed, the political process leading to them

17. Brazil's influential newspapers include *O Globo*, *O Estado de S. Paulo*, *Folha de S.
Paulo*, *Jornal do Brasil*, as well as dozens of specialized (for example, business) or regional
organs. Together with a handful to magazines with national circulation (including *Veja*,
Istoé, *Época*, *Exame*) as well as national and local television stations, they cover politics
often aggressively and are eager to expose corruption and other irregularities. The Internet
and related new media have also proliferated in Brazil since the 1990s.

18. The international context since the 1990s has been engaged in support of human
rights, democracy, trade and integration, and security issues.

19. Ames (2001) discusses several flaws in the political system, including too many actors
with veto power, rules about party formation, malapportionment and other problems with
the electoral system, the presidency as institution, relations between the central government and subnational governments, corruption, and accountability.

20. A classic and influential argument about the general problem of the relationship
between institutional development and mobilization in changing or modernizing societies is
found in Huntington (1968).

sought to advance the consolidation of democracy. Whether the governments that follow will have the same inclination and capacity to frame, address, and articulate the diversity and fragmentation of political forces in the Brazilian political system is difficult to anticipate.[21]

In the context of a potential systemic overload and a great need for political articulation, the tension between macroeconomic stabilization, the alleviation of social ills, and the accommodation of diverse political forces looms large. Stabilization and fiscal balance are probably vital to sustained development in a country with a recent history of hyperinflation and external vulnerability. However, growth and social development to create jobs and reduce poverty were confirmed as national priorities by the results of the 2002 elections. The ability of political actors to balance social and economic goals in the framework of a new approach to national development will be decisive to political stability.

Decentralized and regionalistic federalism poses its own set of challenges and dilemmas. Decentralized federalism is likely to remain a prominent feature of the political system. The democratic polity of the post-1985 period, the constitution of 1988, and political practice in the 1990s and beyond strongly affirmed it. But federalism is unfinished and faces numerous obstacles. Its precise structure and the very balance between centralization and decentralization were and remain far from settled.[22] As city and state governments hone their roles as centers of authority, the distribution of duties and responsibilities in the federation remains contested terrain. Meanwhile, regionalism and regional differences continue to be sources of political tension, magnifying the debate about national purpose and direction at a time when national unity and focus are needed to address Brazil's reform agenda. They provide incentives for political actors to channel local discontent through populist, clientelistic, or corporatist appeals.

Whenever Brazilians embraced democracy—whether the restricted form of the Old Republic, the populist version after 1945, or the post-1985 polity model—the political shift has often been accompanied by relatively liberal economic policies and decentralized federalism, as well as a salient role for São Paulo. Political conditions through the early years of the new millennium tend to repeat this pattern. If so, the ability of the democratizing regime to

21. Luiz Inácio Lula da Silva won the presidency in part by presenting himself as a conciliator reaching out to all political forces in an effort to unite the country. If sustained, the position would represent a continuation of the strategy introduced by the previous president.
22. Chapters 2 and 3 discuss fiscal federalism. Soon after Lula's election, a number of governors began to press for the renegotiation of the debts to the federal government, a move opposed by São Paulo, which had already succeeded in implementing fiscal adjustment. This would be a major test of the federal insistence on fiscal responsibility, as achieved during the Cardoso government.

consolidate itself may depend on the extent to which Brazilians have learned to ward off the factors that made past attempts at democratization short-lived affairs. The Brazilian polity succumbed to authoritarian centralization in 1930, 1937, and 1964 in the context of unregulated competition among different clusters of the political elite—not infrequently regionally based—bent on prevailing over other groups. In interaction with an economically nationalist or statist political movement, rivalries and animosities within state elites could still contribute to a swing of the political pendulum back toward centralization, though such an eventuality would seem possible only with a rupture in the political system. Preexisting cleavages, added to tensions over fiscal federalism and political reform and ideological differences on how to organize the polity and promote economic development, give some reason for concern. The ability of the political elite—still regionally based, in a state of flux, and under great pressure from the popular sectors—to agree on how to organize the Brazilian state and economy is pivotal.[23]

That ability hinges in part on views about the reform process and its fate. The international financial crises of 1998–1999 and those that followed nearly paralyzed Cardoso's second term, giving credence to arguments against the liberalizing drive and raising fears about governability. Public approval ratings plummeted and sectors of the economic elite began to mobilize against its program. The governing coalition lost ground to the anti-reform opposition in the municipal election of late 2000, as many Brazilians wondered if the deepening of economic restructuring was compatible with social development. The development question took on major significance in the national debate leading to the 2002 elections. The first fifteen years of democratization had not solved the most important structural problems of Brazilian society: poverty, inequality, and public security. Market-friendly polices and globalization seemed to hamper large reductions in poverty or inequality. Social conditions had taken a turn for the worse in the aftermath of the 1998–1999 crisis and then again in 2001-2002, when uncertainty and fears about the Brazilian elections induced a sharp rise of the dollar as well as fiscal and financial threats. Demands for policies that effectively address social needs help explain the move to the left in the 2002 elections.[24]

Political negotiation and concerted action are essential to reconcile perceptions about the country's problems, to arrive at a renewed understanding on processes of state and economic reform, and to integrate the more complex

23. Tensions between units of the federation have risen in the recent past. Elected governor of Minas Gerais in 1998, Itamar Franco defied the federal government on several grounds during his tenure in that office, including the well-publicized and costly moratorium on the state's debt in early 1999, a factor in the international financial crisis setting in that year.
24. Public insecurity, crime, and corruption were also important issues.

political system and civil society. This is largely a task to be accomplished by organized political forces. There is thus a need for enlightened political action based on the existing party system and the political process as a whole to articulate and conciliate interests. From the perspective developed in this volume, Brazilian politicians seeking to align the polity face politically diverse actors, social forces, political institutions, policy paradigms, and changing external conditions—as well as a political party system in need of reform. In the context of so many challenges, negotiations by political leaders and organized political forces are essential for a polity alignment that advances the reform process.

The broad state reform agenda. Before further probing the dynamics of alignment, it should be observed that the changing system of interest intermediation presents its own difficulties. Uncertainty and ambiguity concerning political forms are likely to present challenges for some time. This includes not only the precise character of parties, but also preexisting practices of interest aggregation and political support, including clientelism and corporatism. The redemocratizing governments from 1985 through 1993 reproduced the legacy of clientelism and were unable to reform the Brazilian state and economy. The Cardoso administration battled corporatism, clientelism, and populism, but was forced to make some concessions to the first two. As the Brazilian party system evolves, political factions will continue to press aggressively for selective benefits, just as diverse constituencies will demand protection. Patronage and pork barrel politics may not diminish greatly in the short run, as entrenched sectors of the political class, the bureaucracy, and the armed forces demand payment for their loyalty. Up to a point, clientelism by itself will not block effective policy-making. Beyond a certain threshold, clientelism and fiscal populism sap the strength of the state.

Corporatism may be ending as a system of interest intermediation and conciliation, but some of its legacies endure, generating structural confusion and constraining the reform process. Sectors of the middle class, the working class, and the elites cherish the entitlements afforded by corporatist practices, particularly since an alternative has not yet fully materialized.[25] The liberal model emphasizes a different mix between the rights and responsibilities of groups and individuals. But many Brazilians are still wedded to the idea of a paternalistic state, something particularly appealing at a time when economic restructuring and global capitalism are wreaking havoc on some sectors.

Government policy through 2002 represents a landmark in the search for a more functional state form. But, realistically, only patient political effort sus-

---

25. FIESP and IEDI leaders (see chapter 5) seemed to be encouraging the formation of corporatist arrangements days after the Lula-PT electoral victory.

tained through many years will create a durable new state form. Able political leadership will be necessary to maintain and deepen the commitment to political reform to strengthen the party system, improve the electoral system, and build institutional forms adequate to sustain the reform process, the new approach to development, and the deepening of democracy.

Political Realignment, Reform, and Development

External shocks have shaped economic and development policy throughout Brazilian history and continued to do so after 1998. Still, internal political and institutional factors remain crucial to the state's ability to respond to external shocks and respond to crisis.[26] If the fate of Brazil's effort to reform its polity and arrive at a new development model is intertwined with the completion of a process of political realignment that enhances the overall coherence of political dynamics, the Cardoso years offered grounds for considerable optimism. Innovative political leadership linking its political fate to that of the reform drive gained ground during those years. In the Brazil of the 1990s, Cardoso and the PSDB organized a broad political coalition to advance major reforms and align the Brazilian polity. The 2002 election of Lula da Silva as president seemed to call into question the reform process as it created new political dynamics. The outcome of that election presents new challenges to the process of structural realignment, though they do not appear insurmountable.

Restructuring realignments are defined here as regime changes that are accompanied by a major change in policy paradigm, substantial institutional innovation, the rise of a new dominant coalition, and shifts in support by important political blocs such as regions.[27] Political actors and ideas are central in the articulation and maintenance of these shifts. In Brazil, the birth of statism and dirigisme as a development strategy in the 1930s can be seen in the framework of such a restructuring realignment perspective. Getúlio Var-

26. See also Haggard (1990).
27. A political realignment perspective with particular application to the United States is found in Burnham (1975) (see also Skocpol and Campbell 1995). Examples of political realignment from the experience of the United States are the Progressive Era, the New Deal, and the Reagan revolution of the 1980s. In these cases, policy changes were introduced that marked relatively long periods of political ascendancy by either Republicans or Democrats. The concept of political realignment applied here relaxes assumptions of either a relatively mature democracy or linear political development. Moreover, the context of globalization calls for an extended analysis of realignment processes that takes international and global factors into consideration. As historical processes marking epochal changes, restructuring realignments can be compared to revolutions. Restructuring realignments are concentrated periods of reform marking the rise of new political eras or ruling coalitions. They can take the form or be part of revolutions, but the concept of restructuring realignment makes fewer assumptions about violence, sociopolitical drama, and the nature of the economic, political, and social changes they bring about.

gas and the military and regional elites supporting him in the Revolution of 1930 forged a centralizing coalition that realigned the polity for more than half a century. The state-centered development strategy became the key claim to legitimacy by an emergent alliance of politicians that included many political actors from hitherto peripheral and semiperipheral political currents and regions, the military, and the growing bureaucracy. The elective affinity with authoritarianism resulted from its presumed effectiveness in neutralizing recalcitrant elites and other actors often associated with a regional base or focus. In the process, the interests of important social classes were woven into the fabric of the centralizing corporatist regime. Spatially based political elites played key roles in the events marking the realignment process and its consolidation.[28]

As historical processes of magnitude, restructuring realignments are accompanied by major policy reforms cast in terms of doctrine or policy paradigms claiming to represent a viable alternative perspective previously shunned by power holders and policymakers. In Brazil and various countries in Latin America, *cepalismo* and economic nationalism—paradigms comparable to Keynesianism that had been hitherto ignored or at the margins of official policy-making—provided justification for statist regimes in the 1930s and after. Preexisting policy paradigms based on liberalism and free trade entered into crisis shortly before or during the consolidation of a realignment process.

In the last part of the twentieth century, new economic models converged with criticisms of preexisting states and development strategies in Brazil and Latin America to provide rationales for liberalizing regimes and coalitions. Just as liberal or free-trade doctrine was called into question around 1930, trade regimes based on protectionism faced an avalanche of criticism after the 1970s.[29] The liberalizing zeitgeist affirming itself in the 1980s and 1990s called for scaling down and reforming the state to better reconcile economic efficiency and organizational effectiveness. Welfare reform, institutional modernization, decentralization, and the strengthening of local government, as well as economic opening, are part of this perspective.

---

28. Brazil's Revolution of 1930 has been extensively discussed by diverse authors. My own initial research on the Revolution of 1930 and the 1930s can be found in Font (1990a), Font (1996), and Font (forthcoming).
29. For the United States, Rapley (1996, chs. 2-3) discusses not just the role of the neoliberal school associated with the University of Chicago, but also influential reports by the Organization for Economic Cooperation and Development (OECD), the World Bank, the Inter-American Development Bank, the National Bureau of Economic Research, and the New Political Economy associated with such authors as Anne Krueger and Robert Bates. In Latin America, the impetus came not only from mainstream economics, but also from important strands of Christian democratic (Chile) and social democratic (Brazil) thought.

The Cardoso administration sought to balance liberalizing and social democratic approaches to economic policy. Close to mainstream economic thought, Finance Minister Pedro Malan, presidents of the Central Bank, and other key policymakers defended the primacy of stabilization and a stable currency. Another faction in the government, known as the developmentalists or *grupo crítico,* decried the overvalued currency and higher interest rates, favored economic growth policies over stabilization, and called for a more active government.[30] Debate between these two currents repeatedly came into the open, particularly during times of crisis or electoral competition, but Cardoso himself marshaled his intellectual prowess to preside creatively over this policy duality, denying the existence of a contradiction between stabilization, growth, and social development.

Alternative theories and doctrines provide justifications for new policy paradigms. Neoliberalism emphasizes market over the state and the end of ideology. Brazilian reformers during the Cardoso era did view liberalization as unavoidable, but they embraced a pragmatic social democratic approach that justified state activism to address gross inequalities and persistent forms of poverty. The redistributive function calls for high taxes to promote enhanced public welfare, health, and education. The Cardoso team sought to link this evolving Brazilian perspective to the view, also found in third way or social democratic governments of Western Europe, to balance social justice with emphases on efficiency and fiscal responsibility.

A pragmatic, liberalizing, social democratic approach appears to be close to mainstream thinking in Brazil, in spite of its difficulties in becoming a hegemonic policy paradigm. The evolution of the Workers' Party position toward fiscal responsibility, adherence to stabilization, export promotion, and cautious openness to trade liberalization indicated considerable change from traditional statism. In terms of those basic policy goals, the Workers' Party does not currently appear very different from Cardoso and the PSDB.

Political realignments generally result from shifts in which political actors are able to reposition themselves with respect to voter blocks and other slack political resources to configure a new stable ruling coalition or regime. A new era of Republican preeminence in the United States in the 1980s, for example, was accompanied by a massive shift from Democrat to Republican in the South. In the democratizing Brazil of the turn of the century, the process of political realignment would need to build on a new set of pacts and understandings among regionally based factions and elites. Political fragmentation presents a challenge to alignment processes in Brazil. The alliance

30. See Ribamar Oliveira, "O 'grupo crítico' fragilizado," *O Estado de S. Paulo,* November 27, 1998 [www.estado.com.br/edicao/pano/98/11/27/pol618.html]. The names associated with this group are José Serra, the Mendonça de Barros brothers, Pérsio Arida, and the late Sérgio Motta.

between the PSDB and the PFL—particularly strong in São Paulo and the Northeast—was critical during much of the Cardoso era. However, strains in the dominant coalition intensified during Cardoso's second term, leading to its collapse in 2001-2002—thereby raising questions about political support for the reform process and an enduring realignment. The 2002 process of succession revealed serious cleavages between the national PSDB leadership and dominant political elites from the Northeast, including those of Bahia, Maranhão, and Ceará. Since those of Ceará were affiliated with the PSDB, their independent political stance amounted to a dissidence or a party split. This position, directed at the notion of *paulista* hegemony within the dominant coalition and the PSDB itself, no doubt reflected lingering regionalism in the Brazilian polity. In addition, some political currents in Brazil seem to cling to some form of statism. This is not just true in the Northeast and other peripheral areas dependent on the federal government. Industrialists in São Paulo, the economic heartland of the country, continue to demand government protectionism, something that partly explains the salience of business political activism in the period 1998-2001 and in the debates surrounding the 2002 elections.

Realignment processes center on the ability of a particular political leader or political movement to usher in a new period of reforms and broker a process of coalition formation around them. In the United States, Franklin D. Roosevelt and the Democratic Party presided over the rise of the New Deal in the 1930s, while Ronald Reagan and the Republican Party led the 1980s reverse movement toward neoliberalism. In the Brazil of the 1990s and early years of the twenty-first century, the task of realigning the polity in broad structural terms fell on Cardoso and the centrist PSDB, particularly its *paulista* core. Factions and parties of the left and right lacked the balance between focus and flexibility to lead this process. The PSDB stands for a pragmatic way of approaching development, but the party's *paulista* core is too narrow to rule by itself. It must hence forge alliances with other large parties. Its social democratic character should in principle make the PSDB a natural partner to the Workers' Party; however, through the turn of the century the latter claimed the capacity to rule either alone or via a narrower alliance focused on socialist ideas.[31] The PFL of the 1990s was strong in parts of the country where the PSDB was weak, it was one of the largest and most disciplined parties in Congress, and its liberal ideology was loosely compatible with the liberalizing reforms advocated by the PSDB, regardless of the con-

31. Though the PT provided often vociferous opposition to the Cardoso government and the reform process, it shifted toward a more centrist position several months before the 2002 presidential elections, while Lula picked a business leader from the Liberal Party as his vice presidential running mate. The new stance of the PT, if sustained in 2003 and beyond, created conditions for a broad center-left coalition.

viction and consistency with which it might be applied. The PFL hence emerged as a key partner in the PSDB-centered reform coalition of the 1990s. The PMDB, technically still the largest party and a member of the ruling alliance, was a heterogeneous and often unruly political force, though probably the one closest to the PSDB ideologically and historically.[32] The much smaller PDT and PPB rounded out the original reform coalition. The governing coalition's reliance on diverse and even disparate political forces, a main source of strength as well as vulnerability until 2000, could not be replicated in the context of the 2002 presidential succession.[33] When the PSDB-PFL coalition collapsed in the political turbulence of 2001 and 2002, it confirmed the difficulties of a durable process of realignment and revealed the need for new political configurations. However, the victory of the Workers' Party built on its turn toward a centrist social democratic position. If that turn were sustained, it would not be far-fetched to imagine that a reconfigured reformist coalition that included the PSDB might emerge as a possibility.[34]

Realignment processes in emergent or developing societies are called upon to provide blueprints for redefining integration into the international economy, particularly in the context of globalization. Globalization has generally induced shifts in economic policy and development strategies favoring openings toward the international and global spheres. Contemporary restructuring realignments are hence embedded ever more in a web of global processes and actors. In Brazil, a new understanding of global dynamics and Brazil's global role contributed to the opening of the economy and trade liberalization.[35]

At the same time, contemporary realignment processes are vulnerable to the vicissitudes of the global economy. The international financial crises of 1998-1999 and 2001, as well as external pressures for trade liberalization and overall openness, placed great difficulties and strains on the Brazilian realignment process. But shocks are not without positive consequences. Financial and fiscal crises highlight the need for continuing reform and make them more likely. When in late 1999 and early 2000 the world economy was

32. The PSDB emerged as a splinter of the PMDB.
33. The PSDB attempted a Grand Alliance with the PMDB for the first round of elections and broadened it to include the PFL and other parties for the runoffs.
34. The PSDB remained a powerful party after the 2002 elections. Though fourth in the number of senators and deputies, it elected governors in seven states, had a vision and program to offer, and it had more leaders of presidential stature than any other party. The natural option for the PSDB in 2003 was to play the role of loyal, responsible opposition. That role would allow it to support the reform process while cultivating options for success in 2006. It now had a solid base in the Southeast (except for Rio de Janeiro) and was making progress in other regions. The list of PSDB leaders who could mount major presidential campaigns in 2006 included Aécio Neves (governor of Minas Gerais); Tasso Jereissati (senator from Ceará); and the *paulistas* Geraldo Alckmin (governor of São Paulo), José Serra, and Fernando Henrique Cardoso.
35. F.H. Cardoso articulated influential arguments pressing for Brazil's embrace of opportunities afforded by globalization (see Cardoso 2001).

recovering somewhat and Brazil's exports were poised for expansion, fiscal measures and reforms adopted in response to the crises eased Brazil's process of international reintegration. Negotiations with the IMF were significant in this regard. Faced with social and political crises in Indonesia and other Asian countries, the IMF, the World Bank, and other international agencies relaxed in 1998 the neoliberal recipes associated with structural adjustment packages.[36] Still, crises and pressures would return. In this context, U.S.-led negotiations for the adoption of a Free Trade Area of the Americas pose a dilemma for Brazilian policymakers, who are uncertain about their country's industrial competitiveness and demand a higher degree of openness in the United States to Brazilian agricultural, steel, and other exports.

Still, such phenomena as the political crisis of 2001 bring out the centrality of internal politics. Internal political disarray took center stage mid-year, driven by a political-institutional crisis and the internal debate over who should succeed Cardoso in the late 2002 elections. A detailed review of the internal political crisis and the succession debate illuminate the role of regionalism and other factors in the formation of national alliances able to complete a restructuring realignment in Brazil. Prompted by political rivalries, political infighting erupted between members of the broad ruling coalition in early 2001, leading to a spiral of mutual charges of corruption and wrongdoing by two regionally based political leaders who had provided critical support in the Congress. Public outrage resulted in the resignation of key government allies from the three main parties in the ruling coalition—including Antonio Carlos Magalhães, two other senators, the minister of national integration, and a host of lower level officers—as well as the radical reorganization of Sudene and Sudam, the two superagencies concerned with the development of the Northeast and the Amazon region.[37]

Antonio Carlos Magalhães, the chief political boss from the northeastern state of Bahia, was an unsurpassed master of clientelistic politics. The historical leader of the PFL, he was just completing a term as president of the Senate when it became apparent that the PFL would lose control of the Senate to the PMDB's Jader Barbalho, the main political boss from the North or Amazon region. Magalhães responded with a cascade of accusations of corrupt practices by Barbalho and associates. After sensing that the president would not come to his side, Magalhães directed attacks at Cardoso himself. Barbalho, a powerful and tough leader, responded in kind. For several weeks

36. World Bank senior economist Joseph Stiglitz began to call for flexibility in monetary and fiscal policies. The tone of discussions with Brazil changed in November 1998, when a credit of US$18.1 billion was approved by the IMF for fiscal support, even though the IMF had not agreed with the Real Plan when it was first implemented.
37. Magalhães resigned in May 2001. PSDB's José Roberto Arruda had done so a month earlier. Jader Barbalho resigned from the Senate presidency in September 2001.

Brazilians were subjected to daily headlines of charges and countercharges from these two gladiators bent on destroying each other through escalating accusations of corruption. Normal business in Congress came to a standstill, as politicians of diverse persuasions sought to take advantage of the situation. The opposition demanded a congressional investigation. The executive fought the idea, arguing that a congressional inquiry would virtually paralyze the legislative process and that other mechanisms already existed to deal with the charges being made.[38]

The fight between Magalhães and Barbalho damaged more than the ruling coalition and their political careers. It also affected the federal superagencies set up in previous decades to provide aid and development direction to the Amazon and Northeast regions. Formed in the heyday of the Brazilian developmental state, Sudam[39] and Sudene[40] had become conduits for clientelistic practices and patronage. Brazilians suspected for years that corruption was rife in both.[41] The charges by both senators led to investigations that confirmed vast irregularities at the two agencies. The federal government closed them down, converting them into agencies to develop projects, but with financial and technical supervision from the highly respected BNDES. In the end, this dark episode was thus not without a silver lining. It brought public

38. In the middle of this scandal and minicrisis, the leader of the PSDB was forced to resign when it was revealed that he and Antonio Carlos Magalhães had broken into the Senate's confidential computer system to learn how each senator voted on a previous corruption scandal that had resulted in the resignation of another senator. The PSDB leader was compelled to resign from the Senate and was expelled from the PSDB, a party whose public image centers heavily on claims to honesty.

39. Sudam, Superintendency for the Development of the Amazon, came to life in 1966, replacing a small agency created in 1953 (The Superintendency for the Plan of Economic Valorization of the Amazon, or SPVEA). The "Amazonia Legal" it served, more than 60 percent of Brazil's landmass and 11.9 percent of its population, includes the states of Acre, Amape, Amazonas, Mato Grosso, Para, Rondonia, Roraima, Tocantins, and part of Maranhão.

40. Juscelino Kubitscheck launched Sudene, the Superintendency for the Development of the Northeast, in 1959, following a drought a year earlier. Its first superintendent was the well-known economist Celso Furtado. Sudene provided financing through the program known as FINOR (Fundo de Investimento do Nordeste). Through 1999, the latter approved 3,052 projects—of which 2,157 were completed. The agency was suspected of corruption during much of its existence. A CPI report in April 2001 noted 531 projects with irregularities adding up to R$2.2. billion. Bahia, Pernambuco, and Ceará used 63 percent of the R$15.7 billion distributed since 1978. The Lula administration vowed to bring Sudene and Sudam back to life.

41. The accusations against Barbalho, who had emerged as president of the PMDB, pointed out that several of the individuals he indicated for positions in Sudam operated as a "mafia," using false receipts and projects to embezzle large sums—between R$1.2 billion and R$1.8 billion in the 1998-2001 period. A frog farm to be developed under a grant to Barbalho's wife was considerably smaller than would be expected from the R$9 million she received. Moreover, accusers argued that Barbalho's salary could not explain a known personal fortune of at least R$30 million. Nearly 100 individuals were investigated, and many of them were detained. Barbalho eventually resigned from the Senate.

scrutiny of corrupt practices and helped undermine the rule of remaining traditional bosses or *caciques,* such as Magalhães and Barbalho, who were forced to resign from the Senate.[42] The Cardoso administration used the crisis to bring in much-needed changes in development agencies servicing the country's two main peripheral regions—in effect using the crisis to deepen the state reform drive.

The political system managed to restabilize itself within a few months. In spite of the scandal, Congress reasserted its role as a critical actor. But damage had been done. The political turbulence and the departure of prominent leaders in the ruling coalition contributed to derailing the reform process for the duration of Cardoso's term.[43] With major parts of the reform agenda still incomplete and the 2002 succession rapidly approaching, the PSDB now had to restructure negotiations with other political figures with an eye on the reform process.[44] In the end, much of the incomplete reform agenda would be deferred. The shape and continuity of the reform drive would depend to a large extent on the next president. Economic and social development became political issues both outside and within the reform coalition in the pre-electoral debate.

In that context, selecting an appropriate candidate able to rejuvenate the reform coalition and complete the restructuring realignment presented a great challenge as 2002 opened. Such a leader would need to cement rather diverse intra- and interlevel alliances—that is, ensure the integrity of diverse pacts while incorporating them into a coherent national program.[45] Cardoso gave the nod to José Serra, a long-term ally and a *paulista* political leader better known for his skills in designing and implementing policies than in articulating broad political alliances. In the Northeast, this choice alienated not only regional chiefs José Sarney in Maranhão and Antonio Carlos Magalhães in Bahia, but also the PSDB political establishment in Ceará. Serra faced an uphill battle in that region. By mid-July, Ciro Gomes, a former governor of Ceará and critic of the Cardoso reforms, overtook Serra in the polls. Gomes received a great deal of support from the political establishment in the state of Ceará, the PSDP faction historically led by Tasso Jereissati.[46] The PSDB

42. Both leaders retained support in their respective regions and would return to elected political office in 2002, though with diminished powers.
43. The energy crisis of mid-2001 threatened to cut supply by up to 40 percent. It was caused in large measure by very low levels of rain, particularly in the San Francisco River basin. Since the energy sector had not yet been privatized, it could not have been the cause. The energy crisis reinforced the role of the state as regulator, managing quotas and incentives to address the crisis. The government also announced a plan to invest in new hydroelectric plants.
44. See interview with Fernando Henrique Cardoso in *Jornal do Brasil,* May 27, 2001.
45. That any two parties might be allies in one state, but engaged in bitter rivalry in others, strained the process.

itself was hence unable to maintain unity with respect to the reform process at this critical juncture. This internal crisis within the reform coalition subsided somewhat once Serra regained his standing as a front-runner, but the PSDB lost considerable political ground in the first round of the 2002 elections, as Serra used up his political firepower in beating Ciro Gomes and Anthony Garotinho to the second spot in the runoffs. Front-runner Lula da Silva emerged unscathed from the intense debate to the first electoral round, as all of the other candidates, trailing far behind him, fought each other for the other spot in the runoffs. Viewed as the leading candidate for that position, Serra was the focus of the others' attacks. This phenomenon is one of the reasons for his defeat.[47]

Lula won the election by a wide margin.[48] Had the fledgling realignment process thereby been derailed? The early signals from the victorious PT were that a Lula government would continue the reform process (see also chapter 6), though framing it differently. Indeed, the PT's turn to centrist moderation, its new willingness to form alliances with other parties, and the need for congressional support made this outcome likely. If so, such a government would need to form a reform-oriented political coalition that included decisive support from at least one of the other large parties—PMDB, PSDB, or PFL. Two scenarios were plausible. In one, based on political pragmatism, the PT government would seek to include factions from all other parties, replicating the strategy initially developed by Cardoso. An alternative principled scenario based on programmatic affinity and political coherence would include the PSDB as preferential partner in a center-left coalition. The alliance strategy the Workers' Party had picked and political dynamics in general would probably lead to the first option.

From the structural realignment perspective, the reform process in Brazil faced new, rather substantial, challenges after the 2002 elections. All major political forces were now at a new crossroads. The Workers' Party was not exempt from tensions and dilemmas. Though Lula's political program did not represent a major revision of the basic policy course set by the Cardoso government, the party's programmatic character and the militants within the party could push it toward a distinctive approach entailing a substantial alter-

46. To many observers, Tasso Jereissati would have been the natural presidential PSDB candidate in 2002, and Jereissati and associates expected that much. Why Jereissati was not chosen owes in part to the strength of the Serra group within the PSDB. The choice split the PSDB, since Ciro Gomes was a Jereissati protégé.
47. Other reasons include a superb strategy by Lula's marketing director Duda Mendonça, internal problems in the Serra campaign, and Serra's disinclination or inability to activate a charismatic persona—as well as frustration with the lack of economic growth and the high rates of poverty.
48. Lula received 61.27 percent of the valid votes and Serra 38.73 percent on the second and final round of the elections.

ation in the political system and the process of political alignment. If so, all other large parties would face difficult choices about their own roles.

Issues of governability remain important in this regard. The political system had experienced diverse changes in the recent past—the erosion of corporatism, a more complex and assertive civil society, the apparent demise of the great political bosses or *caciques*, the rearticulation of state-level political machines, state reform, and an evolving though still immature political party system. The political shift added to the air of uncertainty about the political and institutional parameters governing political alignment and the fate of the reform process.[49]

Still, the PT victory ushered in new political dynamics and opportunities for political innovation. The original reform coalition seemed to have disintegrated and the political elite, somewhat divided, appeared focused on what roles to play or how to find an accommodation to the situation. Regenerating the reform agenda was surely a major item on the agenda.

Conclusion

The analysis of Brazil's reforms and shift in development strategy advanced in this volume focuses on the interplay between political dynamics, collective action, ideas, and institutions. It sketches a political process approach in which actors motivated by political interests, focused on political junctures, and shaped by institutions and political cleavages occupy center stage. Emergent paradigms and worldviews shape their political choices. In interaction with underlying elite cleavages and other inducers of interest formation and political mobilization, they affect goal definition and policy decisions. Reformist leaders adhering to the art of the possible cast their own roles in terms of emergent paradigms that respond to the challenges of the times and use the resulting agendas to frame perceptions about the reform process, advance innovative approaches to development, and neutralize disruptive political factionalism.

Whether their actions result in the deepening of democracy depends in part on the values and practices defined in these very paradigms. In the past, efforts to thus reform Brazil contributed to discontinuities in democratic development and the assertion of authoritarianism. Judging by the Cardoso years and the early features of the Workers' Party government taking charge in 2003, Brazil's democratizing politicians of different ideological orienta-

49. The political class in Brazil is still based on states and regions to a considerable extent, there remains considerable fluidity in the decentralized federal system, and the three levels of government shape each other in often unpredictable fashion. In the midst of so much complexity, political outcomes owe a great deal to strategic action by a relatively large number of actors.

tions appear to have drawn lessons that decrease the probability of major turbulence and political discontinuities in their country's search for better political, economic, and social models. But only time will tell.

The Brazilian experience suggests that political dynamics and development processes are surely interconnected, though not in a mechanistic way. Brazil's own history and ongoing transformation deny notions of a simple or linear connection between politics and development. Development and industrialization, as well as economic crises threatening them, have taken place under both authoritarian and democratic regimes. The industrialization model pursued from the 1940s through the 1980s has been associated with centralization and authoritarianism. But the relationship seems to be a case of selective affinity. Industrialization and authoritarianism are both largely explained by other factors, and democratic regimes have also relied on development models, achievements, and discourses as rationales for their programs.

Though development may not induce democracy in a linear fashion, economic performance appears essential to sustain liberalizing coalitions in democratizing regimes over the long run. In Brazil and elsewhere, democratic reformers are judged by their ability to address economic and social needs. Voters will warm up to alternative political forces, even if populist or authoritarian, when frustrated with inadequate economic performance. Economic difficulties associated with the reform process have strained and at times endangered the deepening of democracy in neighboring countries.[50] The impact of economic and state reform on the process of democratization is thus an important, yet still relatively uncharted, aspect of transforming Brazil.

Intertwined, the shape and durability of Brazil's development strategy and process of democratization depend on the ability of political leaders to work with each other and key sectors of civil society, the intelligentsia, and the bureaucracy around a shared vision of the future. Their actions, the coalitions they forge, and their ability to advance a distinctive vision for the nation are the main phenomena to watch for assessments of alignments that promote lasting reforms and development in the context of democracy.

---

50. Argentina's lingering fiscal, economic, social, and political crisis in the context of democratization and early economic reforms makes that point rather clearly, as does the election of Chávez in Venezuela and political tension in other Latin American societies.

Stabilization Plans after 1985

TABLE A-1. Stabilization Plans and Inflation Rates

Plan	Before Plan (12-month, %)	After Plan (12-month, %)
Cruzado Plan (1986–1987)	248	64
Bresser Plan (1987–1988)	167	400
Summer Plan (1989–1990)	993	2,397
Collor Plan I (1990–1991)	3,700	422
Collor Plan II (1991)	1,140	515
Real Plan (1994–2002)	4,922	28

Source: OECD 2001

José Sarney administration (1985–1990)

1985 (Mix of orthodox and heterodox measures). Compromise cabinet organized by Tancredo Neves takes over in early 1985. There is tension in economic policy between advocates of austerity and those who would spend more on social programs via the renegotiation of the debt to reduce constraints on government spending. By the second half of the year, the latter have the upper hand. The deficit/GDP ratio expanded by more than 60 percent, and the money supply by 20 percent. Inflation at year's end is at a record 235 percent.

1986 *Cruzado Plan* (heterodox). "Surprise attack" announced in February: price and exchange rate freeze, new currency, *tablitas* to discount prospective inflation in commercial transactions, policy to restore real wages, expansionary monetary policy. Plan seems to work through November 1986 elections, but shortly after the government is compelled to increase taxes and utility prices (Cruzado II). Prices increase, stock market experiences boom, spread between official and parallel exchange rates increases, inflationary pressures mount.

181

Dramatic acceleration of inflation in January 1987 spells the failure of the program. Brazil declares moratorium on commercial debt interest payments.

1987   *Bresser Plan.* Economist Luiz Carlos Bresser Pereira organizes a new economic team and plan. Goals are to stop inflationary acceleration and reduce the odds of a foreign exchange crisis. Features of plan: Exchange rate devaluation (9.5 percent) and hike in government-administered prices and utilities, prices and wages frozen for three months, indexation preserved, monetary and exchange rate policy adjusted to current inflation rate, steps toward separation of Treasury and Central Bank.

Program has some initial success, but meets bureaucratic resistance. Wages rise under pressure from unions. President vetoes proposal for tax increase. Minister Bresser Pereira resigns in January 1988.

1988   *Rice and Beans (Feijão com Arroz) Plan* (conventional). Newly appointed finance minister Maílson da Nóbrega focuses his plan on modest fiscal, monetary, and exchange rate polity to stabilize the rate of inflation at about 15 percent and reduce public sector deficit to 7 percent of GDP. Brazil seeks return to international financial community: suspends moratorium and reschedules the US$63 billion commercial debt. Large trade surplus of US$20 billion makes this possible. Plan fuels inflation and does not promote growth. Inflation rate is 24 percent by July and reaches 684.6 percent for the year.

1989   Jan. *Summer Plan* (heterodox). Return to ideas of Cruzado Plan: price and exchange freeze after a 17 percent devaluation against the U.S. dollar, a new currency, use of *tablitas*, deindexation of financial assets and contracts, centralization of foreign exchange operations, restoration of real wages. One orthodox tool is extremely high real interest rates. Still no fiscal adjustment, but mild administrative reform seeks to reduce the number of agencies and expenditures. Opposition from executive and legislature. Money base increases due to inflow of foreign capital. Plan came apart by June 1989. Sarney administration reduced to ineffectualness through the nine months remaining of term. Public deficits are huge (more than 12 percent of GDP). Money supply expands by 1,288 percent and thus inflation increases exponentially the second half of 1989, ending at 1,782 percent for the year, a new record for Brazil (but not the last one). In February 1990, Sarney's last month in office, the daily inflation rate approximates 2 percent. His administration leaves an image of laxity and profligacy.

Fernando Collor de Mello administration (1990–1992)

(Collor impeached on September 29, 1992)

1990 Mar. *Collor Plan.* Another "surprise attack," this time much bolder and coercive. Zélia Cardoso de Mello, an economic history professor at the University of São Paulo and political associate of Collor de Mello (no relation), is finance minister as well as planning minister. The plan freezes 70 percent of private monetary and financial assets (including regular checking and savings accounts), with mandatory transfer into Central Bank deposits (real yields of 6 percent) to be returned to depositors in equal monthly installments after eighteen months, starting in September 1991. Plan also calls for administrative reforms and cutbacks, a one-time levy on private financial wealth, a fluctuating exchange rate replacing the pegged exchange rate, and an income policy based on a temporary price freeze. Pledges of privatization, deregulation, and trade liberalization.

The plan brings down the inflation rate, but also paralyzes the economy due to minimal liquidity. Plan required a strong management team, something in short supply. The exchange rate overvalues. By December 1990 inflation returns to 20 percent per month, even with the economy now in crisis. Low public trust in programs and expectation of more surprise attacks.

1991 *Collor Plans II and III.* Collor Plan II goes into effect in January 1991. Heterodox plan consists of frozen tariffs and prices, following increases; more promises of cuts in government expenditures. Inflation resumes after initial reduction. Dissatisfaction with centralized policy-making mounts. On September 30, 1991, the federal government announces Collor Plan III: a 15 percent currency devaluation and an interest rate increase. Very little public support and growing resentment.

After the first revelations in May 1992, the Collor administration is mired in charges of fraud and corruption, which lead to his impeachment on September 29, 1992. At that point, Vice President Itamar Franco becomes acting president, becoming official president in December.

Itamar Franco administration (September 1992–1994)
(following Collor de Mello's impeachment)

1992 Oct. to 1993, April. *Early policies.* The Itamar Franco administration appoints three short-lived (two to three months) ministers of finance—Gustavo Krause, Paulo R. Haddad, and Eliseu Rezende—whose policies fail to bring inflation down from more than 20 percent or to address fiscal problem. Concerns about the effectiveness of the Franco administration generalize.

1993 May *Plano Real.* Franco appoints Fernando Henrique Cardoso, his well-liked and widely respected foreign minister, to be finance minister. The plan had two main parts: fiscal adjustment and monetary adjustment. Proposed in December 1993, the plan was discussed in Congress and the media. Cardoso introduced the first two stages of the *Plano Real* by February 1994. These two stages included a tax increase of 5 percent, a Social Emergency Fund (15 percent of tax collection) for stabilization purposes; cuts of about US$7 billion in government expenditures; and a new indexing system leading to a new currency. The URV (Unidade Real de Valor), a transitional reference value unit linked to the dollar on a one-to-one basis, was used for pricing and wage adjustment purposes—allowing effective deindexing and disallowing freezes in prices or salaries. A new currency, the *real*, was fully introduced on July 1, 1994, whereby URV prices were converted into *real* prices. By then Cardoso had resigned to run for the presidency. The monthly inflation rate came down from 45 percent in June to 1.5 percent in September 1994. Two caretakers— Rubens Ricupero and Ciro Gomes—were finance ministers while the campaign was in progress and before Cardoso took office as president. (The *Plano Real* is discussed in Font 1994; Coes 1995: 167–72; Baer 1995).

Fernando Henrique Cardoso administration (1995–2002)

1995 Cardoso continues priority on stabilization and the *Plano Real.* Economist Pedro Malan appointed finance minister. Inflation remained under check throughout the year, becoming less than 20 percent by year's end, thus matching the inflation levels of the 1950s. By early 1996, the *Plano Real* was a major success. Total inflation for 1995 was under 20 percent. Meanwhile, the Brazilian economy grew by 4.5 percent in 1994 and 4 percent in 1995. Still, consensus had it that the plan would not bring a permanent solution until fiscal adjustment was fully implemented—including a permanent stabilization fund, various constitutional amendments to ensure fiscal austerity and the design of noninflationary mechanisms, and institutions to settle distributional conflicts.

This summary of stabilization plans since 1985 draws in part from Moura (1993), Franco (1993), Coes (1995), and Baer (1995).

Fiscal Adjustment Packages

TABLE B-1. Fiscal Stabilization Fund (March 1996)

Item	Description	Goal
FEF - Fiscal Stabilization Fund	Reduce rigid allocation of federal revenues mandated by constitution of 1988. The FEF amounted to 20 percent of total federal revenues from taxes after deducting the constitutionally mandated transfers to states and municipalities.	Improve federal budget by R$6.7 B or .8% of GDP.

TABLE B-2. Fiscal Adjustment Package (October 1997)

Item	Description	Goal
Finance Ministry	Reduction of the Treasury department expenses Improve collection through better auditing Simplification and consolidation of taxes such as IPI[a] and IOF[b] Improvements in collection of fiscal debts to union	R$2.70 B
Privatization	Revenues to diminish public debt	
State Firms	Reduction on expenses Debt reduction Gains in productivity	R$2.25 B
Public Employee Payroll	Change on the gratification and related systems Staff reduction End of overtime for federal employees	R$1.30 B
Est. Total		R$6.25 B

a. Industrial Production Tax
b. Financial Operations Tax

TABLE B-3. Fiscal Adjustment and Competitiveness (November 1997)

Item	Description	Goal
Expenditures	Reduction of expenditures by 15 percent except Health System, Social Assistance, and Agrarian Reform Reducing number of ministries Review criteria for scholarships	R$5.29 B
Revenues	Raise airport use tax Reduction on exemption of duty free to US$300 Limit of 20 percent on income tax deduction plus an additional 10 percent on due tax Raise taxes on cars and beverages	R$6.73 B
State Firms	Reduction of expenses and increase in revenue	R$5.70 B
States and Counties	Financial restructuring	R$2.00 B
Est. Total		R$19.72 B

TABLE B-4. Fiscal Stabilization Program (October 1998)

Item	Description	Goal
Taxation	Increase Financial Turnover Tax (CPMF) from .20 percent to 0.38 percent Proposed creation of a new tax (IVA[a]) in substitution of the ICMS[b], IPI[c], ISS[d], Cofins[e] and PIS[f]	n.a.
Social Security	Additional contribution of 9 percent for a public worker receiving more than R$1,200 per month.	R$2.6 B
FEF[g]	Maintained until 2006	n.a.
Budget	Reduction of expenses	R$8.7 B in 1999
State Firms	Reduction of expenses	R$2.7 B in 1999-2001
Est. Total	Fiscal Savings	R$28 B in 1999

a. Value Added Tax
b. Goods and Services Circulation Tax
c. Industrial Production Tax
d. Services Tax
e. Social Security Contribution
f. Social Integration Program
g. Fiscal Stabilization Fund

TABLE B-5. IMF Accord (November 1998)[a]

Item	Description	Goal
Nominal Deficit	Reduce deficit in spite of high interest rates	Reduction from 8.1 percent of the GDP in 1998 to 4.7 percent in 1999
Hard Currency Reserves	Limit losses	Minimum reserves of US$20 B
Trade Balance	Increase exports	Increase of 7.1 percent
Privatization	Results from sales/concessions	US$26 B in 1999

a. The agreement included an agenda for six evaluations of performance in 1999 to be done together with the IMF.

TABLE B-6. Fiscal Responsibility Law (May 2000)

Goal	Means
Impose legal restrictions on deficits and expenditures by states and municipalities	Limits on investment Prohibition of expenses not associated with increasing revenues Prohibition of increased payroll expenses during the last six months of each administration Limits on payment a posteriori to suppliers

The above summaries of the stabilization packages and programs were extracted from the "Fazenda" Ministry website [www.fazenda.gov.br]. The discussion of the IMF Accord draws from Maria da Conceição Tavares, "Informações sobre o Acordo com o FMI [http://www. abordo.com.br/mctavares/art30_98.htm].

APPENDIX C	*Planning and Social Development*

Avança Brasil (Forward Brazil) is the name of the multiyear plan (PPA) for the 2000–2003 period—that is, the national plan for Cardoso's second term plus the first year of the subsequent administration, as called for in the Brazilian constitution. PPAs define priorities and allocate resources to them via specific ministries. Cardoso's Forward Brazil organizes its 384 projects into three categories: integrated action plans (3), strategic programs (50), and other programs (331). These programs call for extensive partnership with civil society and private business. Each of these projects has a manager and is driven by a result-oriented management plan. *Avança Brasil* has four main foci: cities, rural development, education, and health. Key programs to alleviate poverty focus on microentrepreneurship, agrarian reform, local development, and civil society.

Microenterprise and Microcredit

- *Brasil Empreendedor (Entrepreneurial Brazil)*
  Coordinated by the office of the president and the Ministry of Development, this program supports micro, small, and medium-sized businesses (SMEs) to increase job availability and self-employment. This system works in two different dimensions: Brazil Entrepreneurship for micro, small, and medium firms (October 1999) and Brazil Rural Entrepreneurship (January 2000). By November 2001, the program had provided training to 4 million prospective entrepreneurs and distributed R$20 billion. By September 2002, the third year and phase, the program sharpened its focus on increasing the role of SMEs with respect to local production clusters, exports, and artisans. Entrepreneurial Brazil coordinates various government spheres to implement projects emphasizing partnership with civil society.

- *Brasil Empreendedor Rural (Rural Entrepreneurship)*
This program aims to: develop human capital, reduce the "Brazil cost," and give financial support through rural credit access, stimulate machinery renewal, and attract foreign capital to help finance the sector. This program includes extending credit to families through banks that work with PRONAF.

- *Micro, Pequeno e Médio Empresário (Micro, Small, and Medium Entrepreneurship)*
The goal of this program is to strengthen micro and small firms and support new businesses, to increase the population's income and create new opportunities. The program is based on: managerial training, low cost credit, and technical assistance. From July 1999 until 2000, R$7.7 billion was designated to 975,000 contracts, at an average of R$7,900 per contract.[1]

- *Sebrae (Serviço Brasileiro de Apoio às Micro e Pequenas Empresas/Brazilian Service of Support for Micro and Medium Firms)*
Created in 1990 by the federal government and big business, Sebrae is predominantly managed by the private sector and functions autonomously to implement public sector tasks without profit aims. The Sebrae system developed PRODER (Programa de Emprego e Renda), a community mobilization program to support local, integrated, and sustainable development (DLIS). Sebrae redirected its mission toward the development of small-scale entrepreneurship in 1999, and DLIS became the main approach to strengthening small-scale enterprises. In 2000, Sebrae had DLIS programs in 220 *municípios* and aimed at 1,000 in 2001[2].

- *PRODER (Programa de Emprego e Renda/Employment and income program)*, is one of Sebrae's programs, which promotes the creation of local agencies, supports their development efforts such as their training, and facilitates access to microcredit. Microenterprises in Brazil account for a large share of the total number of firms. Of the 4.9 million businesses created between 1990 and 1999, 2.7 million were microenterprises. Out of 475,005 firms created in 1999, 267,525 were microfirms, most of them in the Southeast. Proder is meant to encourage this development.

1.   The government defines microenterprises as retail businesses with gross yearly income of less than R$83,700. "Empresas de pequeno porte" are retail businesses with yearly gross receipts between R$83,700 and R$720,000.
2.   See "Desarrollo Local y Microempresa" [www.iadb.org/sds/doc/MicMoreira.pdf].

- *BNDES (Banco Nacional de Desenvolvimento Econômico e Social)*
The National Bank for Economic and Social Development finances development programs in accordance with national government policy. Since its founding in 1952, BNDES has financed large industrial and infrastructure companies and has played a major role in supporting agricultural investments, commerce, and social services, in addition to small and medium-size enterprises. In 1997, BNDES created the Social Fund, bankrolled by a share of its annual profits. This fund aims to support (nonreimbursable) social projects.

Family Farming and Rural Development Programs

- *PRONAF, Agrarian Reform* (including *Banco da Terra*)
PRONAF (Programa Nacional de Fortalecimento a Agricultura Familiar/ National Project for Family Agriculture) was launched in 1996 to support rural development by strengthening family farms, increasing rural employment and income, and introducing a new model of agrarian development. It was prompted in part by social movement demands for agrarian policy. The policies also aim at job creation and decreasing migration flows to cities. PRONAF operates as a line of credit to finance harvests (*custeio*), farm purchases and related investments, infrastructure and services, and research. Funds earmarked for municipal infrastructure and services call for the creation of municipal plans for rural development (PMDR). Funds for PRONAF come from FAT (Fundo de Amparo ao Trabalhador). According to José Eli da Veiga (2002), PRONAF has advanced the most on two fronts: financing production and infrastructure in counties where the role of agriculture is important. Veiga has published a number of other studies related to rural development. He also coordinates the CNDRS (National Council for Sustainable Rural Development).

- *INCRA (Instituto Nacional de Colonização e Reforma Agrária)*
The National Institute for Colonization and Agrarian Reform manages the agrarian reform program and rural development. It is an old institution that has acquired new life in the context of the agrarian reform program pursued since 1995.

Education

- *Bolsa Escola (Public School Scholarship Program)*
Initiated by Cristovam Buarque and approved by Congress in March 2001, this program is part of the Education Ministry and was inspired by similar successful programs with minimum income to poor families in some coun-

ties and states since 1995. The strategy of this program is to associate poverty alleviation with education by giving monthly financial incentives to families who enroll children in school. Its primary goal is to reach 10 million families with incomes of less than half of a minimum wage[3] and is financed by the Fund to Combat Poverty.

- *FUNDEF (Fundo de Manutenção e Desenvolvimento do Ensino Fundamental e de Valorização do Magistério/Fund for Teacher Development)*
  This fund was nationally implemented in January 1998 as a means of improving basic education. The constitution of 1988 obligated states and counties to designate 25 percent of all tax revenue to education. FUNDEF then established that 60 percent of the education budget must be directed to basic education and proportionally distributed among states and counties according to their number of students.

- *FNDE (Fundo Nacional de Desenvolvimento da Educação/Fund for Educational Development)*
  The resources for this fund are administrated by the Ministry of Education, which is responsible for collecting and distributing financial resources to a variety of programs and projects for basic education. It finances school meals, textbooks, libraries, health, services and school transportation. The fund services special groups such as indigenous tribes, Afro-Brazilians, and adults.

- □*Fundescola (Fundo de Fortalecimento da Escola/Fund for School Improvement)*
  This program was also developed by the Ministry of Education, in partnership with state and county secretaries of education to promote collective action to improve basic education in the most populous counties of the North, Northeast, and Center-West regions of the country. The main objective is to improve the quality of teaching and decrease the rate of school drop out. The resources to finance this program come from the federal government and loans from the World Bank.

Civil Society and Local Development

- *Comunidade Solidária (Conselho do Comunidade Solidária)*
  Comunidade Solidária was created in 1995 by First Lady Ruth Corrêa Leite Cardoso with the aim of promoting dialogue between government and civil society in order to build more effective partnership in the fight against poverty. From 1995 to 1998, it focused on 1,369 counties, where it invested R$7.8 billion [www.presidencia.gov.br]. Comunidade Solidária has sup-

---

3.   The minimum wage in Brazil in 2000 was R$151.00.

ported a literacy campaign and the recruitment of college students in programs to address social problems by working directly in the affected communities. The Conselho do Comunidade Solidária convenes ministers and civil society representatives on two year terms to discuss innovative partnerships and projects.

- *Comunidade Ativa/Active Community*
  This program helps poor communities organize and mobilize to make demands and channel government programs. It operates in the poorest counties to induce the process of "sustainable and integrated local development" (DLIS) via partnerships and with direct community involvement in the design and implementation of programs. The emphasis of the program is on human and social capital, entrepreneurial skills, and access to information. Local agendas include agriculture, agro-industry, health, urban development and environment, education and extension education, and infrastructure. President Cardoso reports that it had reached 157 counties in 2001 and 604 in early 2002 (Brasil, Presidente, 2002, 50).

- *Projeto Alvorada (Fundo de Combate à Pobreza/Fund to Fight Poverty)*
  Projeto Alvorada was created in 1999 to enhance decentralized management and planning capabilities with regard to programs for improving living conditions in the poorest counties. It initially focused on fifteen programs in 2,313 counties with the lowest HDI (Human Development Index) scores, for which it mobilized more than R$13 billion through 2002 (Cardoso 2002). Projeto Alvorada's first phase, the Support Plan to States with Low Human Development, focuses on education, health, and socioeconomic development. A second phase concentrates on basic social infrastructure in microregions and counties. The Fund to Fight Poverty, a result of congressional initiatives, complements it.

Statistical Trends

Economic Performance and Social Development

FIGURE D-1. Inflation

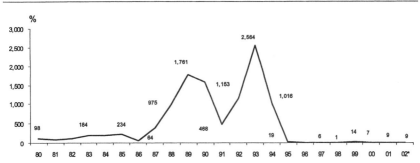

Source: INPC, IPC, IGP-M, IGP-DI (Major four indexes average)
* Annual inflation updated until July.

FIGURE D-2. Gross Domestic Product

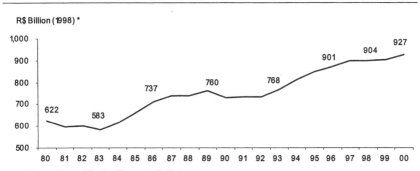

Source: Central Bank - *Economic Bulletin*
* Dec. 1998: 1 *real* = 0.828 US dollar.

195

Appendix D

FIGURE D-3. Interest Rates

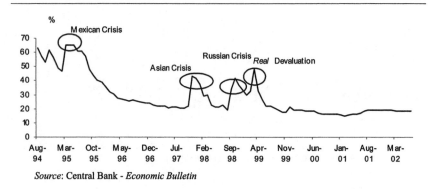

Source: Central Bank - *Economic Bulletin*

FIGURE D-4. Stock Exchange

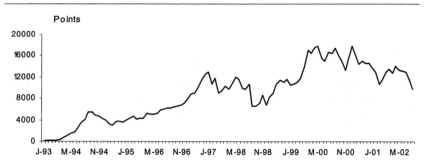

Source: Bovespa - São Paulo Stock Exchange

FIGURE D-5. Mergers and Acquisitions

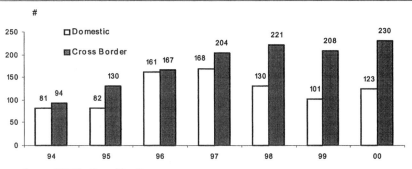

Source: KPMG - Consulting Company

FIGURE D-6. Urbanization

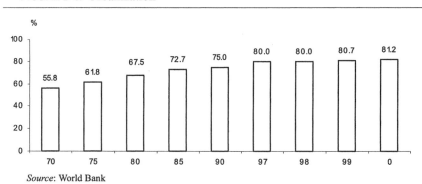

Source: World Bank

FIGURE D-7. Grain Yields, by region, 1973–1999

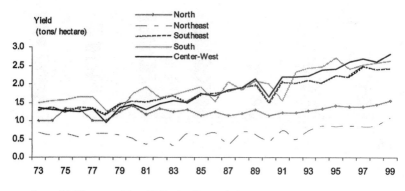

Source: IBGE, extracted from Helfand and Rezende (2000)

FIGURE D-8. Average Monthly Income

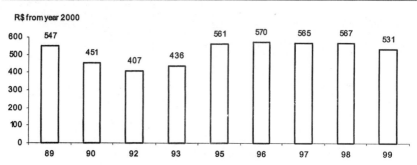

Source: IBGE - Brazilian Institute of Geography and Statistics

FIGURE D-9. Life Expectancy

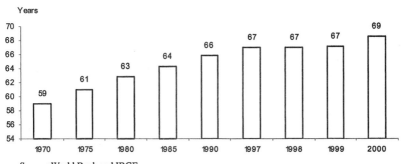

Source: World Bank and IBGE

FIGURE D-10. Industrial Employment, growth rate

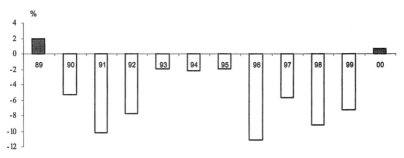

Source: IBGE/DPE/Department of Industry

FIGURE D-11. Monthly Unemployment Rate

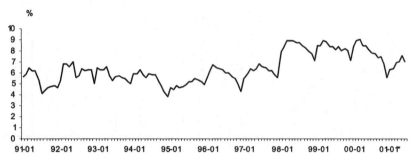

Source: IBGE/Open Unemployment Rate (30 days)
* Updated until June 2001.

FIGURE D-12. Infant Mortality

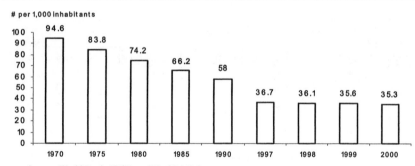

Source: World Bank, IBGE, and Health Ministry

FIGURE D-13. Income Inequality, gini index

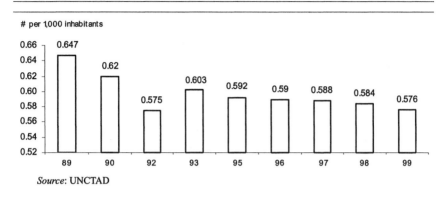

per 1,000 inhabitants

Source: UNCTAD

FIGURE D-14. Inequality, income shares, 1998

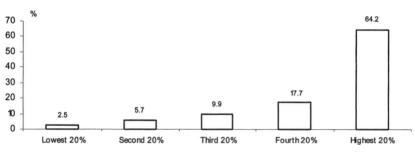

Source: World Bank *Annual Report 1998*

FIGURE D-15. Illiteracy, per age group

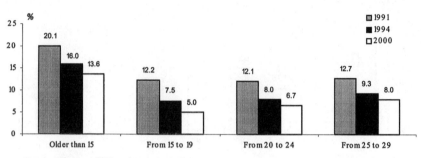

Source: Ministry of Education

FIGURE D-16. School Enrollment, ages 7-14

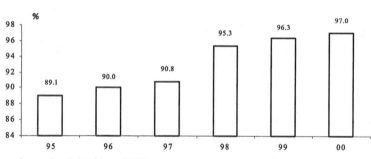

Source: Brasil, Presidente (2001)

FIGURE D-17. Indigence, two-year average trend line

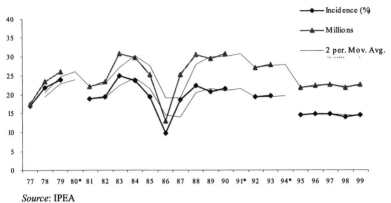

Source: IPEA
* Data not available.

FIGURE D-18. Food Production, two-year average trend line

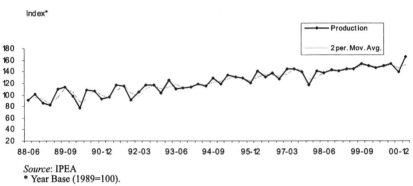

Source: IPEA
* Year Base (1989=100).

204

Appendix D

FIGURE D-19. Human Development Index, South America, 1998

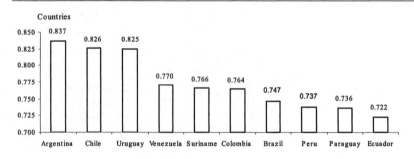

Source: Human Development Report 2000

FIGURE D-20. Population below Poverty Line, selected countries

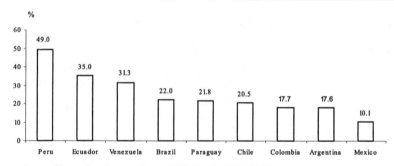

Source: Human Development Report 2001 (data for 1984–1999)

FIGURE D-21. GDP per Capita, selected countries

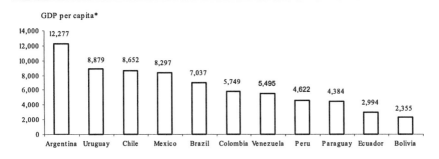

Source: *Human Development Report 2001*
* PPP US$, data for 1999.

FIGURE D-22. *Avança Brasil* Budget, 2000–2003

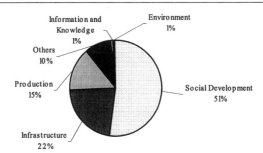

Source: Brasil, Presidente (2001)
Note: Total Budget: R$1,166 Billion.

Fiscal and State Reform

FIGURE D-23. Privatization

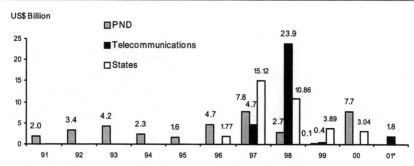

Source: BNDES - National Bank of Economic and Social Development
* Preliminary.

FIGURE D-24. Budget 2000, expenses

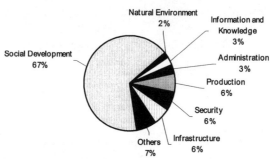

Source: Planning and Budget Ministry

TABLE D-1. Fiscal Deficit–Primary,[1] as percent of GDP

	94	95	96	97	98	99	00	01
All Levels								
Original Goal[2]					0.0	3.1	3.3	3.4
Actual	5.2	0.3	-0.1	-0.9	0.0	3.2	3.5	3.7
Central Government								
Original Goal					0.6	2.5	2.7	2.6
Actual	3.3	0.5	0.4	-0.2	0.6	2.4	1.9	1.9
States and Municipalities								
Original Goal					-0.2	0.2	0.5	0.7
Actual	0.8	-0.2	-0.5	-0.5	-0.2	0.2	0.6	0.9
State Firms								
Original Goal					-0.4	0.4	0.1	0.1
Actual	1.2	-0.1	0.1	-0.2	-0.4	0.7	1.1	1.0

Source: Central Bank
1. Primary Balance excludes service of debt.
2. Established in context of accords with the IMF.

FIGURE D-25. Public Balance, primary

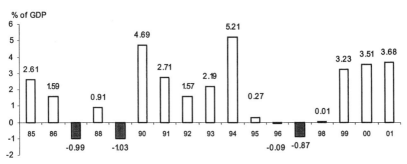

Source: National Treasury Secretariat and Central Bank
Note: Primary balance excludes service of debt; deficits appear with a minus sign.

208

Appendix D

FIGURE D-26. Debt Service

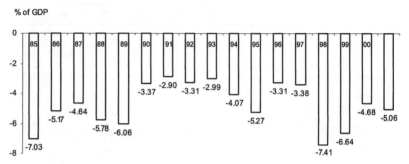

Source: National Treasury Secretariat and Central Bank
Note: Payment of real interest.

FIGURE D-27. Public Balance, operational

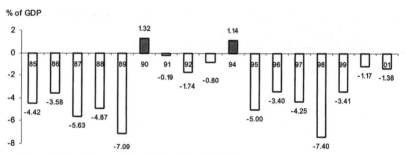

Source: National Treasury Secretariat and Central Bank
Note: Primary balance plus service of debt (real interest).

FIGURE D-28. Primary Deficit, by level of government

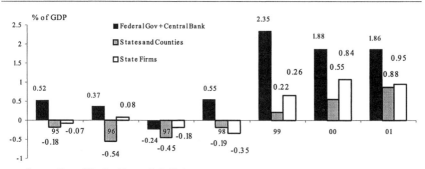

Source: Central Bank - *Economic Bulletin*

FIGURE D-29. Operational Deficit, by level of government

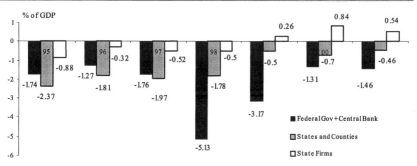

Source: Central Bank - *Economic Bulletin*

FIGURE D-30. Net Total Public Debt

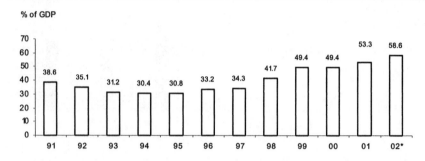

% of GDP

Source: IPEA
* Updated until July 2002.

TABLE D-2. Public Sector Debt, as percent of GDP

Year	States and Municipalities		State Firms		Federal Government and Central Bank	
	Internal	**Foreign**	**Internal**	**Foreign**	**Internal**	**Foreign**
1991	6.18	1.13	10.15	8.21	-2.19	15.12
1992	7.70	1.03	8.96	5.95	0.78	10.71
1993	7.84	0.96	7.94	5.28	1.74	7.39
1994	9.78	0.36	5.18	2.01	6.62	6.43
1995	10.39	0.34	4.94	1.80	9.86	3.51
1996	11.15	0.37	3.89	1.96	14.29	1.56
1997	12.42	0.48	0.89	1.87	16.72	1.95
1998	13.49	0.66	1.24	1.32	20.81	4.20
1999	15.43	0.90	1.28	1.55	22.28	7.95
2000	15.30	0.97	0.88	1.31	23.49	7.50
2001	17.45	1.05	0.40	1.17	24.86	8.32
2002[1]	17.46	1.10	1.02	1.09	26.44	8.92

Source: IPEA
1. Updated until May 2002.

FIGURE D-31. Federal Transfers to States and Counties, by region

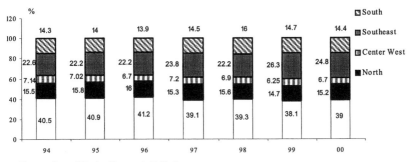

Source: Central Bank - *Economic Bulletin*

FIGURE D-32. Social Security

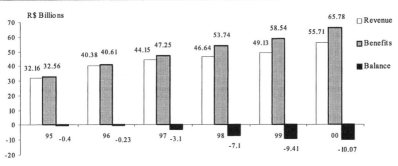

Source: Brasil, Presidente (2001)

Appendix D

FIGURE D-33. Social Security Deficit

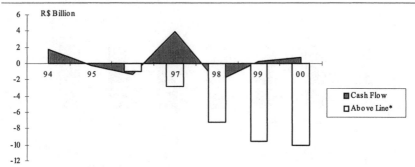

Source: Central Bank - *Economic Bulletin*
* This accurate measure is calculated through the difference between expenses and revenues.

FIGURE D-34. National Congress

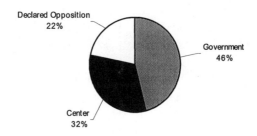

Source: Brazilian Chamber of Deputies

External Sector

FIGURE D-35. Exports and Imports

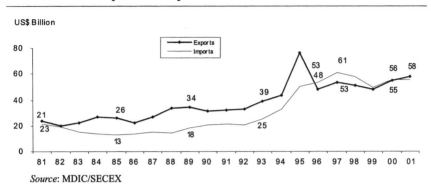

Source: MDIC/SECEX

FIGURE D-36. Trade Balance

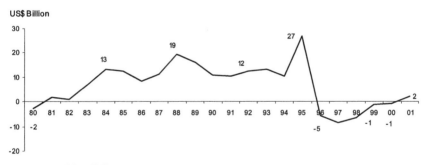

Source: MDIC/SECEX

FIGURE D-37. Current Account

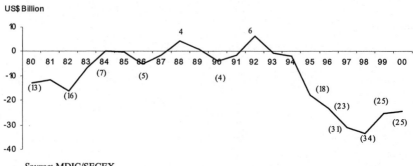

Source: MDIC/SECEX

FIGURE D-38. External Debt

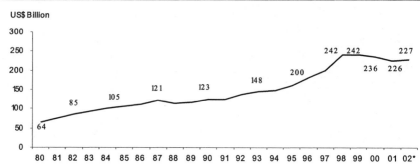

.*Source*: Central Bank - *Economic Bulletin*
* Position updated until March 2002.

FIGURE D-39. External Debt Growth

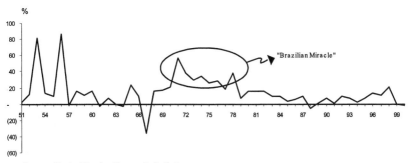

Source: Central Bank - *Economic Bulletin*

FIGURE D-40. Foreign Investment

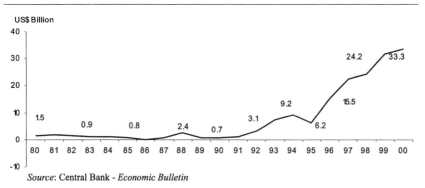

Source: Central Bank - *Economic Bulletin*

Appendix D

FIGURE D-41. Hard Currency Reserves, balance of payments

US$ Billion

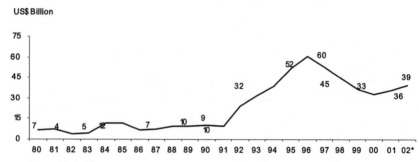

Source: Central Bank - *Economic Bulletin*
* Position updated until March 2002.

FIGURE D-42. Hard Currency Reserves

US$ Billion

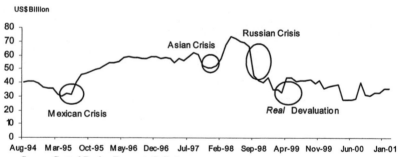

Source: Central Bank - *Economic Bulletin*

FIGURE D-43. Direct Foreign Investment (1980 = 1)

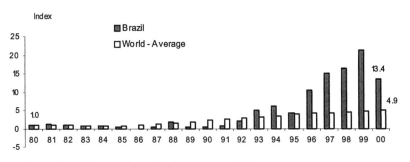

Source: United Nations - *Human Development Report 1999*

FIGURE D-44. Current Account Balance

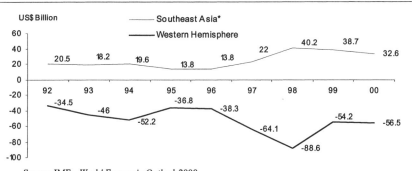

Source: IMF - *World Economic Outlook* 2000
* South Korea, Taiwan, Hong Kong, and Singapore.

Regional Differences

TABLE E-1. Brazil's Five Regions

	States	Area	Population 1996	Population 2000
North	Amazon region and adjacent: Pará, Acre, Amapá, Amazonas, Rondônia, Roraima, Tocantins	45.3%	11,288,259 (7.2%)	12,900,704 (7.6%)
Northeast	Bahia, Pernambuco, Ceará, and six smaller states—Alagoas, Maranhão, Paraíba, Piauí, Rio Grande do Norte, Sergipe	18.2%	44,766,851 (28.5%)	47,741,711 (28.1%)
Southeast	São Paulo, Minas Gerais, Rio de Janeiro, and Espírito Santo	10.9%	67,000,738 (42.7%)	72,412,411 (42.6%)
South	Paraná, Santa Catarina, Rio Grande do Sul	6.8%	23,513,736 (15.0%)	25,107,616 (14.8%)
Center-West	Goiás, Federal District, Mato Grosso, and Mato Grosso do Sul	18.9%	10,500,579 (6.7%)	11,636,728 (6.8%)
Brazil		100%	157,070,163	169,799,170

Source: IBGE

TABLE E-2. Economic and Industrial Output, percent of nation

	Economic				Industrial	
	1970	1985	1995	1998	1970	1985
North	2.2	4.1	4.6	4.5	1.1	4.1
Northeast	11.7	13.6	12.8	13.1	7.0	12.2
Southeast	65.5	59.1	58.8	58.2	79.1	65.8
São Paulo	[39.4]	[35.4]	[35.5]	[35.5]	[56.5]	[44.0]
South	16.7	17.1	17.9	17.5	12.0	15.9
Center-West	3.9	6.0	6.0	6.8	0.9	2.4

Source: IPEA

TABLE E-3. Population

	Share of Brazil (Percent)					Growth Rate in 1996
	1970	1980	1991	1996	2000	
North	4.4	5.6	6.9	7.2	7.6	2.4%
Northeast	30.3	29.2	28.9	28.5	28.1	1.1%
Southeast	42.7	43.4	42.7	42.7	42.6	1.4%
São Paulo	[19.0]	[20.9]	[21.5]	[21.7]	[21.8]	n.a.
South	17.7	16.0	15.1	15.0	14.8	1.2%
Center-West	4.9	5.8	6.4	6.7	6.9	2.2%
Brazil	100	100	100	100	100	1.4%

Source: IBGE

TABLE E-4. Poverty Rates, as percent of region and nation

Period	1995		1997		1999	
Region	Rate	% Brazil	Rate	% Brazil	Rate	% Brazil
North	38.5	5.3	39.6	5.51	39.7	5.6
Northeast	52.1	45.5	52.9	44.9	50.9	42.0
Southeast	26.1	33.2	27.2	34.3	28.6	36.0
South	17.9	8.3	18.1	8.2	19.7	8.7
Center-West	37.4	7.8	34.6	7.1	37.4	7.6
Brazil	33.2	100	34.1	100	35.0	100

Source: Rocha and Albuquerque (1999) and Rocha (2001)

TABLE E-5. Inequality, monthly family income - R$

Period	1992			1999		
Region	10% poorest	40% poorest	10% richest	10% poorest	40% poorest	10% richest
North	17.6	42.7	790.1	27.5	58.0	1,097.3
Northeast	10.1	27.5	605.6	17.5	39.5	900.4
Southeast	30.6	71.7	1,227.3	44.9	96.6	1,784.1
São Paulo	[41.3]	[89.0]	[1,276.4]	[56.6]	[115.7]	[1,926.3]
South	27.5	65.5	1,112.4	37.6	86.3	1,571.6
Center-West	24.5	54.0	1,139.9	36.0	74.7	1,581.5
Brazil	18.4	50.5	1,053.1	28.3	68.3	1,511.7

Source: IBGE

TABLE E-6. Value of Agricultural Production, 1995–1996

	Value of production, in millions of *reais*			Value of production, as percent of Brazil		
	Animal	Vegetal	Total	Animal	Vegetal	Total
North	1,011	1,310	2,321	5.37	4.53	4.86
Northeast	2,723	4,320	7,043	14.46	14.92	14.74
Southeast	5,714	10,820	16,534	30.35	37.36	34.60
São Paulo	[2,403]	[6,010]	[8,413]	[12.76]	[20.75]	[17.60]
South	5,823	9,180	15,003	30.93	31.70	31.39
Center-West	3,557	3,327	6,884	18.89	11.49	14.41
Brazil	18,828	28,957	47,785	100%	100%	100%

Source: IBGE, *Resultados do Censo Agropecuário 1995-1996*

TABLE E-7. Agrarian Reform, 1995–2000

	Number of Families Settled					
	1995	1996	1997	1998	1999	2000
North	10,471	24,682	32,140		24,239	21,251
Northeast	18,551	21,271	26,627		24,482	35,770
Southeast	1,308	3,004	4,583		4,777	5,303
São Paulo	[503]	[822]	[1,063]	[1,833]	[592]	[2,133]
South	2,178	2,007	4,356		5,111	6,433
Center-West	10,404	10,710	14,238		12,220	24,218
Brazil	42,912	61,674	81,944	101,095	70,829	92,975

Source: INCRA-Instituto Nacional de Colonização e Reforma Agrária

TABLE E-8. Urbanization, percent

	1970	1980	1991	1996	2000
North	41.1	51.6	59.0	62.4	69.9
Northeast	41.8	50.5	60.7	65.2	69.1
Southeast	72.7	82.8	88.0	89.3	90.5
São Paulo	[80.3]	[88.6]	[92.8]	[93.1]	[93.4]
South	44.3	62.4	71.1	77.2	80.9
Center-West	48.0	67.8	81.3	84.4	86.7
Brazil	55.9	67.6	75.8	78.4	81.2

Source: IBGE

Glossary

abertura	process of political liberalization during 1974–1985, culminating in the election of a civilian president
autarquia	public or semi-independent corporation or government agency
carioca	native or resident of the city of Rio de Janeiro
comunidades eclesiais de base	Base eclesial communities (CEBs)
coronel	rural political chieftain
dirigisme	statism or state-centered approach to economic development
fazenda	large farm, plantation, or ranch
gaúcho	native or resident of the state of Rio Grande do Sul
heterodox stabilization	stabilization and adjustment programs emphasizing controls on wages, prices, and exchange rates
marajás	public servants receiving exorbitant paychecks
medidas provisórias	provisional measures, a special kind of presidential decree, also known as MPs
mineiro	native or resident of the state of Minas Gerais
município	administrative unit corresponding to county
nordestino	Northeasterner; native or resident of the Northeastern region
orthodox stabilization	stabilization and adjustment plans emphasizing tight monetary policy and fiscal austerity policies
paulista	native or resident of the state of São Paulo
paulistano	native or resident of the city of São Paulo
panelinha	informal political group or clique advancing interests of members
pelego	union or union leader at the service of the state
posseiro	squatter or homesteader
Plano Real	Fernando Henrique Cardoso's stabilization plan, started in 1993
real	Brazilian currency introduced in 1994

Bibliography

Abers, Rebecca. 1998. "From Clientelism to Cooperation: Local Government, Participatory Policy, and Civic Organizing in Porto Alegre, Brazil." *Politics and Society* 26 (4): 511–37.

Abramovay, Ricardo. 1998. "Capital social: Cinco proposições sobre desenvolvimento rural." Paper presented at the II Fórum CONTAG de Cooperação Técnica: *A Formação de Capital Social para o Desenvolvimento Local Sustentável*. Maranhão, Brazil, December 6–8.

Abramovay, Ricardo, and Ana Amélia Camarano. 1999. "Êxodo rural, envelhecimento e masculinização no Brasil: Panorama dos últimos 50 anos." Texto para Discussão *nº 621*. Brasília, Brazil: IPEA.

Abreu, Alzira Alves de, org. 2001. *Transição em fragmentos: Desafios da democracia no final do século XX*. Rio de Janeiro, Brazil: Fundação Getúlio Vargas.

Abreu, Marcelo Dionísio Carneiro, and Marcelo Werneck. 1996. "Brazil: Widening the Scope for Balanced Growth." *World Development* 24 (2): 241–54.

Abrúcio, Fernando Luiz. 1998. *Os barões da federação: Os governadores e a redemocratização brasileira*. São Paulo, Brazil: Hucitec and Departamento de Ciência Política da Universidade de São Paulo.

———. 1996. "Os barões da federação." *Lua Nova* 33: 165–83.

Acuña, Carlos H., and William C. Smith. 1996. "La economía política del ajuste estructural: La lógica de apoyo y oposición a las reformas neoliberales." *Desarrollo Económico* 36 (141): 355–89.

Addis, Caren. 1999. *Taking the Wheel: Auto Parts Firms and the Political Economy of Industrialization in Brazil*. University Park, Pa.: The Pennsylvania State University Press.

Affonso, Rui de Brito Alvares. 1995. "A federação no Brasil: Impasses e perspectivas." In R. de Brito Alvares Affonso and P. L. Barros Silva, eds., *A federação em perspectiva: Ensaios selecionados*. São Paulo, Brazil: FUNDAP.

Albuquerque, José Augusto Guilhon. 1993. "Unfinished Reforms." In Werner Baer and Joseph S. Tulchin, eds., *Brazil and the Challenge of Economic Reform*. Washington, D.C.: Woodrow Wilson Center Press, 149–54.

Albuquerque, Roberto Cavalcanti de. 1995. "Reconstrução e reforma do Estado." In João Paulo dos Reis Velloso and Robert Cavalcanti de Albuquerque et al., eds., *Governabilidade e reformas*. Rio de Janeiro, Brazil: José Oympio, 129–98.

Albuquerque, Rui H. P. L. de. 1982. *Capital comercial, indústria têxtil e produção agrícola*. São Paulo, Brazil: Hucitec.

Alcantara, Lúcio. 1997. "Olhando para o futuro: Perspectivas para o sistema federalista brasileiro." *Revista Brasileira de Estudos Políticos* (85): 89–102.

Almeida, Maria Hermínia Tavares de. 2000. "Não é comigo" (research report at www.werbo.com.br/materia.cfm?materia=65).

———. 1995a. "Pragmatism by Necessity: The Brazilian Path to Economic Reform." Paper presented at the American Sociological Association, Washington D.C., August 19–23. See also: See also: "Pragmatismo por necessidade: Os rumos da reforma econômica no Brasil." *Dados* 39 (2): 213–34.

———. 1995b. "Federalismo e políticas sociais." *Revista Brasileira de Ciências Sociais* 28 (June): 88–107.

———. 1987. "Novo Sindicalismo and Politics in Brazil." In John D. Wirth, Edson de Oliveira Nunes, and Thomas E. Bogenschild, eds., *State and Society in Brazil: Change and Continuity.* Boulder, Colo.: Westview Press.

———. 1983. "O sindicalismo brasileiro entre a conservação e a mudança." In Maria Hermínia Tavares de Almeida and Bernardo Sorj, eds., *Sociedade e política no Brasil pós-64.* São Paulo, Brazil: Brasiliense.

Almeida, Maria Hermínia Tavares de, and Mauricio Moya. 1997. "A reforma negociada: O Congresso e a política de privatização." *Revista Brasileira de Ciências Sociais* 12 (34): 119–32.

Almeida, Maria Hermínia Tavares de, and Bernardo Sorj, eds. 1983. *Sociedade e política no Brasil pós-64.* São Paulo, Brazil: Brasiliense.

Almino, João. 1996. "Del colapso de las ideologías a las ideologías del colapso: La democracia en el Brasil hoy." *Revista Mexicana De Sociologia* (1): 233–41.

Alt, James, Jeffry Frieden, Michael Gilligan, Dani Rodrik, and Ronald Rogowsky. 1996. "The Political Economy of International Trade: Enduring Puzzles and an Agenda for Inquiry." *Comparative Political Studies* 29 (6): 689–717.

Alvarez, Sonia E. 1990. *Engendering Democracy in Brazil: Women's Movement in Transition Politics.* Princeton, N.J.: Princeton University Press.

Ames, Barry. 2001. "A democracia brasileira: Uma democracia em xeque." In Alzira A. Abreu, ed., *Transição em fragmentos: Desafios da democracia no final do século XX.* Rio de Janeiro, Brazil: Fundação Getúlio Vargas.

———. 1995. "Electoral Rules, Constituency Pressures, and Pork Barrel: Bases of Voting in the Brazilian Congress." *Journal of Politics* 57 (2): 324–43.

———. 1987. *Political Survival: Politicians and Public Policy in Latin America.* Berkeley, Calif.: University of California Press.

Armijo, Leslie Elliot. 1999. *Financial Globalization and Democracy in Emerging Markets.* New York, N.Y.: St. Martin's Press.

———. 1997. "Global Change, Regional Response: The New International Context of Development." *American Political Science Review* 91 (4): 982–84.

———. 1996. "Inflation and Insouciance: The Peculiar Brazilian Game." *Latin American Research Review* 31 (3): 7–46.

Avritzer, Leonardo. 2000. "Democratization and Changes in the Pattern of Association in Brazil." *Journal of Interamerican and World Affairs* 42 (3): 59–76.

Azevedo, Sérgio, and Marcus Andre Melo. 1997. "A política da reforma tributária: Federalismo e mudança constitucional." *Revista Brasileira das Ciências Sociais* 12 (35): 75–99.

Baaklini, Abdo I. 1992. *The Brazilian Legislature and Political System.* Westport, Conn.: Greenwood Press.

Bacha, Edmar L. 1991. "Perspectivas econômicas brasileiras em regime de feijão com arroz à la Marcílio." In Maurício Dias, org., *Economia e política da crise brasileira: A perspectiva social-democrata.* Rio de Janeiro, Brazil: Rio Fundo, 79–83.

Baer, Werner. 1995. *The Brazilian Economy: Growth and Development.* 4th ed. Westport, Conn.: Praeger.

Baer, Werner, Isaac Kerstenetzky, and Annibal Villela. 1973. "As modificações no papel do Estado na economia brasileira." *Pesquisa e Planejamento* 3 (4): 883–912.

Baer, Werner, and Joseph S. Tulchin, eds. 1993. *Brazil and the Challenge of Economic Reform.* Washington, D.C.: Woodrow Wilson Center Press.

Balassa, Bela. 1981. "Structural Adjustment Policies in Developing Economies." World Bank Staff Working Papers 464.

Barreto, Maria Inês. 1999. "As organizações sociais na reforma do Estado brasileiro." In L. C. Bresser Pereira and Nuria C. Grau, eds., *O público não-estatal na reforma do Estado.* Rio de Janeiro, Brazil: Fundação Getúlio Vargas.

Barros, A. C. M. 1999. "Capital, produtividade e crescimento da agricultura: O Brasil de 1970 e 1995." Ph.D. diss., ESALQ University, Piracicaba, Brazil.

Barros, Ricardo Paes de, Ricardo Henriques, and Rosane Mendonça. 2000a. "A estabilidade inaceitável: Desigualdade e pobreza no Brasil." In Ricardo Henriques, ed., *Desigualdade e pobreza no Brasil.* Rio de Janeiro, Brazil: IPEA.

———. 2000b. "Evolução recente da pobreza e da desigualdade: Marcos preliminares para a política social no Brasil." In Ricardo Paes de Barros et al., *Pobreza e Política Social.* Cadernos Adenauer 1. São Paulo, Brazil: Fundação Konrad Adenauer.

Bartell, Ernest. 1994. "Privatization: The Role of Domestic Business Elites." In Werner Baer and Melissa H. Birch, eds., *Privatization in Latin America: New Roles for the Public and Private Sectors.* Westport, Conn.: Praeger.

Bartell, Ernest, and Leigh Payne, eds. 1995. *Business and Democracy in Latin America.* Pittsburgh, Pa.: University of Pittsburgh Press.

Bates, Robert, and Anne Krueger, eds. 1993. *Political and Economic Interactions in Economic Policy Reform.* Oxford, London: Basil Blackwell.

Baumann, Renato. 1999a. "Brazil in the 1990s: An Economy in Transition." University of Oxford Centre for Brazilian Studies, Working Paper CBS-07.

———, org. 1999b. *Brasil: Uma década em transição.* Rio de Janeiro, Brazil: Campus.

Becker, David. 1990. "Business Associations in Latin America." *Comparative Political Studies* 32: 114–38.

Bello, José Maria. 1966. *A History of Modern Brazil, 1889–1964.* Stanford, Calif.: Stanford University Press. Based on *História da República.* 4th ed. (1959). Trans. James L. Taylor.

Biderman, Ciro, Luis Felipe Cozac, and José Márcio Rego. 1996. *Conversas com economistas.* São Paulo, Brazil: Editora 34.

Bielschowsky, Ricardo. 1991. "Ideology and Development in Brazil, 1930–1964." *CEPAL Review* 45 (December): 145–67.

———. 1988. *Pensamento econômico brasileliro: O ciclo ideológico do desenvolvimento.* Rio de Janeiro, Brazil: IPEA-INPES.

Bielschowsky, Roberto. 1985. *O pensamento econômico brasileiro: O ciclo ideológico desenvolvimentista.* Rio de Janeiro, Brazil: IPEA/INPES.

Bienen, Henri, and Mark Gersovitz. 1985. "Economic Stabilization, Conditionality and Political Stability." *International Organization* 39 (4): 729–54.

Blake, Charles H. 1998. "Economic Reform and Democratization in Argentina and Uruguay: The Tortoise and the Hare Revisited?" *Journal of Interamerican and World Affairs* 40 (3): 1–26.

Boito, Armando, Jr. 1994. "The State and Trade Unionism in Brazil." *Latin American Perspectives* 21 (80): 7–23.

Bonelli, Regis. 2001. "Políticas de competitividade industrial no Brasil — 1995/2000." Texto para Discussão nº 810. Brasília, Brazil: IPEA.

Bonelli, Regis, and Robson R. Gonçalves. 1998. "Para onde vai a estrutura industrial brasileira?" Texto para Discussão nº 540. Brasília, Brazil: IPEA.

Bonfim, Antúlio, and Anwar Shah. 1994. "Macroeconomic Management and the Division of Powers in Brazil: Perspectives for the 1990s." *World Development* 22 (4): 535–42.

Boschi, Renato R. 1995. "Politics and Economic Reform in Brazil: The Views of Entreprenuers." IUPERJ, Rio de Janeiro, Brazil, October 4–6. Paper presented at the international seminar, "The Challenge of Democracy in Latin America: Rethinking State/Society Relations."

———. 1987. *A arte da associação: Política de base e democracia no Brasil.* São Paulo, Brazil: Vértice and IUPERJ.

———. 1979. *Elites industriais e democracia.* Rio de Janeiro, Brazil: Graal.

———. 1978. *Empresariado nacional e Estado no Brasil.* Rio de Janeiro, Brazil: Forense Universitária.

———, ed. 1991. *Corporativismo e desigualdade: A construção do espaço público no Brasil.* Rio de Janeiro, Brazil: IUPERJ and Rio Fundo.

Boschi, Renato R., Eli Diniz, and Fabiano Santos. 2000. *Elites políticas e econômicas no Brasil contemporâneo: A desconstrução da ordem corporativa e o papel do Legislativo no cenário pós-reformas.* São Paulo, Brazil: Fundação Konrad Adenauer.

Brasil, Ministério do Planejamento, Orçamento e Gestão, Secretaria de Planejamento e Investimentos Estratégicos. 2001a. *Plano Avança Brasil.* Brasília, Brazil: MP.

———. 2001b. *II Forum Global: Democratic State and Governance in the XXIst Century.* Brasília, Brazil: MP.

———. 2001c. *Avança Brasil: Programas estratégicos.* Brasília, Brazil: MP.

———. 2000. *Avança Brasil: Estruturas de desenvolvimento para o investimento.* Brasília, Brazil: MP.

Brasil, Presidente. 2002. *Mensagem ao Congresso Nacional.* Brasília: Presidência da República, Secretaria de Comunicação de Governo.

———. 2001. *7 Anos de Real. Estabilidade, crescimento e desenvolvimento social.* Coleção Documentos da Presidência da República.

———. 2000. *Mensagem ao Congresso Nacional: Abertura da segunda sessão legislativa ordinária da 51ª legislatura.* Brasil: Presidência da República, Secretaria de Comunicação de Governo.

———. 1998. *Avança Brasil: Proposta de Governo.* Brasília, Brazil. s. ed.

Bressan, Silvio. 2002. "Reforma Administrativa." In Bolívar Lamounier and Rubens Figueiredo, eds., *A Era FHC, Um Balanço.* São Paulo, Brazil: Cultura Editores Associados.

Bresser Pereira, Luiz Carlos. c1997. "Interpretações sobre o Brasil." In Maria Rita Loureiro, org., *50 anos de ciência econômica no Brasil.* Rio de Janeiro, Brazil: Vozes.

———. 1997. "Estratégia e estrutura para um novo Estado." *Revista de Economia Política* 17 (3): 24–38.

————. 1996. *Economic Crisis and State Reform in Brazil: Toward a New Interpretation of Latin America*. Boulder, Colo.: Lynne Rienner Publishers.

————. 1994a. "Empresários, suas origens e as interpretações do Brasil." *Revista Brasileira de Ciências Sociais* 9 (25): 52–63.

————. 1994b. "A economia e a política do Plano Real." *Revista de Economia Política* 14 (4): 129–49.

————. 1993. "Uma interpretação da América Latina: A crise do Estado." *Novos Estudos CEBRAP* 37 (November): 37–57.

————. 1992. *A crise do Estado: Ensaios sobre a economia brasileira*. São Paulo, Brazil: Nobel.

————. 1978. *O colapso de uma aliança de classes: A burguesia e a crise do autoritarismo tecnoburocrático*. São Paulo, Brazil: Brasiliense.

————. 1977. *Estado e subdesenvolvimento industrializado*. São Paulo: Brasiliense.

Bresser Pereira, Luiz Carlos, and José Márcio Rego. 1993. "Um mestre da economia brasileira: Ignácio Rangel." *Revista de Economia Política* 13 (2): 98–136.

Bresser Pereira, Luiz Carlos, and Peter Kevin Spink, eds. 1998. *Reforma do Estado e administração pública gerencial*. Rio de Janeiro, Brazil: Fundação Getúlio Vargas.

Bresser Pereira, Luiz Carlos, Jorge Willeim, and Lourdes Sola, eds. 1999. *Sociedade e Estado em transformação*. São Paulo: UNESP and Brasília: ENAP.

Bruneau, Thomas C., and W. E. Hewitt. 1989. "Patterns of Church Influence in Brazil's Political Transition." *Comparative Politics* 22 (1): 39–61.

Büllow, Marisa von. 1995. "Algunas hipótesis alrededor de las elecciones brasileñas de 1994." *Estudios Sociológicos* 13 (38): 433–47.

Bulmer-Thomas, Victor. 1996. *The New Economic Model in Latin America and Its Impact on Income Distribution and Poverty*. London, U.K.: Institute of Latin American Studies, University of London.

————.1994. *The Latin American Economies in the 1930s. The Cambridge History of Latin America*, vol. 6, part 1. Cambridge, Mass.: Cambridge University Press.

————. 1987. "The Balance of Payments Crisis and Adjustment Programmes in Central America." In R. Thorp and L. Whitehead, eds., *Latin American Debt and the Adjustment Crisis*. Pittsburgh, Pa.: University of Pittsburgh Press.

Burnham, Walter Dean. 1975. "Party Systems and the Political Process." In William N. Chambers and Walter Dean Burnham, eds., *The American Party System: Stages of Political Development*. New York: Oxford University Press.

Cadernos, Adenauer I. 2000. *Pobreza e Política Social*. São Paulo, Brazil: Fundação Konrad Adenauer.

Caixeta, Nely. 2002. "Educação." In Bolívar Lamounier and Rubens Figueiredo, eds., *A Era FHC: Um Balanço*. São Paulo, Brazil: Cultura Editores Associados.

Caldeira, Teresa P. R. 2001. *City of Walls: Crime, Segregation, and Citizenship in São Paulo*. Berkeley, Calif.: University of California Press.

Callaghy, Thomas M. 1990. "Lost between State and Market: The Politics of Economic Adjustment in Ghana, Zambia, and Nigeria." In Joan M. Nelson, ed., *Economic Crisis and Policy Choice: The Politics of Adjustment in the Third World*. Princeton, N.J.: Princeton University Press.

————. 1989. "Toward State Capability and Embedded Liberalism in the Third World: Lessons for Adjustment." In Joan M. Nelson, ed., *Fragile Coalitions: The Politics of Economic Adjustment*. New Brunswick, N.J.: Transaction Books.

Camargo, Aspácia, et al. 1989. *O golpe silencioso: As origens da república corporativa*. Rio de Janeiro, Brazil: Rio Fundo.

Camargo, Aspácia, and Eli Diniz, eds. 1989. *Continuidade e mudança no Brasil da Nova República*. São Paulo, Brazil: IUPERJ/Vértice.

Cammack, Paul. 1982. "Clientelism and Military Government in Brazil." In C. Claphan, ed., *Private Patronage and Public Power*. New York, N.Y.: St. Martin's.

Campos, Iris Walquiria. 2002. "Defesa nacional." In Bolívar Lamounier and Rubens Figueiredo, eds., *A Era FHC: Um Balanço*. São Paulo, Brazil: Cultura Editores Associados.

Campos, Roberto. 1994. *A lanterna na popa*. Rio de Janeiro, Brazil: Topbooks.

Cano, Wilson. 1995. "Auge e inflexão da desconcentração econômica regional." In R. de Brito Alvares Affonso and P. L. Baros Silva, eds., *A federação em perspectiva: Ensaios selecionados*. São Paulo, Brazil: FUNDAP.

Carciofi, Ricardo, Guillermo Barris, and Oscar Cetrangolo. 1994. *Reformas tributarias en América Latina: Análisis de experiencias durante la década de los años ochenta*. Santiago de Chile, Chile: CEPAL.

Cardoso, Adalberto Moreira. 2000. "Brazilian Central Union Federations at the Crossroads." Paper presented at the conference of National Labor Confederations in Brazil and South Korea, Berkeley, Calif., May 13–14.

———. 1999a. *A trama da modernidade. Pragmatismo sindical e democratização no Brasil*. Rio de Janeiro, Brazil: Revan.

———. 1999b. *Sindicatos, trabalhadores e a coqueluche neoliberal: A era Vargas acabou?* Rio de Janeiro, Brazil: Fundação Getúlio Vargas.

———. 1998. "Novos e velhos sindicalistas? Revisitando o 'mercado sindical' brasileiro na década perdida." Paper presented at the 1998 Meeting of the Latin American Studies Association. Chicago, Ill., September 24–26.

———. 1997a. "O sindicalismo corporativo não é mais o mesmo." *Novos Estudos* 48 (July): 97–119.

———. 1997b. "Um referente fora de foco." *Dados — Revista de Ciências Sociais* 40 (2): 169–98.

Cardoso, Adalberto Moreira, and Alvaro A. Comin. 1995. "Câmaras setoriais, modernização produtiva e democratização nas relações entre capital e trabalho no Brasil." In Nadya A. Castro, org., *A máquina e o equilibrista: Tecnologia e trabalho na indústria automobilística brasileira*. São Paulo, Brazil: Paz e Terra.

Cardoso, Eliana A. 2001. "Brazil's Monetary and Fiscal Reforms in the 1990s." Bildner Center for Western Hemisphere Studies, The Graduate Center, City University of New York, N.Y., May 16–19. Paper presented at the conference "Reforming Brazil I: A Preliminary Assessment."

———. 1981a. "Celso Furtado Revisited: The Postwar Years." *Economic Development and Cultural Change* 30 (1): 117–28.

———. 1981b. "The Great Depression and Commodity-Exporting LDCs: The Case of Brazil." *Journal of Political Economy* 89 (6): 1,239-49.

Cardoso, Eliana A., and Albert Fishlow. 1992. "Latin American Economic Development: 1950–1980." *Journal of Latin American Studies* 24 (supplement): 197–218.

———. 1989. "The Macroeconomics of the Brazilian External Debt." In J. D. Sachs, ed., *Developing Country Debt and the World Economy*. Chicago, Ill.: University of Chicago Press.

Cardoso, Eliana A., and Ann Helwege. 1991. "Populism, Profligacy, and Redistribution." In R. Dornbusch and S. Edwards, eds., *The Macroeconomics of Populism in Latin America*. Chicago, Ill.: University of Chicago Press.

Cardoso, Fernando Henrique. 1994. "Plano Fernando Henrique Cardoso: Exposição de Motivos n° 395, de 7 de dezembro de 1993." *Revista de Economia Política* 14 (2): 114–31.

———. 1991. "Caminhos para o novo milênio." In Maurício Dias, org., *Economia e política da crise brasileira: A perspectiva social-democrata.* Rio de Janeiro, Brazil: Rio Fundo, 217–28.

———. 1986. "Entrepreneurs and the Transition Process: The Brazilian Case." In P. C. Schmitter and L. Whitehead G. O'Donnell, eds., *Transitions from Authoritarian Rule: Comparative Perspectives.* Baltimore, Md.: Johns Hopkins University Press.

———. 1975. *Autoritarismo e democratização.* São Paulo, Brazil: Paz e Terra.

———. 1972. *Empresário industrial e desenvolvimento econômico no Brasil.* São Paulo, Brazil: Difel. Originally published in 1964.

———. 1971. *Política e desenvolvimento em sociedades dependentes: Ideologias do empresariado industrial argentino e brasileiro.* Rio de Janeiro, Brazil: Zahar.

Cardoso, Fernando Henrique, and Enzo Faletto. 1979. *Dependency and Development in Latin America.* Berkeley, Calif.: University of California Press.

Cardoso, Fernando Henrique, and Mauricio Font, eds. 2001. *Charting a New Course: The Politics of Globalization and Social Transformation.* Boulder, Colo.: Rowman and Littlefield.

Cardoso, Ruth. 2000. "A experiência brasileira no cenário latino-americano." In *Estratégias de parceria no combate à exclusão social: Avaliação, diálogo e perspectivas.* Brasília, Brazil: Conselho da Comunidade Solidária, PNDU, and UNESCO.

———. 1995. "Mudança sociocultural e participação política nos anos 80." In Lourdes Sola and Leda M. Paulani, eds., *Lições da Década de 80.* São Paulo, Brazil: Universidade de São Paulo; Genebra, Swiss: UNRISD.

———. 1994. "A trajetória dos movimentos sociais." In Evelina Dagnino, org., *Os Anos 90: Política e Sociedade no Brasil.* São Paulo, Brazil: Brasiliense.

———. 1988. "Movimentos sociais urbanos: Balanço crítico." In Maria Hermínia Tavares de Almeida and Bernardo Sorj, eds., *Sociedade e política no Brasil pós-64.* São Paulo, Brazil: Brasiliense.

Cardoso, Ruth, et al. 2000. *Um novo referencial para ação social do Estado e da sociedade.* Brasília, Brazil: Conselho da Comunidade Solidária and PNDU.

Carvalho, José Murilo de. 1998. "Educação e cidadania." In João P. R. Velloso, org., *O Brasil e o mundo no limiar do novo século.* Rio de Janeiro, Brazil: José Olympio.

———. 1991. "The Unfinished Republic." *Americas* 48: 139–57.

Cason, Jeffrey. 1999. "Democracy Looks South: Mercosul and the Politics of Brazilian Trade Strategy." In P. R. Kingstone and T. J. Power, eds., *Democratic Brazil.* Pittsburgh, Pa.: University of Pittsburgh Press.

Castro, Antônio Barros de. 1971. *7 ensaios sobre a economia brasileira.* Rio de Janeiro, Brazil: Forense.

Castro, Paulo Rabello de, and Marcio Ronci. 1991. "Sixty Years of Populism in Brazil." In R. Dornbusch and S. Edwards, eds., *The Macroeconomics of Populism in Latin America.* Chicago, Ill.: University of Chicago Press.

Cavarozzi, Marcelo. 1992. "Beyond Democratic Transitions in Latin America." *Journal of Latin American Studies* 24 (3): 665–84.

Cehelsky, Marta. 1979. *Land Reform in Brazil: The Management of Social Change.* Boulder, Colo.: Westview Press.

Chagas, Helena. 2002. "Relações executivo-legislativo." In Bolívar Lamounier and Rubens Figueiredo, eds., *A Era FHC: Um Balanço*. São Paulo, Brazil: Cultura Editores Associados.

Chalmers, Douglas A., Scott B. Martin, and Kerianne Piester. 1996. "Associative Networks: New Structures of Representation for the Popular Sectors?" In D. Chalmers et al., eds., *The New Politics of Inequality in Latin America: Rethinking Participation and Representation*. Oxford, London: Oxford University Press.

Chalmers, Douglas A., Carlos M. Vilas, Katherine Hite, Scott B. Martin, Karianne Piester, and Monique Segarra, eds. 1997. *The New Politics of Inequality in Latin America: Rethinking Participation and Representation*. Oxford, London: Oxford University Press.

Cleaves, Peter S., and Charles J. Stephens. 1991. "Businessmen and Economic Policy in Mexico." *Latin American Research Review* 26 (2): 187–202.

Coes, Donald V. 1995. *Macroeconomic Crises, Policies, and Growth in Brazil, 1964–1990*. Washington, D.C.: The World Bank.

Collier, Ruth Berins, and David Collier. 1991. *Shaping the Political Arena: Critical Junctures, the Labor Movement, and Regime Dynamics in Latin America*. Princeton, N.J.: Princeton University Press.

Collor de Mello, Fernando. 1989. *Diretrizes de Ação do Governo*. Brasília, Brazil: mimeo.

Comin, Alexandre. 1998. *De volta para o futuro: Política e reestruturação industrial do complexo automobilístico nos anos 90*. São Paulo, Brazil: Annablume/FAPESP.

Conde, Luís Paulo. 1998. "O projeto Favela-Bairro." In João P. R. Velloso, org., *O Brasil e o mundo no limiar do novo século*. Rio de Janeiro, Brazil: José Olympio.

Conniff, Michael L., ed. 1982. *Latin American Populism in Comparative Perspective*. Albuquerque, N.Mex.: University of New Mexico Press.

Conselho Nacional de Desenvolvimento Rural Sustentável. 2002. *Plano para o desenvolvimento sustentável do Brasil rural*. Brasília, Brazil: Plano Nacional de Desenvolvimento Rural Sustentável.

Corbo, Vittorio. 1992. *Development Strategies and Policies in Latin America: A Historical Perspective*. San Francisco, Calif.: ICS Press.

Cornelius, Wayne A., and Ann L. Craig. 1991. *The Mexican Political System in Transition*. San Diego, Calif.: Center for U.S. Mexican Studies.

Cousineau Adriance, Madeleine. 1995. *Promised Land: Base Christian Communities and the Struggle for the Amazon*. Albany, N.Y.: SUNY Press.

Cruz, Sebastião Velasco, ed. 1988. "Empresários, economistas e perspectivas de democratização no Brasil." In F. W. Reis and G. O'Donnell, eds., *A democracia no Brasil*. São Paulo, Brazil: Vértice.

Dagnino, Evelina, ed. 1994. *Os Anos 90: Política e sociedade no Brasil*. São Paulo, Brazil: Editora Brasiliense.

Dallari, Dalmo de Abreu. 1986. *O Estado federal*. São Paulo, Brazil: Ática.

Danaher, Kevin, and Michael Shellenberger, eds. 1995. *Fighting for the Soul of Brazil*. New York, N.Y.: Monthly Review Press.

Di Tella, Torcuato S. 1990. *Latin American Politics: A Theoretical Framework*. Austin, Tex.: University of Texas Press.

———. 1965. "Populism and Reform in Latin America." In Claudio Véliz, ed., *Obstacles to Change in Latin America*. New York, N.Y.: Oxford University Press.

Diamond, Larry, and Marc F. Plattner, eds. 1995. *Economic Reform and Democracy*. Baltimore, Md.: Johns Hopkins University Press.

Diamond, Larry, Marc F. Plattner, Yun-han Chu, and Hung-mao Tien, eds. 1997. *Consolidating the Third Wave Democracies: Themes and Perspectives*. Baltimore, Md.: Johns Hopkins University Press.

Dias, G. L. S., and C. M. Amaral. 1999. "Mudanças estruturais na agricultura brasileira, 1980–1998." *Serie Desarrollo Productivo* 99. Santiago, Chile: CEPAL.

Dias, Maurício. 1991. *Economia e política da crise brasileira: A perspectiva social-democrata*. Rio de Janeiro, Brazil: Rio Fundo.

Díaz-Alejandro, Carlos F. 1976. *Foreign Trade Regimes and Economic Development*. New York, N.Y.: Columbia University Press.

Dimenstein, Gilberto. 1996. *Democracia em pedaços: Direitos humanos no Brasil*. São Paulo, Brazil: Companhia das Letras.

Diniz, Eli. 2000. *Globalização, reformas econômicas e elites empresariais: Brasil Anos 1990*. Rio de Janeiro, Brazil: Fundação Getúlio Vargas.

———. 1997. *Crise, reforma do Estado e governabilidade: Brasil, 1985–1995*. Rio de Janeiro, Brazil: Fundação Getúlio Vargas.

———. 1995a. "Governability, Reform of the State and Democratic Consolidation in Brazil." IUPERJ, Rio de Janeiro, Brazil, October 4–6. Paper presented at the international seminar: "The Challenge of Democracy in Latin America. Rethinking State/Society Relations."

———. 1995b. "Governabilidade, democracia, e reforma do Estado: Os desafios da construção de uma nova ordem no Brasil nos anos 90." *Dados* 38 (3): 385–416.

———. 1995c. "Reformas económicas y democracia en el Brasil de los años noventa: Las cámaras sectoriales como foro de negociación." *Revista Mexicana De Sociología* 57 (4): 61–93.

———. 1994. "Empresariado, regime autoritário e modernização capitalista: 1964–1985." In Gláucio Ary Dillon Soares and Maria Celina D' Araujo, eds., *21 anos de regime militar*. Rio de Janeiro, Brazil: Fundação Getúlio Vargas.

———. 1992. "Neoliberalismo e corporativismo: As duas faces do capitalismo industrial no Brasil." *Revista Brasileira de Ciências Sociais* 20 (7): 31–46.

———. 1991. "Empresariado e projeto neoliberal na América Latina: Uma avaliação dos anos 80." *Dados* 34: 349–77.

Diniz, Eli, and Renato Boschi. 1992. "Lideranças empresariais e problemas da estratégia liberal no Brasil." In E. Diniz, ed., *Empresários e modernização econômica: Brasil anos 90*. Florianópolis, Brazil: UFSC/IDACON.

———. 1991. "Corporativismo na construção do espaço público." In Renato Boschi, ed., *Corporativismo e desigualdade: A construção do espaço público no Brasil*. Rio de Janeiro, Brazil: IUPERJ.

———. 1989. "A consolidação democrática no Brasil: Atores políticos, processos sociais e intermediação de interesses." In E. Diniz, R. Boschi, and R. Lessa, eds., *Modernização e consolidação democrática no Brasil: Dilemas da Nova República*. São Paulo, Brazil: IUPERJ/Vértice.

———. 1979. *Agregação e representação de interesses do empresariado industrial: Sindicatos e associações de classes*. Rio de Janeiro, Brazil: IUPERJ.

———. 1978. *Empresariado nacional e Estado no Brasil*. Rio de Janeiro, Brazil: Forense-Universitária.

Diniz, Eli, and Sérgio Azevedo, eds. 1997. *Reforma do Estado e democracia no Brasil: Dilemas e perspectivas* Brasília, Brazil: Universidade de Brasília.

Doimo, Ana Maria. 1995. *A vez e a voz popular: Movimentos sociais e participação política no Brasil pós-70*. Rio de Janeiro, Brazil: ANPOCS.

Dornbusch, Rudiger, and Sebastian Edwards, eds. 1991. *Reform, Recovery, and Growth: Latin America and Middle East.* Chicago, Ill.: University of Chicago Press.

Draibe, Sônia. 2000. "Análise qualitativa dos programas inovadores da Comunidade Solidária." In Ruth Cardoso, W. Franco, J. Werthein, and S. M. Draibe, org., *Estratégias inovadoras de parceria no combate à exclusão social.* Brasília, Brazil: Comunidade Solidária/UNESCO/PNUD.

———. 1998. "A política brasileira de combate à pobreza." In João P. R. Velloso, org., *O Brasil e o mundo no limiar do novo século.* Rio de Janeiro, Brazil: José Olympio.

———. 1985. *Rumos e metamorfoses: Estado e industrialização no Brasil: 1930–1960.* Rio de Janeiro, Brazil: Paz e Terra.

Drake, Paul. 1989. "Debt and Democracy in Latin America, 1920s–1980s." In B. Stallings and R. Kaufman, eds., *Debt and Democracy in Latin America.* Boulder, Colo.: Westview Press.

Dreifuss, René Armand. 1986. *1964: A conquista do Estado: Ação política, poder e golpe de classe.* Petrópolis, Brazil: Vozes.

Ducatenzeiler, Graciela, and Philip Oxhom. 1994. "Democracia, autoritarísmo y el problema de la governabilidad en América Latina." *Desarrollo Económico* 133 (34): 31–54.

Dupas, Gilberto. 1993. "Competitive Integration and Recovery of Growth: Risks and Prospects." In Werner Baer and Joseph S. Tulchin, eds., *Brazil and the Challenge of Economic Reform.* Washington, D.C.: Woodrow Wilson Center Press, 9–30.

Duquette, Michel. 1999. *Building New Democracies: Economic and Social Reform in Brazil, Chile, and Mexico.* Toronto, Canada: University of Toronto Press.

Edwards, Michael, and David Hulme, eds. 1996. *Beyond the Magic Bullet: NGO Performance and Accountability in the Post-Cold War World.* West Hartford, Conn.: Kumarian Press.

Elias de Castro, Iná. 1992. *O mito da necessidade: Discurso e prática do regionalismo nordestino.* Rio de Janeiro, Brazil: Editora Bertrand Brasil.

Erickson, Kenneth P. 1977. *The Brazilian Corporative State and Working Class Politics.* Berkeley, Calif.: University of California Press.

Erickson, Kenneth P., and Kevin J. Middlebrook. 1982. "The State and Organized Labor in Brazil and Mexico." In Sylvia Ann Hewlett and Richard S. Weinert, eds., *Brazil and Mexico: Patterns in Late Development.* Philadelphia: Institute for the Study of Human Issues.

Evans, Peter. 1996. "El Estado como problema y como solución." *Desarrollo Económico* 35 (140): 529–62.

———. 1995. *Embedded Autonomy: States and Industrial Transformation.* Princeton, N.J.: Princeton University Press.

———. 1992. "The State as Problem and Solution: Predation, Embedded Autonomy, and Structural Change." In S. Haggard and Robert R. Kaufman, ed., *The Politics of Economic Adjustment: International Constraints, Distributive Conflicts, and the State.* Princeton, N.J.: Princeton University Press.

———. 1989. "Predatory Developmental and Other Apparatuses: A Comparative Analysis of the Third World State." *Sociological Forum* 4: 561–87.

———. 1982. "Reinventing the Bourgeoisie: State Entrepreneurship and Class Formation in Dependent Capitalist Development." *American Journal of Sociology* 88 (supplement): 210–47.

———. 1979. *Dependent Development: The Alliance of Multinational, State, and Local Capital in Brazil.* Princeton, N.J.: Princeton University Press.

Evans, Peter, Dietrich Rueschemeyer, and Theda Skocpol, eds. 1985. *Bringing the State Back In*. Cambridge, Mass.: Cambridge University Press.

Falcone, Andres Pablo, and Roberto Vilela. 2001. *Recursos privados para fins públicos: As grantmakers brasileiras*. São Paulo, Brazil: GIFE.

Faoro, Raymundo. 1958. *Os donos do poder: Formação do patronato político brasileiro*. São Paulo, Brazil: Globo.

Farah, Marta F. S. 1998a. "O programa Gestão Pública e Cidadania." In João P. R. Velloso, org., *O Brasil e o mundo no limiar do novo século*. Rio de Janeiro, Brazil: José Olympio.

———. 1998b. "Gestão pública e cidadania: Experiências recentes de governos subnacionais." Programa de Gestão Pública e Cidadania, Proposta n°78.

Faria, Vilmar. 2000a. "Brasil: Compatibilidade entre a estabilização e o resgate da dívida social." In *Cadernos Adenauer 1*. São Paulo, Brazil: Fundação Konrad Adenauer.

———. 2000b. "Importância das estratégias inovadoras de parceria." In Ruth Cardoso, W. Franco, J. Werthein, and S. M. Draibe, org., *Estratégias inovadoras de parceria no combate à exclusão social*. Brasília, Brazil: Comunidade Solidária/ UNESCO/PNUD.

———. 1983. "Desenvolvimento, urbanização e mudanças na estrutura de emprego: A experiência brasileira dos últimos trinta anos." In Maria Hermínia Tavares de Almeida and Bernardo Sorj, eds., *Sociedade e política no Brasil pós-64*. São Paulo, Brazil: Brasiliense.

Faria, Vilmar, and Eduardo Graeff. 2000. *Progressive Governance for the 21st Century: The Brazilian Experience*. Brasília: Presidency of the Republic, Senior Advisory Body.

Faucher, Philippe. 1993. "Políticas de ajuste ou erosão do Estado no Brasil?" *Dados* 36 (3): 393–418.

Fernandes, Rubem César. 1998. "O movimento Viva Rio." In João P. R.Velloso, org., *O Brasil e o mundo no limiar do novo século*. Rio de Janeiro, Brazil: José Olympio.

Fernández, Roque B. 1991. "What Have Populists Learned from Hyperinflation?" In Rudiger Dornbusch and Sebastian Edwards, eds., *The Macroeconomics of Populism in Latin America*. Chicago, Ill.: University of Chicago Press.

Fico, Carlos. 1999. *Ibase: Usina de idéias e cidadania*. Rio de Janeiro, Brazil: Garamond.

Figueiredo, Argelina C., and Fernando Limongi. 1999. *Executivo e legislativo na nova ordem constitucional*. Rio de Janeiro, Brazil: Fundação Getúlio Vargas.

———. 1998. "Reforma da previdência e instituições políticas." *Novos Estudos CEBRAP* 51: 63–90.

Figueiredo, R., and Bolívar Lamounier. 1996. *As cidades que dão certo: Experiências inovadoras na administração pública brasileira*. Brasília, Brazil: MH Comunicação.

Fiori, José Luís. 1993. "Ajuste, transição e governabilidade: O enigma Brasileiro." In Maria da Conceição Tavares and José Luís Fiori, eds., *Desajuste global e modernização conservadora*. Rio de Janeiro, Brazil: Paz e Terra.

Fishlow, Albert. 1997. "Is the Real Plan for Real?" In Susan Kaufman Purcell and Riordan Roett, eds., *Brazil under Cardoso*. Boulder, Colo.: Lynne Rienner Publishers.

———. 1990. "The Latin American State." *Journal of Economic Perspectives* 4 (summer): 61–74.

————. 1972. "Origins and Consequences of Import Substitution in Brazil." In L. E. di Marco, ed., *International Economics and Development*. Essays in Honor of Raul Prebish. New York, N.Y.:Academic Press. See also: "Origens e consequências da substituição de importações no Brasil." *Estudos Econômicos* 2 (6): 7–76.

Fleischer, David. 1998. "The Cardoso Government's Reform Agenda: A View from the National Congress, 1995–1998." *Journal of Interamerican and World Affairs* 40 (winter): 119–36.

————. 1996. "Poder local e o sistema eleitoral brasileiro." In *Poder local face às eleições municipais de 1996*. São Paulo, Brazil: Konrad Adenauer Stiftung.

————. 1994. "Manipulações casuísticas do sistema eleitoral durante o período militar, ou como usualmente o feitiço se voltava contra o feiticeiro." In Gláucio Ary Dillon Soares and Maria Celina D' Araujo, eds., *21 anos de regime militar*. Rio de Janeiro, Brazil: Fundação Getúlio Vargas.

Flynn, Peter. 1986. "Brazil: The Politics of the Cruzado Plan." *Third World Quarterly* 8 (October): 176–77.

————. 1978. *Brazil: A Political Analysis*. London: Ernest Benn.

Font, Mauricio A. (forthcoming). *Rise and Twilight of Brazilian Dirigisme*. Lanham, MD.: Rowman and Littlefield.

————. 1996. "Failed Redemocratization: Region, Class, and Political Change in Brazil, 1930–1937." In F. Devoto and T. Di Tella, eds., *Political Culture, Social Movements, and Democratic Transitions in South America in the Twentieth Century*. Rome, Italy: Annali Feltrinelli. Note: Earlier version available as a 1992 Working Paper, Bildner Center for Western Hemisphere Studies, City University of New York.

————. 1994. "A Sociologist Turns to Politics." *Hemisphere* (winter/spring): 20–24.

————. 1992a. "Failed Redemocratization: Region, Class, and Political Change in Brazil, 1930–37." Working Paper, Bildner Center for Western Hemisphere Studies, City University of New York.

————. 1992b. "City and Countryside in the Onset of Brazilian Industrialization." *Studies in Comparative International Development* 27 (3): 26–56.

————. 1991. "Agricultura exportadora e industrialização." *Revista Brasileira de Ciências Sociais* 6 (15): 5–26.

————. 1990a. *Coffee, Contention, and Change*. Oxford, London: Basil Blackwell.

————. 1990b. "Export Agriculture and Development Path." *Journal of Historical Sociology* 3 (4): 329–61.

Fontes, Breno Augusto Souto-Maior. 1996. "Estrutura organizacional das associações políticas voluntárias." *Revista Brasileira de Ciências Sociais* 11 (32): 41–59.

————. 1995. "Clientelismo urbano e movimento popular: A construção das redes do poder." *Revista Brasileira de Estudos Políticos* 81 (July): 119–59.

Forman, Shepard, and Joyce F. Reigelhaupt. 1979. "The Political Economy of Patron-Clientship: Brazil and Portugal Compared." In Maxine Margolis and William E. Carter, eds., *Brazil: Anthropological Perspectives*. New York, N.Y.: Columbia University Press.

Foxley, Alejandro. 1983. *Latin American Experiments in Neoconservative Economics*. Berkeley, Calif.: University of California Press.

Foxley, Alejandro, and Laurence Whitehead. 1980. "Economic Stabilization in Latin America: Political Dimensions—Editor's Introduction." *World Development* 8 (11): 823–32.

Franco, Gustavo H. B. 1993. "Brazilian Hyperinflation: The Political Economy of the Fiscal Crisis." In M. D. G. Kinzo, ed., *Brazil: The Challenges of the 1990s*. London: The Institute of Latin American Studies, University of London and British Academic Press.

French, John D. 1993. *The Brazilian Workers' ABC: Class Conflict and Alliances in Modern São Paulo*. Chapel Hill, N.C.: University of North Carolina Press.

Frieden, Jeffry A. 1991. *Debt, Development and Democracy: Modern Political Economy and Latin America, 1965–1985*. Princeton, N.J.: Princeton University Press.

Fritsch, Winston. 1991. "Obstáculos à modernização industrial." In Maurício Dias, org., *Economia e política da crise brasileira: A perspectiva social-democrata*. Rio de Janeiro, Brazil: Rio Fundo, 119–21.

Furtado, Celso. 1963. *The Economic Growth of Brazil: A Survey from Colonial to Modern Times*. Berkeley, Calif.: University of California Press.

Garcia-Zamor, Jean Claude, ed. 1978. "Regionalism and Political Stability." In Jean Claude Garcia-Zamor, ed., *Politics and Administration in Brazil*. Washington, D.C.: University Press of America.

Garrison, John. 2000. "From Confrontation to Collaboration: Civil Society-Government-World Bank Relations in Brazil." World Bank paper.

Garrison, John, and Anabela Abreu. 2000. "Government and Civil Society in the Fight against HIV and AIDS in Brazil." Case presented at the Europe and the Americas Forum on Health Sector Reform: "The Challenge of Health Reform: Reaching the Poor." San José, Costa Rica, May 24–26.

Gasques, José Garcia, and Júnia Cristina P. R. da Conceição. 2000. "Transformações estruturais da agricultura e produtividade total dos fatores." Texto para Discussão *n° 768*. Brasília, Brazil: IPEA.

Gay, Robert. 1988. "Political Clientelism and Urban Social Movements in Rio de Janeiro." Ph.D. diss., Brown University.

Geddes, Barbara. 1995. "The Politics of Economic Liberalization." *Latin American Research Review* 30 (2): 195–214.

———. 1994. *Politician's Dilemma: Building State Capacity in Latin America*. Berkeley, Calif.: University of California Press

———. 1990. "Building 'State' Autonomy in Brazil, 1930–1964." *Comparative Politics* 22 (2): 217–35.

Geddes, Barbara, and Artur Ribeiro Neto. 1999. "Institutional Sources of Corruption." In Keith Rosenn and Richard Downes, eds., *Corruption and Political Reform in Brazil: The Impact of Collor's Impeachment*. Miami, Fla.: North-South Center Press.

Gereffi, Gary, and Donald L. Wyman, eds. 1990. *Manufacturing Miracles. Paths of Industrialization in Latin America and East Asia*. Princeton, N.J.: Princeton University Press.

Giambiagi, Fabio, and Maurício Mesquita Moreira. 1999. *A economia brasileira nos anos 90*. Rio de Janeiro, Brazil: BNDES.

GIFE — Grupo de Institutos, Fundações e Empresas. 2001. *Investimento social privado no Brasil: Perfil e catálogo dos associados GIFE*. São Paulo, Brazil: GIFE

Glade, Wiliam. 1989. "Privatizations in Rent-Seeking Societies." *World Development* 17 (5): 673–82.

Goetz, Anna Marie. 1996. "Gender and Development: Rethinking Modernization and Dependency Theory." *American Political Science Review* 90 (1): 225–26.

Gohn, Maria da Glória. 1995. *História dos movimentos e lutas sociais*. São Paulo, Brazil: Loyola.

———. 1991. *Movimentos sociais e luta pela moradia.* São Paulo, Brazil: Loyola.

Goldenstein, Lídia. 1994. *Repensando a dependência.* São Paulo, Brazil: Paz e Terra.

Goldsmith, William W., and Robert Wilson. 1991. "Poverty and Distorted Industrialization in the Brazilian Northeast." *World Development* 19 (5): 435–55.

Gomes, Ciro, and Roberto Mangabeira Unger. 1996. *O próximo passo.* Rio de Janeiro, Brazil: Topbooks.

Gomes, Eduardo R., and Fabrícia Corrêa Guimarães. 2001. "Entre a ação política e a ação social: O Pensamento Nacional das Bases Empresariais (PNBE) e a nova democracia brasileira." Bildner Center for Western Hemisphere Studies, The Graduate Center, City University of New York, N.Y., May 16–19. Paper presented at the conference "Reforming Brazil I: A Preliminary Assessment."

———. 1999. "Empresários, o Brasil em reformas e o corporativismo em transição: Um estudo sobre o PNBE—Pensamento Nacional das Bases Empresariais." In Ana Maria Kirschner and Eduardo R. Gomes, eds., *Empresa, empresários e sociedade.* Rio de Janeiro, Brazil: Sete Letras.

Gonçalves, Reinaldo. 1991. "Grupos privados nacionais e o futuro do capitalismo no Brasil: Uma visão alternativa." In Maurício Dias, org., *Economia e política da crise brasileira: A perspectiva social-democrata.* Rio de Janeiro, Brazil: Rio Fundo, 109–18.

Goodman, David. 1986. "Rural Economy and Society." In E. L. Bacha and H. S. Klein, eds., *Social Change in Brazil, 1945–1985.* Albuquerque, N.Mex.: University of New Mexico Press.

Gourevitch, Peter. 1986. *Politics in Hard Times: Comparative Responses to International Economic Crises.* Ithaca, N.Y.: Cornell University Press.

Gouvêa, Gilda Portugal. 1994. *Burocracia e elites burocráticas no Brasil.* São Paulo, Brazil: Paulicéia.

Graham, Douglas H. 1982. "Mexican and Brazilian Economic Development: Legacies, Patterns, and Performance." In Sylvia Ann Hewlett and Richard S. Weinert, eds., *Brazil and Mexico: Patterns in Late Development.* Philadelphia, Pa.: Institute for the Study of Human Issues.

Graziano da Silva, J. 1998. *A nova dinâmica da agricultura brasileira.* Campinas, Brazil: Instituto de Economia, Unicamp.

Greenfield, Gerald Michael. 1984. "Patterns of Enterprise in São Paulo." *Social Science History* 8 (3): 291–312.

Grindle, Merilee S. 1986. *State and Countryside: Dependent Policy and Agrarian Politics in Latin America.* Baltimore, Md.: Johns Hopkins University Press.

Ground, Richard Lynn. 1988. "The Genesis of Import Substitution in Latin America." *CEPAL Review* 36: 179–203.

Guimarães, César. 1977. "Empresariado, tipos de capitalismo e ordem política." *Dados* 14: 34–47.

Guimarães Neto, Leonardo. 1995. "Dimensões, limites e implicações da desconcentração espacial." In R. de Brito Alvarez Affonso and P. L. Barros Silva, eds., *A federação em perspectiva: Ensaios selecionados.* São Paulo, Brazil: FUNDAP.

Haber, Stephen, ed. 1997. *How Latin America Fell Behind.* Stanford, Calif.: Stanford University Press.

Haber, Stephen, and Herbert S. Klein. 1997. "The Economic Consequences of Brazilian Independence." In Stephen Haber, ed., *How Latin America Fell Behind.* Stanford, Calif.: Stanford University Press, 243–59.

Haddad, Eduardo, and Carlos R. Azzoni. 2000. *Trade Liberalization and Location: Geographical Shifts in the Brazilian Economic Structure.* NEMESIS Document [www.nemesis.org.br].

Haggard, Stephan. 1990. *Pathways from the Periphery: The Politics of Growth in the Newly Industrializing Countries.* Ithaca, N.Y.: Cornell University Press.

Haggard, Stephan, and Robert R. Kaufman. 1995. *The Political Economy of Democratic Transitions.* Princeton, N.J.: Princeton University Press.

————. 1992a. "Economic Adjustment and the Prospects for Democracy." In Stephan Haggard and Robert R. Kaufman, eds., *The Politics of Economic Adjustment: International Constraints, Distributive Conflicts, and the State.* Princeton, N.J.: Princeton University Press.

————. 1992b. "Institutions and Economic Adjustment." In Stephan Haggard and Robert R. Kaufman, eds., *The Politics of Economic Adjustment: International Constraints, Distributive Conflicts, and the State.* Princeton, N.J.: Princeton University Press.

————. 1989. "Economic Adjustment in New Democracies." In Joan M. Nelson et al., eds. *Fragile Coalitions: The Politics of Economic Adjustment.* New Brunswick, N.J.: Transaction Books.

————, eds. 1992c. *The Politics of Economic Adjustment: International Constraints, Distributive Conflicts, and the State.* Princeton, N.J.: Princeton University Press.

Haggard, Stephan, and Sylvia Maxwell. 1996. "The Political Economy of Financial Internationalization in the Developing World." In Robert O. Keohane and Helen V. Milner, eds., *Internationalization and Domestic Politics.* Cambridge, Mass.: Cambridge University Press, 203–39.

Haggard, Stephan, Sylvia Maxwell, and Ben Ross Schneider. 1997. "Theories of Business and Business-State Relations." In Sylvia Maxwell and Ben Schneider, eds., *Business and the State in Developing Countries.* Ithaca, N.Y.: Cornell University Press.

Haggard, Stephan, and Steven Webb, eds. 1994. *Voting for Reform: Democracy, Liberalization, and Economic Adjustment.* Oxford, London: Oxford University Press.

Hagopian, Frances. 1998. "Democracy and Political Representation in Latin America in the 1990s: Pause, Reorganization, or Decline?" In Felipe Agüero and Jeffrey Start, eds., *Fault Lines of Democracy in Post-Transition Latin America.* Miami, Fla.: North-South Center Press.

————. 1996a. "Brazilian Indutrialists and Democratic Change." *American Political Science Review* 90 (1): 221–22.

————. 1996b. *Traditional Politics and Regime Change in Brazil.* New York, N.Y.: Cambridge University Press.

————. 1990. "Democracy by Undemocratic Means? Elites, Political Pacts, and Regime Transition in Brazil." *Comparative Political Studies* 23 (2): 147–70.

————. 1986. "The Politics of Oligarchy: The Persistence of Traditional Elites in Contemporary Brazil." Ph.D. diss., Massachusetts Institute of Technology.

Helfand, Steven M., and Gervásio Castro Rezende. 2001. "Brazilian Agriculture in the 1990s: Impact of the Policy Reforms." *Texto para Discussão n° 785.* Rio de Janeiro, Brazil: IPEA. Paper previously presented at the XXIV International Conference of Agricultural Economists, Berlin, August 13–18, 2000.

————. 2000. "Padrões regionais de crescimento da produção de grãos no Brasil e o papel da região Centro-Oeste." *Texto para Discussão n° 621.* Rio de Janeiro, Brazil: IPEA.

Hellmann, Michaela. 1995. "Democratização e movimentos sociais no Brasil." In Michaela Hellmann, org., *Movimentos sociais e democracia no Brasil: "Sem a gente não tem jeito."* São Paulo, Brazil: Marco Zero, 9–23.

Henriques, Ricardo, ed. 2000. *Desigualdade e pobreza no Brasil.* Rio de Janeiro, Brazil: IPEA.

Hewitt. W. E. 1991. *Basic Christian Communities and Social Change in Brazil.* Lincoln, Nebr.: University of Nebraska Press.

Hewlett, Sylvia Ann, and Richard S. Weinert, eds. 1982. *Brazil and Mexico: Patterns in Late Development.* Philadelphia, Pa.: Institute for the Study of Human Issues.

Hira, Anil. 1999. *Ideas and Economic Policy in Latin America: Regional, National, and Organizational Case Studies.* Westport, Conn., and London: Praeger Publishers.

Hirschman, Albert O. 1987. "The Political Economy of Latin American Development." *Latin American Research Review* 22 (3): 7–36.

———. 1979. "The Turn to Authoritarianism in Latin America and the Search for its Economic Determinants." In David Collier, ed., *New Authoritarianism in Latin America.* Princeton, N.J.: Princeton University Press.

———. 1977. "A Generalized Linkage Approach to Development, with Special Reference to Staples." *Economic Development and Cultural Change* 25 (supplement): 67–98.

———. 1968. "The Political Economy of Import-Substituting Industrialization in Latin America." *The Quarterly Journal of Economics* 82 (1): 1–32.

———. 1963. *Journeys Toward Progress: Studies of Economic Policy-Making in Latin America.* New York, N.Y.: Twentieth Century Fund.

Hochstetler, Kathryn. 1999. "Democratizing Pressures from Below? Social Movements in the New Brazilian Democracy." In P. R. Kingstone and T. J. Power, eds., *Democratic Brazil.* Pittsburgh, Pa.: University of Pittsburgh Press.

———. 1997. "The Evolution of the Brazilian Environmental Movement and Its Political Roles." In D. Chalmers et al., eds., *The New Politics of Inequality in Latin America: Rethinking Participation and Representation.* Oxford, London: Oxford University Press, 192–216.

Holston, James, and Teresa P. R. Caldeira. 1998. "Democracy, Law and Violence: Disjunctions of Brazilian Citizenship." In Felipe Agüero and Jeffrey Start, eds., *Fault Lines of Democracy in Post-Transition Latin America.* Miami, Fla.: North-South Center Press.

Houtzager, Peter P. 1998. "State and Unions in the Transformation of the Brazilian Countryside, 1964–1979." *Latin American Research Review* 33 (2): 103–42.

Human Development Report. 2002. "Deepening Democracy in a Fragmented World." New York, N.Y.: Oxford University Press.

———. 2001. "Making New Technologies Work for Human Development." New York, N.Y.: Oxford University Press.

Huntingon, Samuel P. 1991. *The Third Wave: Democratization in the Late Twentieth Century.* Norman, Okla.: University of Oklahoma Press.

———. 1968. *Political Order in Changing Societies.* New Haven, Conn.: Yale University Press.

Jacobi, Pedro. 2000. *Políticas sociais e ampliação da cidadania.* Rio de Janeiro, Brazil: Fundação Getúlio Vargas.

Jaguaribe, Hélio. 1991. "Desafios do projeto social-democrata nas presentes condições do mundo e do Brasil." In Maurício Dias, org., *Economia e política da crise brasileira: A perspectiva social-democrata*. Rio de Janeiro, Brazil: Rio Fundo, 11–25.

Jaguaribe, Hélio, et al. 1989. *Brasil reforma ou caos*. Rio de Janeiro, Brazil: Paz e Terra.

Jenkins, Rhys. 1991. "The Political Economy of Industrialization: A Comparison of Latin American and East Asian Newly Industrializing Countries." *Development and Change* 22: 197–231.

Kahler, Miles. 1992. "External Influence, Conditionality, and the Politics of Adjustment." In S. Haggard and R. R. Kaufman, eds., *The Politics of Economic Adjustment: International Constraints, Distributive Conflicts and the State*. Princeton, N.J.: Princeton University Press.

———. 1990. "Orthodoxy and Its Alternatives: Explaining Approaches to Stabilization and Adjustment." In Joan M. Nelson, ed., *Economic Crisis and Policy Choice: The Politics of Adjustment in the Third World*. Princeton, N.J.: Princeton University Press, 33–61.

Kandir, Antonio. 1998. *O caminho do desenvolvimento: Do Brasil hiperinflacionário ao Brasil competitivo e solidário*. São Paulo, Brazil: Atlas.

Karatnycky, Adrian. 2000. "The State of Democracy: 2000." *American Educator* (summer): 23–31, 49–50.

Kaufman, Robert R. 1990. "Stabilization and Adjustment in Argentina, Brazil, and Mexico." In Joan M. Nelson, ed., *Economic Crisis and Policy Choice: The Politics of Adjustment in the Third World*. Princeton, N.J.: Princeton University Press.

———. 1989. "The Politics of Economic Adjustment Policy in Argentina, Brazil, and Mexico: Experiences in the 1980s and Challenges for the Future." *Policy Sciences* 22 (3–4): 395–413.

———. 1985. "Democratic and Authoritarian Reponses to the Debt Issue: Argentina, Brazil, and Mexico." *International Organization* 39: 473–503.

Keck, Margaret. 1992. *The Workers' Party and Democratization in Brazil*. New Haven, Conn.: Yale University Press.

Keck, Margaret, and Kathryn Sikkink. 1998. *Activists beyond Borders: Advocacy Networks in International Politics*. Ithaca, N.Y.: Cornell University Press.

Kingstone, Peter R. 2001. "Re-inventing Business: Commercial Liberalization and the Response of Industrialists in Brazil." Bildner Center for Western Hemisphere Studies, The Graduate Center, City University of New York, N.Y., May 16–19. Paper presented at the conference "Reforming Brazil I: A Preliminary Assessment."

———. 1999a. *Crafting Coalitions for Reform: Business Strategies, Political Institutions, and Neoliberal Reform in Brazil*. University Park, Pa.: Pennsylvania State University Press.

———. 1999b. "Muddling through Gridlock: Economic Policy Performance, Business Response, and Democratic Sustainability." In P.R. Kingstone and T.J. Power, eds., *Democratic Brazil*. Pittsburgh, Pa.: University of Pittsburgh Press.

———. 1998. "Corporatism, Neoliberalism, and the Failed Revolt of Big Business in Brazil: The Case of IEDI." *Journal of Interamerican and World Affairs* 40 (4): 73–95.

Kingstone, Peter R., and Timothy J. Power, eds. 1999. *Democratic Brazil: Actors, Institutions, and Processes*. Pittsburgh, Pa.: University of Pittsburgh Press.

Kinzo, Maria D'Alva. 1997. "Governabilidade, estrutura institucional e processo decisório no Brasil." *Revista Parcerias Estratégicas* 1 (3): 19–37.

Kinzo, Maria D'Alva, and Victor Bulmer-Thomas, eds. 1994. *Growth and Development in Brazil: Cardoso's Real Challenge.* London: Institute for Latin American Studies, University of London.

Kirschner, Ana Maria, and Eduardo R. Gomes, eds. 1999. *Empresa, empresários e sociedade.* Rio de Janeiro, Brazil: Sette Letras.

Kugelmas, Eduardo, Brasílio Sallum Jr., and Eduardo Graeff. 1989. "Conflito federativo e transição política." *São Paulo em Perspectiva* 3 (3): 95–102.

Lal, Deepak, and Sylvia Maxfield. 1993. "The Political Economy of Stabilization in Brazil." In R. H. Bates and Anne O. Krueger, eds., *Political and Economic Interactions in Economic Policy Reform.* Oxford, London: Basil Blackwell.

Lamounier, Bolívar. 1996. "Brazil: The Hyperactive Paralysis Syndrome." In J. I. Dominguez and A. F. Lowenthal, eds., *Constructing Democratic Governance: Latin America and the Caribbean in the 1990s.* Baltimore, Md.: Johns Hopkins University Press.

———. 1994. "A democracia brasileira de 1985 à década de 1990: A síndrome da paralisia hiperativa." In João P. R. Velloso, org., *Governabilidade, sistema político e violência urbana.* Rio de Janeiro, Brazil: José Olympio.

———. 1993. "Institutional Structure and Governability in the 1990s." In Maria D'Alva G. Kinzo, ed., *Brazil: The Challenges of the 1990s.* London: University of London and British Academic Press.

———. 1992a. "Estrutura institucional e governabilidade na década de 1990." In J. Paulo dos Reis Velloso, ed., *O Brasil e as reformas políticas.* Rio de Janeiro, Brazil: José Olympio.

———. 1992b. "El modelo institucional de los años treinta y la presente crisis brasileña." *Desarrollo Económico* 32: 185–98.

———. 1989. "Authoritarian Brazil Revisited: The Impact of Elections on the 'Abertura.'" In Alfred Stepan, ed., *Democratizing Brazil.* New York, N.Y.: Oxford University Press.

———. 1985. "Apontamentos sobre a questão democrática brasileira." In Alain Rouquier et al., eds., *Como renascem as democracias.* São Paulo, Brazil: Brasiliense.

Lamounier, Bolívar, and Rubens Figueiredo eds. 2002. *A Era FHC: Um Balanço.* São Paulo, Brazil: Cultura Editores Associados.

Lamounier, Bolívar, and Edmar L. Bacha. 1994. "Democracy and Economic Reform in Brasil." In Joan Nelson, ed., *A Precarious Balance: Democracy and Economic Reform in Latin America.* San Francisco, Calif.: Institute for Contemporary Studies.

Lamounier, Bolívar, and Dieter Nohlen, eds. 1993. *Presidencialismo ou parlamentarismo. Perspectivas sobre a reorganização institucional brasileira.* São Paulo, Brazil: Edições Loyola-IDESP.

Landau, Georges D. 2002. "The Regulatory-Normative Framework in Brazil." Policy Papers on the Americas, Center for Strategic and International Studies.

"Latin American Finance: The Rollercoaster Region." 1995. *The Economist,* v 337, December 9, 3–4.

Leeds, Elizabeth. 1996. "Cocaine and Parallel Policies in the Brazilian Urban Periphery." *Latin American Research Review* 31 (3): 47–83.

Lembruch, Gerhard. 1985. "Concertation and the Structure of Corporatist Networks." In J. H. Goldthorpe, ed., *Order and Conflict in Contemporary Capitalism: Studies in Political Economy of Western European Nations.* Oxford, London: Clarendon Press.

Leopoldi, Maria Antonieta P. 2000. "Política e interesses na industrialização brasileira: As associações industriais, a política econômica e o Estado." São Paulo, Brazil: Paz e Terra.

———. 1999. "Democracia e reformas econômicas no Brasil desregulando o setor de seguros e previdência privada na Nova República (1985–1999)." In Ana Maria Kirschner and Eduardo R. Gomes, eds., *Empresa, empresários e sociedade*. Rio de Janeiro, Brazil: Sete Letras.

———. 1994. "O difícil caminho do meio: Estado, burguesia e industrialização no segundo governo Vargas (1951–1954)." In Ângela de Castro Gomes, ed., *Vargas e a Crise dos Anos 50*. Rio de Janeiro, Brazil: Relume-Dumará.

———. 1984. "Industrial Associations and Politics in Contemporary Brazil." Ph.D. diss. Saint Anthony's College, Oxford University.

Lessa, Carlos and Rabio Sá Earp. "O insustentável abandono do longo prazo." In João Paulo de Almeida Magalhães, Adhemar dos Santos Mineiro, and Luiz Antônio Elias, eds. 1999. *Vinte anos de política econômica*. Rio de Janeiro, Brazil: Contraponto.

Levine, Robert M. 1978. *Pernambuco in the Brazilian Federation, 1889–1937*. Stanford, Calif.: Stanford University Press.

Lewandowski, Enrique Ricardo. 1990. "Local and State Government in the Nova República: Intergovernmental Relations in Light of the Brazilian Political Transition." In L. S. Graham and R. H. Wilson, eds., *The Political Economy of Brazil: Public Policies in an Era of Transition*. Austin, Tex.: University of Texas Press.

Lima, Maria Regina Soares, and Renato R. Boschi. 1995. "Democracia e reforma econômica: A visão das elites brasileiras." *Dados* 38 (l): 7–30.

Lima, Maria Regina Soares, and Zairo Borges Cheibub. 1996. "Instituições e valores: As dimensões da democracia na visão da elite brasileira." *Revista Brasileira de Ciências Sociais* 31 (June): 83–110.

———. 1994. *Elites: Estratégias e dilemas do desenvolvimento*. Relatório de Pesquisa, IUPERJ/Conjunto Universitário Cândido Mendes, October.

Lima, Olavo Brasil, Jr. 1983. *Partidos políticos brasileiros: A experiência federal e regional, 1945–1964*. Rio de Janeiro, Brazil: GRAAL.

Linz, Juan J., and Alfred Stepan. 1996. *Problems of Democratic Transition and Consolidation: Southern Europe, South America, and Post-Communist Europe*. Baltimore, Md.: Johns Hopkins University Press.

Longo, Carlos Alberto. 1995. "The State and the Liberalization of the Brazilian Economy." In M. D. G. Kinzo, ed., *Brazil: The Challenges of the 1990s*. London: The Institute of Latin American Studies, University of London and British Academic Press.

Lopes, Juarez R. Brandão. 1996. "Obstacles to Economic Reform in Brazil." In Arend Lijphart and Carlos H. Waisman, eds., *Institutional Design in New Democracies: Eastern Europe and Latin America*. Boulder, Colo.: Westview Press.

Loureiro, Maria Rita. 1992. "Economistas e elites dirigentes no Brasil." *Revista Brasileira de Ciências Sociais* 7 (20): 47–65.

Love, Joseph. 1986. "Economic Ideas and Ideologies in Latin America since 1930." In Leslie Bethell, ed., *Ideas and Ideologies in Twentieth Century Latin America*. Cambridge, U.K.: Cambridge University Press.

Lustig, Nora. 1991. "From Structuralism to Neoconstructuralism: The Search for a Heterodox Paradigm." In Patricio Meller, ed., *Latin American Development Debate*.

Neostructuralism, Neomonetarism, and Adjustment Processes. Boulder, Colo.: Westview Press.

Magalhães, João Paulo de Almeida. 1991. "O impasse atual da economia brasileira." In Maurício Dias, org., *Economia e política da crise brasileira: A perspectiva social-democrata.* Rio de Janeiro, Brazil: Rio Fundo, 217–28.

Magalhães, João Paulo de Almeida, Adhemar dos Santos Mineiro, and Luiz Antônio Elias, eds. 1999. *Vinte anos de política econômica.* Rio de Janeiro, Brazil: Contraponto.

Mainwaring, Scott. 1999. *Rethinking Party Systems in the Third Wave of Democratization: The Case of Brazil.* Stanford, Calif.: Stanford University Press.

———. 1995. "Democracy in Brazil and the Southern Cone: Achievements and Problems." *Journal of Interamerican Studies and World Affairs* 37 (1): 113–79.

———. 1993. "Democracia presidencialista multipartidária: O caso do Brasil." *Lua Nova* 28 (29): 24–26.

———. 1989. "Grassroots Popular Movements and the Struggle for Democracy." In Alfred Stepan, ed., *Democratizing Brazil.* New York, N.Y.: Oxford University Press.

———. 1987. "Urban Popular Movements, Identity, and Democratization in Brazil." *Comparative Political Studies* 20 (2): 131–59.

———. 1986a. *The Catholic Church and Politics in Brazil: 1916–1985.* Stanford, Calif.: Stanford University Press.

———. 1986b. "The Transition to Democracy in Brazil." *Journal of Interamerican Studies and World Affairs* 28 (1): 149–79.

Malan, Pedro. 1999. "Brasil: três finais de década. In João Paulo de Almeida Magalhães, Adhemar dos Santos Mineiro, and Luiz Antônio Elias, eds. 1999. *Vinte anos de política econômica.* Rio de Janeiro, Brazil: Contraponto.

Malin, Mauro. 2002. "Agricultura e Reforma Agrária." In Bolívar Lamounier and Rubens Figueiredo, eds., *A Era FHC: Um Balanço.* São Paulo, Brazil: Cultura Editores Associados.

Malloy, James M. 1987. "The Politics of Transition in Latin America." In James M. Malloy and Mitchell A. Seligson, eds., *Authoritarians and Democrats: Regime Transition in Latin America.* Pittsburgh, Pa.: Pittsburgh University Press.

———. 1979. *The Politics of Social Security in Brazil.* Pittsburgh, Pa.: University of Pittsburgh Press.

Mantega, Guido. 1984. *A economia política brasileira.* Petrópolis, Brazil: Vozes.

Maravall, José Maria. 1994. "The Myth of the Authoritarian Advantage." *Journal of Democracy* 5 (October): 17–31.

Markoff, John, and Silvio R. Duncan Baretta. 1990. "Economic Crisis and Regime Change in Brazil: The 1960s and the 1980s." *Comparative Politics* 22 (4): 421–44.

Marks, Siegfried, ed. 1993. *Political Constraints on Brazil's Economic Development.* New Brunswick, N.J.: Transaction Publishers.

Martin, Scott. 1996a. "As câmaras setoriais e o meso-corporativismo." *Lua Nova* 37: 139–70.

———. 1996b. "Beyond Corporatism: New Patterns of Representation in the Brazilian Auto Industry." In D. Chalmers et al., eds., *The New Politics of Inequality in Latin America: Rethinking Participation and Representation.* Oxford, London: Oxford University Press.

Martínez-Lara, Javier. 1996. *Building Democracy in Brazil: The Politics of Constitutional Change, 1985–1995.* New York, N.Y.: St. Martin's Press.

Martins, José de Souza. 2000. "The Agrarian Reform: The Impossible Dialogue on the Possible History." Ministério de Desenvolvimento Agrário and INCRA. Originally published in *Tempo Social*, Revista de Sociologia da Universidade de São Paulo 11 (October 1999).

Martins, Luciano. 1995a. *Crise do poder, governabilidade e governança*. Rio de Janeiro, Brazil: José Olympio.

———. 1995b. *Reforma da administração pública e cultura política no Brasil: Uma visão geral*. Brasília, Brazil: Escola Nacional de Administração Pública, Cadernos ENAP, n°8.

———. 1994. "Instabilidade política e governabilidade na construção democrática." In João P. R. Velloso, org., *Governabilidade, sistema político e violência urbana*. Rio de Janeiro, Brazil: José Olympio.

———. 1993. "Three Dimensions of the Crisis: A Political Analysis." In Werner Baer and Joseph S. Tulchin, eds., *Brazil and the Challenge of Economic Reform*. Washington. D.C.: The Woodrow Wilson Center Press and Johns Hopkins University Press.

———. 1986. "The 'Liberalization' of Authoritarian Rule in Brazil." In P. C. Schmitter and L. Whitehead G. O'Donnell, eds., *Transitions from Authoritarian Rule*. Baltimore, Md.: Johns Hopkins University Press.

———. 1985. *Estado capitalista e burocracia no Brasil pós-64*. Rio de Janeiro, Brazil: Paz e Terra.

Martins Rodrigues, Leôncio, and Adalberto M. Cardoso. 1993. *Força sindical: Uma análise sócio-política*. São Paulo, Brazil: Paz e Terra.

Maxfield, Sylvia. 1997. *Gatekeepers of Growth: The International Political Economy of Central Banking in Developing Countries*. Princeton N.J.: Princeton University Press.

———. 1991. "Bankers Alliances and Economic Policy Patterns. Evidence from Mexico and Brazil." *Comparative Political Studies* 23 (4): 419–58.

Maxfield, Sylvia, and Ben Schneider, eds. 1997. *Business and the State in Developing Countries*. Ithaca, N.Y.: Cornell University Press.

Maybury-Lewis, Biorn. 1994. *The Politics of the Possible: The Brazilian Rural Workers' Trade Union Movement, 1964–1985*. Philadephia, Pa.: Temple University Press.

McQuerry, Elizabeth. 1995. "Economic Liberalization in Brazil: Business Responses and Changing Patterns of Behavior." Ph.D. diss. University of Texas.

Medeiros, Antonio Carlos de. 1985. "Da mediação burocrática à mediação partidária: Aspectos políticos das relações centro-periferia no Brasil." *Revista de Administração Pública* 19 (4): 76–97.

Médici, André. 2002. "Health Reforms and Federalism in Brazil." Bildner Center for Western Hemisphere Studies, The Graduate Center, City University of New York, N.Y., April 8–9. Paper presented at the conference "New Approaches to Social Reform in Brazil."

———. 1997. "A economia política das reformas em saúde." Porto Alegre, Brazil: IAHCS.

Melo, Marcus André B. C. 1993a. "Municipalismo, nation-building e a modernização do Estado no Brasil." *Revista Brasileira de Ciências Sociais* 8 (23): 85–100.

———. 1993b. "Anatomia do fracasso: Intermediação de interesses e a reforma das políticas sociais na Nova República." *Dados* 36 (1): 119–64.

———. 1990. "A formação de políticas e a transição democrática: O caso da política social." *Dados* 33 (3): 443–70.

Merquior, José Guilherme. 1991. *O liberalismo antigo e moderno*. Rio de Janeiro, Brazil: Editora Nova Fronteira.

———. 1986. "Patterns of State-Building in Brazil and Argentina." In John A. Hall, ed., *States in History*. Oxford, London: Basil Blackwell.

Mesa-Lago, Carmelo. 1994. *Changing Social Security in Latin America*. Boulder, Colo.: Lynne Rienner.

Meyer, David R. 1980. "A Dynamic Model of the Integration of Frontier Urban Places into the United States System of Cities." *Economic Geography* 56: 121–40.

Moisés, José Álvaro. 1994. "A escolha democrática em perspectiva comparada." *Lua Nova* (33): 17–37.

Momsen, Richard P. 1964. *Routes over the Serra do Mar: The Evolution of Transportation in the Highlands of Rio de Janeiro and São Paulo*. Rio de Janeiro, Brazil: Xerxes Books.

Montero, Alfred P. 2001. "Elaboração de políticas econômicas em nível subnacional no Brasil: Uma colcha de retalhos." In Alzira A. Abreu, ed. *Transição em fragmentos: Desafios da democracia no final de século XX*. Rio de Janeiro, Brazil: Fundação Getúlio Vargas.

———. 1999a. "Devolving Democracy? Political Decentralization and the New Brazilian Federalism." In P. R. Kingstone and T. J. Power, eds., *Democratic Brazil*. Pittsburgh, Pa.: University of Pittsburgh Press.

———. 1999b. "A Delicate Game: The Politics of Reform in Brazil." *Current History* 98 (626): 111–15.

———. 1998a. "Assessing the Third Wave Democracies." *Journal of Interamerican and World Affairs* 40 (summer): 117–34.

———. 1998b. "State Interests and the New Industrial Policy in Brazil: The Privatization of Steel, 1990–1994." *Journal of Interamerican and World Affairs* 40 (fall): 27–62.

Moore, Barrington, Jr. 1967. *Social Origins of Dictatorship and Democracy: Lord and Peasant in the Making of the Modern World*. Boston, Mass.: Beacon Press.

Moraes, Marcelo Viana Estevão de. 1995. "Reforma da previdência." In João Paulo dos Reis Velloso and Roberto Cavalcanti de Albuquerque et al., *Governabilidade e reformas*. Rio de Janeiro, Brazil: José Oympio, 219–42.

Morales, Juan Antonio. 1996. *Economic Policy and the Transition to Democracy*. London, U.K.: MacMillan Press.

Motta, Helena. 2000. *Crise e reforma do Estado brasileiro*. Juiz de Fora, Brazil: UFJF.

Moura, Alkimar R. 1993. "Stabilization Policy as a Game of Mutual Distrust: The Brazilian Experience in post-1985 Civilian Governments." In M. D. G. Kinzo, ed., *Brazil: The Challenges of the 1990s*. London: The Institute of Latin American Studies, University of London and British Academic Press.

Mouzelis, Nicos P. 1986. *Politics in the Semi-Periphery: Early Parliamentarism and Late Industrialization in the Balkans and Latin America*. New York, N.Y.: St. Martin's Press.

Muller, A. E. G. 1987. *Desenvolvimento agro-exportador e estruturação espacial: Análise comparativa de dois "territórios vazios" latino-americanos (1870/1880–1930)*. São Paulo, Brazil: IPE/Universidade de São Paulo.

Nassif, Luís. 2002. "Política Macroeconômica e Ajuste Fiscal." In Bolívar Lamounier and Rubens Figueiredo, eds., *A Era FHC: Um Balanço*. São Paulo, Brazil: Cultura Editores Associados.

Nassif, Maria Inês. 2002. "Previdência Social." In Bolívar Lamounier and Rubens Figueiredo, eds., *A Era FHC: Um Balanço*. São Paulo, Brazil: Cultura Editores Associados.

Navarro, Zander. 1999. "Democracia e controle social de fundos públicos—o caso do 'orçamento participativo' de Porto Alegre." In L.C. Bresser Pereira and Nuria C. Grau, eds., *O público não-estatal na reforma do Estado*. Rio de Janeiro, Brazil: Fundação Getúlio Vargas.

Nazmi, Nader. 1995. "Inflation and Stabilization: Recent Brazilian Experience Perspective." *The Journal of Developing Areas* 29 (4): 491–506.

Nelson, Joan M., ed. 1994. "Labor and Business Roles in Dual Transitions: Building Blocks or Stumbling Blocks?" *Intricate Links: Democratization and Market Reforms in Latin America and Eastern Europe*. Washington, D.C.: Overseas Development Council, and New Brunswick, N.J.: Transaction Publishers.

———. 1992. "Poverty, Equity, and the Politics of Adjustment." In Stephan Haggard and Robert R. Kaufman, eds., *The Politics of Economic Adjustment: International Constraints, Distributive Conflicts, and the State*. Princeton, N.J.: Princeton University Press.

———. 1984. "The Politics of Stabilization." In Richard E. Feinberg and Valeriana Kallab, eds., *Adjustment Crisis in the Third World*. New Brunswick, N.J.: Transaction Books.

———, ed. 1990a. "Conclusions." In *Economic Crisis and Policy Choice: The Politics of Adjustment in the Third World*. Princeton, N.J.: Princeton University Press.

———, ed. 1990b. "Introduction: The Politics of Economic Adjustment in Argentina, Brazil, and Mexico." In *Economic Crisis and Policy Choice: The Politics of Adjustment in the Third World*. Princeton, N.J.: Princeton University Press.

———, ed. 1989. "The Politics of Long-Haul Economic Reform." In *Fragile Coalitions: The Politics of Economic Adjustment*. New Brunswick, N.J.: Transaction Books.

Nelson, Roy C. 1995. *Industrialization and Political Affinity: Industrial Policy in Brazil*. New York, N.Y.: Routledge.

Néri, Marcelo. 2000. "Políticas estruturais de combate à pobreza no Brasil." In Ricardo Henrique, ed., *Desigualdade e pobreza no Brasil*. Rio de Janeiro, Brazil: IPEA.

Nunes, Edson André Nogueira, and Paulo Tafner. 1995. "Economia política do poder e modernização da democracia brasileira." In João Paulo dos Reis Velloso and Roberto Cavalcanti de Albuquerque et al., *Governabilidade e reformas*. Rio de Janeiro, Brazil: José Oympio, 87–126.

Nunes, Edson de Oliveira. 1978. "Legislativo, política e recrutamento de elites no Brasil." *Dados* 17: 53–78.

Nunes, Edson de Oliveira, and Barbara Geddes. 1987. "Dilemmas of State-Led Modernization in Brazil." In John Wirth et al., eds., *State and Society in Brazil*. Boulder, Colo.: Westview Press.

Nylen, William R. 1999. "The Making of a Loyal Opposition: The Workers' Party (PT) and the Consolidation of Democracy in Brazil." In P. R. Kingstone and T. J. Power, eds., *Democratic Brazil*. Pittsburgh, Pa.: University of Pittsburgh Press.

———. 1993. "Selling Neoliberalism: Brazil's Instituto Liberal." *Journal of Latin American Studies* 25 (2): 301–12.

O'Donnell, Guillermo. 1996. "Illusions about Consolidation." *Journal of Democracy* 7 (2): 34–51.

———. 1994. "Delegative Democracy." *Journal of Democracy* 7 (2): 34–51.

————. 1974. "Corporatism and the Question of the State." In James Malloy, ed., *Authoritarianism and Corporatism in Latin America*. Pittsburgh, Pa.: University of Pittsburgh Press.

————. 1973. "Modernization and Bureaucratic-Authoritarianism." In *Studies in South American Politics*. Berkeley, Calif.: University of California Press.

OECD. 2001. *OECD Economic Surveys: Brazil*. Paris, France: OECD.

Oliveira, Amaury Porto de. 1993. "Liberalizing into Development." In Werner Baer and Joseph S. Tulchin, eds., *Brazil and the Challenge of Economic Reform*. Washington, D.C.: Woodrow Wilson Center Press, 39–68.

Oliveira, Francisco de. 1994. *Estado, sociedade, movimentos sociais e políticas públicas no limiar do século XXI*. Rio de Janeiro, Brazil: FASE.

————. 1981. *Elegia para uma re(li)gião: SUDENE, Nordeste, planejamento e conflito de classes*. Rio de Janeiro, Brazil: Paz e Terra.

Oliveira, Francisco de, and Alvaro Comin, eds. 1999. *Os cavaleiros do antiapocalipse: Trabalho e política na indústria automobilística*. São Paulo, Brazil: CEBRAP/ Entrelinhas.

Oliveira, Miguel Darcy de. 2000. "O que é o conselho da Comunidade Solidária." In Ruth Cardoso, W. Franco, J. Werthein, and S. M. Draibe, org., *Estratégias inovadoras de parceria no combate à exclusão social*. Brasília, Brazil: Comunidade Solidária/UNESCO/PNUD.

Ottmann, Götz. 1995. "Movimentos sociais urbanos e democracia no Brasil." *Novos Estudos CEBRAP* 41 (March): 186–207.

Packenham, Robert A. 1994. "The Politics of Economic Liberalization: Argentina and Brazil in Comparative Perspective," Kellogg Institute Working Paper #206.

————. 1992. "Freedom and Development in Latin America." *World Affairs* 155 (summer): 3–12.

Pastor, Manuel, Jr., and Eric Hilt. 1993. "Private Investment and Democracy in Latin America." *World Development* 21 (4): 489–507.

Payne, Leigh A. 1994. *Brazilian Industrialists and Democratic Change*. Baltimore, Md.: Johns Hopkins University Press.

————. 1991. "Working Class Strategies in the Transition to Democracy in Brazil." *Comparative Politics* 23 (2): 221–38.

Peixoto, João Paulo M., and Antonio C. Pojo do Rego. 1998. *A política das reformas econômicas no Brasil*. Rio de Janeiro, Brazil: Expressão e Cultura.

Peliano, Anna Maria, and Nathalie Beghin. 2000. "A iniciativa privada e o espírito público." *Políticas Sociais* 1 (June): 55–59.

Peliano, Anna Maria, et al. 1998. "O programa Comunidade Solidária." In João P. R. Velloso, org., *O Brasil e o mundo no limiar do novo século*. Rio de Janeiro, Brazil: José Olympio.

Pereira, Anthony W. 2001. "Agrarian Reform in Brazil, 1995–2001." Bildner Center for Western Hemisphere Studies, The Graduate Center, City University of New York, N.Y., May 16–19. Paper presented at the conference "Reforming Brazil I: A Preliminary Assessment."

————. 1999. "An Ugly Democracy? State Violence and the Rule of Law in Postauthoritarian Brazil." In P. R. Kingstone and T. J. Power, eds., *Democratic Brazil*. Pittsburgh, Pa.: University of Pittsburgh Press.

————. 1997. *The End of the Peasantry: The Rural Labor Movement in Northeast Brazil, 1961–1988*. Pittsburgh, Pa.: University of Pittsburgh Press.

Perz, Stephen G. 2000. "The Rural Exodus in the Context of Economic Crisis, Global-ization and Reform in Brazil." *International Migration Review* 34 (3): 842.

Pessanha, Charles. 1981. "Estado e economia no Brasil: A campanha contra a estatiza-ção 1974–1976." Master's thesis, IUPERJ.

Pinheiro, Paulo Sérgio. 1997. "Popular Responses to the State-Sponsored Violence in Brazil." In Douglas A. Chalmers, Carlos M. Vilas, Katherine Hite, Scott B. Martin, Karianne Piester, and Monique Segarra, eds., *The New Politics of Inequality in Latin America: Rethinking Participation and Representation.* Oxford, London: Oxford University Press, 261–80.

Pinheiro, Paulo Sérgio, and Michael Hall. 1981. *A classe operária no Brasil, 1889–1930.* São Paulo, Brazil: Brasiliense.

Pinto, Almir Pazzianotto. 1994. "Sindicatos, corporativismo e política." In G.A.D. Soares and M.C.D'Araujo, eds., *21 anos de regime militar.* Rio de Janeiro, Brazil: Fundação Getúlio Vargas.

Portes, Alejandro. 1997. "Neoliberalism and the Sociology of Development: Emerging Trends and Unanticipated Facts." *Population and Development Review* (June): 229.

Portes, Alejandro, and Richard Schauffler. 1993. "Competing Perspectives on the Latin American Informal Sector." *Population and Development Review* 19 (1): 33–60.

Power, Timothy J. 2001. "Blairism Brazilian Style? Fernando Henrique Cardoso and the 'Third Way' in Brazil." *Political Science Quarterly* 116 (4): 611-36.

———. 1998a. "Brazilian Politicians and Neoliberalism: Mapping Support for the Car-doso Reforms, 1995-1997." *Journal of Interamerican Studies and World Affairs* 40 (winter): 51-72.

———. 1998b. "The Pen Is Mightier than the Congress: Presidential Decree Power in Brazil." In John Carey and Matthew Soberg Shugart, eds., *Executive Decree Author-ity.* Cambridge, Mass.: Cambridge University Press.

Power, Timothy J., and J. Timmons Roberts. 1999. "A New Brazil? The Changing Socio-demographic Context of Brazilian Democracy." In P. R. Kingstone and T. J. Power, eds., *Democratic Brazil.* Pittsburgh, Pa.: University of Pittsburgh Press.

Przeworski, Adam. 1991. *Democracy and the Market: Political and Economic Reforms in Eastern Europe and Latin America.* Cambridge, Mass.: Cambridge University Press.

———. 1985. *Capitalism and Social Democracy.* Cambridge, Mass.: Cambridge Uni-versity Press.

Purcell, Susan Kaufman. 1997. "The New U.S. Brazil Relationship." In Susan Kaufman Purcell and Riordan Roett, eds., *Brazil under Cardoso.* Boulder. Colo.: Lynne Rienner Publishers.

Purcell, Susan Kaufman, and Riordan Roett, eds. 1997. *Brazil under Cardoso.* Boulder. Colo.: Lynne Rienner Publishers.

Ranis, Gustav. 1990. "Contrasts in the Political Economy of Development Policy Change." In Gary Gereffi and Donald L. Wyman, eds., *Manufacturing Miracles.* Princeton, N.J.: Princeton University Press.

Rapley, John, 1996. *Understanding Development: Theory and Practice in the Third World.* Boulder, Colo.: Lynne Rienner Publishers.

Reilly, Charles A. 1999. "Redistribuição de direitos e responsabilidades—cidadania e capital social." In L. C. Bresser Pereira and Nuria C. Grau, eds., *O público não-estatal na reforma do Estado.* Rio de Janeiro, Brazil: Fundação Getúlio Vargas.

Reis, Elisa P. 2000. "Percepções da elite sobre pobreza e desigualdade." In R. Hen-riques, org., *Desigualdade e Pobreza no Brasil.* Rio de Janeiro, Brazil: IPEA.

————. 1989. "Brasil: Cem anos de questão agrária." *Dados* 32 (3): 281–301.

————. 1985. *Bureaucracy and the Demise of Authoritarianism in Brazil.* Rio de Janeiro, Brazil: IUPERJ, Série Estudos, n° 43 (November).

Reis, Fábio Wanderley. 1995. "Governabilidade, instituições e partidos." *Novos Estudos CEBRAP* (41): 40–59.

————. 1994a. "Notas sobre a reforma do Estado." *Revista do Serviço Público* 45 (3): 17–26.

————. 1994b. "Governabilidade e instituições políticas." In João Paulo dos Reis Velloso, ed., *Governabilidade, sistema político e violência urbana.* Rio de Janeiro, Brazil: José Olympio.

————. 1993. "Estado liberal, projeto nacional, questão social." *Planejamento e políticas públicas* (9): 143–68.

————. 1989. "Estado, economia, ética, interesses: Para a construção democrática do Brasil." *Planejamento e políticas públicas* 1 (1): 33–56.

————. 1988. "Consolidação democrática e construção do Estado" In F. W. Reis and G. O'Donnell, eds., *A democracia no Brasil: Dilemas e perspectivas.* São Paulo, Brazil: Vértice.

Reis, Fábio Wanderley, and Mônica Mata Machado de Castro. 1992. "Regiões, classe e ideologia no processo eleitoral brasileiro." *Lua Nova* 26: 81–131.

Reis, Fábio Wanderley, and Guillermo O'Donnell, eds. 1988. *A democracia no Brasil: Dilemas e perspectivas.* São Paulo, Brazil: Vértice.

Remmer, Karen L. 1991. "The Political Impact of Economic Crisis in Latin America in the 1980s." *American Political Science Review* 85 (3): 777–800.

————. 1990. "Democracy and Economic Crisis: The Latin American Experience." *World Politics* 42 (3): 315–35.

————. 1986. "The Politics of Economic Stabilization: IMF Stand-by Programs in Latin America, 1954–1984." *Comparative Politics* 19 (1): 1–24.

————. 1978. "Evaluating the Policy Impact of Military Regimes in Latin America." *Latin America Research Review* 13 (2): 39–54.

Resende, André Lara. 1991. "O processo hiperinflacionário e as reformas modernizadoras." In Maurício Dias, org., *Economia e política da crise brasileira: A perspectiva social-democrata.* Rio de Janeiro, Brazil: Rio Fundo, 85–92.

Rocha, Geisa Maria. 1994. "Redefining the Role of the Bourgeoisie in Dependent Capitalist Development: Privatization and Liberalization in Brazil." *Latin American Perspectives* 21 (1): 72–98.

Rocha, Sônia. 2001. "Poverty in Brazil: What Is New at the Onset of the 21st Century?" Bildner Center for Western Hemisphere Studies, The Graduate Center, City University of New York, N.Y., April 8–9. Paper presented at the conference "New Approaches to Social Reform in Brazil."

Rocha, Sônia and Roberto C. de Albuquerque. 1999. "Sobre estratégias de redução da pobreza." In João P. dos Reis Velloso and Roberto C. de Albuquerque, eds., *Pobreza, cidadania e segurança.* Rio de Janeiro, Brazil: José Olympio.

Rodrigues, José Albertino. 1968. *Sindicato e desenvolvimento no Brasil.* São Paulo, Brazil: Difel.

Rodrigues, Leôncio Martins. 1995. "Eleições, fragmentação partidária e governabilidade." *Novos Estudos* 41 (March): 78–90.

————. 1990. *CUT: Os militantes e a ideologia.* São Paulo, Brazil: Paz e Terra.

Rodrigues, Leôncio Martins, and Adalberto M. Cardoso. 1993. *Força sindical: Uma análise sócio-política.* São Paulo, Brazil: Paz e Terra.

Roett, Riordan. 1997. "Brazilian Politics at Century's End." In Susan Kaufman Purcell and Riordan Roett, eds., *Brazil under Cardoso*. Boulder, Colo.: Lynne Rienner Publishers, 19–41.
————. 1972. *Brazil: Politics in a Patrimonial Society*. Boston, Mass.: Allyn and Bacon.
Rogowski, Ronald. 1981. "Political Cleavages and Changing Exposure to Trade." *American Political Science Review* 81 (4): 1,121–37.
Rojas, Mauricio. 1991. "Review of the Debate over the Origins of Latin American Industrialization and Its Ideological Context." In Patricio Meller, ed., *Latin American Development Debate. Neostructuralism, Neomonetarism, and Adjustment Processes*. Boulder, Colo.: Westview Press.
Rosenn, Keith, and Richard Downes, eds. 1999. *Corruption and Political Reform in Brazil: The Impact of Collor's Impeachment*. Coral Gables, Fla.: North-South Center Press.
Saborio, S. 1990. "Central America." In J. Williamson, ed., *Latin American Adjustment*. Washington, D.C.: Institute for International Economics.
Sachs, Jeffrey. 1994. "Life in the Economic Emergency Room." In John Williamson, ed., *The Political Economy of Policy Reform*. Washington, D.C.: Institute for International Economics.
Sadek, Maria Tereza. 1999. "Terceiro setor: O que mudar?" In Carlos F. C. Cuenca, org., *Mudança social e Reforma Legal: Estudos para uma nova legislação do terceiro setor*. Brasília, Brazil: Conselho da Comunidade Solidária: UNESCO: BID: FBB.
Sallum, Brasílio, Jr. 1996. *Labirintos: Dos generais à Nova República*. São Paulo, Brazil: HUCITEC.
————. 1994. "Transição política e crise de Estado." *Lua Nova* 32: 133–67.
————. 1988. "Por que não tem dado certo: Notas sobre a transição política brasileira." In Lourdes Sola, ed., *O Estado da transição: Política e economia na Nova República*. São Paulo, Brazil: Vértice.
Sallum, Brasílio, Jr., and Eduardo Kugelmas. 1993. "O Leviatã acorrentado: A crise brasileira dos anos 80." In Lourdes Sola, ed., *Estado, mercado e democracia: Política e economia comparadas*. São Paulo, Brazil: Paz e Terra.
Samuels, David Julian. 1999. "Reinventing Local Government? Municipalities and Intergovernmental Relations in Democratic Brazil." In P. R. Kingstone and T. J. Power, eds., *Democratic Brazil*. Pittsburgh, Pa.: University of Pittsburgh Press.
————. 1998. "Careerism and Its Consequences: Federalism, Elections, and Policy-Making in Brazil." Ph.D. diss. University of California, San Diego.
Sandoval, Salvador. 1998. "Social Movements and Democratization: The Case of Brazil and the Latin Countries." In M. Guigni et al., eds., *From Contention to Democracy*. Lanham, Md.: Rowman and Littlefield.
————. 1994. *Os trabalhadores páram: Greves e mudança social no Brasil, 1945–1990*. São Paulo, Brazil: Ática.
————. 1993. *Social Change and Labor Unrest in Brazil since 1945*. Boulder, Colo.: Westview Press.
Santos, Theotonio dos. 1972. *Brasil: Origenes y perspectivas de una crisis*. Buenos Aires, Argentina: Documento de Trabajo.
Santos, Wanderley Guilherme dos. 1994. "Democracia contrafactual ou Estado efetivo?" In João P. R. Velloso, org., *Governabilidade, sistema político e violência urbana*. Rio de Janeiro, Brazil: José Olympio.

————. 1982. "A elite invisível: Exploração sobre a tecnocracia federal brasileira." *Revista do Serviço Público* (Fundação Centro de Formação do Serviço Público) 39 (110).

————. 1978. *A práxis liberal no Brasil: Proposta para reflexão e pesquisa*. São Paulo, Brazil: Duas Cidades.

Schamis, Hector E. 1999. "Distributional Coalitions and the Politics of Economic Reform in Latin America." *World Politics* 51 (2): 236–68.

Schmidt, Benício Viero, Danilo Nolasco Marinho, and Sueli Couto Rosa, eds. 1998. *Os assentamentos da reforma agrária no Brasil*. Brasília, Brazil: Universidade de Brasília.

Schmidt, Vivian A. 1995. "The New World Order, Incorporated: The Rise of Business and the Decline of the Nation State." *Daedalus* 124 (2): 75–106.

Schmitter, Phillipe C. 1992. "The Consolidation of Democracy and the Representation of Social Groups." *American Behavioral Scientist* 35: 422–49.

————. 1979a. "Paths to Political Development in Latin America." In Douglas A. Chalmers, ed., *Changing Latin America*. New York, N.Y.: Academy of Political Science.

————. 1979b. "Modes of Interest Intermediation and Models of Social Change in Western Europe." In P. C. Schmitter and G. Lehmbruch, eds., *Trends Toward Corporatist Intermediation*. Beverly Hills, Calif: Sage.

————. 1974. "Still the Century of Corporatism?" *The Review of Politics* 36: 85–131.

————. 1971. *Interest Groups, Conflict, and Political Change in Brazil*. Standford, Calif.: Stanford University Press.

Schmitter, Phillipe C., and Gerard Lembruch, eds. 1979. *Trends toward Corporatist Intermediation*. Beverly Hills, Calif.: Sage.

Schneider, Ben Ross. 1998. "Elusive Synergy: Business-State Relations and Development." *Comparative Politics* 31 (1): 101–22.

————. 1997. "Organized Business Politics in Democratic Brazil." *Journal of Interamerican Studies and World Affairs* 39 (2): 95–127.

————. 1995a. "Collective Action, the State, and Business Politics in Brazil and Mexico." IUPERJ, Rio de Janeiro, Brazil, October 4–6. Paper presented at the international seminar, "The Challenge of Democracy in Latin America: Rethinking State/Society Relations."

————. 1995b. "La burguesía desarticulada de Brasil." *Revista Mexicana de Sociología* 57 (4): 135–53.

————. 1991a. *Politics within the State: Elite Bureaucrats and Industrial Policy in Authoritarian Brazil*. Pittsburgh, Pa.: University of Pittsburgh Press.

————. 1991b. "A política de privatização no Brasil e no México nos anos 80: Variações em torno de um tema estatista." *Dados* 34: 21–51.

————. 1988. "Partly for Sale: Privatization and State Strength in Brazil and Mexico." *Journal of Interamerican Studies and World Affairs* 30: (4): 89–116.

Schwartzman, Simon. 2000. "Brazil: The Social Agenda." *Daedalus* 129 (2): 29.

————. 1982. *As bases do autoritarismo brasileiro*. Rio de Janeiro, Brazil: Campus.

————. 1975. *São Paulo e o Estado nacional*. São Paulo, Brazil: Difel.

Selcher, Wayne A. 1998. "The Politics of Descentralized Federalism, National Diversification, and Regionalism in Brazil." *Journal of Interamerican and World Affairs* 40 (4): 25–50.

————. 1989. "A New Start Toward a More Decentralized Federalism in Brazil?" *Publius* 19 (summer): 167–83.

Senghaas, Dieter. 1985. *The European Experience: A Historical Critique of Development Theory.* Leamington, N.H.: Berg Publishers.

Serra, José. 1993. *Reforma política no Brasil: Parlamentarismo x presidencialismo.* São Paulo, Brazil: Siciliano.

————. 1979a. "Three Mistaken Theses Regarding the Connection between Industrialization and Authoritarian Regimes." In David Collier, ed., *The New Authoritarianism in Latin America.* Princeton, N.J.: Princeton University Press.

————. 1979b. "As desventuras do economicismo: Três teses equivocadas sobre autoritarismo e desenvolvimento." *Dados* (20): 3–45.

Shafer, Michael D. 1990. "Sectors, States, and Social Forces: Korea and Zambia Confront Economic Restructuring." *Comparative Politics* 22 (2): 127–50.

Shapiro, Helen. 1994. *Engines of Growth: The State and Transnational Auto Companies in Brazil.* New York, N.Y.: Cambridge University Press.

Sheahan, John. 1980. "Market-Oriented Economic Policies and Political Repression in Latin America." *Economic Development and Cultural Change* 28 (2): 267–91.

Siegel, Gilbert B. 1978. *The Vicissitudes of Governmental Reform in Brazil: A Study of the DASP.* Washington, D.C.: University Press of America.

Siekman, Phillip. 1964. "When Executives Turned Revolutionaries; A Story Hitherto Untold: How São Paulo Businessmen Conspired to Overthrow Brazil's Communist-Infested Government." *Fortune* 70 (3): 147-49.

Siffert Filho, Nelson. 1998. *Governança corporativa: Padrões internacionais e evidências empíricas no Brasil nos anos 90.* BNDES Document.

Sikkink, Kathryn. 1993. "Las capacidades y la autonomía del Estado en Brasil y la Argentina: Un enfoque neoinstitucionalista." *Desarrollo Económico* 32 (128): 543–74.

Silva, Carlos Eduardo Lins. 2002. "Política e Comércio Exterior." In Bolívar Lamounier and Rubens Figueiredo, eds., *A Era FHC: Um Balanço.* São Paulo, Brazil: Cultura Editores Associados.

————. 1995. "Plato in the Tropics: The Brazilian Republic of Guardians." *Current History* (February): 81–85.

Silva, Nelson V., and Carlos Hasenbalg. 2000. "Tendências da desigualdade educacional no Brasil." *Dados* 43 (3): 423–45.

Simão, Azis. 1981. *Sindicato e Estado: Suas relações na formação do proletariado de São Paulo.* São Paulo, Brazil: Ática.

Singer, André. 2002. "Saúde." In Bolívar Lamounier and Rubens Figueiredo, eds., *A Era FHC: Um Balanço.* São Paulo, Brazil: Cultura Editores Associados.

Singer, Paul. 1996. "Desemprego e exclusão social." *São Paulo em Perspectiva* 10 (1): 3–12.

Síntese de Indicadores Sociais. 2000. *IBGE,* Departamento de População e Indicadores Sociais. Rio de Janeiro, Brazil: IBGE.

Skidmore, Thomas E. 1999. "Foreword: A New Test for Brazilian Democracy." In P. R. Kingstone and T. J. Power, eds., *Democratic Brazil.* Pittsburgh, Pa.: University of Pittsburgh Press.

————. 1977. "The Politics of Economic Stabilization in Postwar Latin America." In James M. Malloy, ed., *Authoritarianism and Corporatism in Latin America.* Pittsburgh, Pa.: University of Pittsburgh Press.

Skocpol, Theda, and John L. Campbell, eds. 1995. *American Society and Politics: Institutional, Historical, and Theoretical Perspectives.* New York, N.Y.: McGraw-Hill.

Smith, William C., Carlos Acuña, and Eduardo Gamarra, eds. 1994a. *Democracy, Markets, and Structural Reform in Latin America: Argentina, Bolivia, Brazil, Chile, and Mexico*. Coral Gables, Fla.: North-South Center.

———, eds. 1994b. *Latin American Political Economy in the Age of Neoliberal Reform: Theoretical and Comparative Perspectives for the 1990s*. Coral Gables, Fla.: North-South Center.

Smith, William C., and Messari Nizar. 1998. "Democracy and Reform in Cardoso's Brazil: Caught between Clientelism and Global Markets." *North-South Agenda* 33 (September): 1–28.

Sola, Lourdes. 1998. *Idéias econômicas, decisões políticas: Desenvolvimento, estabilidade e populismo*. São Paulo, Brazil: Editora da Universidade de São Paulo/ FAPESP.

———. 1994a. "The State, Structural Reform, and Democratization in Brazil." In W. C. Smith, C. H. Acuña, and E. A. Gamarra, eds., *Democracy, Markets, and Structural Reform in Latin America: Argentina, Bolivia, Brazil, Chile, and Mexico*. New Brunswick, N.J.: Transaction.

———. 1994b. "Estado, reforma fiscal e governabilidade democrática: Qual Estado?" *Novos Estudos CEBRAP* 38 (March): 189–205.

———. 1994c. "Qual Estado? Ajustamento estrutural como política e como História: O Brasil em perspectiva comparada." Tese de livre-docência, Political Science, University of São Paulo, March.

———. 1993. "Estado, transfomação econômica e democratização no Brasil." In L. Sola, ed., *Estado, mercado e democracia*. São Paulo, Brazil: Paz e Terra.

———. 1989. "Limites políticos ao choque heterodoxo no Brasil: Técnicos, políticos, democracia." *Revista Brasileira de Ciências Sociais* 9 (3): 38–69.

———. 1988. "Choque heterodoxo e transição democrática sem ruptura: Uma abordagem transdisciplinar." In L. Sola, ed., *O Estado da transição: Política e economia na Nova República*. São Paulo, Brazil: Vértice.

———, ed. 1993b. *Estado, mercado e democracia: Política e economia comparadas*. São Paulo, Brazil: Paz e Terra.

Sorensen, Georg. 1993. *Democracy and Democratization*. Boulder, Colo.: Westview Press.

Sorj, Bernardo. 2000. *A Nova Sociedade Brasileira*. Rio de Janeiro, Brazil: Zahar.

———. 1988. "Reforma agrária e democracia." In Fábio W. Reis and Guillermo O'Donnell, eds., *A democracia no Brasil: Dilemas e perspectivas*. São Paulo, Brazil: Vértice.

———. 1980. *Estado e classes sociais na agricultura*. Rio de Janeiro, Brazil: Zahar.

Souza, Amaury de. 1997. "Redressing Inequalities: Brazil's Social Agenda at Century's End." In Susan Kaufman Purcell and Riordan Roett, eds., *Brazil under Cardoso*. Boulder, Colo.: Lynne Rienner Publishers.

Souza, Celina. 1997. *Constitutional Engineering in Brazil: The Politics of Federalism and Decentralization*. New York, N.Y.: St. Martin's Press.

———. 1996. "Redemocratization and Decentralization in Brazil: The Strength of the Member States." *Development and Change* 27 (3): 529–55.

Spalding, Hobart. 1992. "Devastation in the Southern Cone: The Inheritance of the Neo-Liberal Years." *Latin American Issues*, vol. 14. Meadville, Pa.: Allegheny College.

Stallings, Barbara. 1992. "International Influence on Economic Policy: Debt, Stabilization, and Structural Reform." In Stephan Haggard and Robert R. Kaufman, eds.,

The Politics of Economic Adjustment: International Constraints, Distributive Conflicts, and the State. Princeton, N.J.: Princeton University Press.

―――. 1990. "Politics and Economic Crisis: A Comparative Study of Chile, Peru, and Colombia." In Joan M. Nelson, ed., *Economic Crisis and Policy Choice: The Politics of Adjustment in the Third World.* Princeton, N.J.: Princeton University Press.

Stepan, Alfred. 1989. *Democratizing Brazil: Problems of Transition and Consolidation.* New York, N.Y.: Oxford University Press.

―――. 1988. *Rethinking Military Politics: Brazil and the Southern Cone.* Princeton, N.J.: Princeton University Press.

―――. 1971. *The Military in Politics: Changing Patterns in Brazil.* Princeton, N.J.: Princeton University Press.

―――, ed. 1973. *Authoritarian Brazil: Origins, Policies and Future.* New Haven, Conn.: Yale University Press.

Sunkel, Osvaldo, ed. 1991. *El desarrollo desde adentro: Un enfoque neo-estructuralista para América Latina.* Mexico, DF: Fondo de Cultura Económica

Suzigan, Wilson. 1993. "Industrial Policy and the Challenge of Competitiveness." In Werner Baer and Joseph S. Tulchin, eds., *Brazil and the Challenge of Economic Reform.* Washington, D.C.: Woodrow Wilson Center Press, 119–47.

―――. 1986. *Indústria brasileira: Origem e desenvolvimento.* São Paulo, Brazil: Brasiliense.

Tavares, Maria da Conceição. 1974. *Acumulação de capital e industrialização no Brasil.* Rio de Janeiro, Brazil: Universidade Federal.

―――. 1972. *Da substituição de importações ao capitalismo financeiro.* Rio de Janeiro, Brazil: Zahar Editores.

Tavares, Ricardo. 1989. *Reforma e contra-reforma agrária na transição política: Brasil, 1979–1988.* Rio de Janeiro, Brazil: IUPERJ, Série Estudo, n° 70.

Tendler, Judith. 1997. *Good Government in the Tropics.* Baltimore, Md.: Johns Hopkins University Press.

Thomas, John W., and Merilee S. Grindle. 1991. *Public Choices and Policy Change: The Politics of Economic Reform in Developing Countries.* Baltimore, Md.: Johns Hopkins University Press.

Thorp, Rosemary, and Lawrence Whitehead, eds. 1989. *Latin American Debt and the Adjustment Crisis.* Pittsburgh, Pa.: University of Pittsburgh Press.

Tilly, Charles. 1978. *From Mobilization to Revolution.* Reading, Mass.: Addison-Wesley.

Torre, Juan Carlos. 1996. "O encaminhamento político das reformas." *Lua Nova* 37: 57–76.

Tufte, Edward R. 1978. *Political Control of the Economy.* Princeton, N.J.: Princeton University Press.

Unger, Roberto Mangabeira. 1990. *A alternativa transformadora.* Rio de Janeiro, Brazil: Guanabara Koogan.

Veiga, José Eli. 2002. "Cidades imaginárias: O Brasil é menos urbano do que se calcula." Campinas, Brazil: Autores Associados.

Veiga, José Eli, et al. 2001. "O Brasil rural precisa de uma estratégia de desenvolvimento." Brasília, Brazil: Convênio FIPE-IICA (MDA/CNDRS/NEAD).

―――. 2000. "A face rural do desenvolvimento: Natureza, território e agricultura." Porto Alegre, Brazil: Ed. Universidade/UFRGS.

―――. 1998. "Diretrizes para uma nova política agrária." Paper presented at the Seminário sobre Reforma Agrária e Desenvolvimento Sustentável, MDA/NEAD, Fortaleza, Brazil.

Velloso, João Paulo dos Reis, ed. 1994a. *Inovação e sociedade: Uma estratégia de desenvolvimento com eqüidade para o Brasil.* Rio de Janeiro, Brazil: José Olympio.
————, ed. 1994b. *Governabilidade, sistema político e violência urbana.* Rio de Janeiro, Brazil: José Olympio.
————, ed. 1993. *Brasil: A superação da crise.* São Paulo, Brazil: Nobel.
————, ed. 1991a. *A questão social no Brasil.* São Paulo, Brazil: Nobel.
————, ed. 1991b. *Crescimento com redistribuição e reformas: reverter a opção pelos não-pobres.* Rio de Janeiro, Brazil: José Olympio.
————, ed. 1990. *A crise brasileira e a modernização da sociedade.* Rio de Janeiro, Brazil: José Olympio.
Velloso, João Paulo dos Reis, and Roberto Cavalcanti de Albuquerque, eds. 2001. *Soluções para a questão do emprego.* Rio de Janeiro, Brazil: José Olympio.
————, eds. 2000. *Pobreza, cidadania e segurança.* Rio de Janeiro, Brazil: José Olympio.
————, eds. 1995. *Governabilidade e reformas.* Rio de Janeiro, Brazil: José Oympio.
————, eds. 1994. *Modernidade e pobreza.* São Paulo, Brazil: Nobel.
————, eds. 1993. *Pobreza e mobilidade social.* São Paulo, Brazil: Nobel.
Velloso, João Paulo dos Reis, Roberto Cavalcanti de Albuquerque, and Joachim Knoop, eds. 1995. *Políticas sociais no Brasil: descentralização, eficiência e eqüidade.* Rio de Janeiro, Brazil: Inae/Ildes.
Vial, Joaquin, ed. 1992. *Adonde va América Latina? Balance de las reformas económicas.* Santiago, Chile: CIEPLAN.
Vianna, Luiz Werneck. 1984. "Atualizando uma bibliografia: Novo sindicalismo, cidadania e fábrica." *Boletim Informativo e Bibliográfico de Ciências Sociais* 17: 53–68.
————. 1978. *Liberalismo e sindicato no Brasil.* Rio de Janeiro, Brazil: Paz e Terra.
Vieira, Evaldo. 1981. *Autoritarismo e corporativismo no Brasil.* São Paulo, Brazil: Cortez.
Waterbury, John. 1989. "The Political Management of Economic Adjustment and Reform." In Joan M. Nelson, ed., *Fragile Coalitions: The Politics of Economic Adjustment.* New Brunswick, N.J.: Transaction Books.
Weffort, Francisco. 1992. *Qual democracia?* São Paulo, Brazil: Companhia das Letras.
————. 1985. "Nacionalismo, populismo e o que restou do legado político de Getúlio Vargas." In T. Szmerecsányi and R. Granziera, org., *Getúlio Vargas e a economia contemporânea.* São Paulo, Brazil: Unicamp.
————. 1980. *O populismo na política brasileira.* Rio de Janeiro, Brazil: Paz e Terra.
Weyland, Kurt. 1996a. *Democracy without Equity: Failures of Reform in Brazil.* Pittsburgh, Pa.: University of Pittsburgh Press.
————. 1996b. "How Much Political Power Do Economic Forces Have? Conflicts over Social Insurance Reform in Brazil." *Journal of Public Policy* 16 (1): 59–84.
————. 1995a. "Latin America's Four Political Models." *Journal of Democracy* 6 (4): 125–39.
————. 1995b. "Social Movements and the State: The Politics of Health Reform in Brazil." *World Development* 23 (10): 1,699–712.
Whitehead, Laurence. 1993. "On Reform of the State and Regulation of the Market." *World Development* 21 (8): 1,371–93.
————. 1992. "The Alternatives to Liberal Democracy: A Latin American Perspective." *Political Studies* 40 (2): 146–59.

Williamson, John, ed. 1990a. *Latin American Adjustment: How Much Has Happened?* Washington, D.C.: Institute for International Economics.

————. 1990b. "The Progress of Policy Reform in Latin America." In *Latin American Adjustment: How Much Has Happened?* Washington, D.C.: Institute for International Economics.

Willis, Eliza. 1995. "Explaining Bureaucratic Independence in Brazil: The Experience of the National Economic Development Bank." *Journal of Latin American Studies* 27 (3): 625–61.

Willis, Eliza, Christopher Garman, and Stephan Haggard. 1999. "The Politics of Decentralization in Latin America." *Latin America Research Review* 34 (1): 7–56.

World Bank. 2002. *World Development Report.* New York, N.Y.: Oxford University Press.

World Bank. 2001. *World Development Report.* New York, N.Y.: Oxford University Press.

World Bank. 2000. *World Development Report.* New York, N.Y.: Oxford University Press.

World Bank. 1999. *World Development Report.* New York, N.Y.: Oxford University Press.

World Bank. 1998. *World Development Report.* New York, N.Y.: Oxford University Press.

World Bank. 1997. *World Development Report.* New York, N.Y.: Oxford University Press.

Index

Weyland, Kurt, 116
Workers' Party (PT), 37, 68, 87, 89, 129, 157–58, 163, 172, 174, 178, 179; formation by CUT of, 85; social pact of, 164;

victories of, 161, 163
World Bank, 65, 150, 175
World Trade Organization, 147, 155
Wyman, Donald L., 11, 75

About the Author

Mauricio A. Font is director of the Bildner Center for Western Hemisphere Studies and professor of sociology at The Graduate Center and Queens College, City University of New York. His books on Brazil include *Coffee, Contention, and Change* (1990) and *Rise and Twilight of Brazilian Dirigisme* (forthcoming). He is editor of *Charting a New Course: The Politics of Globalization and Social Transformation* (2001).